D0908289

Lexicon of garden and
landscape architecture

Meto J. Vroom

lexicon

 of garden and landscape
architecture

Birkhäuser – Publishers for Architecture
Basel • Boston • Berlin

'When I use a word', Humpty Dumpty said, in a rather scornful tone,
'it means just what I choose it to mean – neither more nor less.'
'The question is', said Alice, *'whether you can make words mean so many different things.'*
'The question is', said Humpty Dumpty, *'which is to be master – that's all.'*

(Lewis Carroll: Through the looking glass)

Introduction

A lexicon is 'the vocabulary proper to some department of knowledge or sphere of activity' (*Oxford English Dictionary*) or: 'the vocabulary of a language, an individual speaker, or a subject' (*Webster*).

This lexicon contains parts of the vocabulary 'proper to' landscape architecture, but also to that of an individual author, arranged in alphabetical order. It is based on the experience gained by the author over a period of more than thirty years of teaching and research, not to mention his consultation of selected books and journals.

It contains both definitions and essays. The former are taken from dictionaries or encyclopaedias, and may claim to be 'an exact statement or description of the nature, scope or meaning of something'. They therefore carry a generally accepted meaning (*Encyclopaedia Britannica 2000*). The essays that follow these definitions are, as Webster defines them, 'non-fictional, usually short literary compositions dealing with its subject from a limited or personal point of view.' Each essay presents a brief outline and a comment on a subject area, and also refers to a number of books and articles in professional journals that generally support and enlarge upon its content.

7

This lexicon is written primarily for students of landscape architecture, whatever their age. Because it is a translated and adapted version of the original Dutch edition, *Lexicon voor de Landschapsarchitectuur*, a number of descriptions, examples and illustrations apply to situations in the Netherlands, or otherwise represent a Dutch outlook on professional theory and practice. It differs from the Dutch edition in that a number of specific Dutch procedures and examples have been omitted, and that references from English-language sources have been substituted for most of the original Dutch-language references.

The reader will encounter items that are sometimes a discussion and sometimes an illustration of the components of gardens or landscapes, and of the theoretical, historical, symbolic and iconographic aspects of landscape design. This mix of items means that the lexicon can be used in various ways: to clarify words and notions used by designers, as a source of background information, and as a general introduction to at least some of the current and historical literature.

Although individual items are described briefly, more information can be gained on each subject through the cross-references. For example, a fuller description of the content of the subject 'analysis' will be found by checking the headwords for 'behaviour', 'design method', 'layer', 'topography'. Similarly, the notion of 'aesthetics' can be expanded by following the eight cross-references stated after the headword.

This lexicon does not contain all possible items of interest. For example, there is no description of types of land-use and their impact on the land. Nor is there a discussion of neighbouring disciplines such as architecture and town planning, sociology or ecology. However, due to their interrelationships and overlaps with landscape architecture, these disciplines and their contributions to the field are frequently cited or mentioned in this lexicon.

In this context it should be added that no practical or technical information is provided on subjects such as plant materials, soils, water, and construction techniques, which can be found in many other reference books.

Which vocabulary is exclusive to landscape architects? The overlaps between the activities of landscape architects, architects, urban designers and planners are so great that we cannot feasibly delineate and delimit a field which belongs exclusively to landscape architecture. The lines as they have been drawn in this lexicon are therefore somewhat arbitrary.

Language – including professional language – is very much alive. New words are introduced all the time. While some are here to stay, others are merely fashionable, and are bound to disappear within a short time. Every lexicon therefore needs to be updated regularly, with additions, deletions and other changes.

All entries are presented here in alphabetical order. To allow for cross-referencing, the headwords of related entries included elsewhere in the lexicon are given in italics. Some concepts can be described in a few sentences, while others – the more central concepts – have a wider context and need more explanation. In order to avoid excessive length and complexity, a number of entries have been distributed under separate sub-headings. Thus, under 'design', the reader will find 'design: (design critique, -objectives, -strategy, -theory, -method, -style, -tools).'

8

What is landscape architecture?

Any attempt to present professional terminology inevitably leads to the question 'what is landscape architecture all about? What is its domain, its 'core-business'?'

Defining the area of expertise of landscape architecture is a difficult task. Both the history of the discipline and its relationship with neighbouring and older disciplines are complicated. Thanks to the rapid expansion of the profession during the 20th century in terms of the scope and scale of its assignments, its limits are hard to pin down. Its activities have expanded from the design of private gardens to the design of public outdoor spaces, to landscape planning, and even to town and country planning. The title used by its practitioners vary from 'garden designer' through 'landscape architect' to 'environmental designer'.

Garden and/or landscape?

Strictly speaking, garden design, urban open-space design, and regional landscape architecture and planning are different pursuits, and the name 'landscape architecture', which for insiders nowadays covers all of these activities, is misleading to outsiders. Gardens, whether private or public, are outdoor spaces of limited size and a very special character, laid out for particular purposes.The design of gardens and parks involves the creation of outdoor spaces of a very special character. Art, nature and functionality are merged into spatial compositions.

Landscapes cover vast territories and are not normally based on overall design concepts, but show the outcome of an interaction between natural factors – soils and climate, for instance – and the decisions, activities and interventions of a great many people.

Landscape architecture in the sense of ' the architecture of landscape' therefore seems an almost impossible concept. Landscapes are not normally based on overall design concepts, but are the outcome of an interaction between natural factors – soils and climate, for instance – and the decisions, activities and interventions of a great many people. In most countries, towns alone are carefully planned (though typically Dutch exceptions can be found in the layout of polders in reclaimed land, and in specific government-sponsored rural reconstruction or reallocation schemes). Few regional landscape plans attempt to impose the same fixed-dimension order on outdoor spaces that pertains in the layout of housing areas, parks and gardens. Instead, they usually indicate main contours or outlines that serve as a structural framework which envelops, contains and supports continuous development. They may also indicate selected areas of special scenic or ecological quality that are to be protected or conserved.

Despite these differences in scope and content, however, garden art and landscape design appear to have a common root.

The triad of garden, landscape and nature

In his analysis of the history of the 'first, second and third nature' (Hunt 2000), John Dixon Hunt does much to clarify the relationship between garden and landscape, as well as the way landscape architects attempt to deal with planning and design tasks in both domains.

First nature is what we call pure wilderness, that is, nature untouched by human hand. Throughout history, first nature has been valued in different ways. To the ancient Greeks, wilderness represented the sublime, the divine world of Olympus. In medieval Western Europe, nature represented a hostile and dangerous world. In more recent times, the cultivation of landscape and the disappearance of the fear of the unknown has led to a contempt for what is called 'waste land' – something that has led to abuse and despoliation. However, the longing for nature has never entirely disappeared; in the second half of the 20th century, it even underwent a revival.

As early as the 15th-century Italian Renaissance, with its geometric layout of gardens, a longing for nature images was demonstrated in the presence of the '*bosco*' or '*barco*'. Rediscovered in our contemporary landscapes, nature has achieved the status of a rare and valuable phenomenon which must be protected and conserved. In order to experience real nature, we organise 'nature trips' to remote countries – and in recent years the Dutch have devoted considerable energy to laying out 'new nature' areas near their homes. Many people hardly realise that such a wilderness remains an artifice, a construct. It is no longer first nature.

Second nature is the agrarian landscape, the ordered world of ploughed fields and orchards, of terraced and subdivided landscapes, and of rural settlements. People have lived and worked here over many centuries. The Roman writer Cicero described the landscape of his time thus: 'we sow corn, we plant trees, we fertilise the soil by irrigation, we dam the rivers and direct them where we want. In short, by means of our hands we try to create as it were a second nature within the natural world' (Hunt op cit p 33). In the 21st century, many urbanites are hardly able to distinguish this second nature from the first.

Third nature is represented by man-made places with their totems, symbols, holy spots and gardens. A garden is the result of 'ingenious connections' between culture and nature (Puppi 1991). Gardens are meant not only for the production of food and other agricultural products, but also to meet the need for protection, safety, symbolic interaction, the display of status and power, and the search for perfection (Mosser 1990). Garden-making involves the creation of places of high quality, and requires intensive maintenance.

The relationship between the three natures

There are many examples of interconnections between the second and the third forms of nature. In paintings of the 15th-century Tuscan landscape we find transitions in the sense of 'certain elements of an essentially agrarian layout treated in ways that give them added value – whether that value is privacy, protection or aesthetic shaping by way of spacing and grouping' (Hunt op cit p 69). The 18th-century English estate is a superb example of this phenomenon.

The layout, form and equipment of gardens and parks is in constant dialogue with the surrounding countryside, even if their relationship is extremely complex. The relationship between gardens and nature – whether second or first – is displayed in sculptured and emblematic objects and forms, such as hills, ponds, dams and other elements that have been derived from nature. These elements are copied and imitated, while views are constructed and atmospheres created.

Thus, in the Japanese garden, the relationship between inside and outside takes the form of a 'borrowed scene'; while, in the Italian Renaissance garden, the vista or sightline to the horizon is a connecting element. In the English landscape style, visible boundaries between park and landscape are removed, allowing for distant views of the second and first natures.

Eighteenth-century English authors such as William Gilpin (1724-1804) and William Chambers (1723-1796) used the word 'zoning' to indicate the three successive types of nature as 'pleasing, enchanted and sublime' (Hunt op cit. pp 45). This ideal caused Uvedale Price (1747-1829) to condemn landscape gardener Lancelot 'Capability' Brown (1716-1783) for his decision to remove third nature from his estates as part of his 'levelling business' by placing country houses in the middle of a large open park-like space without any margin or transition between one and the other. It was Humphry Repton (1752-1818) who reintroduced the outdoor terrace as a margin between dwelling and landscape.

With regard to the Netherlands, the cultivation of the landscape over many centuries resulted in the virtual extinction of first nature. The end of the 20th century saw a revival in the form of 'new nature'. This followed the implementation of the Government's Nature Policy Plan of 1990, which established nature target types, projected ecological networks, and constructed ecotypes. Images of nature are now visible again both in Dutch landscapes and in urban park systems laid out according to ecological principles.

Admittedly, descriptions of situations in which the three natures co-exist date back many centuries, and contemporary examples of such situations are rare. Nonetheless, the distinction between the three helps formulate a definition of nature that 'actively discourages the belief that nature is normative rather than culturally constructed. It allows place-making to be seen as essentially related to immediate topography, and by the virtue of its emphasis on graduated modes of mediation, urges more subtle adjudications of landscape architecture than the habitual ones of "formal" and "informal"' (Hunt op cit p 51).

Many entries in this lexicon illustrate the relationship between garden design and regional landscape architecture, both in the past and in the present

11

(Kerkstra 2003). There are analogies and symbolic relationships between objects and forms within the garden and those in the landscape. References, borrowings and mimesis abound. Gardens and landscapes are intertwined. Names of territories and boundaries in the landscape are derived from those in the garden: 'the marks of distinction must be borrowed from a garden... as evidence of the domain' (Hunt op cit p 45). Knowledge of the one is a prerequisite for understanding the other. Garden design is a source of inspiration for landscape planners. There is no dividing line between the two, and they in fact constitute an inseparable discipline that is 'a branch of knowledge; subject of instruction' (*Oxford English Dictionary*).

For many 20th-century architects and landscape architects, 'freedom from the garden meant freedom to imagine a new mode of living in which landscape and architecture were different in degree rather than kind. In this new mode, the structure of both landscape and architecture is spatially open, unencumbered by delimiting garden walls...' (Dodds 2002).

The history of garden design remains an important source of information for contemporary landscape architecture. This lexicon thus contains many historical examples that illustrate or provide background information. Gardens from centuries ago constitute a collection of examples that are not only enjoyable as museum pieces, but which also represent an archive from which information can be drawn. Specific elements can be dissected, and parts can be combined or abstracted for re-use in a different context. In their layout and form, gardens, like buildings, represent a world view of the society that existed at the time of their creation. They thus contain a lesson for contemporary designers (Jencks 1995).

Dutch art historian Eric de Jong concludes: 'Many design principles applied in contemporary problems of scale and order may be distilled from 17th and 18th-century gardens [...]. The value of these designs lies in the way nature is abstracted, demonstrating in an original way the connection between iconic and compository principles [...]. Regional coherence in the Dutch Randstad could be restored by making use of historic examples of landscape architecture' (de Jong 1993).

The development of the profession and its language

A survey of the history of the profession shows how its origins, identity and strength lie in the art and craft of garden design. 'The power of the profession lies in the art of creating places that stimulate the senses, evoke joy, embody paradox, reflect tradition and inspire hope, places whose aesthetic qualities endure (and are valued) beyond the specific economic and social context from which they arose,' says landscape architect Sven Ingvar Andersson (Weilacher 1996).

As described in the 17th century by the Dutchman Jan van der Groen, the nurseryman, horticulturalist or gardener is an autodidact who occupies himself with plants and soils, with cultivation and tillage. He also designs 'models of flower beds, parterres and trellises etc', and implements these designs himself. He is concerned primarily with the private domain. Drawing, tilling and planting are his major activities. His vocabulary is limited to the subject he deals with. In his eyes, first nature has been conquered (Groen 1683).

While such gardeners still exist, they have been joined by others who have established themselves as designers of outdoor space. They serve as independent advisors to their clients, who leave the implementation of a design to the gardener. To avoid mistakes or misunderstanding, they therefore need to pass on information, to communicate, to lay down design proposals (in both the graphic and the verbal sense) with a great deal of exactitude. Elaborate technical drawings, accompanied by an accurate brief and a cost estimate, are part of every project. A concise terminology has also become important, partly because the landscape architect must explain his design proposals to private and public audiences.

The profession has continued to develop over time. Design theories have led to explorations into a variety of themes, including the principles of aesthetics, the rules of composition and the technique of perspective. Publications have addressed the iconographic and functional aspects of garden design, dating back to the 17th century. And 20th insights on human perception and behaviour have underlain new concepts of the design of public outdoor space.

One result of the broadening theoretical basis of design activities is that successors of the former autodidacts have needed professional training and intellectual development. In various European countries, and also elsewhere, professional institutes or associations have been set up. In the Netherlands, the Association of Garden Architects (BNT) was founded in 1922 (Boer 1990).

Early in the 20th century, professional schools were established at both college and university levels. Students also started to receive educational programmes addressing a range of technical and scientific subjects, each with its own paradigm and vocabulary. The expansion of the language of landscape was truly under way.

At the same time, by undertaking assignments of varying scale and complexity, professional practice underwent further expansion, with projects addressing the private domain, public space, and the landscape as a whole, thereby covering all levels of scale. 'Landscape architecture is simply the design and planning of physical environments'. (Olin 1997).

This meant that the 'three natures' often required equal attention.

Two components of such projects became increasingly important: natura

Somewhat strikingly, the ambition of Dutch landscape architects to move to larger-scale work was slow to develop. It was only after the Second World War that this challenge was taken up, by a new generation of designers led by Jan Bijhouwer (van der Wal 1997).

It was thus some time before the growing demand for designers of large-scale rural development was met by an adequate number of trained landscape architects. Initially, their contribution was limited to roadside planting and shelterbelts – in other words, to embellishing the works of others. In the 1960s, an expanding theoretical basis helped underpin a methodical approach to the planning and design approach of landscape plans and master-plans.

Analysis and synthesis techniques developed, concepts were founded. The horizon was broadened by collaboration, initially with architects and urban designers, and later with planners, ecologists, social scientists and civil engineers. Similarly, insights essential to landscape planning and the design of outdoor spaces were provided by geographers, psychologists and art historians, while ecologists revealed the vital connections between the three natures.

Contemporary landscape architects need to master the language of all these disciplines and apply their principles in their work – and, at times, unexpected problems are created by the discipline's greatly expanded vocabulary. 'The broad range of problems that landscape architects are now tackling – from a garden to a toxic waste dump, a regional planning study, or an urban renewal site – tend to draw them away from the physical locations and the social, cultural or educational milieux where their values and beliefs were initially formed' (Walker 1994).

The distinction between the domain of landscape architecture and that of planning and urban design is becoming blurred. The growth of the profession leads some observers to marvel: 'I know of no other profession,' Ian McHarg states, 'which escalated as swiftly from oblivion to international significance, nor one where so few persons have accomplished so much' (1998). During the 20th century, landscape architecture evolved from an arts and crafts movement into an academic discipline with its own schools, research institutes and professional journals, and also with an association within which the 'why' and 'how' of design are in constant debate.

A body of theory keeps developing. In many countries, landscape architects are now involved in government planning policy – preparing regional and municipal plans, drawing up environmental impact statements, planning greenways and conducting coastal studies. All these activities require analysis and evaluation. For landscape design is no longer a matter of conceiving, and then drawing, a new situation. It involves establishing guidelines for the types of development that will 'fit in with', or improve on, an existing situation. Models and scenarios must be composed, and public hearings organised and reported. And because a well-written statement has become as important as a map, the lack of a clear and concise set of definitions has recently become increasingly apparent.

In the meantime, the paradigm of landscape architects no longer appears to represent a unified vision of reality, especially where the relationship between man and nature is concerned. The impact of ideologies and dogmas has started to become visible. Some professionals form alliances, either with the nature conservation movement, or with the builders and engineers. Others try to bridge the gap between opposing views while collaborating with planners. This means that points of view may diverge according to the type of client and the nature of the assignment (Spirn 1977).

There is also a danger that concepts of how to intervene in the three natures will become increasingly divergent. So is garden design still recognised as the basis for landscape architecture? Pessimistically, John Dixon Hunt concludes: 'landscape architecture [...] has lost touch [...] with gardens, not as items to be designed and built, but as models or ideas for larger enterprises' (Hunt op. cit. p. xi). The attention of landscape architects, say some Dutch observers, may recently have shifted excessively from detailed design work to large-scale regional projects. Others, however, believe that a turning point has been reached. In recent years a number of landscape architects have been actively engaged in implementing new regional design strategies which include the revitalisation of older parks and gardens (de Jong 1993). Landscape architecture is again 'emerging as a discipline which has mastered design assignments across all levels of scale – in contrast to architecture and urban design this' (Steenbergen 1990)., and things are changing for the better (de Jong 2001).

References

- Boer W.C.J. 1990. 'Changing ideals in urban landscape architecture'. In: Vroom M.J.; Meeus J.H. (ed). *Learning from Rotterdam.* Mansell. Alexandrine Press, London pp. 44-69
- Dodds G. 2002. 'Freedom from the Garden'. In: Hunt J.D.; Conan M. (ed). *Tradition and Innovation in French Garden Art. Chapters of a New History*, The University of Pennsylvania Press pp. 185-202
- Groen J. van den 1683, reprint 1988. *Den Nederlandsen Hovenier.* Matrijs, Utrecht.
- Hunt J.D. 2000. Greater Perfections. The Practice of Garden Theory. Thames & Hudson, London
- Jencks Ch. 1995. *The Architecture of the Jumping Universe.* Academy Editions, London
- de Jong. 1993. *Natuur en Kunst. Nederlandse tuin-en landschapsarchitectuur 1650-1740.* Thoth, Bussum
- Kerkstra K. 2003. 'Geometry and Genius Loci'. In: Kerkstra K. (ed). *The Landscape of Symbols.* Blauwdruk publishers, Wageningen
- McHarg I. 1998. 'Landscape Architecture'. In: McHarg I, Steiner F.R. (ed). 1998. *To Heal the Earth. Selected writings of Ian McHarg.* Island Press, Washington D.C. pp.188-193

15

- Mosser M.; Teyssot G. 1991. *The History of Garden Design*. Thames & Hudson, London p. 11
- Olin L. 1997. 'What is landscape architecture?'. In: Thompson G.; Steiner F. (ed) *Ecological Design and Planning*. John Wiley & Sons, New York p.115
- Poppi L. 1991. 'Nature and artifice in the sixteenth-century Italian garden'. In: Mosser M.; Teyssot G. *The History of Garden Design*. Thames & Hudson, London pp. 47 ff.
- Spirn A. 1977. 'The authority of Nature: Conflict and Confusion in Landscape Architecture'. In: Wolschke-Bulmah J. *Nature and Ideology. Natural Garden Design in the Twentieth Century*. Dumbarton Oaks, Washington pp. 249-261
- Steenbergen C.M. 1990. *De stap over de horizon*. TU Delft p.184
- van der Wal C. 1997. *In praise of common sense. A physical planning history of the new towns in the IJsselmeerpolders*. 010 publishers, Rotterdam p.129
- Walker P.; Simo M. 1994. *Invisible Gardens. The Search for Modernism in the American Landscape*. MIT press, Cambridge p.4
- Weilacher U. 1996. *Between Landscape Architecture and Land Art*. Birkhäuser, Basel

For the initial definition of each item, the following dictionaries and encyclopaedias were consulted. In the text these are indicated by means of the following abbreviations:

(van Dale) Van Dale Groot Woordenboek van de Nederlandse Taal. 12th edition 1992

(Britannica) Encyclopaedia Britannica CD. 2000. Bristol

(Goulty) Goulty G.A. 1991. A Dictionary of Landscape. Avebury Technical Avebury

(Hachette) Dictionnaire Hachette Encyclopédie. 1997. Hachette Livre Paris

(Larousse) Le petit Larousse Grand Format. 2001. Larousse Paris.

(Oxford Companion) The Oxford Companion to Gardens. 1986. Oxford University Press

(Oxford Advanced) Oxford Advanced Learner's Dictionary. 1992. Oxford University Press

(Oxford English Dictionary) The Compact Edition of the Oxford Dictionary of the English Language. 1979. Book Club Associates

(Penguin) The Penguin Dictionary of Architecture and Landscape Architecture. Fifth edition. 1999. Harmondsworth Middlesex

(Robert) Le Petit Robert. Le Robert Paris

(Webster) Webster's New Encyclopaedic Dictionary. 1993. Könemann Köln

Acknowledgements

This lexicon could not have been written without the active support of a number of people.

Firstly, the support and encouragement of Harry Harsema was indispensable.

Valuable advice on the content of the English-language edition was received from Marc van Grieken, Michael Hough, Yusuck Koh, David Lowenthal and Frederick Steiner. None of them, of course, are responsible for my actual text, either in part or as a whole.

Logistical support was received from the Department of Landscape Architecture at Wageningen University. Librarians Gerard van der Moolen and Wieske Meijer showed enormous patience in helping me find new sources of information.

Annemarie Roetgerink checked all references and weeded out errors in names and dates. Maarten Ettema took care of the final editing and David Alexander undertook the laborious task of checking the quality of the English translation with great enthusiasm and expertise.

Abstract

see also > mimesis, reduction

'Having only generalised form with little or no attempt at precise representation' (*Webster*).

Abstract art – also called non-figurative art – avoids the representation of recognisable objects. Manifold in expression, it arises from the need to reduce a reality that is all too complex. 'The need for abstraction... seeks gratification in the beauty of all that which denies an organic existence, in the crystalline world, quite simply in the abstract world of laws and necessities.' The painter Cézanne (1839-1906) defines Cubist painting as the depiction of 'nature by means of the cylinder, the sphere, and the cone, all placed [...] so that every facet of an object is turned towards the central point of an object' (Wentinck 1979).

Landscape components such as mountains, hills, rivers, lakes are often represented in gardens in an abstracted or generalised form. Architect Frank Lloyd Wright expressed his reverence for nature by abstracting landscape features: 'the real artist imposes his will on natural form.' This action implies 'a progressive geometrisation of outward form,' while 'natural features can be seen as

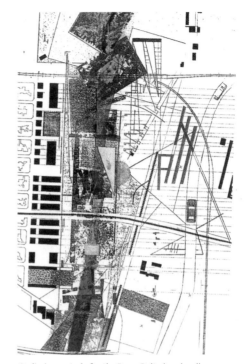

Preliminary study for the Besos Delta brook valley, Barcelona, using coloured planes to indicate not only areas that vary in character but also the outline of housing areas. Design by Maria Goula.
Source: Geometria. Monographs of architecture and urban planning no. 20, Barcelona, 1995

19

Buxus plants in a geometric pattern. Weldam Estate near Goor, Province of Gelderland, the Netherlands.

underlain by an essential geometry' (Spirn 1998). Mountains become knolls, and rivers are represented by cascades. In Japanese gardens, mountains are represented by carefully stacked piles of stone, and the ocean by raked sand.

Abstracted form may also be used in design drawings. Planes in different colours show the shape of areas and elements of a particular character, providing an overall view of a composition at first glance. The detailing process follows.

Abstraction may also be used in planting design. The natural form of individual plants can be subordinated to the composition of larger elements. One of the characteristic aspects of a particular plant species is given a dominant role – for example, ground-cover plants that form continuous planes whose visual effect is determined by the texture of the leaves. In the same way, the specific form of individual specimens within a clump of

trees is no longer recognisable. They are mere parts of a larger whole.

A radical type of abstraction is the deformation of plants through clipping, pruning or shearing, which thus creates a completely different form (Kluckert 2000). Trees and shrubs become geometric blocks, or Cubist forms such as pyramids, cones or columns; sometimes they are clipped to represent animals (Weilacher 1976). In this way, plants can be used to develop a new design grammar (Ogrin 2003)

· Kluckert E. 2000. 'Topiary'. In: *The Gardens of Europe*. Könemann, Köln pp. 347-349
· Ogrin D. 2003. 'The symbolism of artefacts in the landscape'. In: *The Landscape of Symbols*. Blauwdruk, Wageningen
· Spirn A. 1998. 'Abstraction and invention'. In: *The Language of Landscape*. Yale University Press New, Haven p. 198
· Weilacher U. 1996. 'The antidote to virtual reality – Sven Ingvar Andersson'. In: *Between landscape architecture and land art*. Birkhäuser, Basel pp. 157 ff.
· Wentinck C. 1979. 'Abstraction and empathy'. In: *Modern and Primitive Art*. Phaidon, London pp. 12-14

Columnar Trees in Parc Citroën, Paris.

Access, Gate

see also > bridge, dynamic, infrastructure, pattern, terrace

'Permission, liberty, or ability to enter, approach, communicate with, pass to or from, or make use of. A way or means of approach' (*Webster*).

Accessibility in the geographical sense implies movement, connection, flow, and arrival at places of destination. People search for ways and routes to move towards preset goals. The layout of roads, paths, lanes and promenades is focused on providing efficient access (Broadbent 1973). Accessibility is also associated with direction, scale and safety (Motloch 2001). An accessible landscape is opened up and can be viewed and experienced.

The opening up of rural areas in Europe began in the late 18th century with the construction of paths, roads and canals, and later on also of railways. Rural areas became accessible, thereby providing urban dwellers with options for a dynamic experience of landscape (Hoskins 1955).

In England, the drawings of William Gilpin

(1724-1804) introduced scenic landscapes to a larger public. Tourism began to flourish and travellers could see 'how variously nature works upon the scenery' (Batey 1996; Hunt 1992). In 1786 Johan Wolfgang von Goethe (1749-1832) undertook his famous coach journey across the Alps from Germany; he travelled to such Italian cities as Rome and Naples, taking notes and sketching carefully observed landscapes and monuments. These notes were published afterwards, and had an enormous impact (Goethe 1829).

Although the extension of the road system all over Europe in the 19th century stimulated economic development, increased travel also caused a loss of regional identity and authentic scenery. Historians and other writers deplored the loss of romantic images (Huizinga 1945).

In the Netherlands the bicycle became popular after 1900, followed by the motorcar. Picturesque villages and other sites began to be swamped by tourists; local culture, previously an innocent phenomenon, became a destination for curious sight-seers.

The arrival of too many visitors became a menace. A travel account dating from 1905 warned 'if you want to see fishing villages at their best, you'd better hurry'; much later, in 1993, a French advertisement urged tourists to come and 'see France while it is still there' (Lowenthal 2003).

The positive aspect of improved accessibility to the countryside – both overall and to specific sites – is that it provides an opportunity for a direct experience of scenery. It means that stories are created and told (Potteiger 1998), consisting of a succession of experiences and happenings, from the beginning to the end of the road or path, with curves, diversions, branching sections and loops (Alexander 1977/1; Moore 1989). 'Paths meandered into the woods beyond the house with a beckoning siren charm' (Elizabeth George 1989, *A Great Deliverance*).

English landscape parks such as Stourhead in Wiltshire contain a 'circuit walk', from which a changing scenery can be viewed. 'A path is a series of foregrounds; and to adapt

The pedestrian landscape: sandy road near Wekerom, the Netherlands.

21

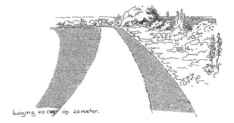

buiging 40 cm op 20 meter.

In perspective view, the bend of a path seems sharper.
Source: Bijhouwer J.T.P. 1954. Waarnemen en ontwerpen in tuin en landschap. Argus Amsterdam. Blz. 58-59

each part of this to the various combinations of the distant objects, which always result from the change of place or aspect, is the proper business of art' (Batey 1996).

Site access

Creating access to a site involves answering questions such as how to reach, enter and move around within it. Access can be classified according to the elements and features of the site to which access is given, and also according to the people or things to whom it is afforded: e.g. other people, human activities, material resources, places of interest, or information (Lynch 1981). As well as the elimination of barriers, the conditions to be met include efficiency, continuity, variety, spatial orientation, flexible use, and visual attractiveness (Lynch 1960; Lynch 1984; Motloch 2001).

Points of entry to a site may be clearly defined, highly visible, and of imposing size and character, such as the entrance to a palace; but they may also be practical, modest and even unsightly, such as the entrance to a car park. In order to enter a site, one usually needs to pass a gate, i.e. 'an opening in a wall or fence; a means of entrance or exit' (*Webster*).

Gates contribute to our experience of space and time. Not merely transitions or breaks in our movement from one space to the next, or from outside to inside (and vice versa), they can evoke feelings of expectation, fear, of drastic change. Emotional responses are

The gate as metaphor: Puerto del Europa, Madrid.

The perspective view of a rectilinear path is enlivened by changes in relief and light. Hyde Park, London.

22

quickly evoked by an appearance that is forbidding or inviting, dominant or hidden, imposing or humble (Anonymous 1996): after all, we may be allowed in, or be shut out. The gates of heaven or hell may beckon us, but we need a 'pass-port' to get in.

Gates in housing areas indicate the transition from public to private: 'to pass through a gate, a portal, or a front door, or to park in a private driveway is more than merely entering: it affirms membership in a well-established group' (Jackson 1997). As landmarks, gates are sometimes visible from afar, the culmination-point in a three-dimensional composition such as the entrance to a royal palace or to a chateau such as Vaux le Vicomte at Melun (Hazlehurst 1980).

Places of entry that lead the visitor gradually to a culmination-point may take the form of an access lane with changing perspective views, such as those on some of the 18th-century English estates. Others may feature a succession of porches and vestibules within a built-up space, which

23

Gates that are meant to overawe: Palace Gate, Vienna, and Arc de Triomphe Caroussel, Paris.

The successive steps taken when entering a square that lead to a climax: Plaça Real, Barcelona .

together create a feeling of expectancy. 'Buildings, and especially houses, with a graceful transition between the street and the inside, are more tranquil than those which open directly off the street' (Alexander 1977/2).

Town gates used to be the place of entry, marking the difference between outside and inside. Gates were also defensive constructions that could withstand attacks. The contemporary 'gated community' offers its residents a safe haven from a hostile urban environment. Gates in urban environments may also be metaphorical objects such as the two leaning office towers in Madrid that form the 'Puerto del Europa'.

At a regional scale, a gate may be the entrance between promontories to a bay or harbour, such as the Bosporus or San Francisco's Golden Gate. It may also be a river mouth, such as at Rotterdam, 'the Gateway to Europe'.

- Alexander C. (et al). 1977/1. 'Entrance transition'. In: *A Pattern Language.* Oxford University Press, New York. pp. 549 et seq.
- Alexander C. (et al) 1977/1. 'Paths and goals'. In: *A Pattern Language.* Oxford University Press, New York pp. 585 ff.
- Anonymous. 1996. 'Pathways'. In: Topos European Landscape Magazine (theme number 20) Callwey, München
- Batey M. 1996. *Jane Austen and the English Landscape.* Barn Elms, London pp. 52, 57
- Broadbent G. 1973. *Design in Architecture.* John Wiley & Sons, New York pp. 45-46
- George E. 1989. *A Great Deliverance.* Bantam Books p. 57
- Goethe J.W. 1829 (reprint 1987). *Italienische Reise.* Rütten & Loening, Berlin
- Hazelhurst F. Hamilton. 1980. *Gardens of Illusion.* Vanderbilt University Press, Nashville, Tennessee. pp. 24-28
- Hoskins W.G. 1955. 'Roads, canals and railways'. In: *The Making of the English Landscape.* Pelican Books pp. 233-269
- Hunt J.D. 1992. *Gardens and the Picturesque.* MIT press pp. 5-9
- Huizinga J. 1945. *Geschonden wereld.* Tjeenk Willink, Haarlem p. 108
- Jackson J.B. 1997. 'The accessible landscape'. In: *Landscape in Sight.* Yale University Press, New Haven pp. 68 -77
- Lowenthal D. 2003. 'Landscape as living legacy'. In: *The Landscape of Symbols.* Blauwdruk publishers, Wageningen pp.12-37
- Lynch K. 1960. *The Image of the City.* MIT Press, Cambridge pp. 49-62
- Lynch K. 1981. 'Access'. In: *A Theory of Good City Form.* MIT Press, Cambridge pp.187-204
- Lynch K.; Hack G. 1984. *Site Planning (third Edition).* MIT Press, Cambridge pp.193-222
- Moore C.W. (et al) 1989. 'Connecting'. In: *The Poetics of Gardens.* MIT Press, Cambridge p. 35

• Motloch J.L. 2001. *Introduction to Landscape Design (second edition)*. Wiley & Sons, New York pp. 158 ff.
• Potteiger M.; Purinton J. 1998. 'Opening'. In: *Landscape Narratives*. John Wiley & Sons, New York pp.187 ff.

Adaptation, Fit, Anchor, Merge

see also > analysis, context, geomancy, infrastructure, layer, soils, system

Adaptation means 'adjustment to environmental conditions' (*Webster*). To fit means: 'suited for something; well adapted for something; good enough for something', or 'suitable and right, usually according to accepted social standards' (*Oxford English Dictionary*).

The adaptation of organisms to their environment is part of their struggle for survival (Darwin 1859/1979). The need to adapt, to fit in, is also deeply anchored in the human subconscious, both in the quantitative sense ('to fit') and in the qualitative sense ('to be adapted to'). One way this is expressed is in our choice of clothes, which must not only be of the right size, but should also be adapted to considerations of fashion.

Within 'closed' mechanical systems, such as tools and machines, the various parts should fit precisely in order to allow the whole to function properly. 'Open' systems such as outdoor spaces also need to fit, in the sense that their dimensions should be appropriate to different uses and demands (Alexander 1964).

One of the basic considerations in the planning and design of outdoor space is the need to adapt, fit or merge types of land-use. Over the years, the 'why' of adapting settlements to environmental conditions (i.e. soils, water and topography) has evolved from the inevitable (as dictated by the lack of construction techniques that would overcome natural constraints) through the urgent (as dictated by need for protection against natural hazards and enemies) to the normative (i.e. ecological reasons and aesthetic preferences). Before the 19th century, the lack of the technical knowledge and equipment that could overcome natural constraints usually made it inevitable that building sites and roads would be adapted to existing conditions.

As soon as new construction techniques

26

Medieval settlement pattern, adapted to physical conditions. De Vlist, the Netherlands.

EXISTING VEGETATION

FOREST:ECOLOGICAL ASSOCIATIONS

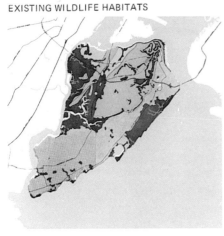

EXISTING WILDLIFE HABITATS

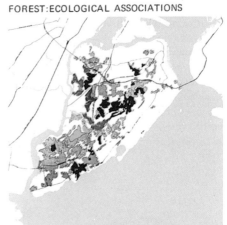

FOREST:EXISTING QUALITY

27

SOIL LIMITATIONS:FOUNDATION

SOIL LIMITATIONS:WATER-TABLE

An adjustment to ecological conditions requires careful landscape analysis (map).
Source: McHarg I. 1963. Design with Nature. History Press New York, p. 107

became available, large-scale interventions in landscapes became the rule. As historic patterns and natural process were ignored, and often eradicated, a loss of diversity ensued.

During the 1970s, however, attitudes changed radically: existing landscape values were too important, and should not be overridden by indiscriminate transformation. In the Netherlands, major land reclamation projects were stopped, and the building of new coastal dikes and the expansion of the national motorway system were reconsidered. The pioneering spirit of earlier decades was discarded, and all new construction was met with suspicion and resistance. From now on, landscapes would be seen as 'vulnerable'. This was the point at which biodiversity, identity, and historical continuity became important values.

Currently, all major projects in the Netherlands are subjected to Environmental Impact Statements, which usually propose so-called 'compensating and mitigating' measures. Local authorities accept the construction of new roads and other works only grudgingly, usually on the condition that they are invisible, or almost. Sunken roadbeds and planting screens have become almost standard measures. The aim of designers to proudly show off their work, and their ability to adapt new forms to local landscape idiom, is often ill-understood (Vrijlandt 2001).

How to adapt

Landscape architecture, states Dixon Hunt, 'is above all else grounded. Its sites are rooted and located, and that locality – either in itself or in the reinvention of it by a designer – must feature in the experience of the place' (Hunt 2002). After the analysis of horizontal relations, new development is therefore adjusted to – or merged into – an existing environment (Josselin de Jong 2004) (see *Context*). The study of layers in the subsoil and subterranean water resources brings an understanding of vertical relations. Combined investigation of the horizontal and vertical relations, as required in many

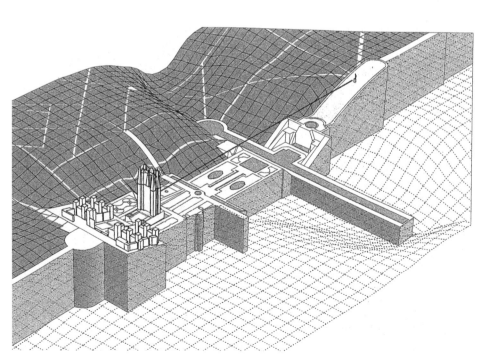

The layout of a Classicist park adjusted to the underlying topography: Vaux le Vicomte, Melun, France.
Source: Steenbergen C.; Reh W. 1996. Architecture and Landscape. Thoth publishing, Bussum

cases, will result in an 'ecological planning approach' (McHarg 1963).

Medieval settlements along streams in marshy areas were built on stable natural banks that could support buildings. In this way, natural conditions formed the basis for settlement patterns, thereby resulting in a legible differentiation. The *genius loci* was apparent (Norberg Schulz 1980).

Classicist parks were laid out according mainly to internal rules of composition, but even in these cases adaptation was sometimes needed. Some of the major examples of designs by André le Nôtre, such as at Vaux le Vicomte at Melun, have been fitted to some degree into the existing topography. The canals are fed by an existing stream, and changes in level are exploited to create a perspective view (Steenbergen 1996).

'Anchoring' is also a form of adaptation. This is defined as 'to secure firmly' (*Webster*).

In site-planning, anchoring involves a search for a firm and visible relationship between a building and its site, and also between that site and its surroundings. Each site is part of a larger whole. While a designer may decide to ignore the surroundings and create an internally oriented and self-contained spot, in most cases he or she looks for a relationship between the physical conditions within the site and those in the surrounding land – the 'context'. Making use of these conditions helps establish a 'spirit of place' (Baljon 1992; Leatherbarrow 2004/1).

The anchoring of a site may be pursued by creating visible connections between the inside and the outside, as they are formed by the alignment of paths, ditches, hedgerows and tree-lined lanes (Harsema 1996). Sightlines or vistas towards a distant landmark such as a church tower may also be used. A more subtle method is to relate the composition of the vegetation inside a site to that outside. In rural situations this normally involves the use of indigenous plant materials.

To anchor a building in a site means to create an ensemble in which the building becomes an integral part of the site. In medieval towns this was a normal procedure:

villages and buildings were part of the site, creating an architectural quality that is now highly valued. In the 20th century, these relations were ignored – with decay and ugliness as a result.

The American architect Frank Lloyd Wright (1867-1959) was famous for the way he anchored his buildings (Kaufmann 1989). 'The architect who is sensitive to his site is not content with merely digging a foundation [...] as a further means of site-anchoring, he may send out tentacles of structure to catch or hook some surrounding feature of the land' (Frampton 1988). However, modernist architect Richard Neutra (1892-1970) was accused of 'viewing the building as an object d'art for which the site is merely a subservient setting' (Leatherbarrow 2004/2).

Symbolic adaptation

Large-scale urban development cannot be fitted into existing land patterns, and in such cases planners may revert to symbolic

The site as a 'subservient setting': Kaufmann house, Santa Barbara, California, USA. Designed in 1946 by architect Richard Neutra; photographed in 1957.

A famous building anchored to the site: architect Frank Lloyd Wright's 'Fallingwater' at Bear Run, Pennsylvania; designed in 1936. This photograph 1956.

29

adaptation, whereby the main outlines of former patterns are reproduced in the new layout in a simplified, symbolic way. In this way the history of a site is still legible. A famous example is the central district of the city of Amsterdam, where the mouth of Amstel river was blocked by a dam in order to connect the two parts of the town. A concentric pattern of canals was developed around this point in order to form a natural drainage system (Vroom 1976). The story of how all this came about is still visible to the discerning eye.

- Alexander C. 1964. 'Goodness of Fit'. In: *Notes on the Synthesis of Form.* Harvard University Press pp. 15-28
- Baljon L. 1992. *Designing Parks.* Architecture & Natura, Amsterdam pp. 67-68
- Darwin C. 1859. *The Origin of Species.* Abridged and introduced by Richard Leaky. Book Club Associates, London pp. 46, 48,49 (reprint 1979)
- Frampton K. 1988. 'In Search of the Modern Landscape'. In: Wrede S; Adams W.H. (ed). *Denatured Visions. Landscape and Culture in the Twentieth Century.* Museum of Modern Art, New York. pp. 47-51
- Harsema H. (ed). 1996. 'Gas storage near Langelo'. In: Landscape architecture and town planning in the Netherlands 1993-1995?. Thoth Publishers, Bussum pp.70-73
- Hunt J.D. 2002. 'Reinventing the Parisian Park'. In: Hunt. J.D.; Conan M. *Tradition and Innovation in French Garden Art. Chapters of a New History.* The University of Pennsylvania Press, Philadelphia pp. 212 ff
- Josselin de Jong F. 2004. 'Prinsenland Rotterdam. New housing district with an agricultural plot layout'. In: Blauwe Kamer Magazine for Landscape and Urban Development. Special issue August 2004, Blauwdruk ,Wageningen pp. 12-16
- Kaufmann E. 1989. *Falling Water, a Frank Lloyd Wright Country House.* Butterworth, Sevenoaks, Kent
- Leatherbarrow D. 2004/1. 'Earthwork as framework'. In: *Topographical Stories. Studies in Landscape and Architecture.* University of Pennsylvania Press, Philadelphia pp. 16-58
- Leatherbarrow D. 2004/2. In: *Topographical Stories. Studies in Landscape and Architecture.* University of Pennsylvania Press, Philadelphia p. 62
- McHarg I. 1963. *Design with Nature.* History Press, New York
- Norberg-Schulz C. 1980. *Genius Loci.* Academy Editions, London pp. 23 ff.
- Steenbergen C.; Reh W. 1996. *Architecture and Landscape.* Thoth Publishers, Bussum p. 161
- Vroom M.J. 1976. 'Landscape planning: a cooperative effort; a professional activity'. In: Landscape Planning number 3 pp. 377 et seq.
- Vrijlandt P.; Kruit J. 2001. 'Motorways and landscape patterns: new concepts explored'. Conference Paper ECLAS Larenstein, Velp

Aesthetics

see also > classicism, functionalism, modernism, perception, proportion, quality, romanticism, value

'Concerned with beauty and the appreciation of beauty.... Pleasing to look at; artistic; tasteful' (*Oxford English Dictionary*)

Immanuel Kant (1724-1804) drew a distinction between two kinds of beauty: the free and unhampered, and the conditional. The first assumes ignorance of the nature of objects perceived – a disinterested way of perceiving and enjoying. The second assumes an understanding of such objects. This makes various points of view possible – for example, the functionalist view that 'form follows function' (i.e. that beauty lies in things being just what they are), or the moralist view that 'beauty lies in goodness' (i.e. that a nuclear power plant looks horrible and a wind turbine is a thing of beauty).

The word aesthetic is derived from the

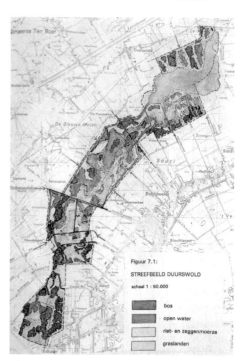

A 'nature development plan' near Duurswold, Groningen, the Netherlands. A disorderly collection of wet and dry spots. Around 1990.

Source: Feddes F. et al 1998. Oorden van Onthouding. Nieuwe natuur in verstedelijkend Nederland. NAI publishers, Rotterdam

Greek *aisthesis*, meaning sensory perception, experience as well as feeling. Characteristics of an object or a space that may give one person an experience of beauty do not necessarily produce the same effect in someone else. But while the characteristics of a beautiful horse cannot be transferred to a beautiful woman, both may have something in common with a variety of objects such as a flower, a Ferrari automobile, or a Mondrian painting. What they share is a high level of perfection, of completeness, of achievement. These notions underlie a certain purpose, such as reproduction or speed (or both) (Baumeister 1999).

The notion of 'Venustas', as introduced by Vitruvius in the first century, points to the beauty of Venus, eliciting feelings of love and erotics (Wöbse 2004). According to Vitruvius, many a beautiful form points to functionality, where proportion and harmony prevail (Eco 2005). In the Dutch landscape, the fertile clay polders in the north of the country have been described as 'the wide, rectilinear landscape where I feel so much at home with its wind and its sails, and also the area where farmers so skilfully sow and harvest their beet (sugar) and grain (fodder, beer); the beauty of efficiency, when will alphas learn to see this? Where these two landscapes merge, harmony prevails' (Kok 1979).

While geometric works of art dominated in gardens during the Renaissance period, the Romantic Age considered the beauty of nature and its imitations to be greater than any geometric form. 'The passion caused by the great and sublime in nature, when those causes operate most powerfully, is astonishment; and astonishment is that state of the soul in which all its motions are suspended, with some degree of horror' (Burke 1753; Olwig 2002). Complexity and elusiveness contribute to the sense of the

31

The beauty of a functional landscape: Zuid Flevoland polder, the Netherlands.
Photo Peter van Bolhuis, Pandion

sublime (Bell 1999). 'The place was covered with a wonderful profusion of flowers, which without being disposed into regular borders and parterres, grew promiscuously, and had a greater beauty in their natural luxuriance and disorder than they would have received from the checks and restraints of art' (Hunt 1975).

The Romantic period passed, and during the second half of the 19th century values changed again. At the beginning of the Machine Age, the sublime character of technology, and the geometry of the built environment was again highly valued (Nye 1993). Then, in the 20th century, the 'feeling for nature' returned (Biese 1905), beautiful forms in nature – whether they were clouds, mountains, or vegetation patterns – reflecting the way they came into being.

Throughout Western history, the succession of design styles and their conflicting values may have suggested that timeless aesthetic criteria in architecture and design do not exist. However, there is evidently some kind of 'eternal beauty' and permanent ugliness.

In the Orient, the aesthetic aspects of famous oriental gardens are extremely complex. In a description by Jusuck Koh (Koh 1984) of the Katsura garden in Kyoto, Japan, conditions for beauty are specified in terms such as this:
· Total harmony between house and garden, combined with inclusive unity, which means there is an ecological and perceptual fitness to the environment.
· Asymmetry, imperfection and contradiction. There is a contradiction between the geometry of the building and the organic of the garden, while the use of rustic natural materials indicates imperfection.
· Sensitivity to change and sequential experience. The garden can be experienced only through movement, through successive revelations.
· Reverence for nature and naturalness. The use of local indigenous materials helps create a sense of place and character.
· Simplicity, restraint and understatement. The simplicity of the Katsura residence contrasts with the rustic quality of the tea

huts. Crispness, purity, cleanliness and austerity are evident. Appreciation of the understated, restrained and subtle design invites user-participation.
· Attention to detail. There are endless surprises and charms in the details, from garden fences to stepping stones. All these objects make human creativity, skill and labour significant.
· Multimodal perceptual experience: a sensitivity not merely to visual experience, but also to the effects of tactile, aromatic, kinesthetic, acoustic and thermal variations.

Though all these conditions may contribute to the appreciation of beauty in gardens anywhere in the world, there is one aspect that may elude the Western eye: the emphasis on the existence of the void. This is not the same as space as it applied in modern architecture. The void is 'not tangible but open-ended, awaiting the completion by garden and user before it can live as an art experience... in the aesthetics of the void it is people and their activities that become the focus' (Koh 1984).

· Baumeister T. 1999. *De filosofie van de kunsten* (i.e. *the philosophy of art*): *Van Plato tot Beuys*. Damon pp. 226-227
· Bell S. 1999. 'The Aesthetics of the Landscape'. In: *Landscape. Pattern, Perception and Process*. Routledge, London pp. 63-96
· Biese A. 1905. *The Development of the Feeling for Nature. In the Middle Ages and Modern Times*. Burt Franklin, New York (undated reprint).
· Burke E. 1753. *A Philosophical Enquiry into the Origins of our Ideas on the Sublime and the Beautiful*. Oxford University Press (reprint 1990)
· Eco U. 2005. *Storia della Bellezza*. Libri s.p. A., Bompiani. Chapter III
· Hunt J.D.; Willis P. 1975. 'Joseph Addison'. In: *The Genius of the Place. The English Landscape Garden*. Paul Eleck, London p. 140
· Koh J. 1984. 'Katsura, why is it so beautiful?'. In: Landscape Architecture USA September/October 1984 pp. 115-125
· Kok H. 1979. *Het zoeken naar een passende woning* (i.e. *The search for a fitting home*). Querido, Amsterdam pp. 41
· Nye D. 1993. 'The Geometrical Sublime: the Skyscraper'. In: Kristensen C. (ed). *City and Nature. Changing Relations in Time and Space*. Odense University Press pp. 29-45
· Olwig K.R. 2002. 'Natural Landscape Aesthetics'i. In: *Landscape Nature and the Body Politic*. The University of Wisconsin Press pp. 159-164
· Wöbse H.H. 2002. 'Ästhetik-Erotik-Schönheit' (i.e. Aesthetics-eroticism-beauty). In: Landschaftsästhetik. Eugen Ulmer Verlag Stuttgart pp.106-112

Katsura Palace grounds Kyoto, Japan. Harmony between palace and garden...
Photos taken in 1987

... contrast between the geometry of the building...

... a sequence of revealing scenes...

33

... and the organic layout of the garden....

... emphasis on detail.

Aesthetic theories confront the question of beauty either empirically or through formal aesthetics (Lang 1987). The empirical approach may be based on fields of expertise such as the following:

- information theory: the search for a balance between order and complexity, both in nature and in a designed environment (Spirn 1988). The idea is that aesthetic pleasure is based on the ability to understand and judge the environment. This requires that the diversity of natural process be reduced into basic concepts.
- semantics (signs, significance). In the 'Principles of Beauty' of Alexander Corens (1778), sixteen ways of describing beauty (of trees) are expressed as adjectives: attractive, modest, delicate, balanced, good-natured, haughty, penetrating, artful, lively, majestic, melancholic, innocent, tender, shy, sensible, good-humoured (Ponto 1990).
- psychobiology: sensory perception as related to the biological need for adaptation. This concept underlies the 'prospect and refuge theory', according to which aesthetic satisfaction is dependent on environmental characteristics that are favourable to survival (Appleton 1975). The extent to which biological factors relate to the cultural remains uncertain (Bourassa 1991).
- public hearings and polls: so far, clear and univocal results are lacking: 'beauty is in the eye of the beholder'.

Formal aesthetics is occupied with subjects such as the following:

- Gestalt laws: the assembly of elements into a coherent image as part of the perception process.
- clarity of expression and economy of communication
- the analysis of the notion of spatial structure
- the study of the rules of proportion.

Too much emphasis on a formal investigation into the sense of beauty may lead away from the basic premise that such an experience is a very emotional one. One

source that puts sensory delight, beauty, delight, the pretty and the picturesque into words is poetry (Drabble 1979).

- Appleton J. 1975. *The Experience of Landscape.* John Wiley & Sons,. London pp. 68-74
- Bourassa S.C. 1991. *The Aesthetics of Landscape.* Belhaven Press, London pp. 48-51
- Drabble M. 1979. *A Writer's Britain. Landscape in Literature.* Thames and Hudson, London
- Lang J. 1987. 'Aesthetic Theory'. In: *Creating Architectural Theory.* Van Nostrand Reinhold, London pp. 181-216
- Ponto A. 1990. 'The character of the tree: from Alexander Corus to Richard Payne Knight'. In: Mosser M.; Teyssot G.T. (ed.) *The History of Garden Design.* Thames and Hudson, London pp. 344 -360.
- Spirn A. 1988. 'The Poetics of City and Nature: Towards a New Aesthetic for Urban Design'. In: Landscape Journal. The University of Wisconsin Press, Madison, Wisconsin pp. 108-126

Allegory

see also > reference, symbol

'A story in which the characters and events are symbols expressing truths about human life' (*Webster*).

Such a story allows for different levels of interpretation. The intention is to engage, to

The grotto at Stourhead Wiltshire, England with the sculpture of Neptune.
Source: Kluckert. 2000. Gardens of Europe. Könemann Köln

admonish; there is a moralising undertone. A fully developed allegorical landscape is found in miniaturised Chinese stone arrangements in Chinese Zen Buddhist gardens. This represented the progress – in time and space – of the soul in the world, which finally comes to rest in the reflective sand gardens (Jellicoe 1970).

The works of Renaissance painters and their 17th-century successors were full of allegorical representations. The painters of the day distinguished themselves from their predecessors by replacing 'rural folk by river gods and Arcadian herdsmen; picturesque farms and hovels by classic temples and pavilions' (de Leeuw 1997). Renaissance and Romantic gardens abound with allegory. (Mosser 1991; Rogers 2001).

In some Romantic parks, visitors are required to follow a circuitous and somewhat demanding track beset by objects that refer to other times and faraway places (the *fabriqués* or follies) before they reach their final destination, a paradise garden (Saudan 1997). The intention is to help the visitor transcend everyday life. A maze or a labyrinth is also an allegorical object, designed to amuse but also to provide spiritual enlightenment (Spirn 1998).

All over Europe, contemporary allegorical representations can be found in the form of war memorials, with their reference to bravery, courage and suffering. 'The public graveyard is a reminder of duties constantly recurring; in the true meaning of the word, it is a monument, a 'bringing to mind' (Jackson 1997).

· Jackson J.B. 1997. 'From monument to place'. In: *Landscape in Sight*. Yale U.P., New Haven pp. 163-174
· Jellicoe G. 1970. 'The landscape of allegory'. In: *Studies on Landscape Design*. Oxford University Press. pp. 17-33
· de Leeuw R. 1997. 'De verbeelding van het landschap in de 18de en 19de eeuw' (i.e. *Imagining landscapes in the 18th and 19th centuries*). In: *Langs Velden en Wegen*. V+K publishing, Blaricum p. 13
· Mosser M.; Teyssot G. 1991. 'The Humanist Garden: from Allegory to Mannerism'. In: *The History of Garden Design*. Thames and Hudson, London pp. 26-44
· Rogers E.B. 2001. *Landscape Design*. Abrams, New York. pp. 126,132
· Saudan M.; Saudan-Skira S. 1997. *From Folly to Follies. Discovering the World of Gardens*. Benedikt Taschen Verlag, Köln pp. 175-185
· Spirn A. 1998. *The language of Landscape*. Yale University Press, New Haven p. 229

Allotment Garden
see also > garden

'Small piece of land that is rented by a private individual (usually from the local council) for growing vegetables, fruit, flowers etc (*Oxford Advanced*).

Allotments have existed in Europe ever since the 14th century (Spirn 1988). In the Netherlands there are different types of allotment, each based on the objectives at the time of its founding:
· The charitative type is the oldest. Benefactors or local governments put a site at the disposal of the poor so that they could grow their own vegetables.
· The utilitarian type followed later. The land was leased, and used mostly for growing potatoes and vegetables for sale at market. The revenues were used to pay for the tenancy.
· The recreational type is currently the dominant one: the garden and its shed, hut or small chalet serves as place of relaxation and pleasure for a whole family (Zantkuil 1972).

In Amsterdam, a Committee for Allotment gardens was established in 1909; its first action was to found the Tuinwijck garden complex (van Rooijen 1984). Contemporary allotment garden complexes are organised in larger units of approximately ten hectares, with an average area per garden of 220 to 300 square metres. Many are located on the urban fringe, meaning they have to be re-established somewhere else at every phase of city expansion.

The more permanent complexes are located within park zones or green belts, and are laid out in conjunction with the whole recreation area. In such cases, municipalities have a broader objective: a well-balanced recreational system with a well-ordered layout. One example of a well-designed allotment complex is that in Naerum, Denmark, where garden architect Sørensen's composition of elliptical hedges creates a strong contrast between inside and outside (Andersson 1993).

The allotment garden has developed over time from a small garden with a toolshed and shelter to self-designed, self-built gazebos of highly individual form and expression (Weeber 1999). Over recent decades, planning controls and environmental standards have led them to

Allotment gardens in 's-Hertogenbosch, the Netherlands.
Photo: by Frank Meijer

be more orderly and uniform in appearance – and also to be markedly more hygienic. But the charm of the individual expression appearance has been lost.

- Andersson S.I.; Hoyer S. 1993. *C.Th Sørensen – en Havekunstner.* Arkitektenforlag, Copenhagen p. 136
- van Rooijen M. 1984. *De groene stad* (i.e. *the green town*): *Een historische studie over de groenvoorziening in de Nederlandse stad.* Cultuurfonds van de Bank voor Nederlandse Gemeenten, The Hague pp. 94-96
- Spirn A. 1988. 'The poetics of City and Nature'. In: Landscape Journal. The University of Wisconsin Press, Urbana, Illinois p. 116
- Weeber C; van Stipthout M. 1999. *Het wilde wonen* (i.e. *Wild living*). De Hef, Rotterdam p. 48
- Zantkuil F. 1972. *Van coelghaerde tot vrijetijdstuin* (i.e. *From cabbage garden to leisure garden*). Algemeen Verbond van Volkstuinverenigingen in Nederland, Amsterdam

Amphitheatre

An amphitheatre is a 'round or oval building with seats rising in curved rows around an open space on which games and plays take place'. It can also be 'something resembling a theatre, such as a piece of level ground surrounded by hills' (*Webster*).

Allotment gardens in Naerum, Denmark, designed around 1960 by landscape architect C.Th.Sørensen.
Source: Andersson S.I. Hoyer S. 1993. C.Th Sørensen – en havekunstner. Arkitektenforlag København p. 139

The oldest remaining examples of amphitheatres were constructed in Greece. They were excavated in mountain slopes, such as at Delphi and Epidauros. The audience could watch performances while enjoying a panoramic view of the surrounding landscape (Crandell 1993; Rogers 2001).

In Italian Renaissance gardens, outdoor amphitheatres were constructed in stone, such as those designed by Raphael at Villa Madama and the Boboli Gardens in Florence (van der Ree 1992; Steenbergen 1996). The application of the rules of perspective guaranteed the proper visibility of the stage, and also helped form illusionist space. (see *Perspective)*

In 17th-century France, symmetrically curved grassy slopes with flower beds were called amphitheatres. In 18th-century England, Charles Bridgeman also laid out amphitheatres in grass (*Oxford Companion*). In the gardens at Stowe, Buckinghamshire, the amphitheatre was an important element in the total composition: 'There was the Temple of Apollo, a Triumphal Arch, a Garden of Venus and an Amphitheatre replete with statues of Gods and Goddesses' (Clifford 1962). A more recent example can be found in

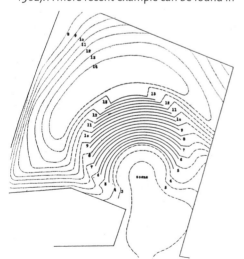

Amphitheatre in Boeslunde, Denmark, by landscape architect C.Th.Sørensen (1893-1979).
Source: Andersson I.; Hoyer S. 1993. C.Th Sørensen – en havekunstner. Arkitektenforlag Copenhagen Denmark.

Boeslunde, Denmark, where landscape architect C.Th Sørensen (1893-1979) designed a carefully composed earth sculpture (Andersson 1993).

- Andersson S.I. 1993. *C.Th.Sørensen – en Havekunstner.* Arkitektensforlag, Copenhagen
- Clifford D. 1962. *A History of Garden Design.* Faber & Faber, London p. 137
- Crandell G. 1993. *Nature Pictorialized. 'The view'. In landscape history.* Johns Hopkins University Press New York. pp. 31-34
- van der Ree P. (et al). 1992. *Italian Villas and Gardens.* Thoth publishers, Amsterdam pp. 36-41
- Rogers E.B. 2001. *Landscape Design. A Cultural and Architectural History.* Harry Abrams, New York p. 66
- Steenbergen C.; Reh W.: 1996. *Architecture and Landscape.* Thoth publishers, Bussum pp. 67-69

Anachronism

see also > anomaly, authentic, folly

An anachronism is 'the placing of persons, events, objects or customs in times to which they do not belong'. Or: a person or thing, especially from a former age, that is out of place in the present' (*Webster*).

On urban and rural sites alike, anachronisms are found wherever new constructions have been added to ancient settlements or between old buildings. While our sense of authenticity is disturbed by vernacular farm buildings with modern plastic silos, or by shiny new office blocks amidst 17th-century gabled façades, these things also remind us of the passing of time.

If an object is 'outdated', this is not necessarily a negative characteristic. A functionalist architect may find the old less efficient, and thus no longer valuable, but art collectors and historians and many other people may think otherwise.

Anachronisms are consciously applied in architecture and garden art, by combining contemporary elements with elements copied from ancient building styles. Gothic buildings and follies such as Palladian bridges are especially abundant in 18th and 19th-century Romantic parks and gardens (Hunt 1992).

The contemporary garden of Little Sparta by Ian Hamilton Finlay in Edinburgh, Scotland is renowned for its many objects that refer to

37

different times, from Palladian columns to models of modern aircraft carriers (Bann 2000). Here, anachronism is intended to stimulate the imagination.

Anachronisms are also found in park layouts which mix samples of historic styles: Parc Buttes Chaumont in Paris, designed by Alphand in 1865; and the gardens at Villandry on the river Loire, which were restored in 1920 (Hunt 1992). However, in their vegetation, growth, and decay, most gardens contain elements that in some way refer to the passing of time. 'All gardens therefore constitute, *a fortiori*, what Umberto Eco referred to as 'open works': multiple, changing, virtual entities existing and

Palladian columns feature together with scale models of aircraft carriers in Ian Hamilton Finlay's sculpture garden 'Little Sparta', in Edinburgh, Scotland.

changing over time. Gardens are, essentially, anachronistic' (Weiss 1998).

• Bann S. 2000. 'The Gardens of Ian Hamilton Finlay'. In: Mosser M. (et al). *The History of Garden Design*. Thames & Hudson, London pp. 522-524
• Hunt J.D. 1992. *Gardens and the Picturesque*. MIT Press, Cambridge
• Weiss A.S. 1998. 'In Praise of Anachronism'. In: *Unnatural Horizons. Paradox & Contradiction in Landscape Architecture*. Princeton Architectural Press, New York. pp.109 ff.

Analogy

see also > association, metaphor, model, symbol

'Partial similarity between two things that are compared' (*Oxford English Dictionary*)

The recognition of similarities in form between objects and spaces stimulates a designer's imagination and intuition. Certain parts or aspects of objects show a strong resemblance with those of other objects, and can be dissected and re-used in a different context. To the designer, analogy is thus a source of inspiration.

The difference between an analogy and a metaphor is that the metaphor is a linguistic notion, in the sense that the name of one object is transferred to another. The connection between analogy and metaphor is that the perception of analogies may lead to the creation of metaphors.

The forms of various objects on Rotterdam's Schouwburgplein show an analogy to that of derricks and ships' decks, and the whole square thereby becomes a symbol of a seaport.

There are also visible analogies in work by imitators of such great architects as Le Corbusier and Mies van der Rohe. These imitators copy the master's form principles for application in their own designs (Broadbent 1973).

There is a distinction between direct analogies and symbolic analogies (Gordon 1961). Direct analogy shows similarity in form between well-known objects: if, for example, the path system in a park is given the hierarchy of the veins of a leaf, it is called 'organic'. Symbolic analogy relates to the underlying meaning of relationships between phenomena, the design of models that are used to describe human society being founded on symbolic analogies.

• Broadbent G. 1973. *Design in Architecture*. John Wiley & Sons, New York pp. 329; 350-351; 421
• Gordon W.J.J. 1961. *Synectics. The development of Creative Capacity*. Collier Macmillan, London p. 34 ff

Analysis

see also > behaviour, design method, layer, topography

'An examination of a whole to discover its elements and their relations' (*Webster*)

Landscape or site analysis is an essential part of the planning and design process of outdoor spaces. It involves the collection and evaluation of data on a terrain or landscape, and is motivated by the need to know and to understand before intervening in any situation.

It is based partly on logical reasoning, and is partly creative. Logic comes into the search for the individual elements which compose an environment, and also into analysis of the way these elements relate and have related in the past. The creative part is the search for an answer to the question of how all this information can be applied in a design: what can one do with it? This combination requires imagination and deductive power on the part of the analyst.

The landscape architect's initial approach to a design assignment consists of 'reconnoitring a given situation, its meaning and its identity'. The tasks of his design are to 'disengage, reveal, enhance, articulate and modulate' the potentials of the site' (Marot 1994).

Inventive analysis can be compared with detective work. As Edgar Allan Poe states in the first detective novel ever written: 'The analytical power should not be confounded with simple ingenuity, for while the analyst is necessarily ingenious, the ingenious man is often remarkably incapable of analysis. Between ingenuity and the analytic ability there exists a difference far greater, indeed, than that between the fancy and the

39

imagination, but of a character very strictly analogous. It will be found, in fact, that the ingenious are always fanciful, and the truly imaginative never otherwise than analytic' (Poe 1830/1944).

This comparison indicates the relative value of the analysis-synthesis approach: dissecting a complex environment in separate parts does not mean that the relations between these parts can be retrieved in the synthesis phase. As the sum of the parts is not the same as a whole, the designer's intuition and experience must supplement the logical process of a step-by-step process.

Site analysis

This is the collection and evaluation of data needed for the design of a certain piece of land. The nature and scope of the collected data are determined by the brief, in which the types of land-use that must be fitted into a site are summarised (Motloch 2001; Rutledge 1971). It is part of the search towards attuning 'supply' and 'demand', when the optimal location and form of various new elements are laid down in the planning proposal (Lynch 1984).

The 'why' of site analysis is founded on the aim of adapting the territorial claims of new land-use to the size and characteristics of an existing site in order to establish the place's potential, capacity and local identity, and also to ascertain historical continuity. There are also practical considerations such as efficiency of use and the need to cut construction costs. Finally, there is also an aesthetic ideal which holds that the optimal functioning of an object or an environment contributes to a sense of beauty.

The following factors are usually investigated in a site analysis:
· the location of the site and its relation to the surrounding area
· soil conditions and water levels
· elevation, topography, slopes
· existing vegetation elements
· local climate
· existing built objects
· sources of pollution and local climate

40

Other factors may be included, depending on the location, nature and size of the site.

This topographical analysis may be supplemented by a topological study, i.e. 'the history of a region as indicated by its topography' (Webster). This involves the study of vertical relations in a landscape – geology, soils, water, plants, wildlife and human settlement (see Layer). A chorological analysis, as performed in ecology, studies horizontal relations and processes. The two approaches are complements within a landscape analysis (Ahern 2002; Zonneveld 1995).

The registration and assessment of visual aspects requires special attention. Spaces, edges, corridors and sightlines must be registered; references to other times and places be noted, and characteristic elements assessed (Simonds 1998). In 17th-century England, these activities were described as 'a search for the genius of the place' – in other words, taking the existing situation as a starting point for future development.

The English poet Joseph Spence (1699-1768) put it this way: 'What is, is the great guide as to what ought to be... to study the ground thoroughly, one should not only take a view of the whole and all its parts, and consider the laying of it in general, and all its beauties and advantages or inconveniences or impediments, in particular, but also walk around it in the line without your own bounds; to see what beauties may be added by breaking through your outline' (Hunt 1975). This statement confirms once again the compelling need not to analyse an environment without a design concept for future development.

· Ahern J. 2002. 'Spatial concepts, planning strategies and future scenarios, a framework method for integrating landscape ecology and landscape planning'. In: Greenways as Strategic Landscape Planning: Theory and application. Wageningen University.
· Hunt J.D.; Willis P. 1975. 'Joseph Spence'. In: The Genius of the Place. Paul Elek, London p. 268
· Lynch K.; Hack G. 1984. Site Planning (third edition). MIT Press, Cambridge pp. 29-66
· Marot S. 1994. 'On public space as landscape. Landscape architecture in France'. In: Archis Journal. Architecture, urbanism, visual arts. NAi, Rotterdam p. 60
· Motloch J.L. 2001. 'Site design as problem-solving'. In:

Introduction to Landscape Design. Van Nostrand Reinhold, London pp. 286 ff.
- Poe Edgar Allan 1944. 'The Murders in the Rue Morgue'. In: *Tales of Mystery and Imagination.* Penguin Books p. 148
- Rutledge A.J. 1971. 'Site design process'. In: *Anatomy of a Park.* McGraw-Hill, New York pp. 91-105
- Simonds, J.O. 1998. *Landscape Architecture. A Manual of Site Planning and Design.* McGraw Hill, New York. pp. 113-136
- Zonneveld I.S. 1995. *Land Ecology.* SPB, Amsterdam

Landscape analysis

In 1915, the British botanist Patrick Geddes (1854-1932), the proclaimed father of modern regional planning, introduced the concept of regional analysis or regional survey, which was to be based on an objective approach: 'Such surveys must be strictly scientific. Our aim is to see things as they are and apply our knowledge to other matters' (Geddes 1915/1932; Turner 1987).

One of example of this approach was the General Expansion Plan for Amsterdam in 1934. This was preceded by an investigation into planning problems that led to a search for a coherent projection of land-use types such as housing, industry, circulation and outdoor recreation, all on the basis of an analysis of existing conditions. The results were a rational layout of urban neighbourhoods and a 'functional city'. Such a survey normally includes:
- the physical geography of the area under study
- historical developments
- industry and manufacturing
- population and housing statistics
- health conditions
- traffic and infrastructure
- parks and recreation grounds
- agriculture
- public services.

Insight into the future need for space can be gained by the extrapolation of existing trends. In recent examples, surveys have acquired a cyclical character, and have become an integral part of the planning process.

Landscape analysis is similar to a site analysis, with the difference that a brief or a programme prescribing new land-use may be lacking. In such cases, the aim of the analysis may be limited by the determination of suitabilities for potential use (Steiner 2000).

When a landscape analysis is supposed to serve as the basis for a landscape plan, it should be based on – and guided by – previously formulated objectives, concepts or ideas (Sijmonds 1990). Without such a concept, the results tend to be limited in scope, serving only to support arguments for the conservation of valued elements. An example of such a limited analysis is found in McHarg's study of a highway route-selection process that had consisted solely of an evaluation of existing conditions. This process resulted in a plan in which minimum disturbance or damage were emphasised, while creative design opportunities were ignored (McHarg 1969).

- Geddes P. 1915. *Cities in Evolution.* Oxford University Press New York
- McHarg I. 1969. 'A step forward'. In: *Design with Nature.* Natural History Press, New York pp. 31-41
- Steiner F. 2000. 'Inventory and analysis of the biophysical environment'. In: *The Living Landscape. An Ecological Approach to Landscape Planning.* McGraw Hill, New York pp. 51-94
- Sijmonds D. 1990. 'Regional Planning as a Strategy'. In: Landscape and Urban Planning Journal, Elsevier, Amsterdam no. 18 pp. 265-273
- Turner T. 1987. 'Landscape theory'. In: *Landscape Planning.* Hutchinson, London pp. 1-2

Design analysis

This is an investigation into the nature and content of a design process whereby the design product is studied through drawings or completed projects. It involves questions about the way the design process was organised and about the considerations or philosophy on which it was based. Thus, were all relevant data taken into account? If not, why not? What are the iconographic aspects of the design; what does it represent?

In short, design analysis attempts to unravel the rationale behind the design process. Examples of detailed design analyses of historic gardens were published by Steenbergen (Steenbergen 1996). However, there are limitations to the amount of dependable information that can be gained on the basis of a design analysis, as personal interpretation by the analyst is inevitable (Weiss 1998).

One source of additional information is the analysis of a number of different designs drawn simultaneously for a particular site, which allows comparison of different solutions to the same problem. Such comparative analysis can be used to study the entries for a design competition in which several designers base their plans on the same conditions and the same brief (Meeus 1990; Baljon 1992).

• Baljon L. 1992. *Designing Parks. An examination of contemporary approaches to design in landscape architecture.* Architectura & Natura Press, Amsterdam
• Meeus J.H.A. 1990. 'Openness in dense packing'. In: *Learning from Rotterdam.* Mansell, London pp. 123-164
• Steenbergen C.; Reh W. 1996. *Architecture and Landscape.* Thoth Publishers, Bussum
• Weiss A. 1998. 'Dematerialization and Iconoclasm'. In: *Unnatural Horizons. Paradox & Contradiction in Landscape Architecture.* Princeton Architectural Press, New York pp. 44 ff.

Anamorphosis
see > perspective

Anomaly
see also > anachronism, contrast

'Deviation from what is usual or expected' (*Webster*).

An anomaly in a landscape is the 'alien object' which does not fit within its context. It can be experienced as a surprising, interesting object, but also as an alienating, disturbing element (Spirn 1998). For example, a small pond that is laid out on top of a hill and serves as a pretext for building a bridge looks out of place, as are the pretty little

The presence of this bridge, which leads to the entrance of a restaurant on top of a hill, was made plausible by the construction of a mini-pond. Soumatre, Hérault, France 2005.

A building out of place: Battery Park Manhattan N.Y. as it looked in 1986.

Urban elements in a Dutch rural setting. The banks of a stream reinforced with imported stone blocks.
Source: Landwerk Journal no 4, p 32, Blauwdruk, Wageningen

flower park in an agrarian setting, the lovingly restored natural stream whose banks are reinforced with imported stone blocks, or the high-voltage power line running through a nature area (Hough 1990).

Surprising sights may be afforded from the motorway that passes underneath an aqueduct, where motorists see ships passing overhead. There is a similar dissonance between a modest but carefully detailed historic office building and its gigantic glass-panelled neighbours.

In their site-design, landscape architects may introduce anomalies that will catch the visitor's attention, that will surprise and delight – like the bridge in the grounds of the VSB head office in Utrecht, whose practical purpose is not clear (see *Bridge*) (Harsema 1996).

• Harsema H. (ed). 1996. *Landscape architecture and town planning in the Netherlands 93-95*. Thoth publishing, Bussum pp. 120-123
• Hough M. 1990. 'Industrial landscapes and environmental perceptions'. In: *Out of Place. Restoring Identity to Regional Landscapes* Yale University Press, New Haven pp. 122-148
• Spirn A. 1998. *The Language of Landscape*. Yale University Press, New Haven pp. 159-160

Antropocentrism
see > ecocentrism

Arcade, Loggia
see also > margin, pergola

'A row of arches with the columns that support them. An arched or covered passageway' (*Webster*). An arched passageway along a building or between buildings that connects the inside and outside. As the margin between public and private, it plays an important role in the human experience of space, and also in the interaction between humans and buildings (Alexander 1977; Stauffacher 1988; Zerbst 1987).

A loggia is 'a roofed gallery open on at least one side' (*Webster*). It originated in Mediterranean countries, where there was a need for seating space that was open but shaded. During the period of the Italian Renaissance, loggias often faced public squares, such as those in Florence. They were was also an important part of a villa, and were often decorated with frescos

43

The loggia around Plaça Real, Barcelona.

(*Britannica*).

In garden design, the arcade was a connecting element which, together with the loggia, terrace and stairway, constituted an important element in the composition of the whole (Steenbergen 1990). In the gardens at Marly near Paris, the arcades are formed by clipped hedges (*Oxford Companion*).

· Alexander C. 1977. *A Pattern Language*. Oxford University Press pp. 581 ff.

44

- *Parc Guëll, Barcelona; architect Antonio Gaudì.*

Basilica St Paul, Rome.

- Stauffacher Solomon B. 1988. *Green Architecture and the Agrarian Garden.* Rizolli, New York p. 115
- Steenbergen C. 1990. *De stap over de horizon (i.e. The step over the horizon).* Delft p. 41
- Zerbst R. 1987. *Antoni Gaudí.* Taschen Verlag, Köln pp. 158-159

Palace garden Het Loo, Apeldoorn, the Netherlands.
Foto: Harry Harsema

Arcadia

see also > pastoral, poetic, romanticism, suburbia, utopia

'A region or scene of simple pleasure and quiet' (*Webster*).

The origins of Arcadia lie in a rural agrarian setting on the Greek Peloponnese islands. It is a mythical place of pastoral simplicity, where there was harmony between man and nature – a middle landscape between town and country, but without the negative aspects of either. It is a paradisal place where two worlds co-exist: the idyllic or 'pastoral rustic', and the real wilderness, which was 'a labyrinth of madness and death' (Schama 1995).

In 15th-century Tuscany, villas were built in rural sites at some distance from town, onto which they nonetheless had a view. The owners could thus retire from urban life

45

An Arcadian Image. 'The Four Seasons' painted by Hendrick Meyer in 1777.
Rijksmuseum Amsterdam

without turning their backs on it
(Steenbergen 1996). This middle landscape
between town and country or 'the best of
both worlds' became very popular in 19th-
century England (Thomas 1983) and in the
20th century USA, where it led to the
development of vast suburban areas
(Mumford 1963; Rowe 1991).

A special form of arcadia became popular in
18th and 19th-century England when
picturesque parks and gardens were laid out
either amid fertile agrarian land, or in a more
natural setting featuring spectacular
geological phenomena (Clifford 1962).
Contemporary arcadia has become a wider
concept, including a clean environment, a
balance between urbanisation and nature,
and an accessible quasi-wilderness (Pepper
1995).

• Clifford D. 1962. *A History of Garden Design*. Faber, London p.
166
• Mumford L. 1963. 'The suburban way of life'. In: *The City in
History*. Secker & Warburg pp. 493-496
• Pepper D. 1995. *Modern Environmentalism*. Routledge, London
pp.168, 188.
• Rowe P. 1991. *Making a Middle Landscape*. MIT Press,
Cambridge pp.1-28 , 217 ff.
• Schama S. 1995. 'Arcadia Redesigned'. In: *Landscape and
Memory*. Harper Collins, New York pp. 517-578
• Steenbergen C.M.; Reh W. 1996. 'Arcadia as the urban ideal'. In:
Architecture and Landscape. Thoth, Bussum pp. 34-35
• Thomas K. 1983. 'Cultivation and Wilderness'. In: *Man and the
Natural World*. Pantheon Books, New York pp. 242-302

Archetype

'The original pattern of a work or model of a
work from which others are copied'
(*Webster*).

According to psychologist Carl Jung (1875-
1961), archetypes are primordial images
which symbolically express quintessential
meanings that cannot be directly identified
or subjected to control by the conscious mind
(Jung 1964; Rogers 2001).

The archetype of the city is not necessarily
the market place, but often the site of the
temple, a collection of buildings in a
geometric layout which houses the centre of
power (Olwig 1993).

The archetype of the garden is the Garden
of Eden, the symbol of Paradise on Earth. It

was the place where the wilderness was
banned and where one could find 'every tree,
good for food and a pleasure to behold' (Prest
1981).

Archetypes of garden design usually consist
of exemplary solutions derived from a
number of styles, especially Classicist and
Modernist (Meeus 1990). The forms of
objects and spaces are also based on
archetypes such as the line, circle or pyramid
(Weilacher 1996). A geometric form such as
this is 'the most nearly typical of all the
objects it represents, having the most nearly
perfect form' (Krieger 2000).

Archetypical landscapes serve as primeval
examples for cultural currents or style
periods. The archetype for the Romantic park
layout, for instance, is Arcadia (Schama 1995).

• Jung C. 1964. *Man and his Symbols*. Doubleday & Company
Garden City, New York pp. 66-67
• Krieger M. 2000. *What's wrong with plastic trees? Artifice and
Authenticity in Design*. Praeger, New York p. 67
• Meeus J.H.A. 1990. 'Openness in dense packing'. In: *Learning
from Rotterdam*. Mansell, London pp. 152-153
• Olwig K.R. 1993. 'The Archetypical City and the Concept of
Nature before the Industrial Revolution'. In: Kristensen T.M. (et
al) (ed). *City and Nature. Changing Relations in Time and Space*.
Odense University Press pp. 99-100
• Prest J. 1981. *The Garden of Eden. The Botanic Garden and the
Re-creation of Paradise*. Yale University Press, New Haven p. 11
• Rogers E.B. 2001. 'Visions of Paradise'. In: *Landscape Design*.
Abrams, New York. pp. 97 ff.
• Schama S. 1995. 'Arcadia Redesigned'. In: *Landscape and
Memory*. Harper Collins, London pp. 517 ff.
• Weilacher U. 1996. 'Archetypical forms'. In: *Between Landscape
Architecture and Land Art*. Birkhäuser, Basel pp. 19, 20

Articulation

'To express clearly and distinctly' (*Webster*).
'Architecture is the articulation of space so
as to produce in the participator a definite
space experience in relation to previous and
anticipated experiences' (Bacon 1974).

In the design of outdoor spaces, articulation
means the avoidance of hard contrasts
between mass and voids, between 'black and
white'. Spaces in gardens are 'grey zones –
neither open nor enclosed'. Designing with
plant materials results in a stratified space,
'constructed, substantial and articulate' (Rose
1993; Meyer 1997).

Somewhat like the punctuation of words in a sentence, there is also a clearly visible distinction between the parts of an object or a space. To achieve this effect, linear spaces may be subdivided (Hoogstad 1990). An entrance can lead to a climax via a series of accents or special features, and thereby provide a strong sense of space, a feeling of being in the centre, in the heart (Baljon 1992).

Articulation may also be the expression of a relationship between the design problem and site conditions (Lynch 1971). It is a condition for quality in design. However, emphasising relations in form-giving can be overdone, as a margin of uncertainty for interpretation should always remain. By 'de-articulating' a design or an image, an artist may allow the observer to complete, to fill in (Melot 1975).

• Bacon E. 1974. 'Articulating space'. In: *Design of Cities*. Thames and Hudson, London p. 21

• Baljon L. 1992. *Designing Parks*. Architectura & Natura, Amsterdam pp. 71-72
• Hoogstad J. 1990. 'Double articulation versus tripartite articulation'. In: *Space-time-motion*. SDU Uitgeverij, The Hague pp. 79 ff.
• Lynch K. 1971. *Site Planning (second edition)* MIT Press, Cambridge pp. 219-222
• Melot M. 1975. *L'oeil qui rit. Le pouvoir comique des images*. Office du Livre, Fribourg pp. 81-82
• Meyer E. 1997. 'The expanded field of landscape architecture'. In: Thompson G.; Steiner F. *Ecological Design and Planning*. Wiley & Sons, New York pp. 56-80
• Rose J.C. 1993. 'Articulate form in landscape design'. In: Treib M (ed). *Modern Landscape Architecture: a Critical Review*. MIT Press, Cambridge pp. 72-75

Association

see also > analogy, metaphor, sign, symbol, reference

'A feeling, memory or thought connected with a person, a place, or a thing' (*Webster*). A capacity for associative thinking or

Too much articulation can be boring. La Gare or 'Le monde désarticulé' by Paul Klee.
Source: Melot M. L'oeil qui rit. Le pouvoir comique des images. Office du livre. Fribourg, Switzerland, 1975

imagining is an important asset for solving cryptograms. It is also an important asset for designers. Associations are not consciously evoked, they just occur or are sub-consciously activated. In a distant past, European rural landscapes were associated with myths and sagas, with dramatic events. They evoked fear (Schama 1995).

Associations occur whenever there is a similarity in form between different objects. For example, by putting an ordinary corkscrew in different positions, one is able to 'see' various other objects or situations, such as a hold-up, or a rocket on a launch-pad (Jencks 1972). Associations can be evoked by smells and sounds that remind one of former times and other places. Roaring sounds combined with kerosene smells may be associated with airports, or the smell of slurry with intensive farming.

In history, images of landscapes have evoked various associations, from delight to melancholy or nostalgia (Gold 1980). When environments or buildings are consciously designed to refer to other objects or worlds, the observer no longer makes unconscious mental connections, but is the subject of manipulated references.

• Gold J.R. 1980. 'Images of Landscape'. In: *An Introduction to Behavioural Geography*. Oxford University Press pp. 115-126
• Jencks C.; Silver N. 1972. *Adhocism. The Case for Improvisation*. Secker & Warburg, London p. 40
• Schama S. 1995. 'The Verdant Cross'. In: *Landscape and Memory*. Harper Collins, New York pp. 214-226

Authenticity
see also > meaning, romanticism, style

Authentic means 'being really what it seems to be' (*Webster*) and 'known to be true or genuine' (*Oxford English Dictionary*).

Every well-designed environment, meaningful place, lively park, good-looking and properly functioning tool, can be called authentic in the sense of being genuine. 'A well-designed thing has its own way of being, and so we say it is authentic. If it works and if it is satisfying, we come to take it as natural' (Krieger 2000).

In everyday language, however, the notion

is bound to elements around us that date from the past and which appear – to us, at least – to be as they were originally conceived, built or laid out. Because they represent history, they are objects of interest. Authentic villages and century-old buildings are tourist attractions, even if the changes wrought over time may have drastically altered their appearance. 'Isolated from the host environment and the local people, the mass tourist travels in guided groups and finds pleasure in inauthentic contrived attractions, gullibly enjoying 'pseudo-events' and disregarding the world outside' (Urry 2002; York 1988).

Authenticity is often difficult to establish, as it depends on a point of view. In the sense that they are full of imitations of such alien

The facade of a vernacular farm building at Orvelte, the Netherlands.

objects as follies that refer to other places and earlier times, Romantic landscape parks in 18th-century England are 'fake'. To our eyes, however, they nonetheless represent the spirit of the time in which they were laid out – a perspective from which they are authentic. A quest for authentic landscapes is therefore mostly a matter of choice, judgement or preference (Lowenthal 1985).

Authentic gardens date back as far as the 15th-century Italian Renaissance examples that have been lovingly restored, and have also benefited from their durable construction. Older gardens are found only in paintings and other reproductions. Due to the lack of plant lists and precise measurements, these are difficult to reconstruct (Lehrman 1991; Hernández-Bermejo 1991; Hajós 1995).

• Hajós G. 1995. 'Notes on the problem of authenticity in historic parks and gardens'. In: Journal of Garden History. Vol. 15 no. 4 pp. 221-225
• Hernandez-Bermejo E. 1991. 'Botanical Foundations for the restoration of Spanish-Arabic Gardens'. In: Tjon Sie Fat L.; de Jong E. (ed). *The Authentic Garden*. Clusius Foundation, Leiden pp. 153 -158.
• Krieger M. 2000. *What's wrong with Plastic Trees? Artifice and Authenticity in Design*. Praeger, New York p. 84
• Lehrman J. 1991. 'An introduction to the problems and possibilities of restoring historic Islamic gardens'. In: Tjon Sie Fat L; de Jong E. (ed). *The Authentic Garden*. Clusius Foundation, Leiden pp. 105 – 108
• Lowenthal D. 1985. *The Past is a Foreign Country*. Cambridge University Press
• Urry J. 2002. *The Tourist Gaze*. Sage Publications, London p. 7
• York P. 1988. Culture as commodity'. In: Thackara J. (ed). *Design after Modernism*. Thames & Hudson, London pp. 160 -168

Avenue
see also > access, boulevard, promenade

In rural areas: 'Wide road or path, often lined with trees, esp. one that leads to a large house'. In towns: 'Wide street lined with trees or tall buildings' (*Oxford English Dictionary*).

Avenues were a prime feature on many of the great 18th-century English estates; one example is the Great Avenue at Castle Howard. In some cases, as at Woodstock Park, the Grand Avenue stands out as a tree-sculptured element in a vast open space (Steenbergen 1996). In formal designs,

avenues are normally straight.

The most famous urban examples are found in Paris, where tree-lined avenues such as the Champs Elysées were the unifying elements in Haussmann's 19th-century plans for the reorganisation of the city. Their layout is grandiose: 'three times the width of a normal boulevard, flanked by lawns and paths, and punctuated with beds of rare plants' (Joest 1990). Their form and dimensions are motivated by the need not only for pomp and ceremony, but also for order, safety and control in a turbulent city – they are part of what might be called a political landscape in which the expression of central power is always evident (Jackson 1984). Their names often refer to famous people or elevated places, such as the 'Champs Elysées' or 'heavenly fields' (Gaillard

49

Entrance lane to farm in Oldehove Overijssel, the Netherlands.

1990).

Though wide, the avenues that serve as entrance lanes leading to estates or farms in rural areas are nonetheless of more modest proportions.

• Gaillard M. 1990. *Les Belles Heures des Champs Élsées*. Martelle Editions, Amiens
• Jackson J.B. 1984. *Discovering the Vernacular Landscape*. Yale University Press, New Haven pp.12 ff.
• von Joest T. 1990. 'Haussmann's Paris: A Green Metropolis?'. In: Mosser M.; Teyssot G. 1990. *The History of Garden Design*. Thames & Hudson, London pp. 387-398

• Steenbergen C.; Reh W. 1996. *Architecture and Landscape*. Thoth Publishing, Bussum pp. 259, 313

Axis

see also > vista, symmetry

'A straight line with respect to which a body, figure or curve is symmetrical' (*Webster*).

In towns and parks, an axis is a straight line connecting two points and also serving as a sightline. It connects the observer's

The Grand Avenue in Woodstock Park, Blenheim House, England. A free-standing sculptural element.

50

viewpoint with the horizon (Kerkstra 2003). Unlike a vista, an axis is flanked by symmetrical or balanced walls or volumes on both sides, and thereby forms an autonomous unit. The length of an axis by far exceeds the width, creating a linear space such as a street, a boulevard, a monumental avenue or a 'grand canal'. The character of the walls on both sides determine the character of the axis (Ching 1975).

Axes are dominant elements to which all other elements are subordinated, especially in the case of the total symmetry found in Baroque parks (Simonds 1997). When its scale and size exceeds that of the surroundings, a well-balanced axis may become dominant, even if it is asymmetrical, like the axis between the Paris Tuileries and the Round Point in La Défense (Steenbergen 1996). Grand axes like these usually form 'baroque-like and purely honorific urban spaces symbolising the state' (Colquhoun 1989).

Examples are found in Washington DC and New Delhi, and also in Albert Speer's designs for Berlin.

· Ching F.D.L. 1975. *Architecture: Form, Space, Order.* Van Nostrand and Reinhold, London pp. 334-341
· Colquhoun A. 1989. *Modernity and the Classical Tradition.* MIT Press, Cambridge pp. 227-229
· Kerkstra K. 2003. 'Geometry and Genius Loci'. In Kerkstra K (ed). *The landscape of symbols.* Blauwdruk publishers, Wageningen
· Simonds J.O. 1997. *Landscape Architecture.* McGraw-Hill, New York pp. 223-229
· Steenbergen C.; Reh W. 1996. *Architecture and Landscape.* Thoth publishing, Bussum. pp. 215-233

Axonometry

see > perspective

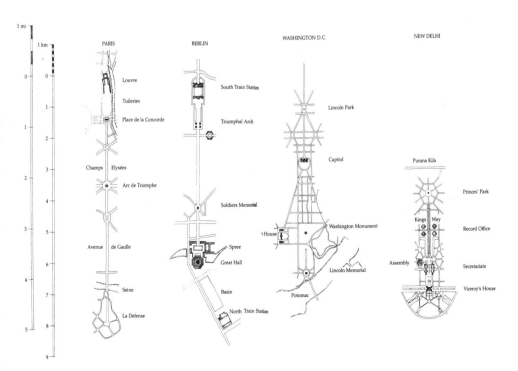

Examples of urban axes in Paris, Berlin, Washington D.C. and New Delhi, all drawn to the same scale.
Source: Colquhoun A, 1989. Modernity and the Classical Tradition. Architectural Essays. MIT press pp 228-229

Baroque

see also > Classicism, geometry, Renaissance

'Of, or relating to, a style of artistic expression, especially of the 17th century, marked by elaborate and sometimes grotesque ornamentation and the use of curved and exaggerated figures in art and architecture' (*Webster*).

The origin of the word baroque lies in the Portuguese *barrocco*, used by jewellers to indicate dented or irregularly shaped pearls that were considered to be exuberant – and even decadent – specimens (Larousse; Petit Robert).

As a design style, Baroque originated in Rome sometime after 1600. It can simultaneously be seen as the final stage of the High Renaissance, and also as a separate style. Baroque towns and buildings are associated with pomp and ceremony, with theatrical effects and exalted feelings. Buildings were plastic in form, enveloping space with their curved fronts, replacing the balanced shape of the Renaissance squares with movement and spatial expansiveness. A symmetrical axis extended to the horizon (Giedion 1967; Gutkind 1969). During the 17th and 18th century, Baroque palaces and gardens were constructed throughout over Europe, giving royal courts sumptuous layouts in which to display their grandeur (Rogers 2002; Kluckert 2000).

In the Netherlands, where majestic dignity and the accompanying grand gestures were less appreciated, Baroque styles never became as popular in garden art as in neighbouring countries. A number of 17th-century gardens were laid out in a Classical style, and included a number of features typical of a Baroque layout, with straight axes radiating from a central point, plus decorative elements, garden sculptures, fountains and other elements designed to amuse (Oldenburger 1999). However, Renaissance and Baroque design principles were adopted in the layout of newly reclaimed territory such as at Borsselle in Zeeland and in the reclaimed Beemster and Schermer polders to the North of Amsterdam (Lambert 1971; van de Ven 1993).

Baroque palace, Sans Souci, Potsdam, Germany.

53

Sensuous curves in Kromhoutpark, Tilburg, the Netherlands. 1991. B+B landscape architects.

In contemporary Dutch parks, Baroque forms – in the sense of a composition of irregular curves and sensuous lines and volumes – are recognisable at sites such as Kromhoutpark in Tilburg (Harsema 1996).

- Giedion S. 1967. 'The undulating wall and the flexible ground plan'. In: *Space Time & Architecture. The Growth of a Tradition.* Harvard U.P. pp. 110-132
- Gutkind E.A. 1969. *International History of City Development* Vol IV: Urban Development in Southern Europe.' The Baroque'. Free Press, New York
- Harsema H. (ed). 1996. 'Kromhoutpark Tilburg'. In: *Landscape architecture and town planning in the Netherlands 93-95.* Thoth publishing, Bussum pp. 164-167
- Kluckert E. 2000. *The Gardens of Europe.* Könemann, Köln pp. 144-347
- Lambert A.M. 1971. *The Making of the Dutch landscape.* Seminar Press, London pp214-220
- Oldenburger C. (et al). 1999. *Gids voor de Nederlandse tuin- en landschapsarchitectuur* (i.e. *Guide for Dutch landscape architecture).* De Hef Publishing, Rotterdam pp. 28-31
- Rogers E.B. 2001. Landscape Design. A Cultural and Architectural History. Harry N. Abrams New York pp. 165- 231
- van de Ven G.P. 1993. (ed). *Man-made lowlands.* Matrijs Publishers Utrecht pp 132-13

Dutch polder landscape with gates and earthen dams.

Barrage, Dam

see also > basin, dike, stream

'An artificial bar or embankment in a river or watercourse (such as that constructed across the Nile) intended to increase the depth of water. With the growth of large-scale irrigation in many parts of the world, the term barrage is commonly applied to large structures designed to conserve a large body of water and thus constructed across the major rivers. The word dam seems to be preferred if water storage is combined with the generation of electricity, and barrage if it is not' (*Goulty*).

Large barrages and dams are not only dominant visual features in mountainous landscapes: in ecological terms, their consequences are often both unforeseen and drastic, especially in underdeveloped countries (Perez 1990).

In the Netherlands during the Middle Ages, the construction of small and medium-sized dams and dikes across and along rivers used to be a prerequisite for building settlements; as with Amsterdam and Rotterdam, the name of many a town or city thus ends in '-dam' (Burke 1956). During the 20th century, large storm-surge barriers were built to enclose and contain large bodies of water such as the Zuyderzee to the east of Amsterdam, and the Delta area in the southwest of the country. The changes were often far-reaching: while safety was improved, ecological conditions were affected over large areas (van de Ven 1993).

In the Netherlands' waterlogged polders, most farms and farmland plots are enclosed by ditches, being accessible only across small earthen dams. With their wooden gates and fences, these dams are distributed in large numbers throughout the polders, and are a characteristic landscape element in the western provinces.

Throughout history, dams have been constructed in gardens and parks, especially in China (Keswick 1991). In England they were used to create ponds, sometime with cascades (Daniels 1999). While their use was popular, the sight of them was not always welcome. Landscape architect Lancelot 'Capability' Brown (1716-1783) attempted to hide his dams, or to fit them into the contours of the terrain, thereby making a pond look like a river (*Oxford Companion*; Moore et al 1989; Turner 1985). Even if their use was welcomed, such works of engineering were not thought to be acceptable in rural settings, a situation that persists today (Colvin 1970).

• Burke G.L. 1956. *The Making of Dutch Towns.* Cleaver-Hume Press, London
• Colvin B. 1970. *Land and Landscape.* Murray, London p. 147
• Daniels S. 1999. *Humphry Repton. Landscape Gardening and the geography of Georgian England.* Yale University Press, New Haven
• Keswick M. 1991. 'An Introduction to Chinese gardens.'. In: Tjon Sie Fat L.; de Jong E. (ed). *The Authentic Garden.* Clusius Foundation, Leiden pp. 189 ff.
• Moore C.W. (et al). 1989. 'Capability Brown's Parks'. In: *The Poetics of Gardens.* MIT Press, Cambridge p. 61
• Perez M.N. 1990. 'Development of Mediterranean agriculture: an ecological approach'. In: Landscape and Urban Planning vl 18, Elsevier, Amsterdam pp. 211-220
• Turner R. 1985. *Capability Brown and the Eighteenth Century English Landscape.* Weidenfeld, New York pp. 81 ff.
• van de Ven G.P. (ed). 1993. 'The Zuiderzee and the Deltaprojects'. In: *Man-made Lowlands.* Matrijs Publishers, Utrecht pp. 237-286

The Oosterschelde storm-surge barrier (above) and Grevelingen dam show just how much the appearance of dams can differ. Zeeland, the Netherlands.

Basin

see also > barrage, garden, island, rock,
source, stream, sustainable

'An enclosed or partly enclosed water area.
The land drained by a river and its branches.
A great depression in the surface of the
lithosphere occupied by an ocean' (*Webster*).

There are basins at all levels of scale, from
pools through ponds, lakes, bays and lagoons
to seas and oceans. All collecting water from
mountains, springs, wells, waterfalls, streams
and rivers, they constitute part of the world's
natural cycle of evaporation, precipitation
and run-off. The eternal movement of the
seas and oceans – the largest basins on earth
– are the source of deep impressions,
emotions, and even fear. They represent the
great depths – desolation, the sublime, the
fairy-like image (Corbin 1988).

Among the smallest basins are the pool, the
pond, and the grand canal in gardens and
parks. In many Italian Renaissance gardens
they are the terminal point for currents of
water that descend from fountains, down
slopes, falls and cascades, to the mirroring
surface of still ponds representing the ocean
(Kluckert 2000), thereby creating an
imposing three-dimensional play of sound,
movement and light reflection, a 'theatre of
water works' (Ogrin 1993).

In historic Chinese gardens, irregularly
shaped ponds were combined with rock
formations. These represented landscapes
with water and mountains, showing a

contrast between hard rock (yang) and the
movement of water (ying) (Keswick 1991).
Ponds are places of pleasure. 'As the water
does its essential, practical work, there will be
occasions for play and celebration – of
glittering surface or drifting mists, of
foaming cascade or silent depth' (Moore
1989).

In Japanese gardens, the composition of
pond, bridge and island creates an ensemble
representing a natural landscape that

'Rapports de l'angle optique avec les eaux' showing the
angle of view that allows the observer to see objects
mirrored in the water.
Source : Edouard André, 1879. Traité Général de la Composition
des Parcs et Jardins. Masson Paris p. 128.

Looking down on water bodies in sloping terrain creates
surprising effects of perspective. The surface of the water
appears to slope towards the observer; a mountain lake in
Austria, and Margraten war cemetery in Limburg, the
Netherlands.

simultaneously functions as a stage for ceremonial and festive occasions (Ito 1972; Thacker 1985). In the Le Nôtre gardens in France, boating on the grand canal was an important pastime (Hazelhurst 1980; Orsenna 2000).

Continuously overflowing in the Patio de la Reja in the Alhambra at Granada is a small basin fed by a fountain. Through its reference to the ocean, its effect by far outstrips its size: 'All rivers run into the sea; yet the sea is not full; unto the place whence the rivers come, thither they return again' (Spirn 1988).

During the Romantic Age, references to nature were made in basins of a totally different character (Laurie 1975). In the parks laid out by Capability Brown (1716-1783) ponds are curvilinear, obscure and somewhat mysterious; these were laid out to appear like a river, its sinuous form fitting within the landscape (Turner 1985).

Water mirrors light. In a flat terrain, the visibility of a water surface depends on circumstances such as its level relative to the surrounding terrain and its length parallel to the angle of vision (Harsema 2000; André 1879).

In the geometric layout of 17th- and 18th-century French gardens, the reflection of light was carefully exploited as a means to manipulate the depth of perspective. The great length of the Grand Canal in Versailles is the central part of a stable composition in which the length of the slope viewed from the main terrace is in balance with the horizontal plane (Steenbergen 1996).

In other cases, a downward view along a slope to a water surface may result in unexpected and disturbing perspective effects, as the water seems to slope towards the observer (Hazlehurst 1980). This effect is strengthened even further when the terrain beyond the water body slopes downwards.

• André E. 1879. *L'Art des Jardins*. Masson Paris p. 128
• Corbin A. 1988. *Le territoire du vide. L'Occident et le désir du rivage*. Aubier-Montaigne, Paris
• Harsema H. (ed). 2000. 'White water lilies in a private city garden'. In: *Landscape architecture and town planning in the Netherlands 97-99*. Thoth, Bussum pp 204-207
• Hazlehurst F. Hamilton 1980. *The Gardens of Illusion. The Genius of André le Nôtre*. Vanderbilt U.P. Nashville, Tennessee p. 142
• Ito T. (et al). 1972. *The Japanese Garden. An Approach to Nature*. Yale Univ Press, New Haven
• Keswick M. 1991. *The Chinese Garden. History, Art & Architecture*. Academy Editions, London p 165 ff.
• Kluckert E.. 2000. 'Villa Lante in Bagnaia'. In: *Gardens of Europe*. Könemann Köln
• Laurie M. 1975. *An Introduction to Landscape Architecture*. Elsevier New York. pp. 31-37
• Moore C.W. (et al). 1989. *The Poetics of Gardens*. MIT press, Cambridge pp 17-20
• Ogrin D. 1993. 'A Theatre of Water Works'. In: *The World Heritage of Gardens*. Thames & Hudson London pp. 50, 76,77
• Orsenna E. 2000. 'Un Canal'. In: *Portrait d'un homme heureux*. *André le Nôtre 1613-1700*. Editions Fayard, Paris pp. 77-78
• Spirn A. 1988. 'The poetics of City and Nature: towards a new aesthetics for Urban Design'. In: Landscape Journal. The University of Wisconsin Press, Urbana, Illinois p. 120
• Steenbergen C.; Reh W. 1996. 'A vista of water, air and light'. In: *Architecture and Landscape*. Thoth Publishers, Bussum p. 205
• Thacker C. 1985. *The History of Gardens*. Croom Helm, London
• Turner R. 1985. *Capability Brown*. Weidenfeld & Nicholson, New York pp. 82 ff

Beauty
see > aesthetics

Behaviour
see also > design theory, determinism, edge, experience, flâneur, norm, utopia

'The way in which a person or thing behaves' (*Webster*).

Human behaviour can be described and explained from a normative viewpoint ('correct' or 'incorrect'; 'decent' or 'indecent') or from a descriptive one – for example, by describing how people react to, and use, an environment.

Usually, designers of buildings and outdoor spaces attempt to base their proposals on an understanding of the needs and the behaviour of users. This understanding may be founded on empirical research such as that carried out since the early decades of the 20th century. One example of such research involved measuring the average distances travelled by pedestrians when visiting public parks from their homes. Knowledge of these distances helps to determine the optimal location and sizes of parks. Similarly, observation has suggested that park visitors prefer to use the edges of open spaces over other areas, a conclusion that was supported by Jay Appleton's 'Prospect and Refuge Theory' (Appleton 1975). In the same way, useful studies of the uses of small neighbourhood parks in Philadelphia (USA) in relation to their location were conducted by Jacobs (Jacobs 1972).

Despite these insights, which have been supported and refined by more recent research, knowledge of human behaviour in relation to designed outdoor spaces remains limited (Lipman 1974). Too often, speculation and fantasy are dominant (Lang 1987). For example, in the early 20th century, adepts of the Modernist Movement in architecture and town planning believed that human behaviour could be guided by 'good' design. However, because they relied too much on utopian visions, their products were disappointing. Open spaces – hopefully labelled 'meeting grounds' – remained empty; public spaces were labelled 'communal', but turned out to be unsafe areas favoured by vandals.

In the 1970s, the idea that human behaviour would be determined largely by

qualitative aspects of the environment was supported by behavioural theories based on the so-called stimulus-response model (Skinner 1971, Rowe 1991; Knox 2000). However, because the human 'behavioural system' is too unpredictable, design processes have not proved equal to the task of creating sustainable and harmonious relationships with the environment: too much irrationality is involved (Simon 1969).

More research into the history of the built environment is needed. 'It should be focused on the interactions which in the course of time connect interests, institutions, conceptual frameworks, design decisions and human relations' (Lefaivre 1990).

In recent years the relationship between human behaviour and the quality (and design quality) of urban environments has acquired a negative meaning. Aggression and vandalism have become so common that some housing areas have been converted into so-called 'gated communities', where residents isolate themselves within protected neighbourhoods. In this way, behaviour affects the layout of housing areas

A sunny spring day in the Jardin des Tuileries Paris in 2005. Visitors move their chairs to a protective wall.

rather than the inverse (Hajer 2000).
Apparently, more research into the actual use
of outdoor space is also needed.

• Appleton J. 1975. *The Experience of Landscape*. John Wiley &
Sons
• Hajer M.; Reijndorp A. 2000. *In search of a public domain.
Analysis and strategy*. NAi Publishers, Rotterdam pp. 8,9
• Jacobs J. 1972. 'The uses of neighbourhood parks'. In: *The death
and life of great American cities*. Pelican Book, Harmondsworth,
Middlesex pp. 99 ff.
• Knox P.; Pink S. 2000. 'Design determinism'. In: *Urban Social
Geography*. Prentice Hall Englewood Cliffs, New Jersey pp. 282-
283
• Lang J. 1987. *Creating Architectural Theory*. Van Nostrand
Reinhold, London pp. 8-12
• Lefaivre L.; Tzonis A. 1990. *De oorsprong van de moderne
architectuur* (i.e. *The origins of modern architecture*) *Een
geschiedenis in documenten*. SUN Publishers, Nijmegen pp.16 ff.
• Lipman A. 1974. 'The Architectural Belief System and Social
Behavior'. In: Lang J. (et al) (ed.) *Designing for Human Behavior:
Architecture and the Behavioral Sciences*. Dowden Hutchinson
& Ross, New York pp. 23-30
• Rowe P.G. 1991. *Design thinking*. MIT Press, Cambridge pp. 44-46
• Simon H.A. 1969. *The sciences of the artificial. Preface*. MIT
Press, Cambridge
• Skinner B.F. 1971. (reprint) *Beyond Freedom and Dignity*. Bantam
Book, Toronto

Belvedere
see > hill

Biodiversity
see > diversity

Border, Boundary, Edge, Margin, Fringe
see also > hedge, wall

   Territories in a town or landscape are
delimited, divided, enclosed or marked by
various means, each with a significant
impact on human perception and behaviour.
These delimitations can be defined in terms
of their form, layout and character, and also
of the abruptness of their transitions with
the neighbouring territories.

   A *border* is a frontier dividing two countries.
In gardens and parks, it is also a strip of
ground along the edge of a lawn or path for
planting flowers or shrubs (*Oxford English
Dictionary*). A herbaceous border is a border
planted with perennial flowering plants,
usually set against a wall (*Oxford
Companion*).

59

*Herbaceous border in grey, brown and rose colours; Moerheim gardens at Dedemsvaart, the Netherlands. Laid out from 1927
onwards. Landscape architect Mien Ruys.*
Photo Cor Rozier.

Edges and margins at the Soetelieve industrial estate, 's-Hertogenbosch, the Netherlands. Buys & van der Vliet landscape architects 1978.

Edges in parks are attractive places for visitors: Vondelpark, Amsterdam, photographed in 2003.

A *boundary* is a 'line that marks a limit; dividing line' (*Oxford Advanced*).

Boundaries around a site, a territory, a land mass, are manifest in many forms. They may delineate the limits of a property, a public space, a town, or a landscape. 'A boundary is what binds us together in a group; that which excludes the outsider or stranger [...] The network of boundaries, private as well a public, transforms an amorphous environment into a human landscape' (Jackson 1980).

Boundaries may appear as edges, fringes or margins.

An *edge* is 'the line where an object or surface begins or ends' (*Webster*), or is 'a line marking the outside limit or boundary of a solid (flat) object, surface or area' (*Oxford Advanced*). A fringe is the 'outer edge of an area, group or activity' (*Oxford Advanced*).

Edges in town and countryside are not solely territorial limits; they may also channel movement. Highly visible borderlines or edges act as lateral references and help clarify the image of a city. The physical characteristics and the legibility of edges of towns vary in terms of texture, form, detailing, symbolic value, building type, use and management (Lynch 1960).

Edges also exist on different scales and at different levels – from local to regional – and consist not only of buildings, town walls, quays, roadside borders, but also of shorelines, dunes or dikes, woodlands, escarpments, or the bottom of steep slopes. Centuries ago, the space-enclosing borders and edges created by hedges and woodlands were relatively dominant features in many landscapes. In recent decades, agricultural development has led most of them to be removed (Hoskins 1973). From an ecological point of view, edges – and especially hedges – are important contributors to ecological diversity (Forman 1995).

Attractive places for visitors are created by the edges inside urban parks that divide dense planting from open meadows, or by those lying along water bodies. And as Appleton proposes in 'Prospect and Refuge theory', woodland edges are agreeable

because of the sense of safety they provide (Appleton 1975); when a holiday crowd enters a park on a sunny day, these are the first areas to be occupied (Dee 2001).

Edges in towns may consist of impenetrable lines, such as the base line of a building complex, or the wall surrounding a garden (Motloch 2001). Such a line is usually softened when a margin is added.

A *margin* is also 'an edge or border: the margin of a lake, pool, pond etc.' (*Oxford Advanced*) The 'ultimate' is the beach – the margin between land and sea (Shields 1999; Corbin 1988).

Margins are important elements, as they influence our perception of the environment. Rather than being a hard and impenetrable line, a margin is more akin to a zone, 'an area, band or stripe that is different from its surroundings in colour, texture, appearance, etc' (*Oxford English Dictionary*).

In towns, margins are the narrow strips formed by the pavements, green fringes or gardens in front of buildings. They form transitional zones, which may for instance help give built-up spaces and outward orientation (Alexander et al 1977). They mark the separation of private and public space, of house and street, and underline the status of the proprietor. They also signify a confrontation between community scale and private scale.

Pavements are the most intensively used parts of the streetscape. They provide safety for pedestrians and constitute important conditions for social life in the city (Jacobs 1972). In daytime, many urban pavements provide vendors with space, thereby creating temporary marginal zones. In other places, residents occupy the margins in front of their house on a more permanent basis by creating small flower beds on the public pavement (Bobic 2004).

Margins may also consist of small private gardens enclosed by fences or low hedges. These are often untidy and cluttered in appearance; sometimes, order is imposed on them through communal layout and maintenance.

Marginal neighbourhoods in a social and economic sense are places that have been

61

unable to keep up with progress in surrounding areas and have thus become part of the social fringe. As peripheral places, they lag behind in social and economic terms – hence their marginal status – though sometimes they may also be valued as picturesque places of historical interest.

In contrast, peripheral zones around a city may also represent margins with exciting prospects, where new development occurs in the form of shopping malls and office districts (Shields 1999). These are places where things seem to happen – where 'the smell of cow-dung mixes with that of businessmen's after-shave (Hajer 2000).' In the eye of many planners, such zones are chaotic, messy and in constant need of tidying up. Traditionally, Dutch planning practice has therefore pursued the strict separation of town and country through the creation of hard edges. Nonetheless, 'despite a century of careful planning aimed at keeping the built environment and rural landscapes apart, the boundaries are

The narrow margin: the edge of a public pavement appropriated by residents in Amsterdam, 2005.

Front gardens forming a margin between house and street.
Photo: Frank Meijer.

becoming blurred' (Lörzing 2004).

- Alexander C. (et al). 1977. 'Building edge'. In: *A Pattern Language*. Oxford U.P. pp 753 ff.
- Appleton J. 1975. 'Behaviour and environment'. In: *The experience of landscape*. Wiley & Sons pp 58-80
- Bobic M. 2004. *Between the edges*. Thoth publishing, Bussum
- Corbin A. 1988. *Het verlangen naar de kust*. (translated from the original French 'Le territoire du vide. L'occident et le désir du rivage') Sun, Nijmegen.
- Dee C. 2001. 'Edges'. In: *Form and Fabric in Landscape Architecture*. Spon Press pp 115-143
- Forman R. T. 1995. 'Windbreaks, hedgerows and woodland corridors'. In: *Land Mosaics*. Cambridge University Press pp. 177-207
- Hajer M.; Reijndorp A. 2001. *In search for a public domain*. NAi Publishers, Rotterdam pp. 21 ff.
- Hoskins W.G. 1973. 'Boundaries in the Landscape'. In: *The Making of the English Landscape*. BBC, London pp. 30-45

An urban margin: Hanevoet, Eindhoven, the Netherlands, photographed in 1985.

63

A hard urban edge; the Dutch town of Purmerend seen from the adjoining polder landscape in the 1980s

• Jackson J.B. 1980 'How to Study Landscape'. In: Jackson J.B. *The necessity for ruins and other topics.* University of Massachusetts, Amherst pp.113-126
• Jacobs J. 1972. *The Death and Life of Great American Cities.* Pelican Book, Harmondsworth pp. 39-98
• Lynch K. 1960 . *The Image of the City.* MIT Press pp 62-66
• Lörzing H. 2004. 'Shifting Boundaries'. In: Blauwe Kamer. Tijdschrift voor landschapsontwikkeling en stedebouw, Stichting Lijn in Landschap, Wageningen. Special issue August 2004
• Motloch J.L. 2001. *Introduction to Landscape Design.* Second edition. Wiley & Sons pp 191-193
• Shields R. 1999. *Places on the Margin. Alternative Geographies of Modernity.* Routledge, London pp 5-10

Boulevard

see also > avenue, promenade

'A broad avenue in or around a city; especially one laid out with trees, shrubs and grass; occupying the site of a former town wall or of fortifications. Also: a wide new road' (*Webster*).

Most boulevards are found in countries where central authority was dominant at the time of their construction. The word is derived from 'bulwark', signifying an interconnected system of fortifications surrounding a town. When Georges Haussmann (1809-1891) cut tree-lined avenues through the medieval urban pattern in Paris, the name 'grand boulevard' was maintained.

The layout of these boulevards was motivated by the need to redevelop slum areas, to improve public safety, and also to express the grandeur of the state (Rasmussen 1951). Forming connecting lines between important buildings and parks, they functioned as 'political parade-grounds driven between wedding-cake mansions and bearing the names of presidents, historical dates, and virtues' as Laurie Lee observes in 'Red Sky at Sunrise' (Benevolo 1980; Joest 1991).

Boulevards are therefore important promenades, whose social function made them popular in 18th-century France. 'Promenading has less to do with seeing the

64

View of the Champs Elysées in Paris from the upper level of the Arc de Triomphe in 1845.
Source: Marc Gaillard: 1990. Les belles heures des Champs Elysées. Editions Martelles Amiens.

countryside and communing with nature, or to do with recreation and edification, than with communication, amusement, conversation and entertainment' (Schröder 2002).

• Benevolo L. 1980. The History of the City. Scolar Press, London pp. 668-669
• von Joest Th. 1991. 'Haussmann's Paris: a Green Metropolis?'. In: Mosser M.; Teyssot G. A. History of Garden Design. Thames & Hudson, London. pp. 387-398
• Rasmussen S.E. 1951. Towns and buildings. MIT Press, Cambridge pp. 109-110
• Schröder C.F. 2002. 'For the pleasure of the people'. In: Topos European Landscape Magazine no 41, Callwey, München pp. 63-64

Bridge

see also > access, pond, threshold

'Thing that provides a connection or contact between two or more things' (*Oxford English Dictionary*).

Bridges connect and reconcile. They are associated with accessibility and contact – after all, we build bridges across waters, chasms and opposing opinions.

Bridges in the landscape stand out as landmarks, often visible from afar. Their form and size ranges between extremes: from high-rise constructions that traverse open water and provide distant views, to unstable planks that float on the waters of a pond, thereby providing a tactile sensation to all those who walk across (Wells 2002). They are often associated with the history of a town or locality, such as the bridge at Avignon and Tower Bridge in London.

In wartime, bridgeheads are amongst the most contested prizes, and John Frost bridge in Arnhem the Netherlands, target of the airborne landings in 1944, became 'a bridge too far'. Some cities are known world-wide for their bridges – Venice, Florence and Sydney to name but three.

Bridges are not famous for their narrative quality alone: their design and construction may also be of exceptional quality. Two examples are the railway bridge across the Firth of Forth in Scotland, a cantilevered steel structure completed in 1890, and the Salginatobel bridge near Bern in Switzerland, a revolutionary hollow box concrete structure designed by Robert Maillart in 1933 (Giedion 1948; Wells 2002; Arcilla 2002).

65

Large bridges spanning river valleys are dominant landmarks. The viaduct across the river Tarn near Millau, Aveyron, France; constructed in 2004. Architect Norman Foster.

Bridges in towns and overpasses in parks help separate traffic flow, such as the ones built in New York's Central Park by Frederick Law Olmsted in the second half of the 19th century (Fein 1981).

Bridges in gardens are constructed in order to enhance – to enliven the experience of the visitor. Bridge, pond and island may form a coherent composition. One leaves the shore, crosses water, experiences various views, and arrives at a place with a special meaning. The idea of constructing bridges as decorative garden features originated in China and Japan, where they often link two conceptually distinct areas (Ito 1972; Symes 1993). Some may consist of simple planking or a simple stone slab; others consist of an arched moss-covered wooden construction. The optimal shape of such a bridge, such as that in Katsura Palace near Kyoto, is the one that forms a full circle with its own reflection in the water.

In Western European gardens, bridges were usual of purely functional design until the Romantic Age, when the influence of Asian culture made itself felt. In the gardens of the 17th and 18th century, many Palladian bridges with heavy colonnaded superstructures offered panoramic views, such as in Stowe and Stourhead in England (*Oxford Companion*). Landscape gardener 'Capability' Brown (1716-1783) accepted bridges as the only ornamental elements in his park designs (Turner 1985).

Recent Dutch examples of pedestrian bridges that connect and provide views in gardens are found in the garden of the office of VSB Bank in Utrecht (Harsema 1996).

Bridges in Japanese gardens are often constructed in wood and covered with moss. Their silhouette mirrored in water can form a perfect circle. Katsura palace garden, Kyoto, Japan. Photographed in 1987.

• Arcilla M.T. 2002. *Bridges/Ponts/Brücken*. Atrium Publishers, Mexico
• Fein A. 1981. *Landscape into Cityscape. Frederick Law Olmsted's Plans for a Greater New York City*. Van Nostrand Reinhold, New York pp. 64-69
• Giedion S. 1948. *Space Time and Architecture. The Growth of a Tradition*. Harvard University Press, Cambridge
• Harsema H. (ed). 1996. 'The site of the VSB head office in Utrecht'. In: *Landscape architecture and Town Planning in the Netherlands 93-95*. Thoth Publishers, Bussum pp.120-124
• Ito T. (et al). 1972. *The Japanese Garden. An approach to Nature*. Yale Univ Press, New Haven
• Symes M. 1993. *A glossary of Garden History*. Shire publications, Princes Risborough, Buckinghamshire
• Turner R. 1985. *Capability Brown and the Eighteenth Century Landscape*. Weidenfeld & Nicholson, London pp. 82
• Wells M. 2002. *30 Bridges*. Laurence King Publishers, London

Bridges may be designed with the sole purpose of providing a three-dimensional effect. Garden of VSB bank, Utrecht, the Netherlands. West 8 landscape architects, 1993.

Cascade

see > stream

Character

see also > association, park, reference, sentiment

'The sum total of the distinguishing qualities of a person, group or thing' (*Webster*).

The character of an environment is a combination of atmospheres, meanings and images presented both by the parts and the whole, evoking a certain mood or expectation in the observer (Baljon 1992, Norberg-Schulz 1980).

A characteristic landscape is 'a particular physical area that creates a overall impression through its unique combination of visual features, such as land, vegetation water and structures, as seen in terms of line, form, colour and texture' (*Goulty*). Character may be the product of natural processes, of human intervention in natural process, of human creativity, or a mixture of these (Goodchild 2005).

Landscape character is often described in terms of metaphors. In biblical terms, a landscape can be 'barren and empty' or 'full of milk and honey'. Contemporary urbanites call every cow-dotted meadow a 'natural landscape'.

The experience of the character of a site involves all the sensory faculties, particularly vision, hearing, smell and feeling, all of which are associated with meaning. A park may not only look spacious and colourful, but also pleasant, festive and appealing – whereas any festive mood will be absent in the presence of ruins, tombs and gravestones that emanate oppressive and melancholic feelings. The layout of parks and gardens may also be described in terms of formal, picturesque or romantic (Teyssot 1990).

From one country to the other, cemeteries are laid out according to rules that are rooted in national culture, and are noted for the way they express the different ways in which different nations deal with questions of life and death and with the memory of the dead.

In Scandinavia, simple horizontal graves may be spread out in a meadow under a canopy of trees, thereby expressing the belief that in death we all are equal, and that we expect to return to nature after life on earth (Hauxner 1993). In southern Europe, graves are more like mausoleums, with abundant sculpture expressing a need to hang onto the memory of individuals and the glory of their past, to which patriotic sentiments are sometimes added (Rogers 2001). In the French Dordogne, graves may be sheltered inside greenhouses full of plants and displays of allegorical texts.

A character is 'consistent' when the

Monumental memorials at Montparnasse cemetery, Paris.

Architectural control. Cemetery at Doorn, the Netherlands.
Landscape architect: W.C.J. Boer, 1954.

response to the sight of a particular site is shared by many. In most cases, however, the experience of an outdoor space by an individual person depends on his disposition or cultural background. Landscape character is called 'strong' whenever there is a visible harmony between natural elements such as soils, vegetation, and wildlife on the one hand, and land-use on the other (Simonds 1997).

Parks designed by Modernist Dutch landscape architects such as Hans Warnau (1922-1995) and Hein Otto (1916-1994) are sober, simple, and rectilinear in character. Visitors who look for strong sensory impressions may find such environments monotonous and boring (Vroom 1990). Amusement parks such as Disneyland provide strong visual and auditory impressions, and therefore exude an adventurous, exotic and sometimes fairy-tale character that is far removed from everyday surroundings. Some critical observers denounce these parks as vulgar, full of false

Graves distributed inconspicuously beneath the trees. Cemetery at Mariebjerg, Copenhagen Denmark. Landscape architect: Sven Hansen, 1935.

69

Protective greenhouses somewhere in the Dordogne, France.

sentiment and lacking authenticity – as 'kitsch' (Dorfles 1968). False sentiment is also expressed in historic monuments that are smartened up and adapted for the gaze of tourists. The desire for a photogenic look can quickly result in 'disneyfication' and thus the destruction of any real character a place may have had.

• Baljon L. 1992. *Designing Parks*. Architecture & Natura, Amsterdam p 72
• Dorfles G. 1968 *Kitsch. An anthology of bad taste*. Studio Vista, London pp. 15-36;
• Goodchild P. 2005. 'Complexities and Critique in Landscape Architecture'. In: Topos European Landscape Journal, Callwey, München no. 49 pp. 66-73
• Hauxner M. 1993. *Fantasiens Have*. Arkitektensforlag, Copenhagen pp. 120-124
• Norberg-Schulz C. 1980. *Genius Loci*. Academy Editions, London pp. 11 ff.
• Rogers E.B. 2001. 'Honoring History and Repose for the Dead'. In: *Landscape Design*. Harry Abrams Publishers pp. 330-337
• Simonds J.O. 1997. *Landscape Architecture*. McGraw Hill,. New York p. 13
• Teyssot G. 1990. 'The eclectic garden and the imitation of nature'. In: Mosser M.; Teyssot G. *The History of Garden Design*. Thames and Hudson, London pp. 359-372
• Vroom M.J. (ed). 1990. *Outdoor Space. Environments designed by Dutch landscape architects since 1945*. Thoth Publishers, Bussum pp. 114, 118, 130,134

Classicism

see also > Baroque, geometry, Renaissance

'The principles or style embodied in the literature, art, or architecture of ancient Greece and Rome'. Also: 'adherence to traditional standards (as of simplicity, restraint or proportion) that are universally and permanently valid' (*Webster*).

Classicism in garden design is connected with all types of geometric layout, the 'formal gardens' that have dominated garden and park design over centuries. Historic examples include the Persian garden, the Italian Renaissance garden, the French 17th-century layout, Baroque parks, and designs in the Neo-Classicist style (Kluckert 2000). They are characterised by their autonomous form and

Villa Lante, Bagnaia, Italy.
Photo: Frank Meijer

by the display of mathematical figures, which symbolises logic. In social terms they express power, status and affluence.

'The Western formal garden came from the paradise garden of Persia, to be perfected in France. From there it became a symbol of aristocracy and authority, to many people an anathema. [...] The rich man owns a garden, the poor man works it' (Stauffacher 1988).

In Western Europe, the Classicist style in architecture and garden design blossomed in 15th-century Italy – at the beginning of the Renaissance – with a geometric layout around an axis, sightlines and vistas that were fitted into the landscape (Jellicoe 1975; Steenbergen 1996; Rogers 2001). In 17th-century France, classical principles were adopted and modified in accordance with the emergence of geography, physics and mathematics. Milestones in classical design were the parks at Versailles and Vaux-le-Vicomte (Melun), which were followed by parks such as the Belvedere in Vienna and

Hohenheim near Munich (Rogers 2001-2002).

Dutch Classicist gardens emerged in the first decades of the 17th century. One great initiator was Frederik Hendrik, prince of Orange (1584-1647), who laid out several palaces and gardens. Only one of these now remains: Huis ten Bosch in the Hague, which dates from around 1650 and is in use as the Queen's residence. The design of its gardens was greatly influenced by the French garden architect André Mollet (Bezemer 2001).

Zorgvliet estate in the Hague was completed in 1675 and the palace gardens at Het Loo near Apeldoorn in 1684 (see *Restoration*). Their layout is much influenced by the flat landscape with its regular patterns of ditches, and by the scarcity of suitable land. This shortage of space, so typical of the Dutch situation, led Pieter de la Cour to describe his 'ideal estate' as triangular in plan, using the effect of perspective shortening to make it look larger than it really is (Bijhouwer 1946).

71

Parc at Versailles, Paris, France.
Source: Kluckert E. 2000. The Gardens of Europe. Könemann Köln

The Classicist design style has four main characteristics:
· in terms of structure: axiality and the use of central perspective; the house and garden form one coherent unit;
· in terms of experience: sharp boundaries, static balance, fixed relationships, the presence of decorative elements;
· in terms of reference: stateliness (home of the dignified bourgeois), prowess, parade ground, theatre (where social inequality is stressed); rationality in its symmetrical layout, as well as mythology in allegoric representations in grottoes and sculptures;
· in terms of design tools: the avenue and the bosket, straight hedges and trees massed into solid volumes, the canal as a long mirroring pool, wide lawns, broderies, sculpture (Baljon 1992).

• Baljon L. 1992. *Designing Parks*. Architectura & Natura,. Amsterdam pp. 139-142 and 158
• Bezemer V. 2001. Courtly Gardens in Holland 1600-1650. *The House of Orange and the Hortus Batavus*. Architectura & Natura Press, Amsterdam
• Bijhouwer J.T.P. 1946. 'Het ideale buiten van de 17e en 18e eeuw'. In: *Nederlandse tuinen en buiten- plaatsen*. Allert de Lange, Amsterdam pp. 15 et seq.

• Jellicoe G. 1975. *The Landscape of Man*. Thames and Hudson, London pp. 154-156
• Kluckert E. 2000. *The gardens of Europe*. Könemann, Köln pp. 51 ff.; pp. 186-208
• Rogers E.B. 2001/1. 'Bramante and the discovery of axial planning'. In: *Landscape Design*. Harry Abrams, New York pp. 133 ff.
• Rogers E.B. 2001/2. 'Bramante and the discovery of axial planning'. In: *Landscape Design*. Harry Abrams, New York pp. 168 ff.
• Stauffacher Solomon B. 1988. *Green Architecture and the Agrarian Garden*. Rizolli, New York p. 57
• Steenbergen C.M.; Reh W. 1996. *Architecture and Landscape*. Thoth Publishers, Bussum

Coherence

see also > composition, dynamic, order

To cohere means 'to hold together firmly as parts' or ' to consist of parts that cohere' (*Webster*).

One of the central objectives of the designer of outdoor spaces is to achieve coherence. The aim is to mould the parts in such a way that some sort of unity is produced, with units that lie close together, yet occupy similar positions in a whole (Arnheim 1969).

Perspective manipulation may make a garden look larger than it is in reality. The Ideal Dutch Garden of the 18th century as described by Pieter de la Cour

Coherence is expressed in both functional and visual terms. Functional coherence means that elements or objects in a site are connected in a practical manner, with optimal movement, transport and communication. The visibility of such connections enables the observer to identify what is where, providing orientation in space, and helping meanings to be recognised. Functional and visual coherence are prerequisites for accessibility and effective action (Baljon 1992).

•Arnheim R. 1969. 'Shape'. In: *Art and visual perception*. Faber Editions, London pp. 32-81
•Baljon L. 1992. 'The layout and spatial coherence of the park'. In: *Designing Parks*. Architectura & Natura Press, Amsterdam pp. 63-104

Collage
see also > fragmentation

'An artistic composition of fragments or material pasted on a surface' (*Webster*).

Cubist painters at the beginning of the 20th century started pasting newspaper cut-outs into more or less ordered compositions which they then called 'collages'. Collage techniques are applied in outdoor design to create a certain amount of coherence in fragmented spaces (Beune 1990; Meeus 1990).

As a technique, collage differs from montage or assembly, where preconceived and complete elements that retain their individual form are mounted together (Reh 1990). Instead, it removes objects from their previous context, and distributes them in a way that is improvised rather than pre-conceived. The accent lies on diversity in form and activity (Rowe 1979; Broadbent 1990).

Unlike urban neighbourhoods laid out by Modernist town planners, whose plans are unified and pre-designed, older urban centres such as Rome and London have plans that can be described as a collage created by the clashing forms of buildings, squares and streets.

•Beune F. 1990. 'Fragmentation of Urban Open Space'. In: Vroom M.J.; Meeus J.H.A. (ed). *Learning from Rotterdam*. Mansell

Publishers, London p. 118
•Broadbent G. 1990. 'Collage City'. In: *Emerging Concepts in Urban Space Design*. Van Nostrand Reinhold, London pp. 263-266
•Meeus J.H.A 1990. 'Openness in dense packing'. In: Vroom M.J.; Meeus J.H.A. (ed). *Learning from Rotterdam*. Mansell Publishers, London p. 152
•Reh W.; Steenbergen C. 1990. Inleiding. In: van der Kooij E. *Het Montagelandschap* (i.e. *The assembly landscape*). Technical University Delft p. 19
•Rowe C.; Koetter F. 1979. *Collage City*. MIT Press, Cambridge, Mass

Colour, Tone, Hue
see also > border, light, sign

The perception of colour is one of the primary sensory experiences. 'Strictly speaking, all visual appearance is produced by colour and brightness' (Arnheim 1969). Colours are a source of sensory delight and also a means of expression in art, fashion, architecture and landscape architecture.

The symbolic functions of colours vary in different cultures round the world. Colour plays an important role in religious and ceremonial events (Lenclos 1999).

In Western cultures, colour has many uses in daily life. For example:
· As a signal: red means danger, green is safe, yellow means 'look out'.
· As an icon: orange represents Dutch royalty and the Dutch national soccer team; black represents sorrow and white a maiden bride; green represents paradise and freshman, red represents left-wing politics, and yellow Roman Catholic. A matter of context and familiarity?
· As a means to aid recognition (e.g. in logos), or to support spatial orientation (e.g. using consistent colours for traffic signs). Consistency creates certainty.
· As an optical stimulant: blue appears to come forward in the field of vision and yellow to recede; warm colours in concentric circles create an eccentric movement, and cold colours a concentric movement (Arnheim 1969).
· As a symbol on thematic maps. Topographical maps use red or black for buildings, green for unpaved areas, blue for

73

water. Planners use colour on maps to emphasise certain aspects of their message. Colours are often used to suggest or even to manipulate (Ormeling 1997).

Flowering fields in Holland.
Photo: Peter van Bolhuis, Pandion

Samples of soil colours in France.
Source: Lenclos J.P. 1989. Les couleurs de la France. Geographie de la couleur. Editions du Moniteur Paris

74

Regional identity expressed in the colours of farm buildings: barn door in Zaanstreek, the Netherlands.

As such, colour does not exist: instead, changing colour effects and moods are created by the luminosity and direction of light, and by its reflection from surfaces such as soil, water and vegetation (Minnaert 1993; Lynch 1995). People all too easily assume that northern landscapes are predominantly green: according to the season, closer inspection reveals woodland to be mostly red-brown and yellow, and river landscapes to be predominately silver, grey and beige (van Maanen 1993). At close range, the shade of trees turns into a blue haze.

Our experience of space is influenced by contrasting and interfering colours acting in combination with light and shadow. Form and space can be dissolved in a play of coloured dots and planes like those in paintings by Impressionists such as Claude Monet (1840-1920) (Clark 1966; Wöbse 2002). 'Colour gives physical landscapes that final dimension of real life, definition and interest' (*Britannica*). From one place to another, earth and rock, natural vegetation and agricultural crops all differ in colour.

The colours of buildings and of construction materials – brick and stone, the pigments in plaster and in paving materials – are determined largely by the local minerals used. In some Mediterranean countries, the influence of climate is also evident in the white-washed buildings (Lancaster 1984; Lenclos 1994). This also contributes to regional identity. In the Netherlands, the colours of brick walls and painted woodwork vary per region. Such a 'geography of colour' is integral to national heritage.

The introduction of concrete and steel in the 20th century meant that regional differences in the use of colour in construction work have diminished, a trend that was also influenced by the International Movement in architecture. Modern architects wish to select colours and colour combinations at will, adding them to their buildings as part of a composition. New colour combinations in architecture were introduced in the 1920s by Bauhaus teachers such as Wassily Kandinsky (1866-1944) and Johannes Itten (1888-1967). They were followed by the Dutch Stijl with Theo van

Doesburg (1883-1931) (Jaffé 1956). Aiming at harmony and contrast, their colour compositions created optical effects and aided the perception of spatial dimensions (Itten 1970).

Landscape designers must learn to select and control the colour compositions of plants and flowers in space and over time, in the awareness that these colours are ephemeral, and that precise and lasting control is difficult. Public gardens can use monochromatic colours covering large surfaces, an art mastered by the Brazilian landscape architect/painter Roberto Burle Marx (1909-1994) (Eliovson 1991). In many Dutch urban parks, flowering bulbs and annual plants are used in large quantities to create 'colour effects' that ignore the individual characteristics of the plants involved.

The art of laying out groups of flowering plants in a harmonious composition is demonstrated in a plant border, where a mixture of flowering perennial plants is situated against a high backdrop such as a hedge, wall or row of shrubs. Such borders,

Flowering border at the Mien Ruys gardens in Dedemsvaart, the Netherlands.
Photo: Dieuwertje Roebers

which were originally introduced in England by Gertrude Jekyll (1843-1932), show a balanced but constantly changing colour scheme from spring to autumn (Bisgrove 1992; Hobhouse 1985; Jekyll 1990; Ruys 1973).

Colours of plants can be identified and labelled with the aid of the Horticultural Colour Chart, in which all plant colours are named in six languages (Anon.1939/1941).

•Anonymous. 1939/1941. *Horticultural Colour Chart*. The British Council and the Royal Horticultural Society, London
•Arnheim R. 1969. 'Color'. In: *Art and Visual Perception*. Faber Editions London pp. 323 ff.
•Bisgrove R. 1992. *The gardens of Gertrude Jekyll*. Frances Lincoln, London
•Clark K. 1966. *Landscape into Art*. John Murray, London pp. 91 ff.
•Eliovson D. 1991. *The Gardens of Roberto Burle Marx*. Saga Press
•Hobhouse P. 1985. *Colour in your Garden*. Collins, London
•Itten J. 1970. *Kleurenleer*. Uitg. Cantecleer, de Bilt
•Jaffé H.L.C. 1956. *De Stijl 1917-1931* Meulenhoff, Amsterdam
•Jekyll G. 1990. *Colour Schemes for the Flower Garden*. Antique Collector's Club, Woodbridge
•Lancaster M. 1984. *Britain in view. Colour and the Landscape*. Quiller Press, London
•Lenclos J.P.; Lenclos D. 1994. *Les couleurs de la France. Géographie de la couleur*. Éditions du Moniteur, Paris
•Lenclos J.P.; Lenclos D. 1999. 'Couleurs et Symboles'. In: *Couleurs du Monde. Géographie de la Couleur*. Éditions du Moniteur, Paris pp. 24-33
•Lynch D.K.; Livingston W. 1995. *Colour and Light in Nature*. Cambridge University Press pp. 1-62
•van Maanen R. 1993. *Kleurenatlas. Schets van de kleur in Nederland*. Uitg. Eisma B.V. Leeuwarden
•Minnaert M. 1993. *Light and colour in the outdoors*. Springer Verlag pp. 131-135
•Ruys M. 1973. *Het Nieuwe Vaste Planten Boek*. (i.e. *The new book of perennials*) Moussault, Amsterdam
•Wöbse H.H. 2002. 'Licht und Farbe' (i.e. Light and colour) in: Landschaftsästhetik Eugen Ulmer Verlag, Stuttgart pp. 44-48

Complexity
see also > contrast, order, oxymoron

Complex means 'having many interrelated parts, patterns or elements that are hard to separate, analyse or solve. It suggests an unavoidable and necessary lack of simplicity and does not imply a fault or failure in designing or arranging' (*Webster*).

Visual complexity in a designed outdoor space results when a particular order combines a variety of sensory impressions with some sort of coherence. Such complexity is created when several themes within a composition occur simultaneously and are interconnected (Dijkstra 2001). The optimal degree of complexity for providing the most pleasant experience lies somewhere between two extremes (between chaos, which leads to uncertainty and anxiety, and total order, which leads to monotony and boredom) (Arnheim 1971; Broadbent 1990/1).

Because it depends both on the disposition of the individual observer and on changes in values in society over time, this optimum is not a constant factor. During the reign of the Modernist Movement in architecture, simplicity and order were in favour ('less is more') (Jencks 1973). With the arrival of post-modernism, however, the need to be confronted with a changing, unpredictable, adaptable or fragmented environment has become fashionable.

Visual complexity in town and country is a matter not only of variation in form and space, colour and texture, but also of meanings and references. Buildings, public squares and parks may simultaneously display openness and enclosure, duality and unity, dynamism and stability, all co-existing in a recognisable way (Broadbent 1990; Venturi 1977). The creation of such a tangle of contradictions and ambiguities may help to enliven the experience of objects and spaces.

Whenever ambiguities are shrouded in an air of secrecy that intentionally produces surprising effects, the result is called 'intricacy'. An intricate space is 'made up of many small parts put together in a complex way, and therefore difficult to follow or understand' (*Oxford Advanced*). For instance, a small valley with a stream running down the middle has interesting features at different scales: the overall space, the immediate surroundings of the stream and its vegetation, the geology and vegetation of the slopes, the fauna in the valley, and the skyline and the changing sky. All these contribute to the intricacy of the landscape (*Goulty*).

The notion of intricacy was introduced in 19th-century English garden design by Humphry Repton (1752-1818) and was copied in Dutch landscape-style parks. 'Intricacy is that disposition of objects which, by a partial and uncertain concealment, excites and nourishes curiosity' (Repton 1806).

• Arnheim R. 1971. *Entropy and Art. An Essay on Disorder and Order.* University of California Press, Berkeley pp. 1-3.
• Broadbent G. 1990/1. 'Kevin Lynch'. In: *Emerging Concepts in Urban Space Design.* Van Nostrand Reinhold, London pp. 227-230
• Broadbent G. 1990/2. 'Venturi'. In: op cit pp. 235-252
• Dijkstra Tj. 2001. 'Helderheid en complexiteit' (i.e. Clarity and complexity) in: *Architectonische kwaliteit.* Uitgeverij 010, Rotterdam pp. 14,15
• Goulty G.A. 1991. *A Dictionary of Landscape.* Avebury Technical, Avebury
• Jencks Ch. 1973. 'The problem of Mies'. In: *Modern Movements in Architecture.* Penguin Books, Harmondsworth, Middlesex pp. 95-108
• Repton H. 1806. *An enquiry into the changes of taste in landscape gardening, to which are added some observations on theory and practice, including a defence of the art.* J. Taylor, London p.162
• Venturi R. 1977. *Complexity and Contradiction in Architecture.* Museum of Modern Art, New York pp.16-32

Composition
see also > coherence, complexity, order, proportion

'Arrangement of elements in a painting, photograph etc' (*Oxford English Dictionary*).

Compositions are also arrangements in music, poetry, the visual arts and architecture. Their most familiar application is in the context of music. Composition has come to mean a creative procedure in which the artist creates out of nothing and arranges his material according to laws generated within the work itself. In architecture, this means 'arranging the parts of an architectonic body in a system of proportions' (Colquhoun 1989). In the design process, it is the counterpart of applied systems analysis, where practical and functional considerations dominate. 'A composition is required to create structure in the visible environment' (Dijkstra 2001).

Compositions are subjected to rules that may change over time. 'An architectonic composition can be analysed as a conceptual scheme or diagram with respect to the physical elements that are active in the spatial effect of the design (the active elements of composition). At the same time, the analysis may concern a number of form principles that regulate the connection between the elements in the composition, such as volumes, rhythm, axiality, zoning, colour, texture, etc' (Steenbergen 2002). Compositions normally have a focal point, a centre, and are enclosed by boundaries and edges (Arnheim 1982).

In terms of the emotional response it elicits, a composition can be described in terms of harmony and contrast, wholeness and integrity, tension and surprise, horror and delight (Leupen 1997).

According to Gordon Cullen 'there is an art of relationship in which all the elements that go into the making of an environment, buildings, trees, nature, water, traffic, advertisements and so on [...] are woven together in such a way that drama is released. This cannot be achieved by scientific research or by the technical half of the brain' (Cullen 1961/1971).

In a design process, compositions of points, lines and planes usually precede a three-dimensional product (Baljon 1992). Most lines in a design drawing for an outdoor space indicate the contours, borders or edges of buildings, pavements, plant beds and trees, as well as the areas set aside for a particular use. These lines may be fluid, sinuous or straight, angular or geometric. While they may be part of a plane surface, they often appear to be three-dimensional, as the difference between 'figure and ground' can oscillate (Arnheim 1969). To the viewer, they express the intentions of the designer by imparting sensory impressions, movement and also symbolic meaning (Motloch 1991). In a romantic design, curved lines are part of a search for the unexpected, whereas most modern designers prefer straight lines, considering the use of curves to be a senseless pursuit.

Regulating lines or sightlines, (also called ley lines) are used to introduce order and rhythm to a design. They direct the view, creating order in a site by helping to locate the optimal relative positions of objects, spaces and volumes. ' Every face, centrepoint

77

Examples of compositions drawn by Humphry Repton in 1840. The two upper two examples show bad combinations of vertical and horizontal masses. The lower examples show good combinations.
Source: Kluckert. 2002. Gardens in Europe. Könemann, Köln p. 394

78

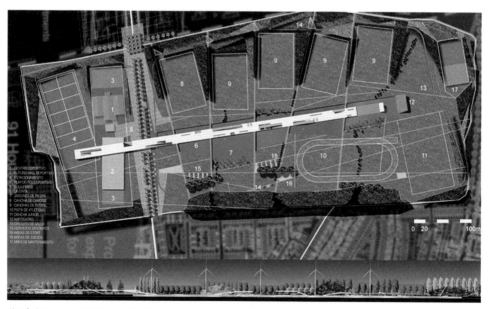

Site design as a composition in plan view: Father Collins Park in Dublin, Ireland.
Source: Diedrich L. (Chief Editor). 2006. Fieldwork. Landscape Architecture Europe. Birkhäuser Basel

and other important crossing is generated by lines, either connecting significant points on the existing building and then projected; or connecting a point on this building with a significant point on the site, or connecting significant points of the new building' (Broadbent 1990).

Planes may form patterns or mosaics. The experience of visual relationships between lines and planes in a composition may range from 'uninspiring' to 'exiting'. The search for an ideal set of proportions dates back to Pythagoras (6th century B.C.). Relative dimensions considered to be ideal include the 'golden section', in which the length of the sides of a rectangle are in accordance with the proportions A:B= B(A+B) (Arnheim 1969/2), a rule to which three-dimensional compositions are also subject. Overlapping and repetition can create enormous variety in sequences of open space (Krier 1988).

Functionalist architecture, which emphasised the content of the 'architectural programme' – where utility, morality and pragmatics prevailed – contested the idea that a composition might be a work of art in its own right. The work of architects such as Le Corbusier and Rietveld nonetheless demonstrates that a functional approach may produce a carefully designed three-dimensional composition (Colquhoun 1989).

Landscapes may be classified according to the typical composition of spaces, patterns, planes and volumes (Litton 1972; Wassink 1999). Dominant elements such as hills, escarpments, water bodies may serve as focal points. Enclosed spaces in landscapes are formed by topographic variety, woodlands or built-up areas. Orientation may be based on parallel geomorphological patterns, such as those along river banks and also by parallel planting belts.

As well as being expressed in terms of mass and volume, coherent compositions in space depend on functional, organisational and ecological factors that are interconnected in time and space. The composition of a landscape design should take account of factors such as speed, time-span and rhythm, and must be adaptable over time (Spirn 1998).

• Arnheim R. 1969/1. *Art and Visual Perception*. Faber Editions, London pp. 213 ff.
• Arnheim R. 1969/2. *Art and Visual Perception*. Faber Editions, London pp. 48-49
• Arnheim R. 1982. *The Power of the Center. A study of Composition in the Visual Arts*. University of California Press, Berkeley
• Baljon L. 1992. 'The Park as a Graphic Composition'. In: *Designing Parks*. Architectura & Natura, Amsterdam pp. 51-62
• Broadbent G. 1990. *Emerging Concepts in Urban Space Design*. Van Nostrand Reinhold, London p. 301
• Colquhoun A. 1989. 'Composition versus the Project'. In: *Modernity and the Classical Tradition. Architectural Essays 1980-1987*. MIT press, Cambridge pp. 33 ff.
• Cullen G. 1971. *The Concise Townscape*. The Architectural Press, London p. 17
• Dijkstra T. 2001. 'Helderheid en complexiteit' (i.e. clarity and complexity). In: *Architectonische kwaliteit*. 010 publishers, Rotterdam pp. 14,15
• Krier R. 1988. 'On architectonic form'. In: *Architectural Composition*. Academy Editions, London pp. 41-68
• Leupen B. (et al). 1997. 'From distribution to composition'. In: *Design and Analysis*. Van Nostrand Reinhold, London/ 010 Publishers, Rotterdam pp. 47-67
• Litton B. 1972. 'Aesthetic Dimensions of the Landscape'. In: Krutilla J.V. (ed). *Natural Environments. Studies in Theoretical and Applied Analysis*. Johns Hopkins, New York pp. 279-283
• Motloch J. 1991. 'Visual Arts as Ordering Mechanisms'. In: *Introduction to Landscape Design*. Van Nostrand Reinhold, London pp. 126-138
• Steenbergen C. (et al). 2002. 'Introduction; Design Research, Research by Design'. In: Steenbergen C. (et al) (ed). *Architectural Design and Composition*. Thoth publishers, Bussum p.21
• Spirn A. 1998. *The Language of Landscape*. Yale U.P., New Haven pp. 85 ff.
• Wassink W. 1999. *Beekdallandschappen* (i.e. *Brook valley landscapes*). PhD thesis, Wageningen University pp. 49 ff.

79

Concept

see also > design method, framework, sketch, theory, vision

A concept is an 'idea underlying something; general notion' (*Oxford English Dictionary*). It is a thought, a notion, an idea (*Webster*). In linguistic terms, it is 'the preliminary phrasing of a piece of writing' (*van Dale*).

A concept is similar to an idea, intellectual conception or representation. In Plato's philosophy, a concept constituted an absolute or ideal form, an absolute pattern (Eaton 2001). Within the field of spatial planning, it is a starting point, the general principle that guides thoughts, plans and designs (Broadbent 1990). 'A spatial planning concept expresses in concise form, in words

Hamilton Finlay's conceptual garden Little Sparta Finlay in Edinburgh Scotland, photographed in 1990.

and images, the way planners and/or landscape architects envisage desirable developments in physical planning as well as the required type of intervention to achieve these' (Hidding 2002). Examples of planning concepts in the Netherlands include 'the Green Heart Metropolis', 'the compact city' and 'urban nodes'. An example in landscape planning is the framework or casco concept (Kerkstra 1990; Ahern 2002).

Concepts applied in site planning and design are similar to those in regional planning: they are the designer's ideas, ideals and views, which respond to the characteristics of the site and guide the design process, including its objectives and its outcome (Pohl 1992). Concepts are based on both normative and positive theories (see *Theory*).

A concept formed during a design process can be defined as the creative and structuring moment at which the first image of the final design arises. It is usually developed and visualised in sketch drawings (Steiner 2000). This is the stage at which the distinction between the intuitive and the rational (i.e. the knowledge gathered on site and from the brief) becomes blurred (Baljon 1992).

In many cases, more than one concept is tested, a process which leads to different results that can be compared and evaluated (Motloch 1991).

'A good concept is instructive, organising, disciplining, productive. It breaks new grounds in terms of the thinkable, it creates new ideas. A good design demonstrates the scope of a concept' (van der Woud 1987). The search for design concepts is exemplified in Ian Hamilton Finlay's conceptual garden 'Little Sparta' in Scotland (*'le paysage moralisé'*) : 'garden and sculpture exist in a site-specific and dialectical relationship, foregrounding the conceptual, symbolic, and allegorical facets of the history of landscape architecture' (Weiss 1998).

A construct is closely related to a concept, but is not quite the same, signifying the drawing of 'a geometrical figure with suitable instruments and under specified conditions' (*Webster*). It is a design concept which has advanced to the stage of a provisional or sketchy spatial structure, and is thereby linked to a visual image. Thus, while an urban network is a concept that can assume a number of different forms, the actual construction of a subterranean rail and road network is something tangible and visible. It is either constructed or not.

• Ahern J. 2002. 'Spatial concepts, planning strategies and future scenarios: a framework method for integrating landscape ecology and landscape planning'. In: *Greenways as strategic landscape planning: theory and application*. Dissertation, Wageningen University pp. 12-36
• Baljon L. 1992. *Designing Parks*. Architecture & Natura, Amsterdam p. 105
• Broadbent G. 1990. *Emerging Concepts in Urban Space Design*. Van Nostrand Reinhold, London
• Eaton R. 2001. *De ideale stad. (i.e. The ideal city)*. Mercatorfonds, Antwerpen p. 11
• Hidding M.C. 2002. 'Planconcepten voor stad en land' (i.e. Planning concepts for town & country). In: *Planning voor Stad en Land*. Coutinho, Bussum pp. 109 ff.
• Kerkstra K., Vrijlandt P. 1990. 'Landscape planning for industrial agriculture: a proposed framework for rural areas'. In: Landscape and Urban Planning, Elsevier, Amsterdam vol 18 no. 3-4 pp. 275-289
• Motloch J.L. 1991. *Introduction to Landscape Design*. Van Nostrand Reinhold, London pp. 132-134, 248-250
• Pohl N. 1992. 'Horizontal articulation in landscape'. In: Topos European Landscape Magazine, Callwey, München pp. 42-47
• Steiner F. 2000. 'Conceptual design from charettes'. In: *The Living Landscape*. McGraw Hill, New York pp. 296 ff.
• Weiss A. 1998. 'In praise of anachronism'. In: *Unnatural Horizons*. Princeton Architectural Press, New York pp. 139-140
• van der Woud A. 1987. 'De Geschiedenis van de Toekomst'. (i.e. the history of the future). In: van der Cammen H. (ed.) *Nieuw Nederland deel I: Achtergronden*. Stichting Nederland Nu als Ontwerp. Staatsuitgeverij, The Hague p. 18

Constructivism

see also > functionalism, modernism

The Constructivist movement in architecture and the plastic arts originated in the Soviet Union during the first decades of the 20th century, and was copied by De Stijl in the Netherlands. Its followers believed that the world could be re-built, reconstructed, in both the spiritual and material sense, and that artists would play a key role in this activity. A constructive universal culture could by itself transcend the tragic conflict between the extremes of capitalism and socialism (Boomkens 1998).

This gospel was translated into mystical language and abstract paintings by Piet Mondriaan (1872-1943), which are characterised by their elimination of the illusionist reproduction of reality, and a return to compositional fundamentals based on coloured planes (Jaffé 1956). At the same time, under the influence of Cubism, spatial concepts in architecture evolved from static enclosure to a continuous interweaving of interior and exterior spaces (Giedion 1950). In its pursuit of purity and elementary form-expression, the avant-gardism of De Stijl considered itself far removed from the chaos and degeneration of everyday culture.

• Boomkens R. 1998. *Een drempelwereld (i.e. A threshold world). Moderne ervaring en stedelijke openbaarheid*. NAi, Rotterdam pp. 140 et seq.
• Giedion S. 1950. *Space, Time & Architecture*. Harvard University Press, Cambridge.
• Jaffé H.C.L. 1956. *De Stijl 1917-1931 The Dutch Contribution to Modern Art*. Meulenhoff Publishers, Amsterdam

Context

see also > access, adaptation, contrast, place, sight line

'The circumstances surrounding an event' (*Webster*).

In visual perception theory, a 'context-effect' is the luminosity of an object relative to its background. A grey surface looks lighter against a dark background, for example, and blacker against a light one. Our perception of differences between objects of different size is also influenced by context effects: a fully grown person looks smaller between giants than between infants (*Britannica*). The same goes for small buildings or trees positioned between much taller ones.

In site design, the notion is derived from the Latin *contexere*; it is associated with coherence and the activity of weaving.. The design of an outdoor space never takes place in a vacuum: there is always an existing environment (Leupen 1997). Events and materials, forms and patterns can be woven into their context. In this way they become part of their surroundings (Spirn 1998).

An architect who designs a new building for a street may adapt his new building to

81

adjoining buildings in terms of dimensions, the proportions of facades and the materials used. In architecture this is called contextualism (Broadbent 1990; Turner 1996). An alternative approach is to start anew with contrasting forms which viewers may experience as surprising or lively – or, conversely, as disturbing or alienating. In landscape architecture, contextualism plays an important role next to topism, i.e. the search for vertical relationships (Pohl 1992).

Enclosed outdoor spaces may be completely isolated from the outside world and have no visual relationship at all. For instance, gardens in medieval times were places of repose and silence, order and enjoyment in a chaotic and hostile world. They were 'sanctified spots from which the wicked were excluded' (Rogers 2001; Aben

2002). Most contemporary gardens, however, are open to their environment, and are visible parts of a larger whole.

One way of 'connecting' the inside and the outside of a site is to continue the linear elements of a landscape pattern – such as borderlines, ditches, quays or hedgerows – inside the site (Harsema 1996). The use of vistas has a similar effect (Leupen 1997). Another way to anchor a terrain is by adapting planting plans to the vegetation in surrounding areas.

Context and place are related notions. Historically, settlements in the Netherlands were woven into their context, and thereby strengthened the Genius Loci (Schulz 1980). Contemporary urban expansion plans may still be woven into the existing topography (Tummers 1998; Meeus 2000), something

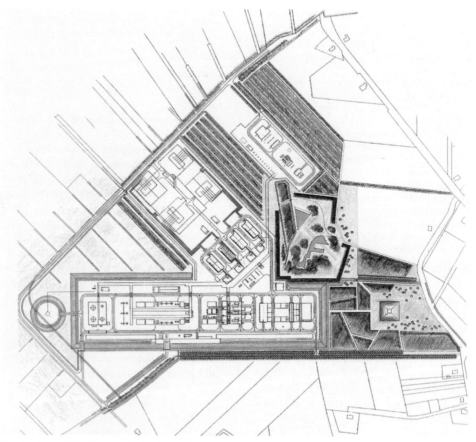

New development fitted into existing landscape patterns. Gas storage facility and pumping station at Langelo, Drenthe, the Netherlands. Alle Hosper landscape architects, 1992-1995.

known in landscape planning as 'critical regionalism' (Frampton 1988).

• Aben R. de Wit S. 2002. *The Enclosed Garden*. 010 publishers, Rotterdam pp. 10-11
• Broadbent G. 1990. *Emerging Concepts in Urban Space Design*. Van Nostrand Reinhold p 253.
• Frampton K. 1988. 'Place-Form and Cultural Identity'. In: Thackara J. *Design After Modernism*. Thames and Hudson, London pp. 51-66.
• Harsema H. 1996. 'Gas storage near Langelo'. In: *Landscape architecture and town planning in the Netherlands 93-95*. Thoth publishing, Bussum pp. 70-73
• Leupen B. (et al). 1997. *Design and Analysis*. 010 Publishers, Rotterdam pp.152 ff.
• Meeus J. 2000. 'How the Dutch city of Tilburg gets into the roots of the agricultural kampen landscape'. In: Landscape and Urban Planning, Elsevier, Amsterdam no. 48 pp. 177-189
• Norberg-Schulz C. 1980. *Genius Loci. Towards a Phenomenology of Architecture*. Academy Editions, London pp. 6 ff.
• Pohl N. 1992. 'Horizontal articulation in landscape'. In: Topos European Landscape Magazine no. 1 September 1992 pp. 42-47
• Rogers E.B. 2001. 'The walled garden'. In: *Landscape Design*. Harry Abrams, New York pp. 121-123
• Spirn A.W. 1998. *The Language of Landscape*. Yale University Press, New Haven pp. 133-168.
• Tummers L. 1998. *Het land in de stad. De stedebouw van de grote agglomeratie*. Thoth publishers, Bussum
• Turner T. 1996. 'Context and design'. In: *City as Landscape*. Spon, London pp. 108 ff.

Continuity
see also > cultural history, coherence, landscape plan

'Going on without stopping or being interrupted' (*Oxford English Dictionary*).

Continuity in time is expressed in landscapes that change gradually under the influence of natural processes and human intervention. The past and the present are visibly connected, a fact that helps us in our search for anchorage in time and space (Lowenthal 1985). 'More than is commonly realised, landscapes are in continual flux. But we sense them as abiding, and need to do so; our very makeup depends on finding our surroundings more durable than ourselves' (Lowenthal 2002). 'Natural processes may transform an ancient landscape, or social shifts cause bizarre dislocations. In the midst of these events, people remember the past and imagine the future' (Lynch 1972; Hoskins 1973).

Although changes in landscapes are of diverse origin and are usually spontaneous, they may also be the result of centralised 'top-down' planning decisions (Pregall 1999). Through the sudden and large changes in scale they bring about, infrastructural projects, building projects, reallotment schemes and the like can lead to a discontinuity that upsets ecological processes and ruptures our experience of time (Meeus 1990). This creates a need for a visible presence of elements and traces from the past in our daily environment, which call in turn for careful planning and the conservation of remnants of earlier forms of land-use.

When the old is allowed to coexist with the new, we can sense the passing of time (Lynch 1971). Adapting new settlements to existing landscape patterns also helps, as some Dutch landscape plans demonstrated in the 1970s (Vroom 1992).

Continuity in space comes into being when a number of different spaces are linked, for instance by a route connecting parts of a town, or connecting a town and a rural area. The experience of such continuity is reinforced by interlocking volumes in urban environments (Cullen 1968), by the use of

83

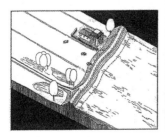 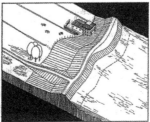 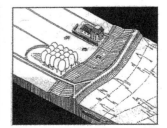

Continuity in time: axonometry of a Dutch river dike before and after reinforcement.

uniform planting, standard paving material and lighting ornaments, and also of other furniture along the road or path (Harsema 2000a; Lynch 1960). Fragmented open spaces may be unified by a continuous pattern of lines or squares on paved surfaces, or by a uniform groundcover planting, such as that used at Amsterdam's Schiphol Airport (Harsema 2000b).

•Cullen G. 1968. *The Concise Townscape*. The Architectural Press, London p. 184
•Harsema H. (ed). 2000/1. 'Blueprint for a clean and attractive city centre'. In: *Landscape architecture and town planning in the Netherlands 97-99*. Thoth Publishers, Bussum pp. 190-194
•Harsema H. (ed). 2000/2. ' 400.000 Birches in a field of clover'.

In: *Landscape architecture and town planning in the Netherlands 97-99*. Thoth Publishers, Bussum pp. 156-159
•Hoskins W.C. 1973. 'Continuity in the Landscape'. In: *English Landscapes*. BBC, London pp. 113-120
•Lowenthal D. 1985. 'How we know the past'. In: *The Past is a Foreign Country*. Cambridge University Press. pp.185 ff.
•Lowenthal D. 2002. 'Landscape as living legacy'. In: Kerkstra K. (ed). *The landscape of symbols*. Blauwdruk, Wageningen pp. 14-37
•Lynch K. 1960. *The Image of the City*. M.I.T. Press, Cambridge pp. 52, 106
•Lynch K. 1971. *Site Planning (second edition)*. MIT Press, Cambridge p. 221
•Lynch K. 1972. *What time is this place?* MIT Press, Cambridge p. 3
•Meeus J. (et al) 1990. 'Transformation of European Landscapes'. In: Changing European Landscapes. Special Issue Landscape and Urban Planning, Elsevier, Amsterdam vol 18 nos 3-4. pp. 325, 326
•Pregall P.; Volkman N. 1999. *Landscapes in History. Design and Planning in the Eastern and Western Traditions* (second edition). John Wiley & Sons, New York
•Vroom M.J. (ed). 1992. 'Landscape plan for Vries land consolidation scheme'. In: *Outdoor Space*. Thoth publishers, Bussum pp.182-185

Contour, Outline

see also > border, composition

'The outline of a figure or body. Shape, form'. 'A contour line connects the points on a

Continuity in space: the planting of thousands of birches at Schiphol Airport, Amsterdam, helps create continuity in a fragmented space. Landscape architect: West 8 landscape architects, 1992.

land surface that have the same elevation' (*Webster*).

Though 'contour' and 'edge' are overlapping notions, they are not identical. Contours are the borderlines of areas or volumes, which are visible in plan or elevation. An edge is both a line and an enclosure, limiting the extent of space (Lynch 1960). In outdoor spaces, contours help determine the composition of the design. They express the intention of the designer, and also carry meaning.

The contours or skyline of a hill, village or building show the characteristic form of the feature in question, and allow identification and orientation. During an insensitive expansion plan, this is the kind of silhouette that a town risks losing.

Perspective and depth are also dependent on perceived contours. Objects with a continuous outline appear to be closer to the observer than those whose outline they interrupt or obscure (Motloch 2001).

Contour lines in a plan are lines of equal

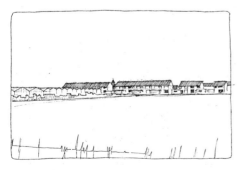

The village of Serooskerke in Zeeland, the Netherlands, silhouetted against the sky, before and after postwar expansion.

elevation with a consistent vertical separation. They help make the topography of a terrain legible (Motloch 2001/2).

• Lynch K. 1960. *The Image of the City*. MIT Press bl 62-66
• Motloch J.L. 2001/1. *Introduction to Landscape Design* (second edition). Wiley & Sons, New York p. 115
• Motloch J.J. 2001/2.. *Introduction to Landscape Design* (second edition). Wiley & Sons, New York pp. 60-61

Contrast

see also > adaptation, context, contour, geometry, order, polarity

'Difference clearly seen when unlike things are compared or put together' (*Oxford English Dictionary*)

In the perceptual field, the ability to perceive contrasts is a general condition for distinguishing forms and creating order. Differences between things makes them more visible. We perceive black because of the existence of white; similarly, we see volumes in space. Contrasts are the opposite of harmony, both in form and colour (Arnheim 1969).

Because contrasts help to enliven our experience of space, their pursuit has been important throughout the history of garden design and town planning. This is the opposite of the equally important urge to adapt, to fit the new into an existing environment (see *Adaptation*). Both ideals are equally valid. Although in certain cases they can be combined, designers sometimes face a fundamental dilemma in which they have to choose between one and the other.

In Chinese cities such as Beijing, but also in Manhattan, there is a contrast between the formal and geometric and the irregular or haphazard. This is also present in Persian gardens, in 15th-century Italian gardens with their *boschi*, and in the formal Palladian structures in English Romantic gardens (Moore et al 1989).

In landscapes around the world, the contrast between the natural (wilderness) and the cultivated (geometric) is a source of wonder and delight (Gombrich 1979). This is especially the case in places where one dominates over the other.

85

'In the wilderness and irregularity of the country, a piece of land laid out and planted according to rule looked very well [...] the human mind yearns for geometry' says Karen Blixen in *Out of Africa*. The inversion of this image is found in Dutch polders, as observed by Dutch author Frank Westerman when describing a farmer's response to the sight of his land: 'He loves this geometric landscape, with its straight rows of poplars, with fifteen paces between one trunk and the next. Rectilinearity means beauty. An oak would fit as badly here as a circle in a Mondrian painting. The farmers are the Creator here,

but, because they are not quite sure of their cause, they lay out curvilinear gardens with kidney-shaped ponds – probably to counterbalance the extreme regularity of the land pattern.'

In most landscapes, the urban contrasts with the rural. The English word 'country' is derived from the Latin contra, which means 'against', or 'on the opposite side' or 'that which is situated opposite the beholder' (*Webster*). The contrast between urban and rural survives changes over time, and marks the difference between repose and unrest, between culture and nature.

Dutch planning policy aims to maintain a contrast between town and countryside. 'The edges of most Dutch towns are clearly marked by canals, rows of trees, open space, and the like. The edges signal the will to maintain the distinction between town and country. Above all, they bear witness to the intention and ability of the Dutch to keep development at bay' (Faludi 1992).

Whether the visibility of contrasting forms in outdoor space elicits a positive or negative response depends on time and circumstance.

A former sand quarry at Crailo near Hilversum, the Netherlands, converted into a nature area. Ecological process contained in a geometrical layout. Landscape architect: Rik de Visser.

After all, a sharp contrast is by definition a disturbing clash between two shapes or spheres, such as 'technology' versus 'nature'. However, in postmodern architecture and landscape architecture, contrast is seen as a desirable quality, as it provides a heightened awareness and a more intense experience of the environment. In urban design, large geometric elements may deliberately be projected between existing highly complex buildings (Broadbent 1990).

Contrasts such as those created by the remnants of buildings or by a rectangular garden layout in the middle of a wilderness can have a strong symbolic effect. They tell stories 'about identity and difference, freedom and control, tradition and invention, use, abuse, and renewal' (Spirn 1998). Contrast make paradox and oxymoron visible. In Dutch nature areas, contrasting geometric forms and patterns remind the visitor of the human hand which guides natural processes (Harsema 1996).

• Arnheim R. 1969. 'The quest for harmony'. In: *Art and Visual Perception.* Faber Editions, London pp. 335-339

Contrasting form: the plaza in front of the former World Trade Center, Manhattan, with a Noguchi sculpture. Photo 1986.

87

Contrasting patterns: semi-natural vegetation versus cultivated fields. View from Mont Ventoux, France.

• Broadbent G. 1990. *Emerging Concepts in Urban Space Design.* Van Nostrand Reinhold, London pp. 183-185
• Faludi A. 1992. 'Dutch growth management: the two faces of success'. In: Landscape and Urban Planning no. 22 p. 93. Elsevier, Amsterdam
• Gombrich E.H. 1979. *The sense of order.* Cornell University Press., Ithaca, New York p. 7
• Harsema H. 1996. 'Field remnants at Vlake Bridges'. In: *Landscape architecture and town planning in the Netherlands 93-95.* Thoth publishers, Bussum pp.150-151
• Moore C.W. (et al). 1989. 'City Gardens: Isfahan and Beijing'. In: *The Poetics of Gardens.* MIT Press, Cambridge pp. 148 ff.
• Spirn A. 1998. 'Transcending Polemics'. In: *The Language of Landscape.* Yale Univ. Press, New Haven pp. 259-262

Convex. Concave

see also > form, hill

Convex: 'With a curved surface like the outside of a ball'. Concave: 'curved inwards like the inner surface of a sphere' (*Oxford English Dictionary*).

In a curved space with parallel walls like a street or a lane, the convex vertical wall faces the concave opposite wall. The resulting sense of enclosure depends on the degree of curvature, but is always much stronger, more visible and inviting, than that produced by a straight linear space (Bacon 1974).

In an undulating landscape, convex forms hide vales and create surprising views (Higuchi 1983). The convex ground-plane of a town square is not only conducive to surface drainage, but also creates optical effects. By offering a protective enclosed space, concave forms in the shape of hollows in the ground attract people and events (Dee 2001). As the following rhyme suggests, there may also be an erotic connotation:

'Everything's either
concave or convex,
so whatever you dream
will be something with sex'

Piet Hein. 1966. Grooks. MIT Press Cambridge

• Bacon E. 1974. *Design of Cities.* Thames and Hudson London p. 27
• Dee C. 2001. 'Bowls and hollows'. In: *Form and Fabric in Landscape Architecture.* Spon London p. 57
• Higuchi T. 1983. 'Depth and convex terrains'. In: *The Visual and Spatial Structure of Landscapes.* MIT Press Cambridge pp. 79-80

Not only is the façade concave, so is the square itself. Piazza del Campo, Siena, Italy.
Photograph by Frank Meier.

Corridor

see also > ecological networks, pattern

'A narrow strip of land especially through foreign-held territory' (*Webster*).

Ecological corridors

The first description of ecological corridors as a landscape unit were made in the US during the 1960s. They are linear zones of great length, such as a river valley, connecting ecotopes and carrying flows of energy, water and wildlife (Lewis 1969). Outside the corridor is the 'foreign' urban and agricultural land. Corridors have a number of characteristic patterns, such as meanders, and courses that weave or branch (Bell 1999; Forman 1995).

In recent years, ecological corridor in the U.S have developed into 'greenways' – large continuous zones that are not only in need of protection, but must also be planned, designed and managed as public grounds that 'link together the rural and urban spaces in the American landscape' (Fabos 1995; Ahern 2002). The Dutch counterpart is the connecting zone within a casco or Econet. An ecological corridor is intended to maintain bio-diversity, and is also characterised by tranquillity, stability and sustainability (Sijmons 1990).

Economic corridors

These are industrialised zones along the main axes of national infrastructure. Consisting of urban developments such as showrooms, offices and warehouses that arose more or less spontaneously along highways, they are dynamic, and often noisy. Located on sites ranging between narrow belts to mega-zones, they are sometimes components of an international transport axis that connects nodes of industrial development. Such corridors might be described as instruments for 'bundling diffuse urban land-use' (Hidding 2002).

An ecological corridor: Drentse Aa brook valley, the Netherlands.

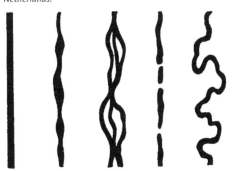

Characteristic patterns in landscape corridors: meandering, interweaving and branching.
Source: Bell S. 1999. Landscape, Pattern, Perception and Process. Spon, London p. 34.

89

Economic corridor in the Netherlands.
Photo: Peter van Bolhuis., Pandion

• Ahern J. 2002. *Greenways as strategic landscape planning*. PhD dissertation, Wageningen University pp. 37 ff.
• Bell S. 1999. *Landscape, Pattern, Perception, Process*. Spon, London p. 34
• Fabos J.G.; Ahern J. 1995. Greenways. Special Issue Landscape

and Urban Planning, Elsevier, Amsterdam vol 33 nos 1-3

• Forman R. 1995. 'Stream and river corridors'. In: *Land Mosaics. The Ecology of Landscapes and Rivers.* Cambridge University Press.

• Hidding M. C. 2002. *Planning voor stad en land.* (i.e. planning for town & countryside) Coutinho publishers, Bussum pp. 127-130

• Lewis P.H. 1969. *Upper Mississippi River Basin Study.* National Park Service. Deparment of the Interior, Washington D.C., Appendix B pp. 68-83

• Sijmons D. 1990. 'Regional Planning as a Strategy'. In: Landscape and Urban Planning, Elsevier, Amsterdam no. 18 pp. 265-273

Criterion, Norm, Standard

see also > value, quality

A criterion is 'a standard on which a judgement or decision may be based' (*Webster*). A norm is 'an authoritative standard' (*Webster*), or a 'standard or pattern that is typical (of a group)' (*Oxford English Dictionary*). In daily use, 'norm' and 'standard' are often confused.

A quantitative criterion is used to determine whether a construction is sufficiently strong, of whether a road or path is wide enough. It is, nearly literally, a yardstick. The standard applied may be based on the dimensions and requirements of the human body, or on the operational requirements of a machine.

The minimum area of land needed for types of land-use is determined on the basis of standards expressed in terms of metres (square or otherwise). Requirements for dimensions of a footpath will depend on its location and use. A garden path should have a minimum width of 30 cm, though the use of a wheelbarrow will require 60 cm, and so forth (Lehr 1997). The profile of streets and roads depends on design speed. The dimensions of car parks are calculated on the basis of the turning circles of cars.

Over the years, various handbooks containing standard measurements and requirements have been compiled on the basis of the experience gained in the construction industry and by the users of buildings and outdoor space (Le Corbusier 1945; Neufert 2000). Standards and guidelines for minimum areas of private and public outdoor space per household or per individual are based partly on research or routine, and partly on ideas about human behaviour and value systems. Such standards vary from place to place, and can also change over time (Lehr 1997; Tandy 1971).

Abstract criteria are principles whereby the real and the good is distinguished from the false or the negative. They are normative – in other words, based on values – and include the criteria used to assess landscape amenity and nature quality (Zube 1975).

There is always some confusion between criteria for visual quality and Environmental Impact Statements, which claim to draw on accepted standards for the objective assessment of the effects of human intervention in landscapes.

• Le Corbusier. 1945. *Le Modulor: essai sur une mesure harmonique a l'échelle humanine app.licable universellement a l'architecture et a la mecanique de l'architecture d'aujourd'hui.* Boulogne, part 1 and 2

• Lehr R. 1997. *Taschenbuch für den Gartenbau, Landschaftsbau und Sportplatzbau.* Parey, Berlin

• Neufert H. (et al) (ed). 2000. *Architect's Data* (third edition). Blackwell, Oxford

• Tandy C. 1973. 'Parks and open spaces'. In: *Handbook for Urban Open Spaces.* Watson-Guptil publications, New York pp. 101-102

• Zube E.H. (et al). 1975. *Landscape Assessment: Values, Perceptions, Resources.* Dowden Hutchinson & Ross Stroudsburg, Penn., U.S.A.

Deconstruction

see also > design, analysis, layer

'A method of critical analysis of philosophical and literary language which emphasizes the internal workings of language and conceptual systems, the relative quality of meaning, and the assumptions implicit in forms of construction' (*Oxford English Dictionary*)

Both in linguistics and in the arts, deconstruction is a form of theoretical (and meta-theoretical) research, a critique of all existing theory and of models of understanding. It attempts to uncover the epistemological assumptions underlying aesthetic values and interpretations of meanings so as to demolish them (Steiner 1997).

As conceived by Jacques Derrida (b.1930-2004), deconstructivism aimed to dissect and deny all self-evident assumptions in philosophy and religion. These included the belief in God, the belief that all problems can be resolved by rational and logical argumentation, and the belief that all thinking is founded in language (Broadbent 1990).

In architecture and landscape architecture, this craze for demolition can be interpreted as 'a breaking up of the established architectonic order, of hierarchical relationships between technical (or functional) demands and aesthetic conditions, in favour of a poetic expressiveness. Existing values are not denied but upturned, allowing for new relations and the discovery of new frontiers' (Reh 1990).

The winning entry for the 1984 Parc de la Villette design competition in Paris can be labelled as an example of a deconstructivist 'unfolded' design. It consists of three intersecting and overlapping geometric patterns of points, lines and planes. Follies are located at intersection points. They form space, not by enclosure but by accentuating points that encompass (Broadbent 1990).

• Broadbent G. 1990. *Emerging Concepts in Urban Space Design*. Van Nostrand Reinhold, London pp. 315-320
• Reh W.; Steenbergen C. 1990. in: Van der Kooij E. (ed). *Het Montagelandschap*. (i.e. *The assembly landscape*). Technical University Delft pp. 19-20
• Steiner G. 1997. *Real presences/Het verbroken contract*. Meulenhoff pp. 124 ff

Decor, Decoration, Decorum

see also > ornament, scene

Decor is the 'furnishing and decoration of a room, stage, etc' (*Oxford English Dictionary*). It is also a setting: 'the scenery used in a play or a movie' (*Webster*). To decorate means 'to make more attractive by adding something beautiful or becoming, or to award a decoration of honour to' (*Webster*); decorum means 'proper behaviour, formal, ceremonial' (*Webster*).

All three notions can simultaneously apply to gardens, which can serve as décor, as theatres, and also as decorated places where social and ceremonial happenings and festivities take place. Such gardens have been known throughout Europe since the Italian Renaissance (Jackson 1980). 'It is the world of suggestion, of illusion, the almost-real' (Hazlehurst 1980).

The decorative elements in 18th-century gardens included fountains, ponds, sculpture, vases and grottoes, which served not only as ornamentation, but also as references to nature and the four seasons, as well as to the propriety and reputation of the owner. They were certainly meant to impress, and also served for ceremonial occasions (de Jong 1993).

• Hazlehurst F. Hamilton 1980. *The Gardens of Illusion. The Genius of André le Nôtre*. Vanderbilt U.P., Nashville, Tennessee
• Jackson J.B. 1980. 'Landscape as theater'. In: *The Necessity for Ruins, and Other Topics*. University of Mass Press, Amherst pp. 67 ff.
• de Jong E. 1993. *Natuur en kunst* (i.e. *Nature and art*). Thoth publishers, Bussum pp. 52, 187 ff.

Design, designing

see also > composition, concept, design objectives, -methods, -theory, -tools, drawing, image, landscape planning, research, style

A design is:
- 'a drawing produced to show the look and function or workings of a building, garment or other object before it is built or made'
- 'the art of action, of conceiving of and producing such a drawing'
- 'an arrangement of lines or shapes created to form a pattern or decoration'
- a technique for deciding 'upon the look and functioning of (a building etc) by making a detailed drawing of it' (*Britannica*)

According to Plato (428-348 BC), to design is 'to create, a manner of production, or to allow to emerge'. What emerges is not only art – the result of production and knowledge – but also the creation of order.

Many authors have stressed different aspects of the notion of design. To Krieger, 'Design is about orderliness and authenticity. Can we deliberately create something that is apparently orderly, purposeful, meaningful – and that works, more or less well?' (Krieger 2000) To Motloch, however, 'Designing is a creative process, it involves a reaction to circumstances and conditions, and brings together sensory impressions and meanings' (Motloch 2001). Meanwhile, Dutch poet Gerrit Komrij calls the designer 'an artist who may give old stories new life with heightened awareness and a different mood, or may spruce them up with a new shine [...] stories that have gone over his head long time ago and can be adjusted only at the last moment'.

In professional practice, designing and planning are regarded as different activities, in the sense that planning is concerned chiefly with the allocation of types of land-use, and designing deals with form and meaning. However, the definition in *Oxford English Dictionary* not only states: 'to plan is to mark out into divisions as in a plan or diagram, but is also 'to devise, contrive, design or make a plan of something to be made or built: planning a garden'..

These contradictory notions therefore mean there is some confusion about the difference between the two activities – especially with regard to the distinction between 'landscape planning' and 'landscape design', as the nature of the activity depends on a personal approach.

Landscape architecture is an applied art form, linked to a site, an objective, and also a patron. As Dutch landscape architect Mien Ruys (1904-1998) complained, 'A painter may create art without an assignment [...] a musician may enjoy his products in solitude [...] but the poor landscape architect cannot do anything all by himself. A garden designer without a commission is like a cook without ingredients' (Ruys 1981).

An assignment accompanied by a brief should logically lead to a predictable and unique design (Steiner 1999). For every situation or problem, however, more than one satisfying design solution is possible. There is more than mere logic involved.

The renowned American educator Donald Schon (1985) gives a succinct description of the whole process: 'Given a programme or a brief and the description of a site, the student must first set a design problem and then go on to solve it. Setting the problem means framing the problematic situation presented by site and programme in such a way as to create a springboard for design inquiry. The student must impose his preferences onto the situation in the form of choices whose consequences and implications he must subsequently work out – all within an emerging field of constraints'.

Central to a design activity is the process of 'reflection-in-action', based on the repertoire of routinised responses that skilful practitioners bring to their practice. It is acquired through training, or through on-the-job experience. It is usually tacit, and it is delivered spontaneously, without conscious deliberation. It is a dynamic knowing process rather than a static body of knowledge, in the sense that it takes the form of continuing detection and correction of error. (Schon 1985/2)

In his essay 'To the students of landscape architecture', French landscape architect Michel Corajoud advises new students of landscape design to observe the following nine rules:
- Work yourself into a state of excitement
- go over the place in every direction

93

- explore the limits, and go beyond them
- leave the problem in order to be able to return
- move crosswise through the scales
- anticipate
- defend open space
- open the project
- keep control of your own design (http//corajoudmichel.nerim.net).

Four aspects of the environment must be considered in every design:
- order: measures such as zoning should be used to improve the visibility of spaces and volumes;
- functionality: spaces should facilitate various uses;
- reference: form and meaning must be connected;
- aesthetics: spaces of beauty should be created.

The main objective of design is to organise elements or parts into a coherent whole, at all levels of scale, and for many uses, from the design of household tools to that of landscapes (Bevlin 1977).

Thanks to the increasing complexity of their assignments during the second half of the 20th century, a landscape architect's activities are no longer based on an applied art-and-craft approach, but on a combination of creative thinking, systematic procedures and applied scientific knowledge.

Their design methods are founded on design theory, in which various assumptions about human behaviour and human values are combined with theories derived from fields such as ecology, geography and geology. A number of design tools are also used. 'Professional design is managed by formal and rational strictures, so that discipline and technique modulate surprise, amazement, and wonder [...]; the dangers of romantic love are balanced by those of method and form and sweet affections' (Krieger 2000).

Describing a number of design approaches from an American perspective, Crewe and Forsyth distinguish between:

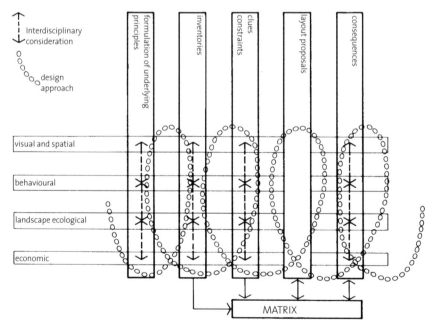

Development of planning process

Complex design assignments require a combination of a design-based approach and an interdisciplinary approach, with continuous feedback to design principles and data.

· Design as a synthetic action, whereby a process of analysis and synthesis is involved in the resolution of the different and sometimes conflicting interests inherent to a design assignment. This approach takes place at all levels of scale, often involving multiple land-use in an urban environment with different clients.
· Design as a cultural expression, in which intuition and artistic expression prevail. Assignments in this case are mostly at a detailed scale.
· Design founded on a landscape analysis, in which natural process and historic development are dissected. In the US, the emphasis lies on providing a basis for the conservation of large areas. Elsewhere, landscape analysis is simultaneously the basis for, and part of, a landscape-design process.
· Interactive design, whereby the designer's expertise throughout the process has to serve the ideas and interests of the public. The aim is to promote a democratic process in planning and design. This approach can succeed only at a local scale, with a limited number of participants and a finite design problem.
· Ecological design, where natural processes serve as a basis for design decisions. This approach works well in degraded or derelict urban areas. Examples have been illustrated by Spirn (1984) and Hough (1995).
· The design of special places with a strong spiritual and emotional context, such as cemeteries, monuments and certain examples of land art (Crewe 2003).

These considerations raise the question of whether landscape architecture should be defined – as it was in the past – as a combination of arts and crafts, or whether it can be viewed as a scientific discipline.

There is no unequivocal answer to this question. Generally speaking, one can state that, unlike in the sciences, no form of architecture aims to discover or further the truth, or bases its knowledge on testing, verifying or falsifying hypotheses. By definition, therefore, they are not scientific pursuits.

On the other hand, however, one may argue that there are analogies between a design process – especially at a regional scale – and scientific research activities.

In both cases, one faces increasing uncertainties regarding the goals to be achieved and how they should be approached. Complexity and chaos theory have become part of scientific research. The design process is influenced by the unpredictability of developments in society; interdisciplinary collaboration helps search for new variables and overcome uncertainties. This approach replaces the traditional linear approach, which aimed to arrive at a fixed final design. Research and design have become overlapping activities, which means that landscape architecture has become an applied science (Prominski 2004).

· Bevlin M.E. 1977. *Design through Discovery*. Holt Rinehart and Winston, New York p. 3-4
· Crewe C.; Forsyth A. 2003. 'LandSCAPES: A typology of approaches to landscape architecture'. In: Landscape Journal, University of Wisconsin Press 22:1-03 pp.37-53
· Krieger M. 2000. 'Discipline and technology'. In: *What's Wrong with Plastic Trees? Artifice and Authenticity in Design*. Praeger, New York pp. 50 -52
· Motloch J.L. 2001. 'Spatial design'. In: *Introduction to Landscape Design*. Wiley & Sons, New York pp. 196 ff.
· Prominski M. 2004. *Landschaft Entwerfen. Zur Theorie aktueller Landschaftarchitektur*. Reimer Verlag
· Schon D. 1985/1. *The Design Studio. An Exploration of its Traditions and Potentials*. RIBA Publications Ltd, London p. 6
· Schon D. 1985/2. *The Design Studio. An Exploration of its Traditions and Potentials*. RIBA Publications Ltd, London p. 24
· Steiner F. 1999. 'Site design'. In: *The Living Landscape*. McGraw Hill, New York pp. 292 ff.

Design concept
see > concept

Design critique
see also > aesthetics, analysis, iconography, taste

Critique is 'a critical estimate or discussion' (*Webster*).

Design critique is applied in two ways:
· As a predominantly contemplative activity or attitude, it is a patient and reflective way

of enjoying a design as a work of art, as a composition. It makes no attempt to categorize the work within an art movement or style, and engages in no search for meanings. Instead, attention is directed towards the internal logic and beauty of form and colour, which stimulate sensory delight.
· In a more precise sense, design critique is not only the joy of beholding but also the demand for truth, for the implicit message. What are the designer's meanings and references; what are the social implications of his work? 'Critique' in this sense is derived from the Greek *krinein*, i.e. the separation of the valid from the illegitimate, the valuable from the useless. It involves a search into the origins and legitimacy of opinions and convictions – whether ethical, metaphysical, scientific, religious or otherwise. It is a matter of judgement (Baumeister 1999).

A critical look at a designed environment – it makes no difference whether it is a real one, or one featuring in a study project – can be taken from different points of view and from different perspectives. A critical judge should be aware of the relative aspects of his views – which indicates the need to study the theoretical basis of landscape design (Treib 2004).

· Baumeister T. 1999. *De filosofie en de kunsten.* (i.e. *Philosophy and the arts*) Damon Best pp. 216; 391-393
· Treib M. 2004. 'Being critical'. In Topos European Landscape Magazine, Callwey, München no. 49 pp. 6-21

Design instrument
see also > drawing, landscape language, simulation

An instrument is 'a means whereby something is done' (*Webster*).

The technical design instruments at a landscape architect's disposal are those that can be used to make internal images visible by translating them into a form that can be shown to others. They are applied mainly in the field of simulation, i.e. in giving 'the appearance or effect of; copy[ing], represent[ing], imitat[ing] the appearance of something' (*Webster*). Traditionally, these

instruments are the stylus, chalk, carbon, brush, pen, sketch block, transparent paper, template etc., all of which are applied in the production of plans, perspective drawings, axonometries and geometric systems (Leupen 1997).

The most important instrument in architectural design is the drawing: 'In a sense one might call the drawing the language of architectural thought; the drawing is the most direct medium of communication about an architectural design. Since designing and communication are inextricably linked, designing without drawing is in fact impossible' (Steenbergen 2002).

In the 19th century, landscape architects were actively engaged in the actual construction phase of a project, and often personally staked out their designs in the field. Nowadays, the activities connected

In the 18th century, landscape architect Humphrey Repton used a folded-paper technique to compare a view before and after improvement.
Source: Daniels. S. 1999. Humphrey Repton. Landscape Gardening and the Geography of Georgian England. Yale University Press, New Haven

1.

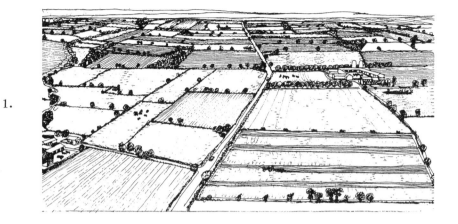

2.

97

3.

Landscape change is often unpredictable. Aerial perspectives of the same landscape show the successive stages of development. 1. The situation in 1972. 2. future change as predicted in 1972. 3. The situation in 1994.
Source: Countryside Commission. Agricultural Landscapes: a Third Look. Technical Report. Walgrave, Northampton, UK

with the work of building and construction is done by others. The finished and detailed drawing serves as an intermediary between the designer and the contractor. This means there is often the risk of a discrepancy between what is represented and what gets built (Corner 1992).

An instrument that helps one compare the current and projected appearances of a site is the type of eye-level perspective drawing used in the 19th century by Humphry Repton in his so-called Red Books (Repton 1813). Landscape changes can also be visualised by means of sketches in bird's-eye view (Anonymous 1997).

The digital storage and manipulation of data brought by Computer Aided Design has had a strong impact, not just on design techniques, but also on communication between designers and their clients. Similarly, the introduction of Geographic Information Systems (GIS) has made the planning process more efficient. Environmental perception has been changed as much by the presentation of virtual landscapes and environments on computer screens as it was changed by the invention of perspective rules during the Italian Renaissance. However, artist's impressions such as those created by the contemporary 'zap-generation' require that an observer is able to interpret the virtual into the real. A negative aspect of this type of display is a tendency towards the theatrical, superficial, or 'flashy' (Lemoine 1988).

The total abandonment of traditional manual modes of sketching by hand with their controlled pencil movements and the intensive interaction between eye, hand, crayon and paper – and their substitution by 'push-button' computer techniques – may mean that designers have lost a means of creative expression. What they have gained, however, are greater opportunities to instantly inspect the effects of new lines, planes and forms: 'we have learnt a great deal from the ease of programming the creation of almost any kind of order and studying its effects' (Gombrich 1979).

• Anonymous. 1997. *Agricultural Landscapes. A third look.*
Countryside Commission, Walgrave ,Northhampton
• Corner J. 1992. 'Representation and Landscape'. In: Swaffield S. 2002. *Landscape Theory. A Reader.* The University of Pennsylvania Press, Philadelphia
• Gombrich E.H. 1979. *The Sense of Order.* Cornell University Press., Ithaca, New York p. 93
• Lemoine P. 1988. 'The demise of classical rationality'. In: Thackara J (ed). *Design after Modernism.* Thames & Hudson, London pp. 190 ff.
• Leupen B. et al. 1997 'Drawing techniques'. In: *Design and Analysis.* 010 Publishers, Rotterdam pp. 204 -215
• Repton H. 1813. *Plans for Sherringham in Norfolk.* Red Books. The Basilisk Press, London
• Steenbergen C. M. 2002. 'The power of drawing'. In: Steenbergen C.M.; Mihl H.; Reh W.; Aerts F. (ed). *Architectural Design and Composition.* Thoth Bussum/Faculty of Architecture TU Delft. p. 158

Design method
see also > analysis, concept, design strategy, design theory, system

A method is 'a regular systematic plan for, or way of doing something.' (*Webster*)

A design process consists of a series of successive phases or stages, going from an assignment and a brief to the final product. It involves a number of decisions based both on deduction (the rational component) and on inductive jumps (the intuitive/creative moments). While a method may be based on logic, it must also must rely on intuition – this is, if we agree with Descartes (1596-1650) that logic serves merely to explain gathered knowledge to others (Simon 1969).

In landscape architecture, two design methods prevail: a linear procedure or cyclical procedure.

The linear procedure
In a simple design assignment, the sequence is as follows: 1.) interpretation of the brief, 2.) a statement of objectives in relation to a budget, 3.) the conception of a design strategy in connection with a site analysis, 4.) the sketching phase, and 5.) the final design with planting plan, construction drawings, specifications and budget.

The non-linear or cyclical procedure
In the case of more complex assignments, many more decisions need to be based on an assessment of interrelated factors. General

goals need to be interpreted into specific objectives, and the relationship between land-use and site characteristics needs to be established. For the latter, matrices are used. The options available are then translated into scenarios or models, whose validity established is tested through feedback to earlier decisions (Halprin 1969; Lynch 1984; Sasaki 1950; Motloch 1991; Steiner 2000).

Historically, the various steps in a design process and the resulting choices depended mainly on the intuition and the craftsmanship of the designer. Considerable attention was devoted to the creation of

formal frameworks, and to order and hierarchy (Hunt 2000).

These days, however, planners and designer are obliged to account for all the decisions taken as a design develops. The design process has therefore become more rational, systematic and 'open', allowing the client and the general public to participate in the process. Designing has become a methodical way of solving problems (Hester 1974; Jones 1980; Lang 1987; Rusch 1973; Rowe 1991).

In 1964, Alexander introduced his ideas on the application of systems theory in environmental design. The existence of a set

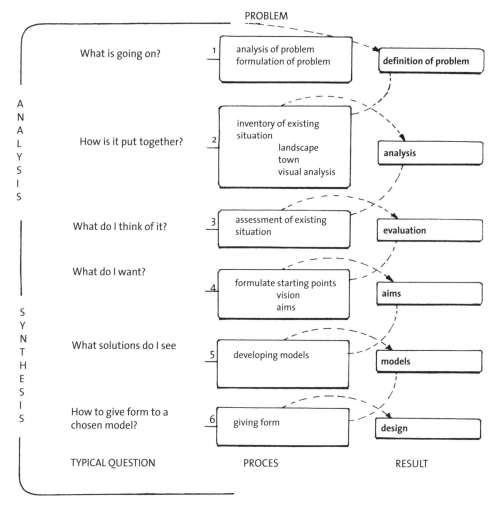

99

Diagram of a design process.
Source: Dekker & Thijsse 1986. De Rode Draad. Student thesis Wageningen University.

of hierarchical relations in design requirements was expected to lead to a logical and computer-supported design process via a top-down approach (see *System*). The idea was tried out on the layout of a housing area, but even the largest computer memory available at the time could not quite solve the problem: designers' intuition and experience were needed to complete a design (Hanson 1969). On other grounds, too, the notional existence of hierarchical relations was soon deemed inadequate, and was replaced by the view that the environment consists of a 'lattice work' of more complex relations (Alexander 1980).

As Donald Schon warns, the ultimate consequence of applying computer-supported logic deduction in the design process is a loss of professional skills: 'The doctrine of technical rationality, promulgated and maintained in the universities and especially in the professional schools, infects the young professional-in-training with a hunger for technique. Many students in urban planning, for instance, are impatient with anything other than 'hard skills' [...] A professional who really tried to confine his practice to the rigorous application of research-based technique would find not only that he could not work on the most important problems but that he could not practice in the real world at all' (Schon 1985).

Generally speaking, the relative position of the rational versus the intuitive part of the design process depends greatly upon the nature of the assignment. In garden design, intuition prevails; in landscape planning, the rational component (Bell 1999; Eastman 1970).

• Alexander C. 1966/1968 (fourth printing). *Notes on the Synthesis of Form.* Harvard University Press, Cambridge pp 60 ff.
• Alexander C. 1988. 'A city is not tree'. Reprint in: Thackara J. 1988 *Design after Modernism.* Thames and Hudson, London pp. 67-84
• Bell S. 1999. 'Design method and practice'. In: *Landscape. Pattern, perception and process.* E&FN Spon pp 101 ff.
• Eastman C. 1970. 'On the Analysis of Intuitive Design Processes'. In: Moore G. (ed).. *Emerging Methods in Design and Planning.* MIT Press, Cambridge pp. 21-38.
• Halprin L. 1969. *The RSVP cycles. Creative Processes in the Human Environment.* George Braziller Inc, New York.
• Hanson K. 1969. 'Design from linked requirements in a housing problem'. In: Broadbent G.; Ward H. *Design Methods in Architecture.* Lund Humphries, London
• Hester R. Jr. 1974. 'Community Design'. In: Swaffield S. (ed). 2002. *Theory in Landscape Architecture.* University of Pennsylvania Press, Philadelphia pp. 49-56
• Hunt J.D. 2000. 'Historical Excursus: Late Seventeenth Garden

Early Warning Maps

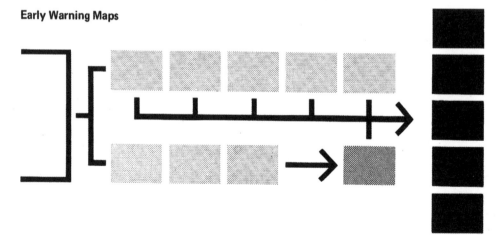

Diagrams from 'Early Warning System'.
The upper maps represent five types of land-use, the lower three show landscape patterns and processes. The vertical row contains maps showing various environmental effects; these are the 'early warning maps'.
Source: Patri T., Streatfield D.C. (et al). 1970. Early Warning System. The Santa Cruz Regional Pilot Study, Berkeley, California

Theory'. In: *Greater Perfections*. Thames & Hudson, London pp.180 ff.
- Jones J.C. 1980. *Design Methods. Seeds for the Future*. John Wiley, New York pp. 2-86
- Lang J. *Creating Architectural Theory*. Van Nostrand Reinhold, London pp. 33-72
- Lynch K.; Hack G. 1984. *Site Planning (third edition)*. MIT Press, Cambridge pp. 1-22
- Motloch J.L. 1991. 'Design as Creative Problem-solving'. In: *Introduction to Landscape Design*. Van Nostrand Reinhold, London pp. 239-256
- Rowe P.G. 1991. 'Staged-Process Models of Problem Solving in Design'. In: *Design Thinking*. MIT Press, Cambridge pp. 46 ff.
- Rusch C. 1973. 'The Role of Graphic Activity in the Design Process. In: Moore G. (ed). 1970. *Emerging Methods in Environmental Design and Planning*. MIT Press, Cambridge pp. 38-48
- Sasaki H. 1950 'Design process'. In: Swaffield S. (ed.) 2002. *Theory in Landscape Archityecture. A Reader*. University of Pennsylvania Press, Philadelphia pp. 35-37
- Schon D. 1985. *The Design Studio. An Exploration of its Tradition and its Potentials*. RIBA Publishing Ltd, London p. 18
- Simon H. 1969. 'The science of design'. In: *The Sciences of the Artificial* .MIT Press, Cambridge pp. 55 ff.
- Steiner F. 2000. 'Site design'. In: *The Living Landscape*. McGraw Hill, New York pp. 292 ff.

Design objectives and goals

see also > design concept, -method

An objective is 'a thing aimed at or wished for'. A goal is the 'object of one's efforts; target' (*Oxford Advanced*).

Both can be approached at two levels, the first approach being made on the basis of the objectives stated in a specified description or brief. These include questions regarding future use, how much of what should go where, how the site is to be managed and at what level of expenditure. Opportunities derived from site characteristics are combined with demands and preferences.

Alternatively, goals and objectives can be approached as general planning goals based on principles and strategies: i.e. what sort of quality should be achieved, and how? Which factors be accounted for? Planning and design goals are often linked to long-term changes (Lynch 1966, 1984; Bell 1999). Over recent decades, for example, the focus of design in urban open space has shifted from decorative through functionalist to ecological (Hough 1995).

However, a purely goal-oriented design process that aims to achieve a final plan through a direct and simple approach does not work. Design goals can be achieved only through phases of learning and feedback in a multivariable and open 'scoring' process that goes through cycles of action and reflection (Halprin 1969).

- Bell S. 1999. 'Design methods and practice'. In: *Landscape. Pattern, Perception and Process*. E& FN Spon, London pp. 101, 102
- Halprin L. 1969. *The RSVP cycles. Creative Processes in the Human Environment*. Braziller, New York
- Hough M. 1995. *Cities and Natural Process*. Routledge London.
- Lynch K. 1966. 'Quality in City Design'. In: Holland L.B. (ed) *Who Designs America?* Anchor Books, New York pp. 125 ff.
- Lynch K.; Hack G. 1984. *Site Planning (third edition)*. MIT Press, Cambridge pp. 107-126.

Design style

see > style.

Design and planning strategy

see also concept, design objective, method

A strategy is: 'a careful plan or method. The art of devising or employing plans or stratagems to achieve a goal' (*Webster*).

In landscape architecture, a design strategy is 'a written statement referred to as the plan, usually accompanied by a map prepared by a planning authority to set out the main long term objectives. A statement of their planning policies include economic, social and environmental considerations. Where these do not coincide, the plan sets priorities and indicates where resources may best be directed, and the principal locations and areas where there is an opportunity to promote significant changes in land-use' (*Goulty*).

A strategy is therefore the rational aspect of a design process, whereby ways are found to achieve a desired situation. It might be termed path-finding. Strategies can be conservative, defensive, offensive or opportunistic (Ahern 2002). An example of an offensive policy for achieving conservation and for strengthening bio-diversity is thus found in the establishment of ecological networks; in the Netherlands, this has replaced conservative or defensive strategies, whereby legal mechanisms or adapted management were used to protect territories of high biological value against economic development.

• Ahern J. 2002. 'Greenways as a planning strategy'. In: *Greenways as Strategic Landscape Planning*. PhD dissertation, Wageningen University pp. 37-52
• Goulty G.A. 1991. *A Dictionary of Landscape*. Avebury Technical, Avebury

Design theory

see also > analysis, design concept, -critique, -method, monitoring.

A theory is a 'set of reasoned ideas intended to explain facts or events' (*Oxford English Dictionary*).

The word is derived from the Greek *theoria*, meaning to supervise, witness and travel, and also to consider, study. 'Travelling' in this case indicates the way in which theory becomes method. Since the time of Descartes (1596-1650), a scientific theory has been defined as a creative, ordering hypothesis that is followed by experimental verification or falsification.

Such a model is not applicable to the arts, or to architecture or landscape architecture, which do not make it possible to test or check theories in the same way. Notions such as truth, authenticity and tenability do not apply. The content and intent of 'theory' differ, and overlap with such concept , visions and paradigms (Corner 1990).

In that it can bridge, mediate or reconcile, theory can play a number of roles in landscape architecture. The bridging role is played by what are effectively 'guidebooks' that describe and locate sites, thereby providing the reader with a descriptive vocabulary and with criteria for appreciating the landscape. The mediating role of theory consists of actively revealing the contradictions underlying a given culture's artistic, political and economic ideologies, thereby influencing perceptions of the landscape in general and of built works in particular. The reconciling role is needed to contain, inscribe, embed, and express within its designed environments a culture's complex and contradictory attitudes about the natural world. It can communicate the tension between those intertwined strands of faith and reason, myth and fact (Meyer 1992).

Theoretical thinking on the subject of garden design has always focused on the how and why of a garden's layout. In essence, the questions concern the nature of good design, and of 'good' environment of the highest possible quality.

This leads to a need to clarify the why and how of the design process (Hunt 2000). Design theories are based on changing standards and values, on ideologies shared by designers. Verification is impossible because of a lack of adequate systematic knowledge of human behaviour, human ideals, expectations and aims. Assumptions are therefore inevitable (Lang 1987; Swaffield 2002).

There is a distinction between positive design theories and normative ones. A positive theory is founded on assumptions and ideas that can be used as a basis for describing and explaining the nature of the design process and the present condition of the natural and the built environment. The greater knowledge of phenomena brought by empirical evidence can deepen a designer's insight into reality. This, together with his own growing experience, can lead him to better decisions (Broadbent 1990). For every landscape architect, the learning process begins during the phase of professional training; it is a life-long process (Corner 1991; Ndubisi 1997; Steiner 1997).

A normative theory is founded on an ideology and on propositions of how reality should be, thoughts on this being guided by notions on human behaviour. Normative theories often lead to utopian design and planning proposals. Architectural history contains many examples of useful innovations and changes that were derived from experiments that were originally utopian in nature. Progress often results from trial and error (Lang 1987; Lynch 1981).

There is also a distinction between instrumental theory and critical theory.

Though the former is typically derived from empirical observation, it often evolves from practical experience, as with Kevin Lynch and John Ormsbee Simons. 'This is what I call the practitioner's knowing-in-action. It can be seen as consisting of strategies of action, understanding of phenomena, ways of framing the problematic situations encountered in day-to-day experience. It is acquired through training, or through on-the-job experience. It is usually tacit [...]' (Schon 1985).

A critical theory challenges taken-for-granted ways of thinking and puts forward alternatives (Meyer 1992).

• Broadbent G. 1990. 'Empiricism'. In: *Emerging Concepts in Urban Space design*. Van Nostrand Reinhold, London pp. 80-81
• Corner J. 1990. 'A discourse on Theory I. Sounding the depths – origins theory and representation'. In: Landscape Journal, University of Wisconsin Press, Madison, Wisconsin Vol 9 no. 2 pp. 61-78
• Corner J. 1991. 'A discourse on theory II: three tyrannies of contemporary theory and the alternative of hermeneutics'. In: Landscape Journal, University of Wisconsin Press, Madison, Wisconsin vol. 10 no. 2 pp. 115-134
• Hunt J.D. 2000. 'Late seventeenth–century garden theory'. In: *Greater Perfections. The Practice of Garden Theory*. Thames & Hudson, London pp. 180 ff.
• Lang J. 1987. *Creating Architectural Theory*. Van Nostrand Reinhold, London pp. 3-21
• Lynch K. 1981. A Theory of Good City Form. MIT Press, Cambridge pp. 73 ff.
• Meyer E. 1992. 'Situating modern landscape architecture'. In: Swaffield S. (ed). 2002. *Theory in Landscape Architecture. A Reader*. University of Pennsylvania Press, Philadelphia pp. 21-31
• Ndubisi F. 1997. 'Landscape ecological planning'. In: Thompson G.; Steiner F. (ed). 1997. *Ecological Design and Planning*. Wiley & Sons, New York p. 37
• Schon D. 1985. *The Design Studio. An Exploration of its Traditions and Potential*. RIBA Publishing, London p. 24
• Swaffield S. 2002. *Theory in Landscape Architecture. A Reader*. University of Pennsylvania Press, Philadelphia 302.
• Steiner G. 1997. *Real Presences/Het verbroken contract*. Meulenhoff, Amsterdam

Design tools and materials

see also > avenue, basin, border, dam, fountain, garden, hedge, hill, path, soil, tree, stream, terrace, water

A tool is 'an instrument or apparatus used in performing an operation or necessary in the practice of a vocation or profession' (*Webster*).

'The content of landscape design is the raw material to be transformed through design: material from which we may derive pleasure and/or significance' (Treib 2002).

The tools and materials used in garden and park design include the following:
• materials such as soils, plants, construction materials, and water
• categories identifying the forms of plants and soils, etc, for example, rectilinear or curved, geometric or loose, sloping or flat, concave or convex
• elements constituting parts of a designed composition: avenues, borders, edges, fountains, hedges, lawns, paths, ponds, terraces, walls, banks, etc. (Steenbergen 1996; 2003)
• dimensions or scales: large or small, high or low, long or short, narrow or wide etc.

These design materials – not to mention the way they are used – help determine the character of a designed environment. As well as being utilitarian, they are also space-forming, decorative and symbolic (Motloch 2001). They may express austerity and simplicity, naturalness, exuberance or diversity (Fairbrother 1974; Vroom 1992; Anonymous 2000). They are also part of architecture in a constructive sense (Booth 1983). As knowledge of these materials and of their properties and use underlies a landscape architect's craft, and thus the identity of the discipline, they are what distinguish a landscape architect from an architect or an engineer.

103

• Anonymous. 2000. Theme Issue 'Materials'. Topos European Landscape Magazine, Callwey, München.nr 32
• Booth N.K. 1983. *Basic Elements of Landscape Design*. Waveband Press, Prospect Heights, Illinois
• Fairbrother N. 1974. 'The elements of landscape'. In: *The Nature of Landscape Design*. The Architectural Press, London pp. 69-130
• Motloch J.L. 2001. *Introduction to Landscape Design* (second edition). Wiley & Sons, New York pp. 77-90
• Steenbergen C.; Reh W. 1996. *Architecture and Landscape*. Thoth publishers, Bussum pp 287, 304
• Treib.M. 2002. 'The content of landscape form'. In: Landscape Journal, University of Wisconsin Press, Madison, Wisconsin no. 20:2-01 pp.119-140

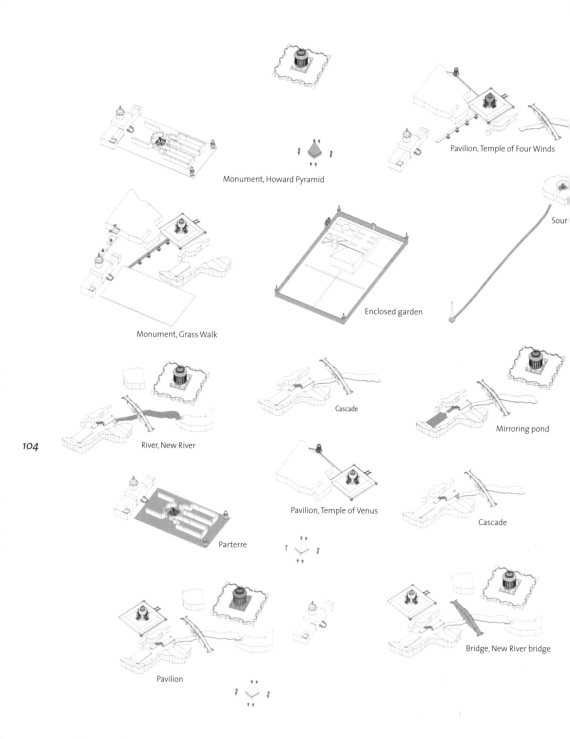

Pavilion, Temple of Four Winds

Monument, Howard Pyramid

Sour

Enclosed garden

Monument, Grass Walk

Cascade

Mirroring pond

River, New River

104

Pavilion, Temple of Venus

Cascade

Parterre

Bridge, New River bridge

Pavilion

Elements such as a parterre, cascade, pond and avenue are among the tools used to create the ensemble at Castle Howard, England.
Source: Steenbergen C. Reh W. 1996. Architecture and Landscape. Thoth publishers, Bussum pp. 304

The character of sculptures and buildings is strongly influenced by the materials used: a sculpture in Parc Guëll by Antonio Gaudi contrasts with a similar one by Mies van der Rohe at the famous Barcelona pavilion built for the 1929 International Exposition.

• Vroom M.J. (ed). 1992 . *Outdoor Space.* Thoth Publishers, Bussum pp. 76-79.

Determinism

see also > adaptation, behaviour, modernism

'A doctrine [which holds] that acts of the will, natural events, or social changes are determined by preceding causes' (*Webster*).

Geographic and ecological determinism are founded on the idea that the natural environment, a landscape or territory, is a precondition for the existence of human society and human culture. A literal application of this idea in landscape design may lead to a persistent search for the natural patterns in the landscape that guide or even determine the layout of settlement patterns, building sites or road patterns.

The opposite doctrine is culturalism, nurtured by anthropology, social geography and archaeology, whereby 'landscapes are primarily considered as cultural constructs, as expressions of a specific order, world view and cosmology of a culture' (Lemaire 1999).

In urban design, determinism is a concept supporting the belief that new environments establish the behaviour and movement of users in fixed patterns. 'Part of the architectural self-image comprises the belief that architects possess the ability to affect social relationships via their work' (Lipman 1974). In extreme cases this doctrine implies the adaptation of the behaviour of users to the ideals of the designer and his sense of order (Ittelson et al 1974; Knox 2000). Human activities may thus be restricted and the amount of private space limited because of its inevitably messy appearance. Public space, preferably labelled as 'communal', dominates.

This ideal was in the ascendancy in Modern Architecture after the Second World War. Due to its inevitably disordered appearance, architects rejected the ideal of the traditional detached house plus garden preferred throughout much of society. Urban neighbourhoods were therefore laid out with regimented high-rise apartment buildings surrounded by public outdoor space. High density prevailed, and was expected to promote social contact. In later years, such

105

ideas were contested by sociologists and psychologists (Webber 1970).

• Ittelson W.H (et al) (ed). 1974. *An Introduction to Environmental Psychology*. Holt, Rinehart and Winston, New York pp. 344-347
• Knox P.; Pink S. 2000. 'Design determinism'. In: Urban Social Geography, Prentice Hall, Englewood Cliffs, New Jersey pp 282-283
• Lemaire T.; Kolen J. 1999. 'Landschap in meervoud: op weg naar een gespleten landschap?'. In: *Landschap in meervoud*. (i.e. *Multiple landscapes*) Jan van Arkel, Utrecht. p 15
• Lipman A. 1974. 'The architectural belief system and social behavior'. In: Lang J. (et al) (ed). *Designing for Human Behavior: Architecture and the Behavioral Sciences*. Dowden, Hutchinson & Ross. Stroudsburg, Penn pp. 23-31
• Webber M. 1970. 'Order in diversity: community without propinquity'. In: Proshansky H.M. *Environmental Psychology. Man and his physical setting*. Holt Rinehart and Winston, New York pp. 533-549

Dike

see also > barrage, polder, stream

'An artificial embankment of earth and rock built to protect low-lying land from flooding, such as the polders in the Netherlands. An embankment in the floodplain of a river parallel to its course, as the Mississippi in the USA and the lower Rhine' (*Goulty*).

Dikes are important features in the Dutch landscape, both visually and functionally: '25% of the surface of the Netherlands is below sea level and about 65% of its total surface would be flooded if it were not for the dikes' (van de Ven 1993). The driver or cyclist who travels the road along the top of a river dike is provided with a continuous panoramic view, the steep slopes on either side contributing a sense of 'floating' over the landscape (Feddes 1988).

Dikes along the North Sea coast are earthworks of huge dimensions – some of them hundreds of meters in cross-section at the base. They are more or less straight. The course of the narrower and steeper river dikes is more sinuous, due mainly to their builders' search for solid ground during the original construction phase in the Middle Ages, and later to the many repairs made after dike bursts. During the 20th century,

Grebbedijk along the Rhine near Wageningen, the Netherlands.
Photo: Harry Harsema

higher peak levels occurred in lowland rivers, and disastrous floods necessitated repeated reinforcements of their dikes.

Over the centuries, these highly visible steep-sided earthworks have had a variety of buildings constructed on them, and now reflect a considerable historical value. They also carry a special type of vegetation, with many rare plants whose seeds arrived on the river waters. All in all, raising and reinforcing such dikes has to be approached with the greatest sensitivity (van Dooren 2001).

A raised path; drawings from a design study on the visual quality of reinforced dikes along the river Rhine.
Source: Feddes Y. Halenbeek F. 1988. Een scherpe grens (i.e. A sharp boundary), Staatsbosbeheer, Utrecht

Dike surrounding the Flevopolder, the Netherlands.

• van Dooren N.; Horlings H. 2001. 'Dike reinforcement in the Netherlands'. In: Topos European Landscape Magazine, Callwey, München.
• Feddes Y.C.; Halenbeek F.L. 1988. *Een scherpe grens. Ontwerpstudie naar de ruimtelijke kwaliteit van verzwaarde rivierdijken.* (i.e. *Design study on spatial quality of reinforced river dikes*) Landschapsarchitectuur Staatsbosbeheer, Utrecht. Chapter 4.1
• van de Ven G.P. (ed.) 1993. *Man-made Lowlands.* Matrijs publishers, Utrecht

Dimension, Measure, Size

see also > grid, proportion, space, scale

A dimension is 'Magnitude of extension in one direction or in all directions. The range over which something extends' (*Webster*). Dimensions can be measured, a measure being the 'standard or system used in stating the size, quantity or degree of something (*Oxford English Dictionary*).

In environmental design, the dimensions of the human body are the basic module for the design of objects and spaces – a reminder not only of the statement by Protagoras (485-410 B.C.) that 'man is the measure of all things', but also of the fact that truth is relative, everything being only as it is perceived. Thus, while physical activities can be accommodated in small spaces that are made-to-measure, larger spaces tend to be dimensioned in relation to basic units or modules related to the size of the human body, which are more recognizable than the metric system. The relationship between the dimensions of buildings or spaces and any standard such as the human body is called scale (Le Corbusier 1945; Peter 1994). Until the end of the 17th century, the proportions and dimensions of objects and planes used to be the prime basis for ordering a design (March 1998).

The size of spaces has always influenced human experience: 'greatness of dimension is a powerful cause of the sublime' (Burke 1990). As well as being determined by natural boundaries, landscape dimensions are determined by topography and vegetation, man-made volumes and linear elements. In a distant past, the sizes of agricultural land lots used to depend on the ability of a farmer to

107

physically cope with a certain area of land. In rocky terrain, size was determined by the distance over which the farmer could carry stones when clearing the land and erecting walls for enclosure. At that time, measurements and boundaries were thus the physical limits for human beings (Corner 1996). Sizes of medieval land lots in western Holland were limited in size by the rate of slope and the relative distance of underground drainpipes. Units within some of the reclaimed 17th-century polders were based not only on functional requirements but also on an architectonic concept (Lambert 1971). (see *Geometry. Polder*)

Sizes of contemporary land lots are purely functional, determined by the requirements of mechanized equipment as well as by the market.

• Burke E. 1990. 'Vastness'. In: *Essays on the sublime and the beautiful.* Cassell, London pp. 80-81
• Corner J. 1996. *Taking Measures across the American Landscape.* Yale University Press, New Haven pp. 7 et.seq.
• Corbusier Le. 1945. *Le Modulor: essai sur une mesure harmonique a l'échelle humanine applicable universellement a l'architecture et a la mecanique.* l'Architecture d'Aujourd'hui, Boulogne
• Lambert A. 1971. *The Making of the Dutch landscape.* Seminar Press, London pp. 212-228
• March L. 1998. *Architectonics of Humanism. Essays on Numbers in Architecture.* Academy Editions, London
• Peter J. 1994. *The Oral History of Modern Architecture.* Abrams, New York p. 11

Discourse

see > paradigm

Diversity

see also > identity, scale.

'The condition of being different or having difference' (*Webster*). Diversity involves the splitting of a homogeneous whole into parts, each with its own character. In biology, it means an increase in complexity and organisation (van Dale).

Diversity is the natural accompaniment of complexity. A blank wall has unity, but no variety, and does not merit lengthy contemplation. A work of art must, as it were, hold in suspension and unify a great diversity of elements; the greater the complexity integrated into this unity, the greater the achievement. This fact is so universally recognized that the two criteria are often stated as one: unity-in-diversity, or variety-in-unity (*Britannica*).

In urban environments, diversity with regard to spaces, facilities, activities, options and atmospheres is a precondition for its citizens' quality of life. A mixture of housing, employment, shopping and consumption stimulates people to circulate. Streets should not be too long, housing should mix various ages, sizes and characters, while people should be present in multitudes (Jacobs 1961; Broadbent 1990).

In regional landscapes, too, quality is underlain by diversity. Historically, the layout and form of settlements was determined by local soil conditions and surface water patterns. Regional building styles and local land-use patterns – the basic components of regional identity – were largely the product of isolation and inaccessibility.

Modern technology has reduced our dependence on soil conditions for building activities; communication is now world-wide. As diversities of form diminish, the size of agricultural lots is tending to become more uniform. Thus, for example, the development of larger lots in the eastern part of the Netherlands and the concentration of settlements in the western part has meant that the earlier disparities of scale have decreased (Kerkstra 1990).

• Broadbent G. 1990. *Emerging Concepts in Urban Space Design.* Van Nostrand Reinhold, London pp. 138-142
• Jacobs J. 1961. *The Death and Life of Great American Cities.* Pelican Book, Harmondsworth, Middlesex
• Kerkstra K.; Vrijlandt P. 1990. 'Landscape planning for industrial agriculture'. In: Landscape and Urban Planning, Elsevier, Amsterdam no. 18 pp. 275-287
• Lynch K. 1976. 'The sensory quality of regions'. In: *Managing the Sense of a Region.* MIT Press, Cambridge pp. 8 et seq.

The definition of biodiversity depends on the level at which it is viewed:
· at a level that considers genetic diversity within a certain species, such as the different strains of wheat that grow in the world's various climate zones

· at a level that considers the total number of types of living organism in the world
· at a level that considers the diversity of ecosystems within a larger area, e.g. marsh ecosystems or forest ecosystems (Schroevers 1999; Anonymous 1998).
  The maintenance of biodiversity is part of the Dutch government's policy as put forward in the Environmental Policy Plan (Anonymous 1993) and the Nature Policy Plan (Anonymous 1990). The establishment of a national ecological network is based on this policy.

· Anonymous. 1990. *Natuurbeleidsplan* (i.e. *Nature policy plan*) Ministerie LNV, The Hague
· Anonymous. 1993. *Nationaal Milieubeleidsplan.* (i.e. National environmental policy plan) Ministerie VROM, the Hague p. 204
· Anonymous. 1998. Environmental Indicators. Towards a sustainable development. Organisation for Economic Cooperation en Development OECD, Brussels pp. 63 et seq.
· Schroevers P. 1999. 'Menselijk bemiddelde natuur' (i.e. *Man-made nature*). In: Kolen J.; Lemaire T. *Landschap in meervoud.* Jan van Arkel, Utrecht pp. 141-161

Drawing, Sketch

see also > design instrument, representation

To draw is 'to produce a likeness of by, or as if by making, lines on a surface: delineate' (*Webster*).

In a design drawing, the outlines, contours or limits of objects, volumes and spaces are made visible in plan. A sketch is 'a rough drawing representing the chief features of an object or a scene, and often made as a preliminary study' (*Webster*).

The activity of sketching is the creative, probing and illustrative part of the design process. The sketching of pencil lines on paper constitutes the trial-and-error phase in which the composition is ordered. Ideas are born, images produced, the expression of feeling aided by the tactile experience of the pen or pencil gliding over paper. A sketch has several functions: 'In painting, sculpture, [...], architecture and garden design [...], the drawing is the essential. In the drawing one finds the basis for the forming of taste, not in terms of impression but of form' (Kant 1790/1978).

Sketch of Villa Reale di Madua by Lodewijk Wiegersma.

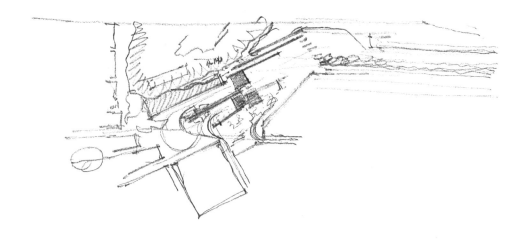

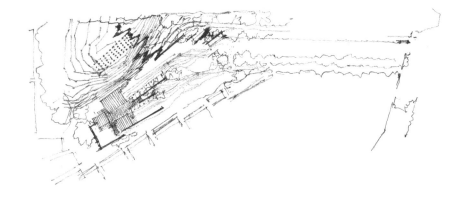

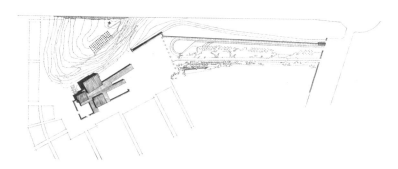

The sketch as an integral part of the design process. Three phases in the development of the design of the chapel at the Malm cemetery in Helsinki. Entry to a design competition by Alvar Aalto (1898-1976).
Source: Fleig K. (ed). 1963 Alvar Aalto. Verlag für Architektur, Zürich

'In a sense, one might call the drawing the language of architectural thought; the drawing is the most direct medium of communication about an architectural design [...] designing without drawing is in fact impossible' (Steenbergen 2002).

When travelling, too, sketching and drawing objects and spaces helps one to learn to see, analyze and imagine the essential characteristics of the layout and the general atmosphere of gardens and landscapes (Cullen 1968). By obliging the observer to look carefully, drawing an environment helps us understand it and recognise its beauty (de Botton 2003). 'Drawing in the landscape creates an awareness of place that is a distinct form of information-gathering and of understanding the landscape setting' (Lavoie 2005).

The sketching of an existing tableau or scene is analogous to the perception process: 'Looking over the shoulder of an artist as he draws an architectural and decorative ensemble, we shall see his perceptual hierarchies at work as he starts from the relationships he finds easy to code in a few lines, re-constructing rather than recording' (Gombrich 1979). Landscapes are thus the inevitable result of cultural interpretation [...] (Corner 2002).

In poetic or critical drawing we aim to find out what is 'really going on', and students should therefore be well-trained in free-hand sketching (Dee 2004; van Haaften 2001). For the registration of scenes, a camera is easier and quicker to handle, but in photography too much information is collected, inhibiting focused observation and a personal connection to the land.

The three-dimensional perspective drawings of a design help illustrate the designer's intentions, both to himself and to others. In other words, they 'project' a future situation (Corner 2002). By emphasising certain details and leaving out inessential items, the designer may clarify his intentions, but he is also able to mislead (Corboz 1988).

Architectural purists in the 1920s considered the sketching pencil a suspect instrument, and preferred to leave illustrative work to others; sketching was thought to be too subjective and inaccurate (Simon 1988). While modern digital techniques may provide greater accuracy and speed in the drawing process, the loss of sensory contact risks an impoverished emotional involvement on the part of the designer. The design process is tending to become a predominantly cerebral activity.

• de Botton. 2003. 'On Possessing Beauty'. In: *The Art of Travel*. Penguin Books, London pp. 217-238
• Corboz A. 1988. 'Le dessin, degré zéro-zéro de l'architecture'. In: Simon J. 1988. *Croquis Perspectifs de 130 Paysagistes*. Collection 'Aménagement des Espaces Libres' Livre no 11, Bourguignon, Turny p. 5
• Corner J. 2002. 'Representation and landscape'. In: Swaffield S. 2002. *landscape theory. A reader*. The University of Pennsylvania Press, Philadelphia pp. 144-164
• Cullen G. 1968. *The concise townscape*. The Architectural Press, London
• Dee C. 2004. 'Poetic-critical drawing in landscape architecture'. In: Topos European Landscape Magazine, Callwey, München no. 49 December 2004 pp. 58-65
• Gombrich E.H. 1979. *The Sense of Order*. Cornell University Press, Ithaca, N.Y. pp. 115-116
• van Haaften A. 2001. *Freehand sketching for students of architecture*. Bouwkunde publishing, Technical University Delft ISBN 90-5269-283-1
• Kant I. 1790 (1978). *Over schoonheid*. (i.e. *On beauty*) Boom, Meppel p. 63
• Lavoie C. 2005. 'Sketching the landscape: exploring a sense of place'. In: Landscape Journal 24:1-05 University of Wisconsin Press pp. 13-31
• Simon J. 1988. *Croquis perspectifs de 130 paysagistes*. Collection: 'Aménagement des espaces libres'. Atelier de Paysage, Bourguignon, Turny
• Steenbergen C.; Aerts F. 2002 'The power of drawing'. In: Steenbergen C. (et al) (ed.) *Architectural Design and Composition*. Thoth publishers, Bussum pp. 158-177

111

Durable

see > sustainable

Dynamic. Sequence. Rhythm.

see also > experience, framework, process

Dynamic is: 'characterized by constant change, activity, or progress' (*The New Oxford Dictionary of English*)

Natural and cultural landscapes develop and change over time. Landscapes are dynamic. An observer witnesses a momentary 'glimpse' of an ever-moving and changing environment.

Natural dynamics are the result of physical processes (such as erosion and sedimentation) and of biological processes (involving growth, blossoming and decay). Some changes can occur suddenly: discontinuities may disrupt the course of certain events, creating a complex situation whereby dynamic change takes place at different speeds – something that is often difficult for the individual observer to grasp.

Society also changes, and shifting views on realities influence our perception of the real world. The passing of time can be perceived in the wider landscape, but also in every garden: 'gardens structure time, with an emphasis on those that are unique' (Miller 1999).

The art of landscape design is therefore an entirely different activity than the architecture of buildings: 'All that landscape art makes available to the senses is never more than the approximation of what is still to be sensed, yet to appear, or still to be shown; for with the passing of the day, the seasons, or simply of time landscapes show themselves to be exactly what they have not been' (Leatherbarrow 2004).

Many of the slower processes in landscapes often remain unnoticed. Dynamic change brought about by human interference now

Giacomo Balla's 'Speed of a motor car', 1913.
Source: Gerhardus M. & D. 1978. Symbolism and Art Nouveau. Phaidon London

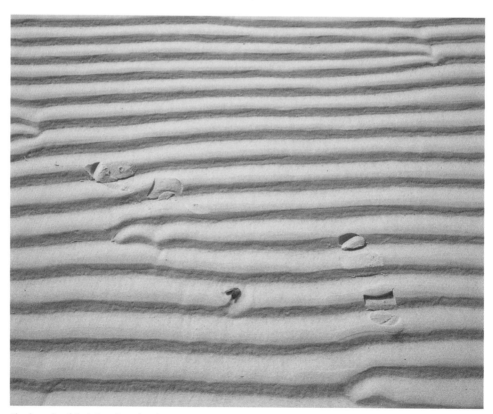

The dynamics of rippled sand on a beach.

predominates, and is the cause of great concern – for while change as such can contribute to bio-diversity, too much dynamic change reduces it (Schroevers 1999). Although Dutch Government landscape conservation policy aims to reduce such change in rural areas, such a policy is hard to maintain, as it leads not only to public protest, but also to a static social and economic environment (Lörzing 1982). Landscape planners attempt to absorb dynamic change by the layout of frameworks. These should be congruent with landscape structure, and demand a new approach to design and simulation (Spirn 1988).

• Leatherbarrow D. 2004. *Topographical Stories. Studies in Landscape and Architecture.* The University of Pennsylvania Press, Philadelphia pp.131-132
• Lörzing H. 1982. *De angst voor het nieuwe landschap.* (i.e. *Fear of a new landscape*). Staatsuitgeverij, The Hague
• Miller M. 1999. 'Time and temporality in Japanese gardens'. In: Birksted J. (ed). *Relating Architecture to Landscape.* Spon Press, London pp. 43-58
• Schroevers P. 1999. 'Menselijk bemiddelde natuur' (i.e. *Man-made nature*). In: Kolen J.; Lemaire T. *Landschap in meervoud.* Jan van Arkel, Utrecht pp. 148-149
• Spirn A. 1988. 'The poetics of City and Nature'. In: Landscape Journal no. 2 University of Wisconsin Press, Urbana, Illinois pp. 124

In painting, the existence of a dynamic society became a source of interest in around 1910 with the advent of Futurism (related to Cubism). One Futurist manifesto denounced the prevailing glorification of the old, and the contempt for the new, young and lively (Giedion 1967; Gerhardus 1979). As dynamics are related to movement, the Futurists concentrated on pictorialising movement, such as in *Speed of a motor car* by Giacomo Balla.

In architecture and town planning, the notion of dynamic space is associated with the experience of space over time (Giedion 1954/1967). In a dynamic space, the walls run from low to high, change continuously in direction, and refer to something higher or further away. The observer is thus invited to move along. Space itself may appear to move (Gombrich 1982).

A dynamic space is the antipode of a static space, which is clearly defined, enclosed and visible from one point of view. While the interior of a Gothic church or a Baroque palace is full of movement, the composition of a Classicist park is very static. The movement of observers through adjoining spaces provides a succession of experiences evoking an emotional response comparable to enjoying music or looking at a film (Bacon 1974). Applicable here are such musicological notions such as interval, metre, cadence and tempo, and also sequence and rhythm.

A sequence is a 'set of events, numbers, actions, etc, with each one following the one before continuously or in a particular order' (*Oxford English Dictionary*).

The sensation of movement depends on the variety of spaces traversed, from open to

113

Dynamic change in the river floodplain near Wageningen, the Netherlands.
Photo Henk van Aggelen

enclosed, from articulated to uniform. It also depends on the speed of the observer, the number of objects visible, and on the time needed to absorb visual stimuli (Arnheim 1969). Traversed at walking speed, urban spaces (including parks) can provide an interesting experience through their succession of changing views, enclosed spaces and gates. Such spaces have a 'human scale' (Cullen 1961).

It takes a pedestrian 20 seconds to traverse a space of 25 metres, during which time he is able to enjoy a particular view. To have the same effect on the driver of a car travelling at 100 kilometres per hour, such a space should be 550 metres in length (Wöbse 2002). During the 1960s, methods developed for the notation of visual sequences along roads helped establish design criteria for the alignment of new roads (Appleyard 1964; Thiel 1970).

Dynamic activities such as walking, running, driving, steering, approaching or entering all contribute to 'visual control' (Gibson 1979). Kinaesthetic sensations – the experience of beauty through movement – are comparable to dancing or sitting in a roller coaster. To design a motorway with its alignment and furnishings, one requires insight into the dynamic experience of such an environment, the speed at which stationary objects are perceived to pass depending on their placing and distance from the road, all against a background of shifting perspectives (Appleyard 1964). As Dutch journalist S. Montag wrote about travelling in the driver's seat of a High-Speed Train: 'This is a wonderful view. Rhythmic music with yourself as the moving object' (*NRC Handelsblad*, 11 March 2000).

Rhythm is 'a movement or activity in which some action or element recurs regularly' (*Webster*).

In music, it implies 'proper perfection in a natural, living and breathing way, as distinct from a merely mechanical accuracy' (Blom 1971). In outdoor space, it is created by a succession in the timing and spacing of accents, objects, views and sensations. It can also be a regular or harmonious repetition of lines, shapes and colours. The natural rhythm of sand ridges on the beach is more irregular than the artificial rhythm of the roofs in rows of houses. In a designed environment, forms and shapes are structured and brought to life by means of rhythm (Bell 1993).

• Appleyard D. (et al). 1964. *The View from the Road*. MIT Press, Cambridge
• Arnheim R. 1969. 'Movement'. In: *Art and Visual Perception*. Faber Editions, London pp. 360 ff.
• Bacon E. 1974. 'Moving through three dimensions'. In: *Design of Cities*. Thames and Hudson, London pp 320-324
• Bell S. 1993. *Elements of Visual Design in the Landscape*. Spon, London pp. 140-144
• Blom E. 1971. *Everyman's Dictionary of Music*. St Martin's Press Inc., New York
• Cullen G. 1961. *The Concise Townscape*. The Architectural Press, London pp. 17 ff.
• Gerhardus M & D. 1979. *Cubism and Futurism*. Phaidon London pp. 19-24
• Gibson J.J. 1979. 'Rule for the visual control of locomotion'. In: *The ecological approach to visual perception*. Houghton Mifflin & Company, Boston pp. 232 ff.
• Giedion S. 1967. *Space, Time and Architecture*. Harvard University Press, Cambridge pp. 430-450
• Gombrich E.H. 1982. 'Moment and movement in art'. In: *The Image and the Eye*. Phaidon, Oxford pp. 40-62
• Thiel P. 1970. 'Notes on the Description, Scaling, Notation and Scoring of the Physical Environment'. In: Proshansky H (et al). *Environmental Psychology: Man and his Physical Setting*. Holt Rinehart Winston, New York pp. 593- 602
• Wöbse H.H. 2002. 'Lebenszeit – erlebte Zeit'. In: *Landschaftsästhetik*. Ulmer Verlag, Stuttgart pp. 69-78

Eclecticism

see > mannerism, post-modern, style

Eclectic means 'selecting what appears to be best from various doctrines methods or styles. Composed of elements from various sources' (*Webster*).

Throughout history, architects have used historic design styles – with varying degrees of success. The best-known period was the 15th century Italian Renaissance, when manifestations of classical Roman and Greek culture that had been lost during the Middle Ages were rediscovered, studied and reconstructed. This led to a revival of Classical ideals and values.

The return to Classicism in the 18th century was of a different nature, when the search for the past was accompanied by nostalgia and poetic dreaming, and arbitrary choices were made. Neo-classicism in garden design meant mixing elements from various periods, for example by juxtaposing broken columns and Gothic ruins with Classical temples (Colquhoun 1989; Teyssot 2000).

20th-century post-modern architecture borrows freely from historic styles, turning them into a refined if slightly superficial play with personal and collective memories (Amsoneit 1991).

While eclecticism can be denounced as a somewhat unoriginal display of false sentiment, it has also been praised: 'We all carry around with us a *musée imaginaire* in our minds, drawn from experience – often as tourists – of other places, and from knowledge culled from films, television, exhibitions, travel brochures, popular magazines etc. It is inevitable that all of these get run together. And it is both exciting and healthy that this should be so. Why, if one can afford to live in different ages and cultures, restrict oneself to the present, the locale? Eclecticism is the natural evolution of a culture with a choice' (Jencks 1977).

• Amsoneit W. 1991. *Contemporary European Architecture*. Benedikt Taschen, Köln
• Colquhoun A. 1989. *Modernity and the Classical Tradition*. MIT Press, Cambridge pp. 6 ff.
• Jencks C. 1977. *The language of Post-Modern Architecture*. Academy Editions, London
• Teyssot G. 2000. 'The Eclectic Garden and the Imitation of Nature'. In: Mosser M.; Teyssot G. (ed). *The History of Garden Design*. Thames & Hudson, London pp. 359-371

The Klein-Gienicke landscape garden in Potsdam, Berlin. The Lion's Fountain is surrounded by decorative objects dating from different periods in history.
From: Kluckert E. 2000. The gardens of Europe, Könemann, Köln p. 428

Ecocentrism, Bio-centrism

see also > nature conservation

Ecocentrism is an attitude, a faith and a lifestyle. Adherents to the belief that human beings are an integral part of the earth's ecosystem include such great names as Charles Darwin (1809-1882) and Thomas Huxley (1825-1895). Ecocentrism is characterised by a prevailing respect for natural process and for other living organisms, and a belief that man should adapt to his natural environment. 'Mother Nature' is nature personified as a creative and controlling force affecting the world and the humans' (*Oxford English Dictionary*).

Contemporary ecocentrism perceives ecology as the main science providing instructions for human conduct, with nature itself supplying the objective guidelines for moral judgement and collective behaviour (Keulartz 1998; Young 2000). Proposing that every landscape constitutes a natural system that should be perceived holistically, ecocentrism has its roots in the Romantic Age of the 18th and 19th century, marking a reaction against industrialisation and urbanisation, and the degradation, despoliation and drastic changes they brought to the landscape. To quote Henry Thoreau (1817-1862): 'In Wildness is the preservation of the World'; 'Culture is the whore and nature the virgin' (Schama 1995).

In 1991, James Lovelock formulated Gaia Theory, which views 'the Earth [...] as a single physiological system, or a set of systems, that is alive at least to the extent that, like other living organisms, its chemistry and temperature are self-regulated at a state favourable for life'. If or when Homo Sapiens becomes too great a polluter, it may be wiped out by Gaia (i.e. Mother Earth) as she jumps to a new level of self-organisation (Jencks 2003; Pepper 1996).

The opposite to ecocentrism is found in anthropocentrism or even technocentrism, i.e. 'interpreting or regarding the world in terms of human values and experiences' (*Webster*). Currently, both are denounced as the underlying cause of our environmental problems, with short-term gain prevailing over long-term quality, and the negative impact of human action on the natural environment being ignored.

• Jencks C. 2003. *The Garden of Cosmic Speculation*. Frances Lincoln London, pp. 99-104
• Keulartz J. 1998. *The Struggle for Nature. A Critique of Radical Ecology*. Routledge, London
• Pepper D. 1996. *Modern Environmentalism. An Introduction*. Routledge, London pp. 21; 168-237.
• Schama S. 1995. *Landscape and Memory*. Harper Collins, London p. 572
• Young T. 2000. 'Belonging, not Containing'. In: Landscape Journal. The University of Wisconsin Press, Madison, Wisconsin, September Issue pp. 46 ff.

Ecological design

see also > design, design theory, ecological network

Ecological design is founded on an increasing concern in society about the world-wide degradation of environmental quality that is now results from the squandering of natural resources, from our immense waste of energy, and from the industrial and traffic-based pollution of water, soil and the air. It is linked with concerns about the despoliation of the countryside, the apparent loss of bio-diversity, and the fragility of the earth as a natural system (McHarg 1969; McHarg 1998; Pepper 1996).

Ecological design is sustainable design, whose basic premise is to 'allow the ongoing process that sustains life to remain intact and to continue to function along with development' (Franklin 1997). One of its instruments is thus the careful analysis of landscape and individual sites as part of every design process.

A secondary aim of ecological design is to provide urban populations with opportunities to enjoy the sensory and symbolic delights inherent to natural and semi-natural environments. As applied in

117

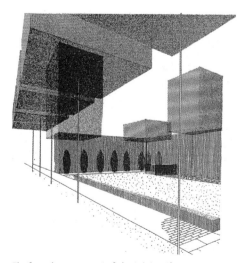

The formal arrangement of plants into a three-dimensional composition in a Modernist design.
Source: Thompson G.F.; Steiner F. 1997. Ecological Design and Planning. John Wiley, New York p. 58

planning and design, it involves the establishment of ecological zones and networks, and a search for topological relationships in the planning of rural areas. Taking a structural approach to guiding landscape processes, it thereby replaces an earlier focus on the design of fixed patterns.

In summary, an ecological design approach involves the following: 1.) the design of sustainable water systems such that full attention is paid to hydrological cycles and the prevention of erosion; 2.) the establishment of connecting zones between urban open spaces and the countryside; 3.) the protection of wildlife and 4.) the application of ecological principles in planting plans (Franklin 1997; Hough 2004).

According to Koh (1987), a new ecological and aesthetic basis should also be developed for design. However, the ideals supporting ecological design are at odds with earlier Modernist views in which the role of plant materials was reduced to formal arrangements and the enclosure of space (Johnson 1997).

- Franklin C. 1997. 'Fostering Living Landscapes'. In: Thompson G.F.; Steiner F. (ed). Ecological Design and Planning. Wiley & Sons, New York pp. 263-292
- Hough M. 2004. Cities and Natural Process. A Basis for Sustainability (second edition). Routledge, London
- Johnson M. 1997. 'Ecology and the Urban Aesthetic'. In: Thompson G.; Steiner F. (ed). 1997. Ecological Design and Planning. John Wiley & Sons, New York pp. 167-184
- Koh J. 1987. 'An ecological aesthetic'. In: Landscape Journal. The University of Wisconsin, Madison, Wisconsin, Spring Issue pp. 177-191
- McHarg I. 1969. Design with Nature. The Natural History Press New York
- McHarg I.; Steiner F. (ed). 1998. To Heal the Earth. Selected Writings of Ian McHarg. Island Press, Washington D.C.
- Pepper D. 1996. Modern Environmentalism. An Introduction. Routledge, London

Ecological networks, Greenways

see also > ecological design, corridor, framework, nature, nature conservation

The establishment of ecological networks in urban and rural areas is intended to reinforce natural processes and increase biodiversity in landscapes (Lammers 1994; Cook 1994). The concept of connecting networks is itself an adaptation and expansion of the island theory of McArthur & Wilson (McArthur 1967).

In current ecological theory, ecosystems cannot exist within isolated areas, but must instead be part of a larger ecological framework, an interconnected pattern of nature areas that allows plant and animal species to migrate. Existing nature areas are therefore being expanded, and new ones laid out and connected by corridors of varying width. The extent to which bio-diversity is increased by these measures is currently uncertain (Ahern 2002).

In the general sense of the word, a network is 'a fabric or structure of cords or wires that cross at regular intervals and are knotted or secured at the crossings' (Webster).

In the Netherlands, there two categories of ecological network or ecological framework. The first consists of branching networks, such as those in river catchment areas (see below).

The second type is the circuit, or 'meshed', type of network, which is established on agricultural land (Vrijlandt 1994) in a

Yearly energy budget of a lawn compared to an alfalfa patch

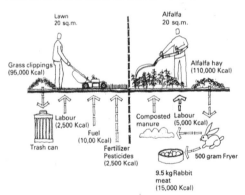

	Energy input Kcal	Energy yield plant	Kcal: Human food
Lawn	15,000	95,000	–
Alfalfa	5,000	110,000	15,000

The ecological design and management of gardens also involves energy-saving measures.
Source: Hough M. 2004 (second edition). Cities and Natural Process. Routledge London p. 225

relatively even, non-hierarchic distribution over the existing landscape pattern. As this must be 'constructed' – in other words, superimposed over the hierarchic, asymmetrical relations already present – it is seldom an easy undertaking. This is especially the case when a landscape pattern is viewed as part of national heritage: for example, when land that has been in agricultural production over centuries is dug up and altered beyond recognition. Ancient patterns in the landscape are bulldozed away, to be replaced with marshes, hummocks and copses – uneven terrain that is suitable for a predetermined type of nature development.

To date, the establishment of the first parts of the network in the Netherlands has not reflected any attempt to integrate the new ecological zones – so-called 'new nature' – into their environment. The domain of 'nature' is separated from that of 'culture', thereby making the establishment of ecological zones a form of contingency planning (Keulartz 1998).

Dutch biologist Koos van Zomeren comments as follows: 'Personally, I see [the expansion of] new nature resembling that of asphalt and concrete. You may react with resignation. My problem is not so much with the phenomenon as with the pretence that accompanies it. I do not see new nature as a victory of nature over farmland, but as a victory of the urban over nature. New nature stands for urban values of change, of a [particularly Dutch conception of a] perfectible environment'.

An alternative approach to the development of ecological networks is seen in the expansion and management of so-called branching networks, hierarchical patterns such as those in stream valleys and other watersheds. In plan, they look like dendritic structures with a hierarchical order. Together with improved management, the protection and expansion of such 'wet' networks should not only help improve biological diversity, but also maintain water quality and control water quantity. Management policy would focus on separating sources of divergent

quality of both surface water and seepage water (Vroom 1994). Overall, the networks involved are much easier to plan and manage: all that is necessary is the reinforcement of their existing structural coherence. Such an approach goes hand in hand with the ecological management of river banks and floodplains, and allows for better water control (van Buuren 1993) (Vrijlandt 1994).

The debate about ecological networks involves some fundamental notions about the interaction between man and nature – whether this is a relationship of subject to object, or a continuum of which man is part. (Soper 1995).

• Ahern J. 2002. *Greenways as strategic landscape planning: Theory and application.* PhD thesis, Wageningen University pp. 37 et seq.

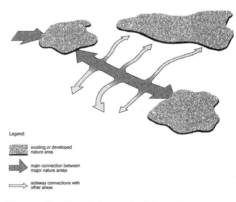

Legend:

existing or developed nature area

main connection between major nature areas

sideway connections with other areas

Diagram of corridors that connect existing nature areas.
Source: Cook E.A.; van Kier H. 1994. Planning and ecological networks, Elsevier, Amsterdam

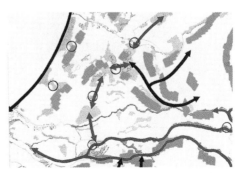

Part of the National Ecological Network in the Netherlands.

119

• van Buuren M.; Kerkstra K. 1993. 'The framework concept and the hydrological landscape structure: a new perspective in the design of multifunctional landscape'. In: Vos C.; Opdam P. (ed). *Landscape Ecology of a Stressed Environment*. Chapman & Hall, London.

• van Buuren M. 1994. 'The hydrological landscape structure as a basis for network formulation; a case study for the Regge catchment'. In: Cook E.A.; van Lier H.N. Landscape Planning and Ecological Networks. ISOMUL. Developments in landscape management and urban planning, no. 6F, Elsevier, Amsterdam pp. 117-134

• Cook E.A.; van Lier H.N. 1994. Landscape Planning and Ecological Networks. ISOMUL. Developments in landscape management and urban planning, no. 6F, Elsevier, Amsterdam

• Keulartz J. 1998. *The Struggle for Nature. A Critique of Radical Ecology.* Routledge, London, Epilogue

• Lammers W. 1994. 'A new strategy in nature policy: towards a national ecological network in the Netherlands'. In: Cook E.A.; van Lier H.N. *Landscape Planning and Ecological Networks. ISOMUL.* Developments in landscape management and urban planning, no. 6F, Elsevier, Amsterdam pp. 283- 309

• Mc Arthur R.H.; Wilson E.O. 1967. *The Theory of Island Biogeography.* Princeton University Press, New York.

• Soper K. 1995. *What is Nature? Culture, Politics and the Non-human.* Blackwell, Oxford, UK

• Vrijlandt P.; Kerkstra K. 1994. 'A strategy for ecological and urban networks'. In: Cook E.A.; van Lier H.N. *Landscape Planning and Ecological Networks. ISOMUL* Developments in landscape management and urban planning no. 6F, Elsevier, Amsterdam

• Vroom M.J. (et al). 1994. 'Landscape planning and water management in the Netherlands'. In: Ekistics: the problems and science of human settlements, Volume 16, no. 364/365

Edge

see > border

Emblem

see also > symbol, sign, reference

'An object or a likeness used to suggest a thing that cannot be pictured' (as a flag is the emblem of one's country). Also: a device, symbol, design or figure used as an identifying mark' (*Webster*).

Landscapes may be viewed as national emblems; thus, Dutch river and polder landscapes demonstrate to foreign visitors how earlier Dutch generations reclaimed and managed their land. Contemporary urbanisation spoils these sites, or otherwise reduces them in size. 'The sub-sea-level Dutch still cherish (but seldom celebrate) the dwindling compage of water meadows, copses, dairy holdings and meandering rivers immortalised by Rembrandt and van Ruysdael' (Lowenthal 1992).

Some of these landscapes have been put on the UNESCO World Heritage list. Meanwhile, in order to advertise their products, some Dutch businesses use traditional emblems such as tulip fields, windmills and clogs in order in order. The Nature Conservation Movement, too, has its emblems, such as the panda, beaver and stork.

• Lowenthal D. 1992. 'European landscapes as national emblems'. In: Paysage & Aménagement / Landscape Research no. 21 October 1992 pp. 14-23

Enclosure

see > boundary

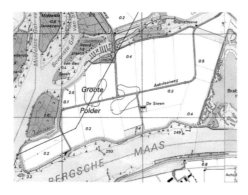

'New nature'. Aakvlaai Polder in the Biesbosch area of the south-western Netherlands, before and after its proposed transformation into part of the National Ecological Network.
Source: Rivierenmagazine no. 6-2001. Provincie Gelderland Arnhem

Holland... Europe As You Imagined.

Holland ▒   The Reliable Airline **KLM**
New Dutch Airlines

Traditional emblematic image of Holland. KLM poster.

Environmental Impact Statement EIS

see also > aesthetics, quality, value

An impact is 'the force of impression or operation of one thing on another' (*Webster*).

In legal language, an EIS is 'a summary of the environmental impacts of an action and alternatives, including no action'. In providing a brief outline of a proposed action and of its likely impact on the environment, an EIS states whether this impact is likely to be adverse or beneficial, short-term or long-term, and reversible or irreversible. It not only uses empirical information to identify and develop methods and procedures for identifying any negative effects, but also to make proposals for countering them. Similarly, it studies the prospects for the so-called 'zero-option' in the area under consideration, i.e. the event that the development plans are cancelled (Steiner 1999).

In the Netherlands, an EIS is required by law for every project that exceeds a

predetermined size or budget. Each EIS must indicate possible damage and formulate proposals both for so-called mitigating measures (i.e. ways of reducing negative impacts) and for compensating measures (i.e. countermeasures), either on the site itself or elsewhere (or both).

An EIS is claimed to be an objective instrument. In the case of environmental impacts which can be measured, such as soil and water pollution and the emission of particles into the atmosphere, this is certainly the case (Anonymous 1981; Dijkstra 1992). In the case of landscape amenity, however, effects are extremely difficult to assess, and a certain amount of arbitrariness is inevitable. One solution to this may involve the use of expert judgement; another, the organisation of opinion polls among a local population.

It might be argued that proposals for mitigation or compensation are primarily a matter of design quality, and not of the number of hectares claimed for nature development or beautification.

- Anonymous. 1981. *Milieueffectrapportage Ontwerp van Wet* (i.e. *Environmental impact statements; preliminary legislation*). Staatsuitgeverij, The Hague
- Dijkstra H. 1992. Milieueffectrapportage. Deel 24. Effectvoorspelling. Hoofdstuk VIa, Landschap. Ministerie VROM, The Hague
- Steiner F. 1999. 'Environmental Impact Assessment'. In: *The Living Landscape*. McGraw Hill, New York p. 391

Ethics

see also > ecocentrism, meaning

'A branch of philosophy dealing with what is good and bad and with moral duty and obligation. The principles of moral conduct governing an individual or a group' (*Webster*).

Designers of outdoor space must serve the interests of their clients. While doing so, they are also obliged to adhere to ethical principles. The interest of the client comes first, as long as this is not in conflict with the interests of the community in terms of environmental quality (Ndubisi 1997; Wolschke 1994). One condition is that landscape architects should have no financial interest in the implementation of projects and the sales of plant materials. Thus, for example, members of the Dutch Association for Landscape Architecture (BNT) must sign a code of honour regarding professional ethics (Boer 1990).

Twentieth-century Modernist architecture and town planning were much influenced by ideals of social equity as a basis for the layout and design of urban neighbourhoods. The ambition was to improve the life of the people by creating a better living environment. This is in stark contrast with the design of contemporary corporate buildings, which often serves primarily as a vehicle for individuals or large corporations to display their wealth and power. Such 'architecture of opulence, [of] the sleek and commanding office buildings, apartment houses, and other structures, [contributes] to long-run political destabilisation, in that such architecture operates on a world-wide scale to reassure the rich, the strong and the self-confident, and to provoke and to radicalise the poor' (Spirn 1998). This might be characterised as aestheticism without ethics.

Environmental ethics

122

Various ideas have resulted from the conflict between recent environmental awareness and older value systems that were concerned merely with social benefit, amenity and aesthetics. They can be divided into an anthropocentric view, in which the human species comes first; and a non-anthropocentric or ecocentric view, in which other members of the biotic community also count. The adoption of the latter could have far-reaching consequences for landscape design (Thompson 1999).

Experience

see > perception

• Boer W.C.J. 1990. 'Changing ideals in urban Landscape Architecture'. In: Vroom M.J.; Meeus J.H (ed). *Learning from Rotterdam*. Mansell, London
• Ndubisi F. 1997. 'Landscape ecological planning'. In: Thompson G.; Steiner F. (ed.). *Ecological Design and Planning*. John Wiley & Sons, New York pp. 9-44
• Spirn A.W. 1998. *The Language of Landscape*. Yale University Press,* New Haven p. 258
• Thompson I. 1999. 'Environmental ethics'. In: *Ecology, Community and Delight. Sources of Values in Landscape Architecture*. Spon, London pp. 137-161
• Wolschke-Bultmann J. 1994. 'Ethics and morality'. In: Journal of Garden History vol. 14 nr. 3 pp. 140-142

Facilitate

see > behaviour, determinism, flexibility, framework

'To make something easy or less difficult' (*Oxford Companion*).

Some types of outdoor space are designed to accommodate specific types of use. Activities there are pre-programmed, and visitors know what to expect. Many parks and playgrounds are laid out like this. However, there are also sites which, though they are not used for a specific planned activity –temporarily or otherwise – are used anyway. Some of them are found on wasteland or in undeveloped areas where industrial development has been postponed. They are freely accessible for people of various ages who use them for fun (Geuze 1993; Andela 1994).

In other places abandoned farmland is exploited for all sorts of activities, whether family picnics, drag racing, or even canoeing in the drainage ditches (Princen 2004). In such cases, users are free to choose – within certain limits – the activity they want to undertake. The sensation of the unprogrammed dominates. Beyond access

roads and occasional garbage collection, facilities are limited, and there is plenty of open space for various uses.

Public parks may be laid out with a minimum of detailed spaces for special activities, and do 'not offer anything but necessary conditions' (Pohl 1993). Whole landscapes may be fitted out with durable frameworks that allow for flexible use within enclosed spaces (see *Framework*).

Inside buildings, too, a flexible layout can help facilitate multiple use. Extreme examples are large exhibition halls such as Mies van der Rohe's Neue Nationalgalerie in Berlin, which contain a vast space under a single roof.

• Andela G. 1994. 'Challenging landscapes for explorers. Estrangement and reconciliation in the work of West 8'. In: Archis Journal for architecture, urbanism, visual arts. NAi, Rotterdam no. 2. pp.38-49
• Geuze A. 1993. 'Accelerating Darwin'. In: Smienk G. (ed). *Nederlandse landschapsarchitectuur. Tussen traditie en experiment*. Thoth, Bussum pp. 12-22
• Pohl N. 1993. 'In which the spirit of the Volkspark also...'. In: Knuyt M. (et al) (ed). *Modern Park Design. Recent trends*. Thoth publishers pp. 71-81
• Princen B. 2004. *Artificial Arcadia*. 010 publishers Rotterdam

Undeveloped land at the perimeter of the port of Rotterdam as freely available space for all sorts of activities.

Fashion

see > style

Fit

see > adaptation

Flâneur, Saunterer

see also > perception, behaviour

'An aimless person. Man-about-town' (*Webster*). Sauntering is 'walking in a leisurely way; strolling.'(*Oxford Companion*)

The word *flâneur* is a word introduced from French into German by the philosopher Walter Benjamin (1892-1940), who expanded the notion to cover the whole complex world of the bohemian – artists with their ambitions, fears and failures, who moved from one social, ritual or topographic event to the next.

To saunter is to seek a leisurely path through the type of urban labyrinth that contains a mixture of use types and a succession of open and enclosed spaces, and that ensures there is always something to see and experience (Jackson 1997): 'the observer is a prince enjoying his incognito wherever he goes' (Broadbent 1990).

The world of the flâneur is that of a voyeur who also feels vulnerable when exposed to the inquisitive eyes of others. He undergoes a multitude of impressions: 'something is happening here'. But he also looks for more; he is in search of the essence of urbanity, of points anchored in the past: 'For the saunterer every street slopes down... to a past which is the more compelling when it is connected with one's own history' (Benjamin 1994).

The presence of flâneurs such as the camera-toting tourist, the day tripper, are proof of urban quality, of ambiance (Urry 1990). This applies to city streets and squares, but also to public parks. Jane Jacobs (Jacobs 1961) identified successful little parks such as Rittenhouse Square in Philadelphia, where the combination of a relatively small size and a location in a neighbourhood with a diversity of shops, restaurants and other facilities made them successful parts of the urban fabric, both in functionally and spatially.

In Europe, larger parks such as Hyde Park in

125

Tourists sauntering on the Barcelona Ramblas.

London, les Jardins des Tuileries in Paris, and Amsterdam's Vondelpark are places where 'things happen', and where many people saunter around all day long. These green spaces have succeeding categories of visitors who – in daytime, at least – between them create a feeling of safety.

• Benjamin W. 1994. *Eenrichtingsstraat (i.e. One-way street). (1928 Einbahnstrasse)* Historische Uitgeverij, Groningen p. 88
• Broadbent G. 1990. *Emerging Concepts in Urban Space Design.* Van Nostrand Reinhold, London p.162
• Jackson J.B. 1997. 'The Stranger's Path'. In: *Landscape in Sight.* Yale University Press, New Haven pp. 19-29
• Jacobs J. 1961. 'The uses of neighbourhood parks'. In: *The Death and Life of Great American Cities.* Pelican, Harmondsworth, Middlesex pp. 99 ff.
• Urry J. 1990. 'Seeing and being seen'. In: *The Tourist Gaze.* Page Publication,s London pp. 136 ff.

Flexibility

see also > facilitate, framework, multiple use

Flexible means 'easily changed to suit new conditions' (*Oxford Companion*).

Flexibility in architecture was fervently pursued by architect Mies van der Rohe (1890-1962), who stated that while buildings may survive over long periods, their use keeps changing. He therefore built large spaces under enormous roofs, thereby allowing the interior to be changed whenever the need arose. Large exhibition halls are still constructed like this.

Flexibility as a design principle in outdoor space design is founded on the same philosophy: landscapes are dynamic, and developments over time often unpredictable. Because each successive generation has different needs, the adaptation of outdoor space to new uses is a permanent process.

Flexibility is achieved through the establishment of fixed and durable elements in a framework that encloses interior spaces or compartments (Baljon 1992; Vroom 1992). Inside them, continuous change can take place, while the overall structure is left intact. These frameworks can be of various size and scale, sometimes covering large areas of land, and consisting of woodland zones or shelterbelts with a long lifespan (Kerkstra

Walls of open concrete blocks form a permanent framework allowing for flexible use, such as changing flower exhibits. Floriade Horticultural Exposition, Rotterdam 1960. Architects van den Broek & Bakema.

1990) or, in small areas such as gardens, of patterns of walls, hedges, terraces and stairs of varying heights.

• Baljon L. 1992 . *Designing Parks*. Architectura & Natura,. Amsterdam pp. 112-116
• Kerkstra K.; Vrijlandt P. 1990. 'Landscape planning for industrial agriculture: a proposed framework for rural areas'. In: Landscape and Urban Planning Journal, Elsevier, Amsterdam vol. 18 nos. 3-4 pp. 275-289
• Vroom M.J. 1992. *Outdoor Space*. Thoth publishers, Amsterdam pp. 34-35

Folly
see > landscape style

Form, shape
see also > function, volume

A. 'Outward physical appearance of something' (*Britannica*).

Every tangible object consists of both matter and form. A three-dimensional volume can be identified through its form (Ching 1979). In a flat plane, forms interact with their background. These forms may be regular and geometric, such as circles, triangles, pyramids, and cylinders; they can also be irregular (Krier 1988). A thing's shape can be described in terms of simple or complex, angular or round, partial or complete, large or small. It can also be described in terms of scale (Arnheim 1969).

B. 'Specific type of arrangement or structure of something' (*Oxford Companion*).

There is a relationship between the shape of an object and its functional properties. This makes recognition possible: what is this, what is it for, how did it originate? Form is related to the identity of an object, whether man-made or of natural origin. Orientation in a space depends on its form, dimensions, and on the rules of perspective.

The modelling and moulding of space is intended to give it a particular functional and eye-catching form. In a design process, modelling is the step at which the concrete form of a new object, site or landscape is imagined and portrayed. Construction, synthesis, style, symbolism and aesthetics are all involved (Gombrich 1971; Leupen 1999; Motloch 1991).

Landscape architects must therefore be 'familiar with a repertoire of forms before they can use them or manipulate them. This includes the forms found in nature and the forms of art, our art and that of others – other media, other cultures, and other periods' (Olin 2002).

• Arnheim R. 1969. *Art and Visual Perception*. Faber Editions, London pp. 32-154
• Ching F.D.K. 1979. *Architecture: Form, Space & Order*. Van Nostrand Reinhold, London pp. 58-63
• Gombrich E.H. 1971. *Norm and Form*. Phaidon Press, London pp. 81 ff.
• Krier R. 1988. 'On architectonic form'. In: *Architectural Composition*. Academy Editions, London pp. 41-68
• Leupen B.; de Zeeuw P. (et al). 1999. In: *Design and Analysis*. Van Nostrand Reinhold, New York
• Motloch J.L. 1991. Introduction to Landscape Design. Van Nostrand Reinhold, New York pp. 126-130
• Olin L. 2002. 'Form, meaning, and expression'. In: Swaffield S. *Landscape Theory. A Reader*. The University of Pennsylvania Press, Philadelphia pp. 77-79

Fragmentation
see also > coherence, collage, order, post-modernism

'To break into small pieces or parts; split up' (*Oxford Companion*).

To designers who look for spatial coherence, the disintegration of space into fragments is a negative process. Advocates of fragmentation may argue in turn that a collection of entities and fragments also possesses a latent design quality, and has a potential for conversion and use within a positive strategy. Fragmentation may be exploited as a virtue rather than approached as a difficult or insoluble problem (Baljon 1992). The underlying philosophy is that a fragmented design mirrors a world of complex forces and counterforces in which the laws of causality no longer count, and from which convention and consensus are absent (Bolle 1992).

When the parts of a fragmented environment can no longer be pieced together, the emphasis may be put on the accentuation of contrasts and the stimulation of variety.

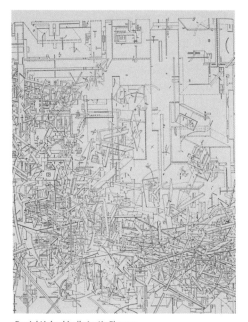

Daniel Liebeskind's Arctic Flowers.
Source: Broadbent G. 1990. Emerging Concepts in Urban Space
Design. Van Nostrand, New York

The designer plays with ruptures and discontinuities, and reinforces them. Relics are set apart, brought together, and placed in a new context with the help of collage techniques, or framed within an overlay. Attempts are made to reduce excessive diversity and complexity into a number of 'readable' contrasts. The result may yet be a subtle form of coherence (Beune 1990).

Daniel Liebeskind's drawing *Arktische Blumen* shows how coherence can be created without the use of conventional tools such as the use of symmetry or the introduction of a dominant element. The total picture is one of unity in diversity (Broadbent 1990). The design of the offices of OMA and landscape architects West 8 for the Chassé site in Breda demonstrates such a contradiction (Harsema 2000).

Landscape fragmentation on a regional scale is a different matter. Expanding linear settlements, new roads, railways and expanding airport runways are increasingly cutting into the existing fabric, thereby

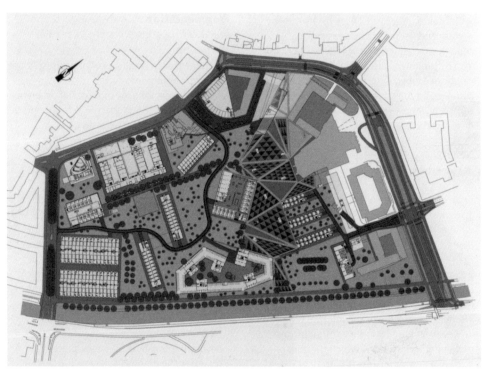

Unity in diversity: Chassé site in Breda, the Netherlands. Designers: OMA + West 8 landscape architects 1998.
Source: Blauwe Kamer Journal no. 2-1998. Stichting Lijn in Landschap, Wageningen

fragmenting space (Yap Hong Sen 2000).
From an economic point of view, this means
damage to properties; from an ecological
point of view it means the destruction of
habitats. The remnants of land left behind
are smaller, as are local plant and animal
populations, while ecological patches
become more thinly spread. The variation in
quality of habitats decreases (Opdam 1993).

Whenever it is impossible to stop the
fragmentation caused by activities such as
road construction, Dutch planning rules call
for 'defragmentation' of the landscape, which
is achieved through so-called compensatory
measures which are financed out of the road
construction budget. Such measures involve
the acquisition of land near a new road and
the on-the-spot transformation of
agricultural land into 'new nature'. These
measures may or may not improve ecological
conditions or stop defragmentation, but they
apparently satisfy many people.

Landscape fragmentation is also a problem
in the visual sense. Open spaces become
smaller, and variations in scale diminish.
Landscape architects attempt to counter this
effect by using design tools such as
perspective views and contrasting elements
(Kerkstra 1990).

• Baljon L. 1992. *Designing Parks*. Architectura & Natura,
  Amsterdam pp. 122-127
• Beune F.; Thus T. 1990. 'Fragmentation in Open Space'. In:
  Vroom, M.J.; Meeus J.H.A. *Learning from Rotterdam*. Mansell,
  New York. pp. 106-121
• Bolle E. 1992. 'De gefragmenteerde ruimte van het
  deconstructivisme' (i.e. *The fragmented space of
  deconstructivism*). In: *Tussen architectuur en filosofie*. VUB Press,
  Brussels p. 47
• Broadbent G. 1990. *Emerging concepts in urban space design*.
  Van Nostrand Reinhold, London p. 246
• Harsema H. (ed). 2000. 'Breda town centre expands onto
  former barracks site'. In: *Landscape architecture and town
  planning in the Netherlands 97-99*. Thoth, Bussum pp. 54-57
• Kerkstra K.; Vrijlandt P. 1990. 'Landscape Planning for industrial
  agriculture' In: Landscape and Urban Planning, Elsevier,
  Amsterdam vol. 18 nr 3-4 pp. 276-279
• Opdam P. (et al). 1998 'Population responses to landscape
  fragmentation'. In: Vos C.C.; Opdam P. *Landscape Ecology of a
  Stressed Environment*. Chapman & Hall pp. 147-167
• Yap Hong Seng. 2000.' Schiphol'. In: *De Stad als uitdaging.
  Politiek, planning en praktijk van de stedebouw*. NAi publishers,
  Rotterdam pp. 45 ff.

Framework

see also > ecological network, flexibility,
structure, sustainable

'Structure giving shape and support'
(Oxford Companion).

A framework in an outdoor space may
consist of walls, hedges, woodland belts or
other elements that enclose and subdivide
space. A framework is by definition a
structural element that is both stable and
durable. It fixes the main outlines of a layout

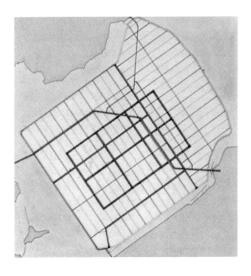

129

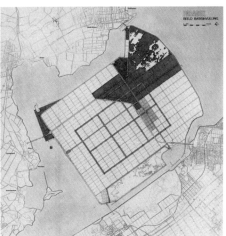

*A belt of trees 100 metres wide creates a framework that
encloses a large part of a new polder.*
*'Paradox': Winning entry for the Markerwaard polder
design competition, the Netherlands, 1984.*
Source: Vroom M.J. (ed) 1992. Buitenruimten / Outdoor Space.
Thoth, Amsterdam

while allowing for the flexible completion of specific areas, where use may change over time without negative effects on the integrity of the whole.

In Italian Renaissance Gardens of the 15th century and onwards, stone constructions such as retaining walls, balustrades, terraces and stairways formed durable frameworks that lasted over centuries, while generations of plant materials went through cycles of growth, blossom and decay (Lazarro 1990; Shepherd 1953). In 17th-century French gardens, the durable elements are the avenues, boskets and bodies of water that subdivide and surround spaces.

Contemporary parks and gardens, meanwhile, contain both durable and changeable elements. One example is found in a design for Bijlmer Park in Amsterdam, where, without loss of character, an existing promenade park had to absorb within its borders a number of new uses such as playing fields, housing, and a festival space. The design proposed a permanent framework of green zones with footpaths, all enveloping an archipelago of islands reserved for various activities (Harsema 2004).

Landscape frameworks usually consist of patterns of roads and waterways, plus edges of land lots with their tree-lined verges, hedges or belts. In pattern these are usually irregular, though they sometimes consist of a grid, as in 17th-century Dutch polders such as Beemster and Schermer to the north of Amsterdam.

In around 1990 Dutch planners reinvented the so-called 'casco' concept for use in landscapes lying on the higher sandy soils, where rapid change in agricultural exploitation was leading to decreased diversity. As a landscape architectural concept, a casco consists of a coherent pattern of belts of tree or woodland of varying width, enclosing spaces of different size within which dynamic change may take place (Kerkstra 1990). Though new frameworks can be designed as geometric elements of a dominant character, such as that in the Markerwaard design competition, in most cases they have been adapted to the existing situation and are less determinant.

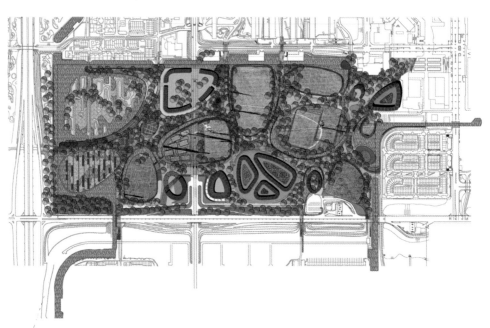

An 'archipelago of islands' – reserved for different uses – is contained within a framework of green promenades. Design for Bijlmerpark, Amsterdam, 2003. Landscape architects Karres and Brands.

Source: Harsema H. (ed.) Jaarboek Landschapsarchitectuur & Stedenbouw in Nederland 01-03 / Landscape Architecture and Town Planning in the Netherlands 01-03. Thoth, Bussum p. 119

This particular casco may overlap with an ecological network, but this is not always the case. The primary objective underlying the ecological network is to create or protect ecologically sound zones that function as buffers between conflicting types of land-use (van Buuren 1993). The desired result is a 'two speed' landscape, in which stable areas and dynamic areas exist side-by-side (Sijmons 1990). In the USA these frameworks are named 'greenways', and also function as outdoor recreation corridors (Ahern 2002).

• Ahern J. 2002. *Greenways as strategic landscape planning: theory and application*. PhD Dissertation, Wageningen University.
• Van Buuren M.; Kerkstra K. 'The framework concept and the hydrological structure: a new perspective in the design of multifunctional landscapes'. In: Vos C.C.; Opdam P. 1993. *Landscape Ecology of a Stressed Environment*. Chapman & Hall, London. pp. 219-243
• Harsema H. (ed). 2004. 'Bijlmerpark – Amsterdam Zuidoost: an archipelago of activity'. In: *Landscape architecture and town planning in the Netherlands*. Thoth, Bussum pp. 118-121
• Kerkstra K.; Vrijlandt P. 1990. 'Landscape planning for industrial agriculture: a proposed framework for rural areas'. In: Landscape and Urban Planning, Elsevier, Amsterdam nr. 18. pp. 257-287
• Lazarro C. 1990. *The Italian Renaissance Garden*. Yale University Press, New Haven pp. 100-108
• Shepherd J.C; Jellicoe G.A. 1953. *Italian Gardens of the Renaissance*. Alec Tiranti, London
• Sijmons D. 1990. Regional planning as a strategy. In: Landscape and Urban Planning, Elsevier, Amsterdam nr. 18, pp. 265-273

Functionalism

see also > modernism, quality

Functionalism is a 'principle in architecture, design, etc. that the purpose and use of an object should determine its shape and construction' (*Oxford Companion*).

This design principle, which was adopted in 20th century architecture, promotes a synthesis of function, materials, construction and form. It is based upon the philosophy of pragmatism, in which truth and authenticity are connected with a properly functioning technology (Broadbent 1990). It is connected with Modernism in architecture and urban design, but existed as far back as the time of Vitruvius. 'An inner necessity took place of analogy as the generator of forms expressive

of the programme or the structure of a building' (Colquhoun 1989).

The purest form of Functionalism is expressed in simplified (and sometimes oversimplified) statements such as 'form follows function' and 'a house is a machine for living' (Peter 1994). Its standards are exemplified in Neufert's *Architects' Data*, which contains a systematic description of tools, objects, spaces, sites, and buildings with their constituent parts, and of the way these should be designed, dimensioned and combined in a standardised and therefore optimally efficient way (Neufert 2000). Man, or rather the human body, is the measure of all things (Leupen 1997).

Functionalism eventually evolved into a phase in which the emphasis came to lie on displaying certain structural parts of a building and shaping different sections of a building in such a way that their function would be legible.

Another characteristic feature of Functionalism is 'Less is More': the pursuit of utter simplicity combined with careful and precise detailing, all adding to the beauty of

Emphasizing the function of parts of a building. Hospital in Aachen, Germany.

the building. 'The poetics of a building must grow out of its legible and fully expressed structure', as architect Norman Foster put it. Thus, when the young woman in Robert Pirsig's *Lila* tells the Captain that her favourite boat has false smokestacks, his response is 'beauty isn't things trying to look like something else [...] Beauty is things being just what they are' (Pirsig 1991).

Functionalism in urban planning was founded on the ideas of the CIAM congress in Athens in 1926, which advocated the separation of housing, industry, traffic and recreation. This development eventually led to monotonous housing areas and boredom, and thus to aversion (Jacobs 1961; Rowe 1991). However, the idea was never entirely abandoned. Nowadays multifunctionality is once more seen as an important condition for a positive experience of urban environments.

In landscape architecture, Functionalism can be applied in site planning and landscape planning.

Functionalism in site planning
Here, the priority lies on a layout suited to the most efficient land-use. Existing site characteristics may be ignored as a matter of principle, even if circumstances would make adaptation possible. Consciously applied Functionalism may rest on the argument that breaking with the past will create contrasts which heighten the intensity of experience of a site. A new and creative approach is also believed to provide a more

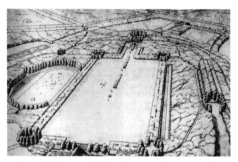

Volkspark Rehberge Berlin, landscape architect: E. Barth, 1926-1929.
Source: Pohl N. 1995. Der kommende Stadtpark.. Doctoral thesis. TU Delft p. 77

Purely functional forms can be beautiful.

durable result than a plan adapted to present circumstances (Baljon 1992).

Functionalism in park design developed in Germany in the years around 1910, when the first so-called *Volksparken* were laid out. Predominant in these were provisions for sports and play, such as a playing field, a children's pond and an athletics track. These examples were followed in other European countries (Chadwick 1966; Pohl 1995). These parks were characterised by a severe, rectilinear and simple layout and a clear hierarchic composition of spaces. The design tools are lanes, meadows, copses, separate flower gardens, and an efficient layout of access roads and paths.

While some Modernist parks are praised for their beauty of composition, other Functionalist gardens are criticised for their sober and uninspiring layout: 'the illusion of grandeur and vastness of Romantic parks, the lack of legibility (lakes looking like rivers, or trees used for camouflage), the mythological references, and the moralising content associated with all this are rejected by the Moderns. The functional garden [...] looks as if it just happened to came about, without the interference of a designer' (Aben 1998).

Despite these drawbacks, it is safe to state that Functionalism brought a clean break with the Romantic and eclectic designs of previous periods – in itself a relief.

Functionalism in landscape planning

The Functionalist ideal in landscape planning emphasises landscape form as a legible result of human use and construction. Form and function, form and process are intimately coupled. A change of function necessitates a change in the landscape. Observers should be able to see the relationship between form and function, which not only makes landscape legible but also represents beauty of form (de Visser 1997).

From this point of view, landscape protection and conservation are irrelevant, as they only hamper development. All additions that lead to a decrease in the visibility of activities are considered to be of negative value. Buildings should be free of arbitrary decorative elements, and landscapes should be free from camouflaging hedgerows or screens (Vroom 1997).

- Aben R.; de Wit S. 1998. *The Enclosed Garden*. 010 Publishers, Rotterdam p. 144
- Baljon L. 1992. *Designing Parks*. Architectura & Natura, Amsterdam pp. 110-112
- Broadbent G. 1990. 'Pragmatism'. In: *Emerging Concepts of Urban Space Design*. Van Nostrand Reinhold, London pp. 84 ff.
- Chadwick. G.F. 1966. 'The Continental Contribution'. In: *The Park and the Town*. The Architectural Press, London pp. 249 - 306
- Colquhoun A. 1989. *Modernity and the Classical Tradition*. MIT Press, Cambridge p. 74
- Jacobs J. 1961. *The Death and Life of Great American Cities*. Penguin, Harmondsworth, Middlesex
- Leupen B. (et al) 1997. 'Functionalism'. In: *Design and Analysis*. 010 Publishers, Rotterdam pp. 84-100
- Neufert E. (et al). 2000. *Architects Data (third edition)*. Blackwell, Oxford
- Peter J. 1994. *The Oral History of Modern Architecture*. Abrams, New York
- Pirsig R.M. 1991. *Lila. An Inquiry into Morals*. Bantam Books, New York p. 150
- Pohl N. 1995. 'Der Volkspark', in: *Der kommende Stadtpark*. PhD Dissertation, Technical University Delft pp. 77-80.
- Rowe P.G. 1991. 'Functionalism and the Modern Movement'. In: *Design Thinking*. MIT Press, Cambridge pp.155 ff.
- de Visser R. 1997 Het landschap van de landinrichting (i.e. *The landscape of land consolidation schemes*). Een halve eeuw landschapsbouw. Blauwdruk, Wageningen p.110
- Vroom. M.J. 1997. 'The Functional Landscape'. In: Thompson G.F.; Steiner F. (ed). *Ecological Design and Planning*. John Wiley & Sons, New York pp. 311-313

133

Garden

see also > icon, metaphor, mimesis, nature, place, theme

'An enclosed piece of ground adjoining a house used for growing flowers, fruit or vegetables'. Also: 'an idyllic spot, a park, or ornamental grounds laid out for public enjoyment and recreation' (*Oxford English Dictionary*).

Gardens have always been defined as enclosed spaces, but the name is sometimes also applied to a charming, pleasant or fertile region (Hunt 2000). 'Gardens men make reflect the essential nature of the society to which they belong' (Clifford 1962)

Gardens have many facets and meanings, and can manifest themselves as an idea or icon, a place, a work of art, a theatre, a *lieu de memoire*, an object of action, or as the presentation of a theme.

• Clifford D. 1962. *A History of Garden Design*. Faber & Faber, London pp.17, 42.
• Hunt J.D. 2000. 'What on earth is a garden'. In: *Greater Perfections*. Thames & Hudson, London pp. 14 ff.

The garden as an icon, a metaphor

Gardens demonstrate how people experience the relationship between nature and culture. They represent the shifting balance over time between wilderness and human control, from safe places in the midst of a hostile nature – order in chaos – to controlled nature (Cooper Marcus 1990; Rowe 1991).

Gardens can represent Paradise, with its harmony, seduction, and the fall of man and angels. Classical gardens contained icons representing people and events from Greek mythology. Those at Villa Lante, laid out for Cardinal Gambara in the 16th century, tells the story of paradise lost and regained (Rogers 2001). In his Garden of Cosmic Speculation laid out during the 1990s, Charles Jenck introduced metaphors from nature – not only living nature, but also the laws and structures of physics and biochemistry with their spirals, waves, order and chaos, fractals and the double helical structure of DNA: 'DNA and RNA are the basic words of nature and therefore suitable

135

The garden as a theatre. Private garden of landscape architect S.I. Andersson.
Photo: Lodewijk Wiegersma

The garden as a theatrical setting for a party of the fashionably dressed. The symbol of luxury, pleasure and love. Painting by a pupil of Esaias van de Velde (1591-1569).
Source: de Jong E.; Dominicus van Soest M. 1996. Aardse Paradijzen. De tuin in de Nederlandse kunst 15de tot 18de eeuw. Uitg. Snoeck-Ducaju & Zoon Ghent p. 132

The garden as a place of action: Springtime, after Pieter Bruegel the Elder (1525-1569). Noord Brabants Museum 's-Hertogenbosch.
Source: de Jong E.; Dominicus van Soest M. 1996. Aardse Paradijzen. De tuin in de Nederlandse kunst 15de tot 18de eeuw. Uitg. Snoeck-Ducaju & Zoon Ghent p. 150

elements for us to celebrate in a garden' (Jencks 2003).

From the great Classicist parks to contemporary affluent suburbs, gardens have also been used to express power and wealth. Paradoxically, they may also show the mental poverty of their owners. Arriving in the Chicago suburbs when tracing the travels of Hemingway, Michael Palin observed 'wide lawns and narrow minds' (Palin 1999).

• Cooper Marcus C. 1990.' The Garden as a Metaphor'. In: Francis M.; Hester R.T. (ed). *The Meaning of Gardens*. MIT Press, Cambridge pp. 26-33
• Jencks C. 2003. *The Garden of Cosmic Speculation*. Frances Lincoln, London pp. 17-19; 145 ff.
• Palin M. 1999. *Michael Palin's Ernest Hemingway*. Weidenfeld & Nicholson, New York
• Rogers E.B. 2001. *Landscape Design*. Harry Abrams, New York p. 145
• Rowe G.P. 1991.'Landscaping and site layout'. In: *Making a Middle Landscape*. MIT Press, Cambridge pp. 92 ff.

The garden as a place

Gardens belong to the inner world of their owners. They are enclosed by hedges, fences or walls, and contain a collection or arrangement of plants and objects among which people like to spend parts of their lives. They show the succession of growth, flowering and decay through the seasons (Bacon 1625). In terms of size and allure they can range from large estate and parks to small terraces decked with flowerpots (Francis 1990).

In all cases, their separation from the outside world requires a place of entry, a threshold, whether real or implicit (Landecker 1997). While total enclosure is found in contemporary patios (McHarg 1998), many gardens are also visible as an integral part of their surroundings that fits into landscape patterns – constituting 'the most condensed units in which historic, functional and spatial complexity of landscape is manifest' (Aben 2002).

• Aben R.; De Wit S. 2002. *The Enclosed Garden*. 010 publishers, Rotterdam p. 10
• Bacon F. 1625.'Over tuinen' (i.e. *On gardens*). In: *Essays*. Boom publishers, Meppel 1978. pp. 189-195
• Francis M.; Hester R.T. (ed). 1990.'The Garden as Idea, Place and Action'. In: *The Meaning of Gardens*. MIT Press, Cambridge pp. 2-20
• Landecker H. 1997. Martha Schwartz. Transfiguration of the Commonplace. Spacemaker Press, Washington D.C. p. 110
• McHarg I.L.; Steiner F. 1998.'The court house concept'. In: *To Heal the Earth*. Island Press, Washington pp. 164 -174

The garden as a work of art, as a three-dimensional ensemble

Gardens as works of art may constitute the oeuvre of a certain artist, or of a group of unknown gardeners (Andersson 2001). Individual gardens may assume the character of a sculpture, fixed in time and form, such as those found in Japan. For instance, the shrine of Royan-ji near Kyoto contains groups of rocks combined with raked sand as an object of contemplation (Kuitert 1988).

Famous 20th-century works of art include the gardens of the Brazilian 'painter with plants' Roberto Burle Marx (1909-1994), and the sculpted forms of the American artist Isamu Noguchi (1904-1989) (Walker 1994). For the landscape architect, such gardens are a place to experiment with new forms and concepts – a place to try out new design ideas (Francis 1990; Stauffacher 1988).

137

• Andersson S.I.; Høyer S. 2001. *C.Th Sørensen Landscape Modernist*. The Danish Architectural Press, Copenhagen
• Francis M.; Hester R.T. (ed). 1990.'The Garden as Idea, Place and Action'. In: *The Meaning of Gardens*. MIT Press, Cambridge pp. 2-20
• Kuitert W.M.1988. *Themes, Scenes and Taste in the History of Japanese Garden Art*. Gieben Publisher, Amsterdam pp. 114 ff.
• Stauffacher Solomon B. 1988. *Green Architecture and the Agrarian Garden*. Rizolli, New York
• Walker P.; Simo M. 1994.'The garden as art'. In: *Invisible Gardens. The Search for Modernism in the American Landscape*. MIT Press, Cambridge pp. 56-91

The garden as a theatre

Historic and modern gardens can both serve as stages for social activities, for play-acting. 'Paintings reveal how gardens have functioned as theatres, not just periodically as places for performances [...] but as sites for role playing' (Hunt 2000). 'Not only were dramatic astonishment and theatrical perspective effectively used in the layout of Italian Baroque gardens, but many of the gardens of this period also contained actual

The garden as a place. Design by Ank Bleeker.

138

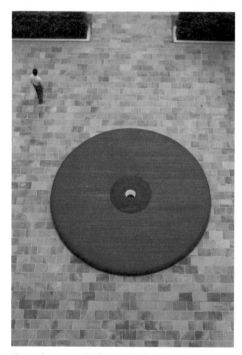

The garden as a work of art. Design by G. Noguchi.
Source: Walker P.; Simo M. 1994. 'Invisible Gardens'. In: The Search
for Modernism in the American Landscape. MIT Press
Cambridge

outdoor theatres with a grassy stage [and]
hedges for wings' (Rogers 2001). Louis XIV
strutted like a peacock with his entourage
through the park of Versailles, and organised
imitation naval battles in the Grand Canal.

Such theatrical activities are expressed
more poetically in the dialogue between man
and plant in the garden of Sven Ingvar
Andersson, where privet hedges 'developed a
sudden desire to become long-necked birds'
and were transformed in accordance with
their wishes. 'Theatre is both flight from
reality and concentration of reality. In that
paradox lies a particular parallel between
theatre and garden' (Spirn 1994).

• Hunt J.D. 2000. *Greater Perfections.* Thames & Hudson, London
 p. 163
• Rogers E.B. 2001. *Landscape Design. A Cultural and Architectural
 History.* Harry Abrams Publishers, New York blz. 179 ff.
• Spirn A. 1994. 'Texts, Landscapes and Life'. In: *Tilegnet Sven
 Ingvar Andersson.* Arkitektensforlag, Copenhagen p. 111

The garden as a place of memory

Gardens are not only linked with references
to Paradise, myths and sagas. Having also
been consciously designed to commemorate
certain persons or special events (historical
and otherwise), they have acquired the
character of a monument (Baridon 1995;
Oldenburger 1990). Memory of past times is
also embodied in historic design styles: 'in
the late 18th century, pathos and memory
came to play an important role in Western
garden design, as Romanticism replaced
Classical order as the dominant cultural
impulse' (Rogers 2001).

* Baridon M. 1995. 'Les mots, les images et la mémoire des
jardins'. In: Mosser M.; Nys P, (ed). 1995. *Le Jardin, art et lieu de
mémoire.* Les éditions de l'Imprimeur, Paris
* Oldenburger-Ebbers C. 1990. 'Garden designs in the
Netherlands in the seventeenth century'. In: Mosser M.; Teyssot
G. 1990. *The History of Garden Design. The Western Tradition from
the Renaissance to the Present Day.* Thames and Hudson, London
* Rogers E.B. 2001. *Landscape Design. A Cultural and Architectural
History.* Harry Abrams, New York p. 23

The garden as a place of action

For many people, gardening is a passionate
pursuit, and also a form of outdoor
recreation. This is demonstrated in allotment

gardens, where tilling the soil, planting, weeding and pruning plants provide direct sensory experiences as well as an inexpensive source of fruit, vegetable and flowers. Private gardens enable gardeners to develop the craft of grafting and nursing. Their layout and maintenance require physical effort. Activities change over the seasons, and every month has its specific demands, with a peak in springtime (de Jong 1996). There is a mixture of 'pleasure with profit, aesthetics with pragmatics' (Hunt 2000) 'The garden is a potent and complex symbol; it embodies pleasure, fertility, sustenance, and renewal. Gardening is a life-embracing act, an act of faith and hope, an expression of commitment to the future' (Spirn 1988).

- Hunt J.D. 2000. *Greater Perceptions*. Thames & Hudson, London p. 160
- de Jong E.; Dominicus-van Soest M. 1996. 'Tuinen en tuinieren' (i.e. *Gardens and gardening*). In: *Aardse Paradijzen I*. Snoek-Ducaju & Zoon publishers, Ghent pp. 87-92
- Spirn A. 1988. 'The poetics of City and Nature: towards a new aesthetic for urban design'. In Landscape Journal, The University of Wisconsin Press, Urbana, Illinois pp. 108-126

The thematic garden

Thematic gardens may be designed for a particular type of use: gardens for the blind, office gardens, play yards, school gardens, allotment gardens – and even traffic gardens. One recent invention is the 'restaurant-garden', where visitors can inspect and select their vegetables before consuming them (Harsema 2002).

Thematic gardens may also accommodate a particular selection of plants, such as rock gardens, herb gardens, botanical gardens, rose gardens, Delphinium gardens or *heemparks*. While the botanical garden or hortus originated in Europe in the 16th century out of a need to create a plant collection for scientific purposes (especially medical ones), it also contributed to the development of gardens in general (Tomasi 2000). The oldest surviving Dutch botanical garden, the Clusius Garden, was founded in Leiden in 1590. Such gardens gradually developed into extensive collections of plants – including decorative ones – from all parts of

the world. They were important sources for the spread and propagation of garden plants (Schnapper 2000).

The *heempark*, a Dutch invention, is a theme garden planted exclusively with indigenous plants. The word defies exact translation, but is derived from the old German word *Heim*, meaning 'home' or 'the surrounding environment'. It is applied to a park that contains an area of natural garden with wild plants. Its vegetation is usually managed just as intensively as formal bedding, with the difference that only selected wild flowers are allowed to remain. The origin of the *heempark* goes back to the early years of the 20th century in the town of Amstelveen, Netherlands, since when it has become an established part of public open space planning in many Dutch towns (Bekkers 2003).

- Bekkers G. (et al). 2003. *Designed Dutch Landscape: Jac P Thijssepark*. Architectura + Natura Press, Amsterdam
- Harsema H. 2002. 'Restaurant in Frankendael Park Amsterdam: a quiet garden restaurant in the city'. In: *Landscape architecture and town planning in the Netherlands 99-01*. Thoth publishers, Bussum pp. 100-103
- Schnapper A. 2000. 'Garden and plant collections in France and Italy in the seventeenth century'. In: Mosser M.; Teyssot G. *The History of Garden Design*. Thames & Hudson, London pp. 175-177
- Tomasi L.T. 2000. 'Botanical gardens of the sixteenth and seventeenth centuries'. In: Mosser M.; Teyssot G. 1990. *The History of Garden Design. The Western Tradition from the Renaissance to the Present Day*. Thames and Hudson, London pp. 81-83

Garden City

see also > constructivism, functionalism, modernism

'A town designed for healthy living and industry; of a size that allows for a full measure of social life, but not larger; surrounded by a rural belt; the whole of the land being in public ownership, or held in trust for the community' (*Goulty*).

The garden city was devised by Ebenezer Howard (1850-1928) and propagated by Patrick Geddes (1854-1932) (Howard 1898; Jacobs 1961). Their ideal was to improve the living conditions for factory workers in unhealthy cities by laying out new garden

139

Tuindorp Vreewijk garden village in Rotterdam. Architects: Granpré Moliere, Verhagen, Kok 1916.
Source: Een beeld van een eeuw. Published by Vereniging Woningcorporaties Hilversum. Photo Martin Thomas

Aerial view of neighbourhoods in the western section of Amsterdam, laid out in the 1950s according to the ideals of the garden city movement. Town planner: C. van Eesteren.
Photo: Peter van Bolhuis, Pandion

cities in which the two counterparts, or 'magnets' – the urban and the rural – were combined in an idyllic environment.

These garden cities were intended to contain large areas of public and private garden, as well as factories, workshops and various other institutes, all connected by a carefully conceived infrastructure of roads and railways, and powered by electricity so as to avoid pollution by smoking chimneys. Agriculture was to be pursued not only outside town, but also inside.

Overall, the idea was founded on extensive economic analysis. Social theories also played a role: life in close-knit communities in touch with nature, where social control would lead to regulated behaviour, was favoured over an open society, with its multiformity and mobility (Keulartz 1998).

The ensemble was contained in a geometric layout. The prototype was Letchworth in 1903, followed by Welwyn Garden City, where building started in 1919. Both of these towns seem to have functioned successfully over a period of more than fifty years (Osborn 1965).

Planner Patrick Geddes (1854-1932) saw the development of garden cities as part of an overall regional plan based on a regional survey. To harmonise with the existing landscape, such a plan would distribute garden cities over large areas (Jacobs 1961; Broadbent 1990).

In the Netherlands, initiatives for planning new garden cities and neighbourhoods were developed in the general Extension Plan for Amsterdam (AUA 1934) of 1934. City planner C. van Eesteren (1897-1980) envisaged a 'continuous city with proud workers living in self-contained garden suburbs at cycling distance from their place of work, who would thus be allowed to freely develop their talents and abilities'. Apartment blocks no more than six floors high were arranged in parallel formation in open park space, with undulating or flat tree-planted lawns dotted with flowerbeds. Communal playgrounds and seating were provided. Traffic areas and green spaces were strictly separated.

• *Algemeen Uitbreidingsplan Amsterdam 1934* (i.e. *General Extension plan for Amsterdam 1934*)

• Broadbent G. 1990. *Emerging Concepts in Urban Space Design.* Van Nostrand Reinhold, London pp. 123-126
• Howard E. 1898. *Garden Cities of Tomorrow.* MIT Press, Cambridge 1965
• Jacobs J. 1961. *The Death and Life of Great American Cities.* Pelican Book, Harmondsworth, Middlesex pp. 28-31
• Keulartz J. 1998. 'Letchworth in Limburg'. In: *The Struggle for Nature. A Critique of Radical Ecology.* Routledge, London pp. 70-89
• Osborn F.J. 1965. 'Preface'. In: Howard E. *Garden Cities of Tomorrow.* MIT Press, Cambridge

Gate
see > access

Genius loci
see > place

Geomancy
see also > adaptation, contrast, place

Geomancy, also known as *feng shui*, originated in China, and has been aptly defined as 'the art of adapting the residences of the living and the dead so as to co-operate and harmonise with the local currents of the cosmic breath' (Yi-Fu Tuan 1972).

Whereas negative consequences follow from siting a building inappropriately, geomancy holds that siting it properly will bring health and prosperity. Adapting the form of buildings to the shapes of hills and the direction of watercourses is beneficial, as both are the product of the forces of wind and water – in other words, feng shui. This philosophy resulted in a preference for natural curves, winding roads, and constructions that are anchored in the landscape rather than contrasting with it. There was an aversion for straight lines and geometric plans (Keswick 1978).

The principle is no longer applied in China, except in new high-rise buildings in major cities such as Hong Kong, where Shinto priests are paid to inspect new buildings and declare them free from harmful forces. Religious, ceremonial and commercial aspects are deceptively combined here. In the West, geomancy is practised in contemporary planning and landscape planning through

141

the adaptation of new developments to existing landscape patterns. The magic foundation has been rationalised in terms of 'genius loci' (Norberg-Schulz 1980).

• Keswick M. 1978. *The Chinese Garden*. Academy Editions, London p. 55
• Norberg-Schulz C. 1980. *Genius Loci. Towards a Phenomenology of Architecture*. Academy Editions, London
• Yi-Fu Tuan. 1972. 'Discrepancies between attitude and behaviour'. In: English & Mayfield. *Man Space Environment*. Oxford University Press, New York. pp. 68-81

Geometry

see also > Classicism, contrast, dimension, pattern, Renaissance, space, symmetry

'From Greek gômetrein: to measure the earth' (*Webster*).

Geometric forms include straight lines, squares, circles and triangles. In 15th-century Italy, the geometric basis of the design of buildings and outdoor spaces was associated with a view of a static cosmos dominated by order, proportion and harmony. To the architect Palladio (1508-1580), the mathematical basis of his designs represented the 'true grace of appearances'. He sought to achieve harmony between his buildings and their surroundings. 'Harmony in the local environment relates to the greater harmony of the earth' (Cosgrove 1993).

Geometric patterns in landscapes have always been associated with mankind and his desire to impose order. 'They stand out against the pleasing medley of the natural environment'. Although, in nature, geometry on a larger scale is rare (Gombrich 1979), architect Frank Lloyd Wright saw natural features in the landscape as underlain by 'an essential geometry' (Spirn 1998).

Euclidian geometry is based on the existence of three dimensions which form volumes and spaces laid down in points, lines and planes (Bell 1999; Motloch 2001). As elaborated by Descartes (1596-1650), the projection of parallel lines on the earth's surface by means of coordinates allowed grids to be created that fix all points on the surface of the earth, as on topographic maps.

Geometry and landscape

Where land is reclaimed from the sea, a marsh, or a lake, it is converted into agricultural polderland, its layout determined by rational and functional considerations. On flat terrain, the straight line is the most practical for the layout of drainage channels, and also for subdividing and using the land.

From the 16th century onwards, most Dutch

Beeckensteijn estate near Velzen, the Netherlands, designed by J.D. Michael in 1776, serves as an example of the transition in garden layout from the geometric style to the landscape style.
Source: Oldenbuger C.S. (et al). 2002. Gids van de Nederlandse tuin en landschapsarchitectuur. De Hef, Rotterdam

polders, were laid out in this manner. In some cases there were other motives: polders such as Beemster and Purmer, north of Amsterdam, were influenced by the geometrical layout of Italian Renaissance gardens. They were subdivided on the basis of proportional relations that aim for 'pure form' (van de Ven 1993; Lambert 1971). Unity was achieved through the application of proportional rules, such as those of the 'Golden Section'. The perfect square, which represents the most balanced form and a perfect universe, was also used as a mathematical design principle (Reh 1999). Geometric patterns are plentiful in the Dutch landscape and may be even considered as national emblems (Lowenthal 1992). 'My love for plane geometry prepared me to feel a special affection for Holland. For the Dutch landscape has all the qualities that make geometry so delightful' (Huxley 1925).

Around the world, most farmyards are square in plan, irrespective of the surrounding land patterns: 'to make a back yard, the farmer usually cuts a regular shape such as a rectangle or a square, out of the fabric of the surrounding fields and the forests. This seems to be an ancient compulsion. In nearly all of the world's cultures, humans mark the four quarters of the world by staking out square districts.. Apparently they do so to 'make a world', to make cosmos out of a chaos' (Franck 1994).

Geometry in towns

Geometry in town planning dates back to ancient times. For the Egyptians, geometry meant pure form, the study of order. The square grid was also used by the Greeks and Romans. Linked to the origins of geometric

143

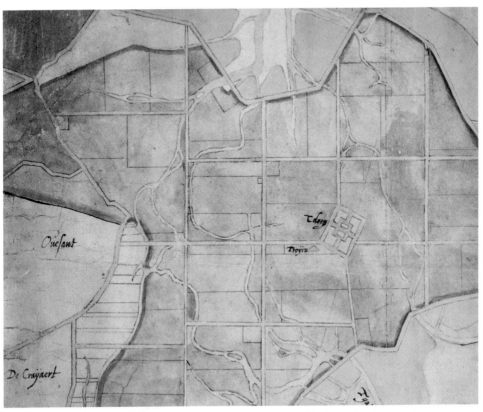

Plan of Borssele polder in the province of Zeeland, the Netherlands, reclaimed and laid out during the 17th century. The dimensions of the grid are 800 x 800 metres.
Source: Geuze A.; Feddes F. 2005. Polders. NAI publishers, Rotterdam p 259

architecture are the names of such architects as Vitruvius (1st century B.C), Alberti (1404-1472) and Palladio (1508-1580). In park design, geometric patterns have been significant since the Italian Renaissance (Broadbent 1990; Steenbergen 1996).

A geometric plan is characterised by:
· a basic scheme formed by matrices, grids, and regulating lines in a well-organised mathematical composition.
· axiality. An axis is a straight regulating line, the central line determining the location of surrounding objects.
· symmetry, in which objects are arranged along a line or axis, or otherwise around a central point, such that they mirror or exchange one another.
· directedness, i.e. a position or movement in one direction, such as a vector in mathematics.

· Bell S. 1999. 'Geometric Principles'. In: *Landscape, Pattern, Perception and Process.* Spon, London pp. 18-19
· Broadbent G. 1990. *Emerging Concepts in Urban Space Design.* Van Nostrand Reinhold, London pp. 5-9, 35-39.

· Cosgrove D. 1993. 'Landscape as theatre'. In: The Palladian Landscape. Leicester University Press. pp. 222 ff.
· Franck K.A.; Schneekloth L.H. 1994. *Ordering Space. Types in Architecture and Design.* Van Nostrand Reinhold, London pp. 90
· Gombrich E.H. 1979. *The Sense of Order.* Phaidon, London p. 5
· Huxley A. 1925. *Along the Road. Notes & Essays of a Tourist.* Paladin, London 1985. p. 64
· Lambert A. 1971. *The Making of the Dutch Landscape.* Seminar Press, London pp. 212-220
· Lowenthal D. 1992. 'European landscapes as national emblems'. In: Paysage & Aménagement/ Landscape Research no. 21 October 1992 pp. 14-23
· Motloch J.L. 2001. 'Geometry as ordering mechanism'. In: *Introduction to Landscape Design.* Van Nostrand, London pp. 147 ff.
· Spirn A. 1998. *The Language of Landscape.* Yale University Press. p. 198
· Steenbergen C.M.; Reh W. 1996. 'The hidden geometry within nature'. In: *Architecture and Landscape.* Thoth, Bussum pp. 39 ff.
· van de Ven C. (ed.) 1993. *Man-made lowlands.* Matrijs, Utrecht pp. 131-136

Geometry and nature
With the beginning of the Romantic Movement, the hitherto predominant Italian and French style in garden design was abandoned. From now on a rectilinear layout was considered to be dull, pompous, and not

Geometry in nature is rare, and usually temporary. Concentric circles created by sand crabs after every high tide on the beaches of Bali, Indonesia.

fitting: 'Nature by presumptuous Art oppressed' (Turner 1985). Geometry in nature is a rare phenomenon, mostly of temporary character (Gombrich 1979).

Dominant in Romantic designs are sinuous lines and undulating fields reminiscent of natural forms. 'Shapes of mountain ranges, riverbanks, sand dunes, trees are poised at a moment in time, their beauty lying in a peculiar combination of order and disorder, harmoniously arranged, form reflecting the processes that produced it' (Spirn 1998).

In the 18th and 19th century, the transformation of the geometric plans of existing parks and estate grounds often resulted in radical change. In some cases, however, gradual change caused the older central part of a garden to be conserved within a geometric pattern surrounded by a new Romantic landscape-style garden. One Dutch example is the Beeckestein estate at Velsen near Haarlem, which was transformed during the course of the 18th century.

During the 19th century, this process was reversed once more. In the so-called mixed style, Romantic elements were combined with geometric counterparts. Some Dutch examples can be found in the work of landscape architect Leonard Springer (1855-1940) (Moes 2002).

Contemporary nature development plans in the Netherlands demonstrate the ecologist's abhorrence of even the merest traces of human presence that a geometric form might betray. The layouts of new nature areas contain an abundance of capricious patterns that seem to attempt to suggest an underlying natural origin. In a reaction to this, designs by some Dutch landscape architects try to demonstrate that newly laid out 'nature' is a product of human culture by incorporating geometric forms in the layout of such areas. These forms vary between circular frog ponds, to square or rectangular islands in a marshy environment (Harsema 1996; Korten 2000).

• Gombrich E.H. 1979. 'The patterns of nature'. In: *The Sense of Order*. Cornell University Press, Ithaca, New York pp. 5 ff.
• Harsema H. (ed). 1996. 'Field remnants at Vlake Bridges'. In: *Landscape architecture and town planning in the Netherlands*

93-95. Thoth, Bussum pp. 150-151
. Korten H.; de Visser R. 2000. 'Natuurontwikkelingsplan zanderij Crailo' (i.e. Nature development plan in the Crailo sand quarry). In: Groen Journal, Doetinchem no. 1 pp. 12-17
• Moes C.D.H. 2002. *L.A. Springer Tuinarchitect Dendroloog*. De Hef publishers, Rotterdam
• Spirn A. 1998. 'Geometries of process'. In: *The Language of Landscape*. Yale University Press, New Haven pp.105 ff.
• Turner R. 1985. 'The Progress of Taste'. In: Capability Brown and the Eighteenth Century English Landscape. Weidenfeld & Nicholson, London pp. 29 ff.

Grid

see also > geometry, matrix, module, network, continuity

A network of lines superimposed on a map and forming squares for referencing. The basis of the network is that each line in the grid is at a known distance either east or north of a selected origin (*Goulty*).

The origin of the grid as a pattern of squares serving as a matrix for the layout of a town goes back many centuries. One example is the Greek town of Olynthus, which dates from 432 B.C (Benevolo 1980).

In the United States, the pattern is applied not only in cities, but also in rural areas,

A connecting and unifying grid pattern in a pavement.
Source: Dreiseitl H. (et al). 2001. Waterscapes. Planning, building and designing with water. Birkhäuser, Basel.

where the national mile-grid was introduced in the Land Ordinance of 1785 (Corner 1996; Rogers 2001). Its popularity is connected with 'its intrinsic ease in surveying, its adaptability to speculative activities and its simple appeal to unsophisticated minds'. The grid pattern was also seen as a means to create order, helping not only to improve access and trade, but also to improve the virtuousness of citizens (Jackson 1997; Jackson 1980; Steiner 2002). The US grid system is in fact one of the most ambitious schemes in history for the orderly creation of landscapes and of small communities. The deeper background is a utopian belief in an egalitarian society in which every citizen participates in the democratic process as it existed during the lifetime of Thomas Jefferson (1743-1825).

Grid patterns also abound in Dutch lowland polders, both in ancient polders and modern reclamation and reconsolidation projects (van de Ven 1993).

Grids have been applied throughout the ages in courtyards, gardens and terraces. In the Renaissance, Leonardo da Vinci (1452-1519) studied the link between a geometric grid plan and a river's natural course. 'In this way the idea evolved that an ideal proportional system, a rational scheme of dimensions and proportions, could be derived in which the relation between humankind and nature could be enhanced' (Steenbergen 1996). As a means of unifying space, modern gardens use grids in pavements and patterns of box hedges. In some cases the grid superimposes a geometric order. One example is the winning entry by Bernard Tshumi for the 1983 Paris Parc de la Villette design competition.

• Benevolo L. 1980. *The History of the City.* Scolar Press, London p.107
• Corner J. (ed). 1996. *Taking Measures across the American Landscape.* Yale University Press, New Haven

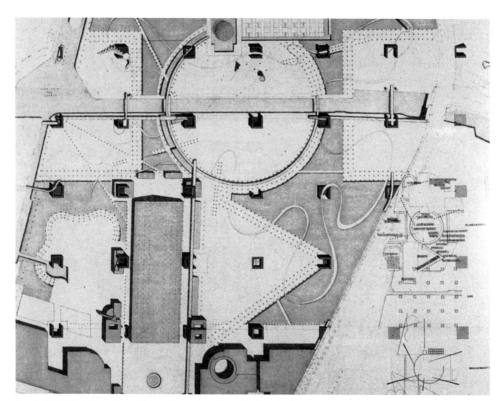

Parc de la Villette in Paris. Bernard Tshumi's winning scheme for the 1984 design competition creates a grid pattern that imposes order within a vast park.

- Jackson J.B. 1997. *Landscape in Sight*. Yale University Press, New Haven p.178
- Jackson J.B. 1980. *The Necessity for Ruins, and Other Topics*. The University of Massachsetts Press, Amherst. pp. 113-126
- Rogers E.B. 2001. *Landscape Design*. Harry Abrams New York pp. 267-268
- Steenbergen C.M.; Reh W. 1996. *Architecture and landscape*. Thoth publishers, Bussum p.14
- Steiner F. 2002. 'The straight and the curved'. In: *Human Ecology*. Island Press, Washington pp.82-84
- van de Ven C. (ed). 1993. *Man-made lowlands*. Matrijs, Utrecht pp. 131-136

Grotto, Cave

see also source, stream, basin

A grotto is 'an artificial recess or structure made to resemble a natural cave' (Italian *grotta*, *grotto*) (*Webster*)

A natural grotto represents security

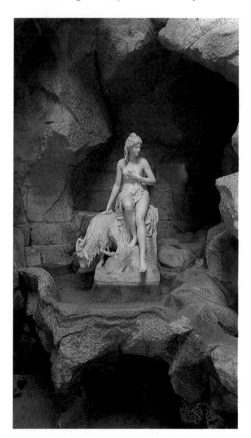

(explaining why Neanderthalers lived in them, for example). It also represents the origin of life, the birthplace of Venus. In Greek mythology is the tale of Odysseus, who defeated the Cyclops in his cave. The grotto of Tiberius in Sperlonga is a theatrical architectural display (Rogers 2001).

In Classical mythology, natural grottoes were the home of nymphs and the muse, thus explaining *nymphaeum* as a name for later grottoes. In gardens, grottoes are dark, humid places, where water-dripping mosses provide pleasant shelters in warm climates.

In gardens of the Italian Renaissance, water ran from a spring through a grotto, and then down a cascade to a pond, a sculpture representing Neptune providing a decorative background (Hunt 1992; Kluckert 2000).

The acme of grottoes or nymphaea, the grotto of Thetis, was built in the gardens at Versailles for the repose and amusement of the King. Numerous niches contained nymphs, tritons and glass globes dripping with water. An atmosphere of secrecy and nostalgia helped stimulate the imagination. During the Romantic Age, the grotto was considered to be a place of inspiration and introspection, stimulating fantasy and controlled reflection (Lang 2000).

- Hunt J. D. 1992. Gardens and the Picturesque. MIT Press, Cambridge pp. 77 ff.
- Kluckert E. 2000. *Gardens of Europe*. Könemann, Köln pp. 58-59
- Lang K. 2000. 'The body in the garden'. In: Birksted J. (ed). *Landscapes of Memory and Experience*. Spon Press, London pp. 107-121
- Rogers E.B. 2001. 'The grotto of Tiberius'. In: *Landscape Design*. Harry Abrams, N.Y. pp. 89-91

The nymph Amalthaea in the salle de fraicheur, Rambouillet Park, Yvelines, Paris.
Source: Saudan M. 1987. From folly to follies. Benedikt Taschen Köln.

147

Ha-ha
see > landscape style

Hedge
see also > abstraction, border, determinism, landscape, side screen, wall

'A fence or boundary formed by a dense row of shrubs or low trees' (*Webster*).

Hedges enclose and subdivide fields, orchards, yards, parks and gardens. In the past, they dominated European farm landscapes, except in places where, owing to climatic and geological conditions, stone walls prevailed (Hoskins 1955). While most hedgerows around fields are allowed to grow wild after occasional pruning, the regularly clipped hedges around gardens and yards are carefully kept in shape. Throughout history, hedges in gardens have been used as a means to create sculptural and optical effects, and to create decorative patterns such as broderies (Kluckert 2000; Ponte 1991). Twentieth-century Danish landscape architects mastered the art of creating three-dimensional compositions with hedges (Andersson 2001; Hauxner 2003). One contemporary Dutch example can be found in the cemetery at Almere Haven in Flevoland (Vroom 1992).

Hedges that enclose farmland and private gardens symbolise private property. During most of the 20th century, Communist regimes in Eastern Europe removed hedges from the landscape as part of their policy of collectivisation (Jackson 1997).

Hedges are also an important design tool. By fixing the height of the hedges separating collective and private space, Dutch town planners attempt to influence the behaviour of the residents of urban neighbourhoods: social contacts can encouraged by allowing neighbours to 'chat to each other over their low fences and hedges' (Nio 2004).

Hedges are also connected with historical events. During the 16th and 17th centuries, dense hedgerow patterns provided shelter for persecuted Protestants in France and Holland to organise their *prêches de plein air* or *hagepreken* – clandestine religious meetings. During the Second World War, the dense *bocage* in Nomandy caused the invading allied forces considerable trouble.

Hedges and hedgerows are of immense ecological importance. They are refuges for mammals, birds and insects, and protect

149

Hedges as ecological niches. Maasheggen protected landscape, Limburg, the Netherlands.

*A hedge as a sculptural element in a Renaissance garden.
Villa Garzoni in Collodi, Italy.*

plants and animals against strong winds
(Forman 1995). Some hedgerow landscapes in
the Netherlands have therefore been given
protected status.

Hedges also create green visual barriers
that can be used to screen unsightly
buildings or car parks – in other words, to
improve the appearance of their
surrounding. Ordinances in some Dutch
provinces require hedgerows at least three
metres deep to be planted around objects
that are considered unsightly or visually
undesirable – factories, greenhouses, freight
yards, trash dumps and the like. As a result,
the landscape looks greener and more rural
than it really is. At the same time it also
becomes less legible; meaning is lost.

• Andersson S.I.; Høyer S. 2001. C.Th. Sørensen. *Landscape
  Modernist.* The Danish Architectural Press, Copenhagen
• Forman R.T. 1995. 'Windbreaks, hedgerows and woodland
  corridors'. In: *Land Mosaics.* Cambridge University Press. pp. 177-
  207
• Hauxner M. 2003. 'Hedges and Groves'. In: *Open to the Sky.*
  Danish Architectural Press, Copenhagen pp. 206-237
• Hoskins W.G. 1955. 'Hedgerows and trees'. In: *The Making of the
  English Landscape.* Pelican Book, Harmondsworth, Middlesex
  pp. 195-200

A perspective view between hedgerows of the landscape near Oldenzaal, the Netherlands.
Photo: Frank Meijer

- Jackson J.B. 1997. *Landscape in Sight*. Yale University Press, New Haven pp. 113 ff.
- Kluckert E. 2000. *Gardens of Europe*. Könemann, Köln pp. 347 ff.
- Nio I. 2004. 'Searching for a new collectivity'. In: Harsema H. (ed). *Landscape Architecture and Town Planning in the Netherlands 01-03*. Thoth Publishing, Bussum
- Ponte A. 1991. 'The Garden of Villa Garzoni at Collodi'. In: Mosser M.; Teyssot G. *The History of Garden Design*. Thames & Hudson, London pp. 181-184
- Vroom M.J (ed). 1992. *Outdoor Space*. Thoth publishers, Bussum p. 20

Heritage landscape

see also > eclecticism, culture, landscape, postmodernism, restoration

'A landscape concerned with historical and cultural influences' (*Goulty*).

Landscapes which appear to have a long cultural history can be viewed from two perspectives. The first is by taking the history of art and architecture as a source of inspiration for artists and designers, and by thus borrowing, copying, adapting or remodelling historical examples. In other words, styles and motifs from the past are imitated (Steenbergen 2002). During the 19th century, this was common practice in eclectic architecture, which produced so-called neo-styles. Though such eclectic styles were banned by the Modernists, carefree borrowing returned in post-modern times.

The second way of looking at history is by studying visible traces and remnants of former land-use that refer to a long history of human settlement – old buildings, land parcels, ancient monuments, graveyards, and so on. Such elements are important sources of information and inspiration for landscape planners who seek to promote historical continuity through their protection and assimilation (Baljon 1992).

Planners and designers often wrestle with the question of how historic identity can be transformed into spatial form. 'History stays alive through story-telling, myth, ritual and language. Language encodes not only important cultural stories but also extensive knowledge of native habitats [...]. Many of these sites have specific landscape elements associated with them, such as a mountain [...]' (Wasserman 2002); 'the spaces we have created over the centuries contain countless stories about our identity – stories we tell ourselves about ourselves' (Kolen 2004).

A reference to the past is often charged with romantic ideas about the way the world was organised in historical times. But our past is not what we think it is. We know very

151

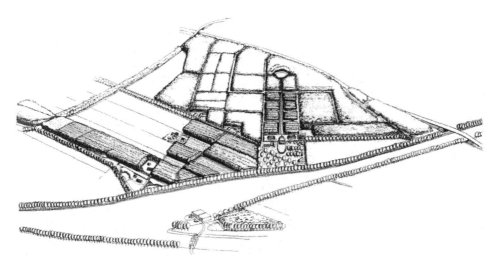

Bos na 2000 design competition, 1985. Around the 17th-century Heemstede estate near Utrecht, new woodland has been laid out in harmony with existing land patterns.
"Koppeling" (competition entry). Design team: Yttje Feddes, Doortje Haan, Wenda Stoffel, Bert Lenten, Henk Volkers.
Source: Nederlands Bosbouwtijdschrift, 27 September 1985, p. 43

little about it, we interpret, and are occupied with nostalgic dreams about our individual and collective past (Lowenthal 1985; Schama 1995). The most reliable sources of information in this respect are the physical objects that were created long time ago, which allow us to deduce how people lived and which tools they used.

How can we conserve and protect elements from the past? In the long run, unless careful and permanent maintenance is assured, all things will perish. Restoring buildings and other structures means that choices have to be made. The authenticity of conserved and restored objects is always doubtful, sometimes involving a break with the past rather than the maintenance of historical continuity (Lynch 1972; Jackson 1980). Any feeling of alienation is increased when conserved objects are identified by labels or signs that carry stories for tourists (Urry 1990).

Landscape planning and history

Historical objects and patterns can be conserved or restored, but they can also be converted and adapted to new uses, all while serving as reminders of the past (Feddes 1999). Entries for a Dutch design competition called *Bos na 2000* (i.e. Woodland after 2000) showed various ways an old estate might be fitted into its environment while new types of land-use are introduced.

Historical defensive strongpoint on a hill. Grebbeberg, Rhenen, the Netherlands. Restoration plan by Michael van Gessel.
Photo: Harry Harsema

- Baljon L. 1992. *Designing Parks*. Architectura & Natura, Amsterdam pp. 106-109
- Feddes F. (ed.) 1999. The Belvedere Memorandum. A policy document examining the relationship between cultural history and spatial planning. Ministry VROM, The Hague
- Jackson J.B. 1980. *The Necessity for Ruins, and Other Topics*. The University of Massachusetts Press Amherst pp.89-102
- Kolen J. 2004. 'Belvedere – or the complicity of the designer in the historical process'. In: Harsema H. (ed.) *Landscape Architecture and Town Planning in the Netherlands 01-03*. Thoth, Publishing pp. 24-33
- Lowenthal D. 1985. *The Past is a Foreign Country*. Cambridge University Press. pp. 35-73
- Lynch K.1972. *What Time is this Place?* MIT Press, Cambridge pp. 29-37
- Schama S. 1995. *Landscape and Memory*. Harper Collins, New York p. 3-19
- Steenbergen C. (et al). 2002. 'The composition of new landscapes'. In: *Architectural Design and Composition*. Thoth, Bussum/Faculty of Architecture, Technical University Delft pp. 192-207
- Urry J. 1990. 'Gazing on History'. In: *The Tourist Gaze*. SAGE publications, London pp.104 ff.
- Wasserman J. 2002. 'Memory embedded'. In: Landscape Journal, The University of Wisconsin Press, Urbana, Illinois 21:1-02 pp.190-200

Hierarchy

see also > pattern, scale, system,
'Systems with grades of authority or status from the lowest to the highest' (*Oxford Advanced*); 'arrangement into a graded series' (*Webster*).

Hierarchy in space

Hierarchy in space means that forms and spaces within a three-dimensional composition have an ascending sequence of size and scale, and thus of importance. The most important space in a hierarchic composition is usually the largest. It may be of a unique form, and also be located in a specific place within the layout (Ching 1979). Users of outdoor space may show a preference for edges with small spaces from which large open spaces are visible (Alexander 1977).

In landscapes, water systems constitute the natural basis for hierarchical patterns, especially where branched pattern of river tributaries emerge into the main watercourses (Litton 1974).

Road systems also have hierarchical

patterns, the alignment of local streets being adapted to their environment, and the whole creating part of the local network. Regional roads connect points at greater distances, and are usually adapted to major changes in landform.

In the north-western European plains, the infrastructure of highways, canals and electric power lines makes up an independent network that entirely ignores the underlying geomorphological pattern. Recognition of the existence of such a hierarchy might lead to a design approach whereby lines at the same level of scale formed a coordinated pattern (Vrijlandt 1980).

Hierarchy in design

During the 1970s, when systems analysis was introduced into the design of outdoor space, attempts were made to optimise not only all functional relations between the

parts of a site, but also the production and maintenance of the objects within it. This could be done only by assuming that hierarchical relations exist between parts and the whole (Alexander 1964; Broadbent 1973; Rowe 1991).

The application of this principle to the design of built environments, however, led to the conclusion that functional and spatial relations are more complex than can be explained on the basis of hierarchy. The awareness of the existence of network relations led to a different approach (Alexander 1988; Turner 1996).

• Alexander C. 1964. *Notes on the Synthesis of Form.* Oxford University Press, New York pp. 60-63
• Alexander C. (et al). 1977. 'Hierarchy of open space'. In: *A Pattern Language.* Oxford University Press, New York pp. 557 ff.
• Alexander C. 1988. 'A city is not a tree'. In: Thackara J. *Design after Modernism.* Thames and Hudson, London pp. 67-84
• Broadbent G. 1973. *Design in Architecture.* John Wiley & Sons, New York pp. 272 ff.
• Ching F.D.K. 1979. *Architecture: Form, Space & Order.* Van Nostrand Reinhold, London pp. 350-357
• Litton B. 1974. 'Classification'. In: *Water and Landscape.* Water Information Centre New, York pp.18 ff.
• Rowe P.G. 1991. 'Problem-Space Planning'. In: *Design Thinking.* MIT Press, Cambridge pp. 65 ff.
• Turner T. 1996. 'A city is not a tree, it is a landscape'. In: *City as Landscape.* Spon, London pp.21 ff.
• Vrijlandt P. (et al). 1980. *Electriciteitswerken in het landschap* (i.e. *Power lines in the landscape). Probleemverkenning en koncept vorming.* Rapport no. 224, De Dorskamp, Wageningen pp. 41 ff.

153

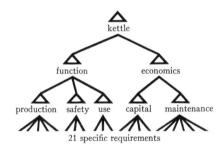

Hierarchical relations within a system as described by Christopher Alexander.
Source: Alexander C. 1964. Notes on the Synthesis of Form. Harvard University Press, Cambridge

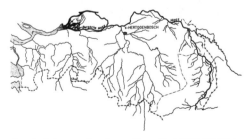

Branched stream valleys form a hierarchic pattern. Province of Brabant, the Netherlands.
Source: 1968. De Bodem van Noord Brabant. Stiboka Wageningen

Hill, Belvedere, Hillock, Mound

see also > geomorfology, land art, monument.

'A usually rounded natural elevation of land lower than a mountain. An artificial heap or mound' (*Webster*).

Most natural hills found in the Low Countries were formed by glaciers or strong winds, and range from linear coastal dunes to circular Pleistocene dunes and ridges. Their limited numbers make them stand out as landmarks, from which one can view the horizon in a flat landscape (Higuchi 1983). They tell a story about the origin of the Dutch landscape, and are highly valued natural elements that are often officially registered as nature monuments.

Hills seem to be generally appreciated as elements that contribute positively to the experience of landscape. A 1968 survey organised in England among a large number of respondents concluded that landscape amenity was directly related to the amount of relief: the more the better. Mountains were considered as superbly beautiful (Fines 1968). One bizarre implication of this research result is that the Dutch polder landscapes and most deserts and prairies were at the bottom of the scale, of no interest to anyone.

Artificial hills around the world demonstrate historical attempts by human beings to put their stamp on the land and to emphasise their immortality. As far back as 3500 BC, the prevailing cosmology in the Mesopotamian region associated mountaintops with divinity, a notion embodied in the artificial mound of the ziggurat (Rogers 2001; Ogrin 2002).

Other well-known examples are pre-historic tumuli, Egyptian pyramids and obelisks, and the tombs of Macedonian kings of the first century BC (Giedion 1971). The pyramids were copied in 19th-century gardens such as the one constructed by prince von Pückler Muskau on his estate at Branitz, Germany, where he was buried in 1871 (Kluckert 2000).

Some low-lying areas in the Low Countries are dotted with more prosaic *terpen*, artificial mounds erected as places of refuge for the population in times of flood (Lambert 1971).

In Chinese gardens of the Tang and Ming dynasty, hills consisted were rockeries representing holy mountains and immortality. Together with ponds, these formed the core of the garden layout (Keswick 1978, Keswick 1991).

In Roman times, and, much later, in 16th-century Tuscany and Veneto, villas, also called belvederes, were constructed on high points

154

The artificial mound as a place of refuge. Oosterwierum, Friesland, the Netherlands.

outside cities, combining the advantages of a distant view combined with a cool breeze; literally, *belvedere* means 'a beautiful view' (Cosgrove 1993).

In medieval Western Europe, artificial mounds carried a raised platform providing a view over the enclosing wall or hedge to the outside of the garden. Initially, their function was to detect and observe unwanted visitors; later they became a source of pleasure, as in 18th-century England, where a belvedere inside a walled garden, often with a gazebo or pavilion on the top, provided a view of the surrounding landscape. One could climb to the top via a spiral path or stairway (Aben 1998).

Belvederes were also a well-known feature in 17th-century Dutch gardens (Diedenhofen 1990). They were copied in German landscape-style gardens, and also at Parc Buttes-Chaumont in Paris, which was laid out in 1865 (Sørensen 1959; Kluckert 2000).

Rounded hills with sensual forms were part of gardens in the 18th-century English landscape style (Burke 1753). They were

The mound as a burial monument. The pyramid lake in Branitz, Germany, burial place of Count Pückler Muskau, 1871.
Source: Kluckert E. 2000. Gardens of Europe. Könemann Köln p. 438

155

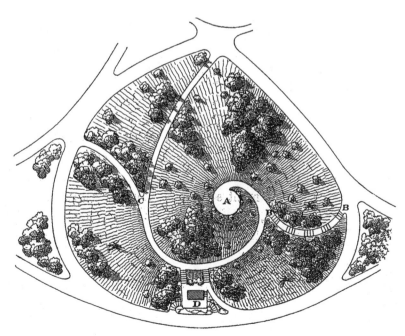

The hill as a viewing place: the Belvédère in Parc Buttes-Chaumont, Paris.
Source: André E. 1879. L'art des Jardins. Traité général de la composition des Parcs et Jardins. Masson Paris p. 386

introduced by 'Capability' Brown (1716-1783) in his park designs, and located between the purely utilitarian rural landscape and the hostile world of rocks and mountains (Turner 1985).

In many contemporary public gardens, hillocks are designed as pieces of sculpture. In playgrounds, they create attractive differences of relief for children's play.

Refuse dumps are more problematic examples of artificial mounds. Sometimes of considerable size, they are difficult to hide from view. Attempts to give them a more attractive form are frustrated by the negative

associations that underlie them. Most Dutch designers therefore try to make them resemble dunes or other natural features – thereby creating anomalies in the flat Dutch landscape. An alternative would be to consider them as 'permissible metaphors for rejected landscapes' by creating sculptural elements out of waste material (Engler 1995).

• Aben R.; de Wit S. 1998. *The enclosed garden*. 010 publishers, Rotterdam p. 80
• Burke E. 1753. A philosophical enquiry into the origins of our ideas on the sublime and the beautiful. Oxford Reprint 1990, Cassell, London
• Cosgrove D. 1993. 'Villa: the Palladian rural landscape'. In: *The Palladian Landscape*. Leicester University Press. p. 93
• Diedenhofen W. 1990. 'Belvedere or the Principle of Seeing and Looking in the Gardens of Johan Maurits van Nassau-Sieger'. In: Hunt J.D. *The Dutch Garden in the Seventeenth Century*. Dumbarton Oaks, Washington, D.C. pp. 49 ff.
• Engler M. 1995. 'Waste Landscapes: Permissible Metaphors in Landscape Architecture'. In: Landscape Journal, The University of Wisconsin Press, Urbana, Illinois vol. 14 no.1 pp.11-25
• Fines K.D. 1968. 'Landscape evaluation: a research project in East Sussex'. In: *Regional Studies* vol. 2 pp. 41-55
• Giedion S. 1971. 'The tumulus'. In: *Architecture and the Phenomena of Transition*. Harvard University Press, Cambridge, Mass pp. 59-68
• Higuchi T. 1983. 'The domain-viewing mountain type'. In: *The Visual and Spatial Structures of Landscape*. MIT press, Cambridge pp. 172 ff.
• Keswick M. 1978. *The Chinese Garden*. Academy Editions, London pp. 39-40
• Keswick M. 1991. 'An introduction to Chinese Gardens'. In: Tjon Sie Fat L; de Jong E. *The Authentic Garden*. Clusius Foundation pp. 189 ff.
• Kluckert E. 2000. *Gardens of Europe*. Könemann, Köln p. 438
• Lambert A. 1971. *The Making of the Dutch Landscape*. Seminar Press, London pp. 30-31
• Ogrin D. 2002. 'Symbolism in man-made landscapes'. In: *The Landscape of Symbols*. Blauwdruk, Wageningen pp. 64-99
• Rogers E.B. 2001. *Landscape Design. A Cultural and Architectural History*. Harry Abrams, New York pp. 34-42
• Sørensen C.Th. 1959. *Europas Havekunst* G.E.C. Gads Forlag, Copenhagen pp. 267-268
* Turner R. 1985. *Capability Brown*. Weidenfeld & Nicholson London pp. 77

Hilllocks in a playground; interior court somewhere in London. Landscape architect Michael Brown, 1970.

The hill as a symbolic element. Centre for Advanced Science and Technology, Japan. Landscape architect: Peter Walker.
Source: Walker P.; Levy L.1997. Minimalist Gardens. Spacemaker Press, Washington D.C. p. 98

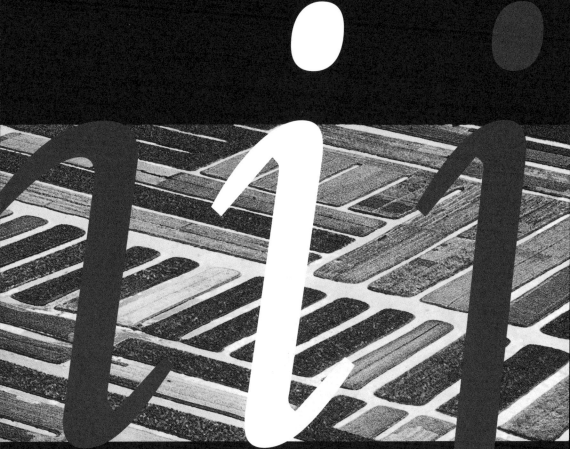

Icon. Iconography. Iconology

see also > metaphor, mimesis, sign, symbol

An icon is 'a usually pictorial representation' or 'a conventional religious image' (*Webster*).

Throughout history, gardens have contained icons, and often a collection of them grouped within iconographic themes. Renaissance gardens abounded with representations from Greek mythology and Arcadian scenes. In French formal gardens, nature was depicted in such contrasting features as the parterre, the *tapis vert* and the forest, mostly in a hierarchical sequence of increasing naturalness. In 18th-century English landscape gardens, nature in all its physicality and impressive growth was set against culture (Steenbergen 1996).

Iconography is 'the branch of knowledge which deals with the representation of persons or objects by any application of the arts of design' (*Oxford English Dictionary*). Iconology is 'that branch of knowledge which deals with the subjects of icons (in any sense of the word); also the subject-matter of this study, icons collectively, or as objects of investigation' (*Oxford English Dictionary*).

While iconography is thus a descriptive activity, iconology is an analytical discipline – academic research into the meaning of a work of art, probing why it was made as it was, the sources of information it was based on, and how it is to be explained or 'read' from a social and cultural background (Gombrich 1972; Peter 1994).

In everyday language, the two notions have been mixed, and the descriptive is blended with the analytical. An 'iconographic programme', for instance, is described as the content of a work of art – such as a garden – composed of objects, spaces and figures with a certain meaning (van der Blom 1997).

A new iconography may emerge in the form of artistic representations of products and inventions of modern science with its crystals, spirals, fractals, helices etc (Jencks 2003).

• van der Blom A. (et al). 1997. Nederlandse Schilderkunst (i.e. Dutch painting). Tussen detail en grandeur. Atrium publishers, Alphen aan de Rijn p. 287
• Gombrich E.H. 1972. 'Iconography and Iconology'. In: *Symbolic Images* . Phaidon London pp. 5 ff.
• Jencks C. 2003. *The Garden of Cosmic Speculation*. Frances Lincoln, London
* Peter J. 1994. *The Oral History of Modern Architecture*· Harry Abrams New York p. 61 ff.
* Steenbergen C.; Reh W. 1996. *Architecture and Landscape. The Design Experiment of the Great European Gardens and Landscapes*. Thoth publishers Bussum pp. 15, 37, 97, 274, 323

The DNA helix as a recently discovered basic element in nature, symbolized in the garden of Charles Jencks at Portrack.
Source; Jencks Ch. 2003. The Garden of Cosmic Speculation. Frances Lincoln, London.

Iconoclasm

see also > analysis

An iconoclast – in the literal sense of the word – is someone who breaks or destroys religious works of art, as happened during the in the Byzantine period (8th Century), when religious objects were considered blasphemous (*Britannica*). Such destructive activity was repeated during the Reformation in the Netherlands in the 16th century, and by the Taliban in Afghanistan in the 21st century.

While, from a cultural point of view, iconoclasm is an extreme form of vandalism, in a more general or abstract sense it means the attacking of established values, of the sacrosanct elements of a culture, thus without necessarily leading to large-scale destruction. Italian Futurists at the beginning of the 20th century, for instance, who regarded the past as superfluous, would have liked to drown the whole city of Venice in the waters of its lagoon. 'Come on', they shouted, 'set the libraries on fire! [...] Change the courses of the canals and let the museums be flooded! [...] What a joy to see the old famous paintings torn up and float away with their colours smeared! [...] Get your pickaxes and hammers and flatten without pity these hallowed places!' But nothing happened (Arnold Heumakers, *NRC-Handelsblad*, 14 December 2003).

In the plastic arts, Marcel Duchamp (1887-1968) was the first to show –and cause shock with – such banal objects as hat racks and urinals in a museum exhibition. He belonged to an avant garde that shifted the accent from the enjoyment of beauty to an intellectualising problem-stating form of art.

In recent architectural history, the demolition of the Pritt-Igoe housing blocks in Chicago can be seen as a symbolic form of iconoclasm. With this action, Post-modernism discarded Modernism (Jencks 1978).

A contemporary Dutch iconoclast is C. Weeber, an architect who attacks the established values of planning authorities, and propagates do-it-yourself home building or 'wild living' (Weeber 1999). Critics who attack some of the consequences of nature conservancy policy may also be considered iconoclasts (Keulartz 1998). Though the planning authorities and the nature conservation establishment considers these people mainly as nuisances, such attacks may very well contribute to debate and renewal.

An entirely different form of iconoclasm is the plan analysis in which a designed site or environment is carefully deconstructed – taken apart – with a view to discovering the designer's true motives (Weiss 1998).

• Jencks C. 1978. 'The Death of Modern Architecture'. In: *The Language of Post Modern Architecture*. Academy Editions, London p. 9
• Keulartz J. 1998. *The Struggle for Nature. A Critique of Radical Ecology*. Routledge, London
• Weeber C.; van Stipthout W. 1999. *Het wilde wonen* (i.e. *Wild living*). 010 publishers, Rotterdam
• Weiss A.S. 1998. 'Dematerialization and iconoclasm'. In: *Unnatural Horizons. Paradox & Contradiction and Landscape Architecture*. Princeton Architectural Press, New York. pp. 44 ff.

Identity

see also > authentic, recognition, typology

'Distinguishing character or personality: individuality' (*Webster*).

Identity can apply to a nation, social group or individual human being, as well as to an object, site, town or landscape. While the identity of a nation depends on language and culture, that of a group depends on shared values and behaviour; and that of an individual on a name, a social function. In social terms, it is the 'process of constructing meaning on the basis of a cultural attribute' (Castells 1997).

The identity of objects and environments is determined by their specific outward appearance, and by the existence of contrasts and their connected meanings. By definition, identity makes identification possible.

Identity may also be established through long familiarity with images and environments. It provides a sense of being at home – is the genius loci (Norberg-Schulz 1980). Stereotypical images of everyday environments such as chain stores also help create identity (Lynch 1960). In public squares in French towns, national identity is often evident in the characteristic buildings, objects and inscriptions.

Because outward appearance and value judgements are involved, the identity of spaces and objects cannot be established objectively. Identity is related to culture and not based on rational criteria. There is an interaction between the observer and the object perceived, and a role is played by individual experience, memories, self-images and even myths. People recognize differences between landscapes by their natural and cultural characteristics. In the past, every region manifested itself by its specific interaction between geology, land use and architecture, all based on the 'bones of the

159

The village square in Eyrargues, Provence, France.

Settlement on the banks of a creek in De Vlist, the Netherlands

landscape, the fundamental structure that gives form and colour to the scene and produces a certain kind of topography and natural vegetation' (Hoskins 1970). The outcome is what is called cultural identity (Frampton 1988).

During the 20th century, such identities were diluted by the arrival of new technologies and by the increasing migration of people (Hough1990). Critical Regionalism, as introduced by Frampton (1988), is therefore an approach to landscape planning which supports regional identity by 'proposing a local culture of (landscape) architecture which is consciously evolved [...] and resists being totally absorbed by forms of optimized production and consumption'. However, cherishing regional identity should not lead to superimposed images founded on false assumptions about the culture of the past. The layout of the land in history was always dictated by what was considered useful and necessary (Herngreen 2002).

• Castells M. 1997. 'The power of identity'. In: *The Information Age. Volume II*. Blackwell, London pp. 5 ff.
• Frampton K. 1988. 'Place-form and cultural identity'. In: Thackara J (ed.). *Design after Modernism*. Thames and Hudson, London pp. 51 ff.
• Herngreen R. 2002. 'Percepties van regionale identiteit' (i.e. *Perceptions of regional identity*). In: *De achtste transformatie*. Blauwdruk publishers, Wageningen pp. 15 ff.
• Hoskins W.G. 1970. *The Making of the English Landscape*. Pelican Boo,k Harmondsworth, Middlesex p.14.
• Hough M. 1990. 'Regional Identity by Necessity'. In: *Out of Place. Restoring Identity to the Regional Landscape*. Yale University Press, New Haven pp. 34-58
• Lynch K 1960. *The Image of the City*. MIT Press, Cambridge pp. 6-7.
• Norberg-Schulz C. 1980. *Genius Loci*. Academy Editions London pp. 20-23

Ideology

see also > ecocentrism, modernism, paradigm, utopia

An ideology is a '(set of) ideas that form the basis of an economic or political theory or that are held by a particular group or person' (*Oxford Advanced*). 'Ideal or abstract speculation, in a deprecatory sense impractical or visionary theorizing or speculation' (*Oxford English Dictionary*).

An ideology represents a certain outlook on reality and on the way this reality is believed to be or ought to be. In the eyes of most people, ideologies consist of abstract, impractical or fanatical theories. While they seem to be based on 'common sense', on objective observation and logic reasoning, they are not: they contain hidden assumptions that are not subject to debate. Their generally accepted characteristics are 'bias, over-simplification, emotive language, and adaptation to public prejudice' (Geertz 1973/1).

World views and shared opinions are expressed in global and compulsive ideas. There is no tolerance for alternative opinions. 'Sensible people trust their own experience, stupid people rely on an ideology' (Williams 1983). The debate on environmental quality in general, and landscape quality in particular, is an almost inextricable maze of reasoning – based on the knowledge of natural process – and on the ideology called ecocentrism.

Ecology rests on scientific theory and method, on empirical and verifiable data, but when research results do not conform to the ideas and objectives of the radical ecologist, they are mistrusted (Pepper 1996).

However, ideologies should not always be judged as negative phenomena, because they can be of positive value in a changing culture, having an important function in helping people to overcome anxiety in a chaotic world. 'Ideology provides a symbolic outlet for emotional disturbances generated by social disequilibrium [...] and [...] bridges the emotional gap between things as they are and as one would have them be, thus insuring the performance of roles that might otherwise be abandoned in despair or apathy' (Geertz 1973/2). Artists and architects connected with the Bauhaus in Germany and pioneers of the Modern Movement were, as Dutch historian van der Woud states 'productive suppliers of essential and normative values that helped renew architectonic culture. Ideology and utopian ideas form an integral part of the arts and architecture' (Van der Woud 1987).

161

• Geertz C. 1973/1. 'Ideology as a cultural system'. In: *The

Interpretation of Cultures. Basic Books Harper, New York pp. 193-233

• Geertz C. 1973/2.'Ideology as a cultural system'. In: *The Interpretation of Cultures.* Basic Books Harper, New York pp. 203-206

• Pepper D. 1996.'Postmodern science and ecocentrism'. In: *Modern Environmentalism. An Introduction.* Routledge, London pp. 240 ff.

• Williams R. 1983.'Ideology'. In: *A Vocabulary of Culture and Society.* Fontana Book, London pp. 153-157

• van der Woud A. 1987.' De geschiedenis van de toekomst' (i.e. *The history of the future*). In: van der Cammen H. *Nieuw Nederland. Onderwerp van Ontwerp. Deel 1 Achtergronden.* Staatsuitgeverij, The Hague pp. 39-40

Idyllic

see > pastoral, utopia

Illusion Illusionism

see also > perspective, reference, renaissance

An illusion is a 'false idea, belief or impression; delusion'. Also:'thing that a person wrongly believes to exist; false perception' (*Oxford Advanced*).

In the pictorial arts, an optical illusion suggests a three-dimensional reality by means of perspective manipulation on a flat plane. This can be achieved via the distortion of perspective, but also with the aid of colour and the effects of light and shade. A special form of illusionist painting is the trompe-

The illusion-filled landscape of a pleasure park: Efteling, Province of Brabant, the Netherlands.
Photo: Guy Ackermans

l'oeil (Lanners 1973, Gombrich 1964, Gombrich 1982). The Venetian artist Veronese (1528-1588) painted scenes on the walls of villa Barbaro which gave visitors the impression of stepping outside the room into an open loggia. The illusion was reinforced by the architectural composition designed by architect Palladio (Andersson 2002).

In garden design, perspective distortion is a well-known tool for suggesting depth in space, for instance through the use of converging lines in the ground plan, whereby a designer exploits the circumstance that observers are accustomed to the idea that all parallel lines converge in the distance (Bijhouwer 1954; Hazlehurst 1980). A different way to deceive the eye of the beholder was used in 18th and 19th-century parks when half-sized gazebos or pavilions were built that made the surrounding space appear much larger (Warnau 1979).

As well as optical illusions there are also ideas based on illusion, which are created through association or a 'dream image'. Past landscapes were filled with illusions of pagan gods floating in the air. In the rituals and spectacle of their courtly theatres, rulers created a make-believe world (Yi-Fu Tuan 2002). In architecture and landscape architecture, a world of illusions can be created by the use of images that refer to other times and places (Gombrich 1964) – a form of deceptive representation that was used both in the Romantic Age and under Postmodernism. The observer is allowed to escape everyday reality and enter another world. These days, the need for such an escape is commercially exploited in entertainment parks such as Disneyland (Metz 2002).

• Andersson S.I. 2002.'Gardens in fantasy and reality – learning from Villa Barbaro'. In: Kerkstra K. (ed). *The Landscape of symbols.* Blauwdruk publishers, Wageningen pp. 38-63

• Bijhouwer J.T.P. 1954. *Waarnemen en ontwerpen in tuin en landschap* (i.e. *Observing and designing gardens and landscapes).* Argus, Amsterdam

• Gombrich E.H. 1964. *Art and Illusion.* Chapter VIII. Phaidon London

• Gombrich E.H. 1982. *The Image and the Eye.* Phaidon, Oxford pp. 180-181

• Hamilton Hazlehurst F. 1980. *Gardens of Illusion. The Genius of André le Nôtre.* Vanderbilt University Press, Nashville,

Tennessee
• Lanners E. 1973. *Illusions*. Holt Rinehart & Winston, New York
• Metz T. 2002. *Fun! Leisure and Landscape*. NAi publishers, Rotterdam
• Warnau H. 1979. 'Een Wandeling' (i.e. A walk). In: *Rapport over de parken Sonsbeek, Zijpendaal en Gulden Bodem in Arnhem*. Wageningen University Vakgroep Landschapsarchitectuur p. 78
• Yi-Fu Tuan. 2002. 'Landscape as cosmic theater and scenery'. In: Olwig K.R. *Landscape Nature and Body Politic*. The University of Wisconsin Press, Madison pp. xiv-xv

Image, imagination

see also > concept, aesthetics, design theory, illusion, recognition, reduction, reference, representation.

An image is 'a mental picture of something not present. A vivid or graphic representation or description.' Imagination is 'the act or power of forming a mental image of something not present to the senses or never before wholly perceived in reality' (*Webster*).

'We picture material and imaginary places in our minds. These images are fuelled not only by our own experiences, but also by the representations of these places in religion, art, literature and popular culture' (Franck 1994). These images may be deceptive. Preconceived images of certain scenes that are based on romantic paintings or literary sources may lead to bitter disappointment in travellers who view the actual scenery. Marcel Proust (1871-1922) describes the reaction of a holidaymaker who visits the seaside expecting to see precipitous cliffs shrouded in mist and fog, and pounded by a furious sea. In reality he is confronted with an unglorious beach resort with a banal collection of restaurants, shops and motor cars. There is a huge gap between reality and the preconceived image. Fortunately for the narrator and his holiday visit, a painter has also arrived on the spot, who is about to create his own images instead of relying on those created by others. He draws the attention to light and colour reflected from the sea, and the beauty of yachts and thereby 'opens the eyes' of others' (de Botton 1997).

In architectural design, an imagined 'new' environment is also based on the designer's notions, associations, thoughts and ideals, usually in combination with a well-defined programme or brief. Most designers also rely on established rules, schemes or assumptions to guide or control their imaginative power (Broadbent 1973, Gombrich 1978; Rand 1970).

The use of one's imagination does not necessarily involve the creation of something totally new; it may also be limited to the discovery of a new form for an existing 'content', or an original concept for an old idea (Arnheim 1969). 'In finding similarities we create new images, we bring them together, are creatively engaged and enlarge our possessions' (Burke 1756).

Environmental design involves the transformation of a mental image into visible, tangible form. 'Imaging' is a creative moment in the design process: 'The mind of man possesses a creative power of its own; either in representing at pleasure the images of things in the order and manner in which they were received by the senses, or in combining those images in a new manner, and according to a different order. This power is called imagination; and to this belongs whatever is called wit, fancy, invention, and the like' (Burke 1756/1990).

In passing on ideas and proposals, the presentation of visualised images, including map drawings, is often more effective than words, as images represent 'virtual reality' – that is, the *seemingly* real, the *imagined*. A virtual landscape is the landscape of imagination, made visible through modern simulation techniques. Older techniques include paintings, sketches, or the type of overlay used by Humphry Repton (Repton 1813). 'Images of gardens, obviously, occur in paintings and drawings but also in photographs, whether they have been deliberately selected either as a main subject or as the apt setting for one' (Hunt 2000).

• Arnheim R. 1969. *Art and Visual Perception*. Faber and Faber, London p. 141
• de Botton A.; 1997. *How Proust Can Change your Life*. Vintage Book, New York pp. 145-148
• Broadbent G. 1973. 'The architect as designer'. In: *Design in Architecture*. Wiley & Sons, New York pp. 1-10
• Burke E. 1756. *A philosophical Enquiry into the origin of our ideas of the sublime and the beautiful*. Oxford reprint 1990.

Cassell, London pp. 21; 50
- Franck K.A.; Schneekloth L.H. 1994. *Ordering Space. Types in Architecture and Design.* Van Nostrand Reinhold, London p.27
- Gombrich E.H. 1978 (third edition). 'Expression and communication'. In: *Meditations on a Hobby Horse.* Phaidon, London pp. 56 ff.
- Hunt J.D. 2000. 'Gardens in word and image'. In: *Greater Perfections. The Practice of Garden Theory.* Thames & Hudson, London pp. 143-179
- Rand P. 1970. 'The beautiful and the useful'. In: *Thoughts on Design.* Van Nostrand Reinhold, London pp. 9 ff.
- Repton H. 1813. *Plans for Sherringham in Norfolk.* Red Books, The Basilisk Press, London

Infrastructure

see also > access, adaptation, node, fit, fragmentation, hierarchy

'Subordinate parts, installations etc that form the basis of a system, an organisation or an enterprise'. Also: 'facilities such as roads, railways, power stations, water supply, telephones, etc, which form the basis for a country's economic growth' (*Oxford Advanced*). Infrastructure consists of lines which connect points and form hierarchical networks (Motloch 2001). These are the carriers of flows of people, goods, water and energy. A city can be viewed as a network of connections between places, objects and spaces. These connections may adopt many forms and patterns such as axis, grids, radial or linear hierarchic patterns (Jackson 1980).

Parts of the network of city streets consist of mono-functional traffic arteries, others create places that also serve as public outdoor space (Jackson 1997; Rudofsky 1969). They may even form an integral part of an urban living environment (Gehl 2001/1). During the second half of the 20th century, many streets that had been taken over by the motorcar in the earlier decades were won back for the pedestrian, often with satisfying effects (Gehl 2001/2).

Movement through a landscape often follows paths taken by others. This is especially true for landscapes that have been designed, in contrast with those that exist by nature: designed sites normally set out line of movement that visitors are expected to follow (Leatherbarrow 2004). A path, however, not only facilitates: it also limits free circulation. When, in *Out of Africa*, Karin

A city street as a pedestrian area. Der Graben in Vienna, Austria.

Blixen flew over Kenyan landscapes, she observed: 'It is a sad hardship and slavery to people who live in towns, that in all their movements they know of one dimension only; they walk along the line as if they were led on a string. The transition from the line to the plane, into the two dimensions when you walk across a field or through a wood, is a splendid liberation to the slaves, like the French revolution'.

Because, in rural areas, networks are created by the conjunction of local infrastructure and the border-lines of land lots, built-up areas and other elements at the same level of scale, infrastructure is a constituent part of the overall landscape pattern (Jackson 1997). While a motorist driving along a motorway is offered a view of an arbitrary cross-section of the landscape, the user of a local country road moves from place to place, via a bend, a corner, a bridge, a hilltop, a road-side terrace. His experience is more direct and more satisfying. The layout and maintenance of a fine-meshed pattern of public paths, tracks, and roads for walking and cycling, occasionally widened to form a resting place, would therefore improve the accessibility of rural scenes for pedestrians (Sijmons 2002).

National infrastructure has been superimposed over local networks. It consists of autonomous lines that cut through the underlying patterns, creating isolation, fragmentation and contrasts (Rowe 1991). In order to avoid interference, all development plans should carefully study the relationships between elements of the highest level in the national hierarchy, such as motorways, railways, canals, pipelines and high-voltage networks. Their individual alignment and form should be based on the aim of creating continuity and legibility, thereby contributing to an acceptable appearance (Harsema 2002).

Road design and landscape

In Britain, Humphry Repton (1752-1818) was the first to recognize that laying out and aligning roads was in fact a design problem. He introduced the notion of 'parkways':

'nothing is more beautiful than the distant glimpse of a road winding up a hill, and nothing more disgusting than the same degree of curvature undulating without reason across a plain' (Daniels 1999).

In the 20th century, the parkway as a means of 'driving for pleasure' was introduced in the USA and Europe (van Winden 2002). The dynamic experience of these parkways and the surrounding landscape by motorists requires a precise adaptation of the road alignment to successive perspective views (Appleyard 1964). Such adaptation is not always pursued, explaining why some parkways are masterpieces of engineering, while others have a disastrous effect on the landscape (Mumford 1953; Rowe 1991).

In the Netherlands, the expansion of infrastructure is slowed by public resistance, the product of the resentment caused by the

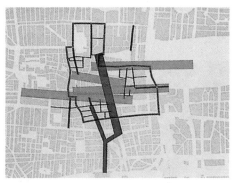

165

Proposed hierarchic pattern of roads and paths in the city of The Hague. Alle Hosper landscape architects, 1987-1989.

Motorways enclosed by sound barriers.
Photo: Frank Meijer

Free circulation in open fields. An example in Kenya.
Source: Yann A.B. 2001. The Earth from the Air: 365 Days. Thames & Hudson, London

Water infrastructure: irrigation canal in Provence, France.

landscape despoliation it often involves. The planning and design of new roads and railroads therefore often resembles contingency planning (Provoost 1995).

A more positive attitude amongst politicians and planners would lead to a different design approach, creating new linear patterns that served as a basis for a different order (Vrijlandt 2001). In the past, such new lines have often formed new corridors along which new development took place. In these cases, the environment eventually adapted itself to the road instead of the other way around (Anonymous 1998).

Canals

Until the 19th century, the role of man-made waterways in the Netherlands' national transport hierarchy was equal to that of roads. However, the original reason for their construction lay in the need not so much to accommodate traffic as to drain excessive water in wet times and to provide irrigation in dry times. In southern Europe, the latter function is dominant (van der Woud 1998).

As traffic systems, canals – with their quays, bridges and locks – have been a characteristic element in the western European landscape for some centuries (Hoskins 1970). While the alignment of older canals and town moats was adapted to local patterns, the vertical and horizontal alignment of the major 19th-century canals contained long, straight stretches. With contrasting straight lines cutting through older landscape patterns, such canals thus belong to the highest

category in the national hierarchy of infrastructural works.

- Anonymous. 1998. Topos, European Landscape Magazine, Callwey, München. Theme Number 24 'Landscape and Traffic'
- Appleyard D. (et al). 1964. *The View from the Road*. MIT press, Cambridge
- Daniels S. 1999. 'On the Road' and Landscapes of Transit'. In: *Humphry Repton. Landscape Gardening and the Geography of England*. Yale University Press pp. 27 ff. and 47 ff.
- Gehl J. 1971. *Livet mellem Husene*. Arkitektensforlag København
- Gehl J.; Gemzøe L. 2001. *New City Spaces*. The Danish Architectural Press, Copenhagen
- Harsema H. (ed). 2002. 'The High Speed Railway, southern link: Design ambitions for a train with self-esteem'. In: *Landscape architecture and town planning in the Netherlands 99-01*. Thoth publishers, Bussum pp. 140-143
- Hoskins W.G. 1970. 'Canals'. In: *The Making of the English Landscape*. Pelican Book pp. 247-254
- Jackson J.B. 1980. 'The discovery of the street'. In: *The Necessity for Ruins*. The University of Massachusetts Press, Amherst pp. 55-66
- Jackson J.B. 1997. 'Roads belong in the Landscape'. In: *Landscape in Sight*. Yale University Press, New Haven
- Leatherbarrow D. 2004. *Topographic Stories. Studies in Landscape and Architecture*. The University of Pennsylvania Press pp. 200 ff.
- Motloch J. 2001. 'Circulations as ordering mechanism'. In: *Introduction to Landscape Design*. Van Nostrand Reinhold, London pp.158 ff.
- Motloch J. 2001. 'Truck and automobile circulation'. In: *Introduction to Landscape Design*. Van Nostrand Reinhold London pp. 170 ff.
- Mumford L. 1953. *The Highway and the City*. Harcourt, Brace & World, New York pp. 234-246
- Provoost M. 1995. 'A "grand projet" for the Netherlands. The love-hate relationship between railway, road, landscape and city'. In: Archis Journal, NAi publishers, Rotterdam 3 1995 pp. 68-80.
- Rowe P.G. 1991. 'Highways'. In: *Making a Middle Landscape*. MIT Press, Cambridge pp. 185 ff.
- Rudofsky B. 1969. *Streets for People*. Doubleday & Company, New York
- Sijmons D. 2002. 'Landschap met beleid' (i.e. Landscape and policy). In: *Landkaartmos*. 010 publishers, Rotterdam pp. 206-214
- Vrijlandt P.; Kruit J. 2001. *Motorways and landscape patterns: new concepts explored*. Conference Paper Europenan Conference of Landscape Architecture Schools, Larenstein, Velp
- van Winden W. 2002. 'Infrastructure with a tendency towards conciliation'. In: Harsema H. (ed). *Landscape architecture and town planning in the Netherlands 99-01*. Thoth publishers, Bussum pp. 144-147
- van der Woud A. 1998. *Het lege land. De ruimtelijke orde van Nederland 1798-1848*. Contact, Amsterdam Chapter 6

From commercial traffic to pleasure-craft: Canal du Midi, Languedoc, France.
Photo: Frank Josselin de Jong

Interaction

see also > behaviour, perception, design process

'Act or have an effect on each other. Act together or co-operatively, especially so as to communicate with each other' (*Oxford Advanced*).

While an outdoor environment may be visible as a series of brief glimpses, the experience may also be an interactive adventure in which a role is played by mental processes such as acquisition, manipulation and transformation, all leading to personal involvement and commitment in relation to an object or an environment. Interaction with an environment in the physical sense such as in gardening activities is a dynamic process.

Interactive planning and design is founded on a desire to legitimise design and planning proposals by involving the client in the planning and design process. After all, whether they are individuals, interest groups or the entire population of a design area, the clients are the ones who will use the designed environment, and who must thus help decide on it. The intention is to improve the effectiveness and efficiency of planning policy (Hidding 2002).

In recent years, the organisation of the design process has exchanged its previous hierarchic, 'top-down' approach – when the client sees only the final product – for an approach whereby projects are discussed in groups with critical and decision-making powers. This requires a design process that is open and transparent: every proposal or decision must be explained and clarified, and its consequences elucidated. Typically, the planner or designer will simultaneously act as an informer, teacher and advocate, and, if there are number of conflicting interests, as decider.

However, the results have often proved disappointing (Lynch 1981). The participation of individual citizens in a design process will work only for projects of limited scale, with discussions in small groups (Alexander 1977; 1979).

• Alexander C. 1977. *A Pattern Language*. Oxford University Press
New York.
• Alexander C. 1979. *A Timeless Way of Building*. Oxford University Press New York.
• Hidding M.C. 2002. 'De interactieve aanpak nader bekeken' (i.e. Another look at the interactive approach). In: *Planning voor stad en land*. Coutinho Bussum pp. 138-140
• Lynch K. 1981. *A Theory of Good City Form*. MIT Press Cambridge pp 43-50

Intricacy

see > complexity

Inventory

see > analysis

Inversion.

'Being reversed in position, direction or

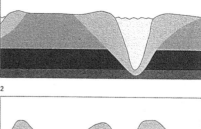

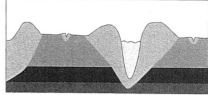

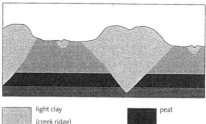

▨	light clay (creek ridge)	■	peat
▨	heavy clay (wetlands)	▨	clay layer before peat formation

The inversion of low-lying creeks into raised ridges.
Source: Ven G.P. van de (ed) 1993. Man-made lowlands. History of water management and land reclamation in the Netherlands. Matrijs Utrecht p 36

relation' (*Oxford Advanced*).

The inversion that occurred in the Dutch landscape over the years still continues today, either as a product of soil compaction, as the result of a conversion from land to water and back to land, or through the enclosure of open rural areas by urban growth.

· Compaction: centuries ago, gullies and tidal creeks cut their channels through marshy landscapes, and slowly filled with clay sediment. In later years, artificial drainage caused the surrounding land to subside, eventually causing the firmer ground of former creek beds to stand above level

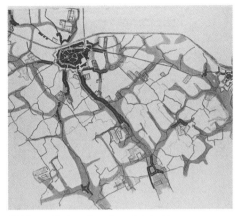

Walcheren: the inversion of creecks into ridges.

169

The inversion of this landscape - from marsh to land to water - was caused by successive stages of drainage and reclamation, peat digging and erosion. Vinkeveen, the Netherlands.
Photo: Henk van Aggelen

ground (van de Ven 1993).

· Conversion: onwards of the 11th century, the great marsh in the western provinces of the Netherlands was drained and reclaimed. Bogs were converted into polderland. Eventually, parts of the peatland were excavated for fuel, creating lakes whose shores eroded under the influence of strong winds. Land became water again, such as in the case of Vinkeveense Plassen (Lambert 1971).

· Enclosure: until the 20th century, towns in the western Netherlands were isolated concentrations of buildings in a large open landscape. Increasing urbanisation has caused these built-up areas to expand so much that large tracts of farmland are now being enclosed by urban fields. The relationship between openness and enclosure has been inverted (Tummers 1997).

· Lambert A. 1971. 'Rural settlement'. In: *The Making of the Dutch Landscape*. Seminar Press, London pp. 89-127
· Tummers L.J.M.; Tummers-Zuurmond J.M. 1997. *Het land in de stad (i.e. The rural in the city). De stedebouw van de grote agglomeratie*. Thoth, Bussum pp. 71 ff.
· van de Ven G.P. (ed.) 1993. *Man-made Lowlands*. Matrijs publishers, Utrecht p. 36

Irony

see also > paradox

'Expression of one's meaning by saying the direct opposite of one's thoughts in order to be emphatic, amusing or sarcastic. Situation, event etc. that is desirable in itself but so unexpected or ill-timed that it appears to be deliberately perverse' (*Oxford Advanced*).

Paradox and irony are closely related, paradox being a contradiction containing grains of truth, and irony the absurd, whereby a first impression conflicts with the underlying truth. An ironic view involves critical distance (Potteiger 1998).

Ironic situations can, for example, arise when a poisonous refuse dump develops intoturns out to be a wildlife refuge containing a highly valued diversity of plants and animals or is converted into an attractive outdoor recreation centre (Spirn 1998).

· Potteiger M; Purinton J. 1998. 'Theming'. In: *Landscape Narratives*. John Wiley, New York p.18
· Spirn A. 1998. *The Language of Landscape*. Yale University Press New Haven pp. 229-230

Island

see also > basin, bridge, dam, stream

' An area of land surrounded by water and smaller than a continent. Something suggestive of an island in its isolation' (*Webster*).

Islands are isolated spots that contrast with their environment – land versus water, for example, or dense versus open. Natural islands occur in the oceans, along coasts, and in rivers and marshes. Streams and islands are the essential components of river landscapes.

Artificial islands abound in waterlogged landscapes in the Netherlands, the result of the numerous drainage ditches dug around land parcels. Each parcel is in fact an island that came into being out of necessity. It is accessible only via earth dams or small bridges.

Contemporary housing areas may be deliberately designed and laid out on islands, such as that in the town of Zaandam. Near Amsterdam, a housing district was also laid out in the water of the IJsselmeer, due not only to the lack of space elsewhere, but also to the attractive location in a contrasting

Every land parcel is an island. Broek op Langedijk (as it was), the Netherlands.

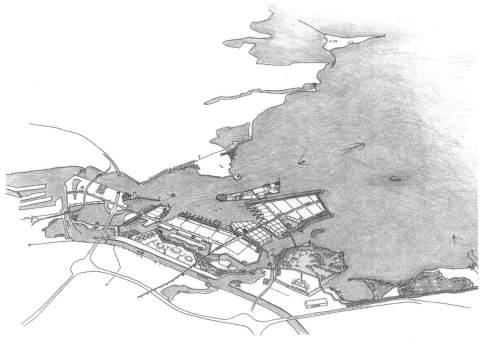

Housing development on a newly created island. IJburg district near Amsterdam. Urban planner: Palmboom & van den Bout. Landscape architects: H+N+S 1995-1996.

171

Japanese island gardens symbolize isolation. Ryoan-Yi Kyoto.

environment (Harsema 1996; 1998).

Islands do not need to be surrounded by water: an isolated copse, or an enclosed farmstead in an open landscape, can effectively be an island in the space surrounding it. In ecological theory, an important role in sustaining bio-diversity is played by nature reserves scattered like islands over an agricultural landscape (McArthur 1967).

In the history of garden design, islands not only symbolise isolation, but also are places for ceremony or festivities, especially in Chinese and Japanese gardens, where the connection between bridge, island and pond is considered important (Rogers 2001). In Asia and Europe alike, they are the background for the events of countless ancient myths (Graafland 2002).

In a more abstracted form, Japanese temples and palaces have their so-called island gardens, where precise patterns raked in gravel symbolise the sea, with scattered islands in the form of rocks or tumuli. They are cleansed soils, the scene of religious activities (Teiji Ito 1972; Kuitert 1988; Keswick 1978, Keswick 1991).

In 17th-century French gardens, beauty was represented on the *Île enchanteè*, the enchanted island. In English landscape-style gardens, Capability Brown (1716-1783) articulated space by means of tree-covered 'islands', situated in ponds, lakes or undulating meadows, his so-called 'clumps' (Turner 1985).

172

• Graafland A. 2002. 'The composition of the garden and the choreogra[phy of the body'. In: Steenbergen C. (ed). *Architectural Design and Composition*. Thoth publishers, Bussum p. 65

• Harsema H. (ed). 1996. ' Zaan Island, Zaandam'. In: *Landscape Architecture and Town Planning in the Netherlands 93-95*. Thoth publishers, Bussum pp. 82-85

• Harsema H (ed). 1998. 'The IJburg housing district in Amsterdam'. In: *Landscape Architecture and Town Planning in the Netherlands 95-97*. Thoth publishers Bussum pp. 90-93

• Keswick M. 1978. *The Chinese Garden*. Academy Editions, London pp. 39-40

• Keswick M. 1991. 'An introduction to Chinese Gardens'. In: Tjon Sie Fat L.; de Jong E. *The Authentic Garden*. Clusius Foundation, Leiden pp. 189 ff.

• Kuitert. W. 1988. *Themes, Scenes and Taste in the History of Japanese Garden Art*. Gieben publishers, Amsterdam pp. 114 ff.

• Mc Arthur R.H.; Wilson E.O. 1967. *The Theory of Island Biogeography*. Princeton University Press, New York.

• Teiji I. (et al). 1972. 'The Island Garden'. In: *The Japanese Garden. An Approach to Nature*. Yale University Press, New Haven

• Rogers E.B. 2001. 'Mountains, Lakes and Islands: Imitations of Immortality in Chinese Gardens'. In: *Landscape Design*. Abrams, New York pp. 282-296

• Turner R. 1985. *Capability Brown and the Eighteenth-century English landscape*. Weidenfeld and Nicholson, London

Labyrinth, Maze, Knot garden

see also> garden, meaning

A labyrinth is a 'place constructed of or full of passageways and blind alleys'; a maze is 'a confusingly intricate network of passages' (*Webster*). Their layout apparently meets some basic human need: 'The unconscious is often symbolised by corridors, labyrinths or mazes' (Jung 1964).

The origin of labyrinths is found in Greek mythology, which tells us how Daedalus constructed a prison for the man-eating Minotaur – a place surrounded by a complex maze of paths and alleys from which it could not escape.

In Renaissance gardens, a labyrinth usually consists of a spiral path between hedges,

Labyrinth. Hortus Palatinus, Frankfurt, Germany 1620.
Source: Mosser M.; Teyssot G. (ed). 1990. The History of Garden Design. Thames and Hudson London

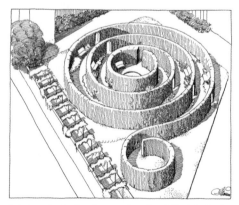

Spirals are 'metaphors for growth and evolution'. Design by C Th Sørensen.
Source: Andersson & Hoyer : Sørensen – en havekunstner. Arkitektensforlag, Copenhagen

leading to a centre that also forms a climax. The labyrinth thereby 'acquired the identity of a topos as much in a practical sense as in a conceptual and theoretical sense' (Carpeggiani 1990). Spirals 'are metaphors for growth and evolution, whether reeling clockwise or counter-clockwise' (Potteiger 1998). For people moving through a labyrinth there is also a reference to Paradise: after a strenuous journey one arrives in the promised land.

Many of the larger 16th and 17th-century gardens in Europe contained a maze or knot garden (Thacker 1985; Whalley 1998). This usually consisted of a complex pattern of man-high hedges flanking either a dead-end or continuous narrow paths. The visitor had to cover a large distance within a limited space (Moore 1989). Such mazes constituted an outdoor puzzle laid out for amusement, allowing for different experiences, including love-making. Sculptures and fountains were located in the centre.

• Carpeggiani P. 1990. 'Labyrinths in the Gardens of the Renaissance'. In: Mosser T.; Teyssot. (ed). *The History of Garden Design*. Thames and Hudson, London pp. 84 ff.
• Jung C. 1964. *Man and his Symbols*. Doubleday New York p. 171
• Moore C.W. (et al). 1989. *The Poetics of Gardens*. MIT Press, Cambridge pp. 46-47
• Potteiger M.; Purinton J. 1998. *Landscape Narratives. Design Practices for Telling Stories*. John Wiley & Sons, New York pp. 126-127
• Thacker C. 1985. 'The verdant puzzle'. In: *The History of Gardens*. Croom Helm, London pp.115-119
• Whalley R.W.; Jemmings A. 1998. *Knot Gardens and Parterres. A History of the Knot Garden and How to Make One Today*. Barn Elms, London

Land Art

see also > monument, symbol

Outdoor sculptures, constructions, earthworks and other art objects that are consciously designed or positioned to form part of their environment are called land art. Land-art objects in the true sense of the word are composed of earth, water and rock, make a strong reference to nature, and absorb the surrounding landscape into the art work. The modelling of a terrain or the sculpturing of ground form may be the work

'Aardwerk' in Noordoostpolder, the Netherlands, by Piet Sleegers.

'Polder-landscape Garden of Love and Fire' by Daniel Liebeskind.
Photo: Harry Harsema

of an artist or a landscape architect (Bann 1991; Jellicoe 1966; Weilacher 1996).

Over time, the notion of land art has expanded to cover all art forms in the landscape, even if the objects are made of concrete or steel. The relationship with the environment is mostly symbolic; in some cases, sightlines in relation to the position of the sun or moon are of importance. Art objects along motorways serve as landmarks that provide a dynamic experience. They form part of attempts to create 'arti-visual landscapes' (Meeus 1992).

• Bann S. 1991. 'The garden and the visual arts in the contemporary period: arcadians, post-classicists and land artists'. In: Mosser M.; Teyssot G. *The History of Garden Design*. Thames & Hudson, London pp. 495-506.
• Jellicoe G. 1966. 'Landscape from Art'. In: *Studies in Landscape Design*. Oxford University Press pp. 1-16
• Meeus J.; Bosch J. 1992. *Genius Regionis and other metaphors. Artivisual Landscapes*. Thoth, Bussum
• Weilacher U. 1996. *Between Landscape Architecture and Land Art*. Birkhäuser, Basel

Landmark

see also > orientation, symbol

Landmarks are highly visible elements in the landscape that are normally remembered as a mental image. They contribute to the viewer's orientation in space, making it easier to distinguish one place from another. In an urban area they may be buildings or structures, or sometimes individual trees, which by virtue of their size, position or character stand out from other elements in the townscape. When announcing the proximity of a destination, they may be a sign of welcome, though in shallow coastal waters they may also indicate a danger to shipping (Moore 1989).

Landmarks serve their purpose best when they visibly contrast against a background in form, height, dimension or colour, or when old contrasts with new (Lynch 1960). They also stand out if their content is symbolic, as with church towers. They may serve as an emblem for a city or even a whole country, such as the Eiffel Tower in Paris.

In various parts of the world, mountain peaks are familiar landmarks, which sometime symbolise the 'land of the gods' (Higuchi 1983).

• Higuchi. T. 1983. *The Visual and Spatial Structure of Landscapes*. MIT Press, Cambridge pp. 183-184

Land art can have a geographical context: ants abound in the Mediterranean landscape. A roundabout in a minor road near Bédarieux, Hérault, France.

• Lynch K 1960. *The Image of the City.* MIT Press, Cambridge pp. 78-83
• Moore C.W. (et al).1989. *The Poetics of Gardens.* MIT Press, Cambridge p. 10

Landscape

see also > the introduction to this lexicon, as well as: analysis, culture, heritage, layer, landscape typology, nature, perception, reduction, space, system, quality, rural, value, wilderness.

'Landscape is our basic heritage. It is all-embracing and relevant to everyone. Most of what we learn and do impinges on it. Landscape is where we all make our homes, do our work, live our lives' (Lowenthal 2003).

Definitions of landscape in *The Oxford English Dictionary* include the following:
· a view or prospect of natural inland scenery, such as can be taken in at a glance from one point of view: a piece of country scenery;
· inland natural scenery or its representation in painting; a view, prospect of something, a vista;
· the object of one's gaze; a sketch, adumbration, outline; a bird's eye view;
· a plan, map.

A landscape may be a piece of territory with a particular character, such as a desert landscape or a polder landscape. In daily language it can also be a collection – loose or otherwise – of items or objects within a defined space, such as an 'office landscape' with its furniture and plants. Other thematic landscapes include sports, traffic, and industrial landscapes. The combination of 'land' and '-scape' indicates an area, an expanse, a space, that has been created or shaped, is visible as such, and therefore can be represented.

In various languages, the etymology of the word is complex (Bourassa 1991; Spirn 1998; Hunt 2000), its elaboration showing the difficulty of formulating a definition which covers all possible angles of view. The Descartian separation between subject and object allows us to describe the 'land' of landscape as a territorial entity, to be analysed objectively in its components, such as soils, water, vegetation and land-use. However, the 'scape' – the landscape of our daily living environment – is what we see, with its meanings, and also with its stories of the past and present, which raise our expectations and emotions.

Though landscape mirrors our vision, we look through spectacles that are coloured by value systems, ideologies, or practical gain and utility. The way we see and define landscape is influenced by knowledge and recognition, ideas and values, objectives and interests.

For some people, landscape represents nature. For others it is an artefact or just attractive open space, or the counterpart of the city (Meinig 1979; Motloch 2001). But a city can also be seen as a part of the total landscape, which happens to be urbanised. 'Unfortunately, people have a very limited notion of what a landscape is. Most people conjure up a forest, waterfalls, the prairie and other pristine or primeval untouched natural environments. In the city, landscape is thought of as parks, waterfronts and plazas. Although these spaces are landscapes, landscape need not be confined to parks, waterfronts and gardens: it must include all the spaces found outside the building footprint – alleys, highways, sidewalks, parking lots, strip malls, suburban tracts, utility corridors – all are constructed artefacts. Our landscape, contrary to our fantasy of the wilderness, is what we determine it to be' (Richardson 2004).

The historical geographer sees the landscape as a rich source of information about our heritage, made legible by the distribution and layout of ancient and modern settlements, as well as other objects (Hoskins 1955). This heritage may also be represented by past manifestations of the visual arts and architecture, with their beauty and symbolic form (Jellicoe 1975).

The 15th-century Italian architect Andrea Palladio (1508-1580) saw landscape as a theatre, the stage of a multitude of human actions and manifestations (Cosgrove 1993). At that time, the perceptions of landscape of various artists varied as much as they do today. Michelangelo (1475-1564), for instance, looked upon landscape as something elevated, glorious: the scene of heroic action he liked to paint. He showed little appreciation for the common-sense approach of Flemish painters such as Jan van Eyk (1385-1441). He wrote: 'On their paintings all one sees is laundry, ruins, green grass, shadows of trees, rivers and bridges, with on one side a horde of people and on the other side a collection of individuals – and that is what they call landscape' (van der Blom 1997).

The final conclusion of all these observations was put into words by the American geographer J.B. Jackson: 'For more than twenty five years I have been trying to understand and explain that aspect of the environment we call the landscape [...], and yet I must admit that the concept continues to elude me. Perhaps one reason for this is that I persist in seeing it not as a scene or ecological entity, but as a poetical or cultural entity, changing in the course of history' (Jackson 1984).

- van der Blom A. et al. 1997. *Nederlandse Schilderkunst* (i.e. *Dutch painting*). *Tussen detail en grandeur.* Atrium, Alphen aan de Rijn p. 28
- Bourassa S.C. 1991. *The Aesthetics of Landscape.* Belhaven Press, London pp. 2-4
- Cosgrove D. 1993. 'Landscape as theatre'. In: *The Palladian Landscape.* Leicester University Press. pp. 222 ff.
- Hoskins W.G. 1970. *The Making of the English Landscape.* Pelican Books, Harmondsworth, Middlesex pp. 13-16.
- Hunt J.D. 2000. 'The idea of a garden and the three natures'. In: *Greater Perfections.* Thames and Hudson, London pp.32 ff.
- Jackson J.B. 1984. 'Concluding with landscapes'. In: *Discovering the Vernacular Landscape.* Yale University Press, New Haven pp.147-157
- Jellicoe G. & S. 1975. *The Landscape of Man. Shaping the Environment from Prehistory to the Present Day.* Thames and Hudson, London
- Lowenthal D. 2003. 'Landscape as living legacy'. In: Kerkstra K. (ed). *The Landscape of Symbols.* Blauwdruk publishers, Wageningen pp. 12-37
- Meinig D.W. 1979. 'The Beholding Eye. Ten versions of the same scene'. In: Meinig D.W. (ed). 1979. *The Interpretation of Ordinary Landscapes.* Oxford University Press, New York. pp. 33-50
- Motloch J.L. 2001. 'Landscape meanings'. In: *Introduction to*

The everyday landscape as painted by Pieter Breugel in 1565: Harvest.
Source: Vöhringer C. 1999. Pieter Breughel. Könemann, Köln

Landscape Design. John Wiley & Sons, New York pp. 7-22
• Richardson T. (ed). 2004. *The Vanguard Landscapes and Gardens of Martha Schwartz.* Thames & Hudson, New York p. 127
• Spirn A 1998. *The Language of Landscape.* Yale University Press, New Haven pp. 16-18

Landscape and culture

'What we call "culture" or "civilisation" refers to the human capacity to create, to invent or discover new and original applications and to make surrogates' (Gombrich 1948).

Human culture is expressed in tradition as well as in renewal. It is manifest in independent thinking, the testing of inventiveness, the conservation of historical continuity – a reflection on what has been done, what others do, and a continuous effort in making and creating new environments.

The creation of new landscapes is rooted in culture. This means that the landscape architect cannot divorce his work from contemporary culture (Schwartz 1993). At the same time, he should be able to open up new horizons. As the Dutch sociologist Hofstee stated: 'there is undoubtedly ample opportunity for him. He may be able to renew culture by designing a new landscape form that is accepted and imitated in society' (Hofstee 1983).

Designs of landscape architects claim to be works of art that are related to contemporary values. These artworks may take the form of a grand gesture – like Le Nôtre's *grand axes*. They may demonstrate a consummate skill in the handling of plants – like the herbaceous borders of the Dutch landscape architect Mien Ruys, which are carefully composed in space and time. They may constitute painterly rearrangements of nature such as those in the Picturesque tradition. They can result in symbols that give meaning to an environment, and appeal to the subconscious processes in the human mind (Thompson 1999).

Man-made landscapes have been reclaimed from nature, in a process of either complete or partial conversion that was carried out for the sake of economic and social improvement. In the Netherlands, this consisted of reclaiming polders, cultivating wildlands, and laying out the land for a particular purpose. In these cases, the notions of culture and cultivation overlap.

Landscape definitions and landscape planning

How we perceive landscape is not determined by conventions and emotions alone. How landscape is defined also depends on the aims and objectives of parties with an interest in manipulating it one way or another. In many people's eyes, what is and what ought to be are inextricably linked.

Contemporary definitions of landscape by nature conservancy organisations stress the presence of a natural process that should be fostered; they reflect some misgiving about the role of humans, and an aversion against the role and presence of technology and urbanisation (Vroom 1997).

This contrasts with the definition of the Dutch Ministry of Agriculture (Anonymous 1992), which tends to support projects involving human intervention: 'Landscape is the visible part of the earth determined by the coherence and mutual influence of soils, relief, climate, flora and wildlife, as well by as human interference.' This definition has been adopted by landscape architects and planners, who must then attempt to

179

Man-made landscapes dominate in the Netherlands: the village of Nagele in the Noordoostpolder. 1940. Architect P. Verhage.
Photo: Peter van Bolhuis, Pandion

understand these factors both separately and as a whole – understand the 'mechanisms' of landscape in order to be able to intervene and guide development. Landscape is viewed as a system whose parts and relationships can be subjected to analysis. However, the absence of emotional or phenomenological aspects makes this definition incomplete or one-sided.

Meanwhile, landscape architects are faced with a double image of landscape. One is the cognisable and dissectable object they attempt to understand and control. The other mirrors their own ideals and longings, the source of meaning. If one of these is ignored, it is impossible to design environments that appeal to people's imagination.

• Anonymous. 1992. *Nota Landschap* (i.e. *Landscape Policy Document*). Ministerie van Landbouw, Natuurbeheer en Visserij. Staatsuitgeverij, The Hague
• Gombrich. E.H. 1948. *Art and Illusion*. Phaidon, London
• Hofstee E.W. 1983. 'Macht en machtsuitdrukking in onze cultuur en hun betekenis voor de landschapsvorming' (i.e. Power and the expression of power, and its meaning for landscape). In: *Economie en Landbouw*. VUGA publishers, The Hague pp. 213-233
• Schwartz M. 1993. 'Landscape and common culture since modernism'. In: Treib M. (ed) *Modern Landscape Architecture: a Critical Review*. MIT Press, Cambridge pp. 260-265
• Thompson I. 1999. *Ecology, Community and Delight. Sources of Values in Landscape Architecture*. Spon, London pp. 71-72
• Vroom M.J. 1997. 'Images of an Ideal Landscape and the Consequences for Design and Planning'. In: Thompson G.F.; Steiner F. (ed) *Ecological Design and Planning*. John Wiley, New York pp. 293-320

Landscape analysis

see > analysis

Landscape architecture

see > introduction

Landscape language

see also > landscape, legibility, meaning, toponymy

The concept of landscape language can be interpreted in two ways: as the 'language of landscape', and as the professional language of landscape designers and managers.

The first of these indicates the existence of a phenomenological and mythological relationship between man and his environment. Landscape talks to us, and we must learn to understand and respond. 'Elements of landscape language are like parts of a speech, each with separate functions and associations [...] These elements do not exist in isolation, but rather combine in significant ways, like words in a phrase, clause or sentence, to make a tree, fountain, street, or a larger, more complex landscape story – garden, town or forest' (Spirn 1998). Landscapes with a long history of human settlement have a more complex and rich language than modern ones.

The question is whether or not landscape speaks to us. In the eyes of many, landscape is just there, remaining silent, a world in itself. Only human beings are able to use words, to attach meanings to landscapes and objects, and to put their ideas and ideals into words, expressing what they see as 'landscape values' (Gregory 1994). The language of landscape is thus the language of humans, which means there are many languages, each based on a different paradigm, which can, in various ways, help understand the 'narrative' aspects of landscape.

An activity promoted by John Ruskin (1819-1900) was 'word painting': using language to express very precisely one's understanding of an environment, as well as one's emotional reaction to it. The following example comes from de Botton (2002): 'Grass is expansive, the earth timid and the true cumulus, the most majestic of clouds [...] is for the most part windless; the movements of its masses being solemn, continuous, inexplicable, a steady advance or retiring [...].Trees on steep slopes stand comfortless, yet with such an iron will that the rock itself looks bent and shattered beside them.'

Another example is found in *Great Expectations*, where Charles Dickens describes the experience of a traveller who takes the early morning coach out of London in 1860: 'I set off [...] before it was yet light, and was out in the open country-road when the day came creeping on, halting and whimpering and shivering, and wrapped up in patches of clouds and rags of mist, like a beggar' (Dickens 1860/1978)

In contrast, when planning and designing, a professional might define landscape language in terms of a vast 'pattern system' which helps filter reality. Patterns in the mind of man form both language and designed environments. Pattern language provides the vital connection between context and the creation of form (Alexander 1977; Drew 1972).

Landscape architects use their own language for explaining their concepts, ideas and designs, for communicating with colleagues and clients and for participating in political debates. Ideas are not communicated if design quality is described with words such as 'nice', 'horrible', 'good', 'screwy' or 'interesting'. A better vocabulary is evolving, however – some of it featuring in this compendium. Much of it is borrowed from neighbouring disciplines, such as geography, soil science, the social sciences, art history, and ecology. Professional debate is facilitated by a more precise and generally accepted terminology on the iconographic aspects of designs – which, of course, is also of vital importance to the teaching of landscape architecture (Schon 1985; Weilacher 1996).

• Alexander C. (et al). 1977. *A Pattern Language*. Oxford University Press, New York pp. IX-XVII
• de Botton A. 2002. 'On possessing beauty'. In: *The Art of Travel*. Penguin Books, London pp. 214-238
• Dickens C. 1860 (reprint 1978). *Great Expectations*. Penguin Books, Harmondsworth, Middlesex p. 368
• Drew P. 1972. 'Pattern language'. In: *Third Generation. The Changing Meaning of Architecture. Chapter 2*. Pall Mall Press, London pp. 21-35
• Gregory D. 1994. 'Postmodern readings and textualities'. In: *Geographical Imaginations*. Blackwell, London pp. 140 et seq.
• Schön D. 1985. *The Design Studio. An Exploration of its Traditions and Potentials*. RIBA Publishing Ltd, London. pp. 63-81
• Spirn A. 1998. 'Is a leaf like a noun, flowing like a verb?'. In: *The Language of Landscape*. Yale University Press, New Haven p. 85
• Weilacher. 1996. ' A new language in the landscape'. In: *Between Landscape Architecture and Land Art*. Birkhäuser, Basel pp. 9 ff.

Landscape planning

see also > analysis, design, structure

The general definition of the verb 'to plan' is 'to design or make a plan of something to be made or built : e.g. planning a garden' (*Oxford English Dictionary*).

Landscape planning can be viewed as part of the regional planning process, a form of 'growth management' which concerns the location, intensity and timing of development (Faludi 1992). It is essentially a strategic process, with an emphasis on the analysis and control of processes and forces that underlie landscape change. Designing new environments in the sense of giving form is not always the main objective, even if one never loses sight of the design element (Ahern 1995). Landscape design and landscape planning are therefore overlapping activities.

The notion was first introduced in England by Brian Hackett (Hackett 1971). With an emphasis on the visual and ecological aspects of planning, it studies landscape form and its impact on human perception. The guidance of land-use takes account of existing patterns and natural processes (Rogers 2001), ideas for optimal harmony between them being illustrated in maps and bird's eye views. 'A landscape plan is more than a land-use plan, because it addresses the overlap and integration of land uses. A landscape plan may involve the formal recognition of previous elements in the planning process, such as the adoption of policy goals. The plan should include a written statement about policies and implementation strategies as well as a map showing the spatial organisation of the landscape' (Steiner 2000/1). In a landscape master plan, detailing is restricted to main outlines; in a landscape plan it is more exact.

In the Netherlands, the emergence of landscape planning as a branch of landscape architecture was closely connected with the large-scale reconstruction (or reconsolidation) of agricultural areas in the 20th century under the auspices of the Land Consolidation Act. These projects were sponsored by the Ministry of Agriculture, and were intended primarily to improve conditions for agricultural production, and thereby to raise farm incomes.

As required by law, landscape plans for

181

these projects specified the location of specific nature areas and historic elements. In the early stages, these plans were usually limited to proposals for roadside tree-planting and the creation of shelterbelts around farmyards.

The experience they gained in this work taught many landscape architects how they could work on a regional scale. This led to planning at a more ambitious level. Historical developments and the deeper structure of landscape were studied, ecological relations analysed, and solutions established. Of prime importance was the conservation of information about the history of places and natural heritage.

All these considerations led to landscape master plans or landscape structure plans that provided a general indication of possible developments (Andela 2000). While aesthetic considerations are always inherent to a designer's motivation, their effect in most cases is hardy discernible. 'The designs of rural areas fit so well into the existing landscape that they are hardly noticeable' (Etteger 2004).

Landscape planning activities may sometimes have a preparatory function, such

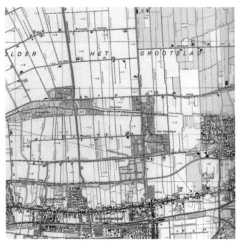

An example of total landscape renovation in the reconsolidation plan for Het Grootslag, province of Noord Holland (started in 1969). Situation before and after implementation.

Source: Visser R. de. 1997. Een halve eeuw landschapsbouw: het landschap van de landinrichting. Blauwdruk, Wageningen

An example of landscape restoration fitted carefully into the existing pattern. Reconsolidation plan (started in 1966); Vries, province of Drenthe, the Netherlands. Situation before and after implementation.

as when a landscape analysis is intended to help develop concepts for projects within the scope of general planning activities. Such plans require intensive co-operation with other disciplines (Vroom 1976).

Dutch landscape planners pay a lot of attention to the interaction between existing land-use and the natural landscape patterns expressed in relief, water systems and soils. This approach is rooted in the conviction that amenity and landscape legibility are determined largely by harmonious relationships between natural patterns and the layout of settlements and farmland.

Developments that disturb this relationship can be corrected through design or planning proposals (Kerkstra 2003). These establish scenarios for possible future developments in infrastructure, housing, agriculture, forestry and nature management, each scenario incorporating general conditions such as water control, tourism and landscape change. A successful plan requires collaboration between all the parties concerned. The final outcome also depends greatly on supervision and guidance by central government, without which many landscape plans remain mere paper products (Harsema 2002).

Environmental planning and ecological planning are closely related to landscape planning. 'Environmental planning is the initiation and operation of activities to manage the acquisition, transformation, distribution and disposal of resources in a manner capable of sustaining human activities, with a minimum distribution of physical ecological and social processes' (Steiner 2000/2).

• Ahern J. 1995. 'Greenways as a planning strategy'. In: Landscape and Urban Planning Journal, Elsevier, Amsterdam vol. 33 pp. 1-3, 131-155
• Andela G. 2000. *Kneedbaar landschap, kneedbaar volk* (i.e. *Malleable land, malleable people*). *De heroïsche jaren van de ruilverkavelingen in Nederland*. Thoth, Bussum pp. 73 ff.
• Etteger R. van 2004. 'The invisible conversion'. In: *Landscape architecture and town planning in the Netherlands 01-03*. Thoth publishing, Bussum pp.210-213
• Faludi A. 1992. 'Dutch growth management: the two faces of success'. In: Landscape and Urban Planning Journal no. 22, Elsevier, Amsterdam pp. 93-106
• Hackett B. 1971. *Landscape Planning. An introduction to Theory*

and Practice. Oriel Press, London
• Harsema H. (ed.) 2002. 'The beauty of the Netherlands' countryside, on paper'. In: *Landscape architecture and town planning in the Netherlands 99-01*. Thoth, Bussum pp. 174-177
• Kerkstra K. (et al.) 2003. 'Verborgen tuin van Midden-Limburg' (i.e. The hidden garden of Noord-Limburg). In: Houwen J.; Farber K. (ed.) *Ontwerpen aan de zandgebieden van Noord- en Midden-Limburg. Drie over dertig*. Published by Provincie Limburg, Maastricht pp. 98-119
• Rogers E.B. 2001. 'Conserving Nature: Landscape Design as Environmental Science and Art'. In: *Landscape Design*. Harry Abrams publishers, New York pp. 481-486
• Steiner F. 2001/1. 'Introduction'. In: *The Living Landscape. An Ecological Approach to Landscape Planning*. McGraw Hill, New York p. 3 ff
• Steiner F. 2000/2. 'Landscape plans'. In: *The Living Landscape. An Ecological Approach to Landscape Planning*. McGraw Hill, New York pp. 253 ff.
• Vroom M.J. 1976. 'Landscape planning: a cooperative effort; a professional activity'. In: Landscape Planning, Elsevier, Amsterdam no. 3 pp. 371-382

Landscape style
see also > park, picturesque, poetic, romanticism, symbol

This design style was developed in 18th-century England, during the Romantic Age, which brought a drastic change in world

A folly at Rousham House, England: a foolish construction in an arbitrary location.
Source: Saudan M. 1987. From Folly to Follies. Benedikt Taschen Verlag Köln

Postmodern follies placed in a grid in Parc de la Villette, Paris

views. Unlike the Classicist style that preceded it – the 'formal mockery of princely gardens' designed to impress and to 'dazzle the eye' – it involved a search for natural form (Saudan 1987). The intention was no longer to overawe the viewer but to let him explore. Alexander Pope (1688-1744) put it this way: 'He gains all ends who pleasingly confounds, surprises, varies, and conceals the bounds' (Moore 1989).

Contemporary literature and paintings reflect this same search for nature images (Crandell 1993).

Landscape style was much influenced by 17th-century Dutch and French painting, and also by the undulating English landscape with its open grassy slopes (Clifford 1962; Dixon Hunt 1975). The representation of nature images became so intertwined with what might be termed the re-presentation of idealised impressions that critics at the time raised the question if this type of park design could be defined as a work of art (Hunt 2000).

Outdoor walks provided a succession of impressions and experiences. 'Elizabeth was delighted,' Jane Austen wrote in *Pride and Prejudice*. 'She had never seen a place for which nature had done more, or where natural beauty had been so little counteracted by an awkward taste.'

To an almost overwhelming extent, symbolism was everywhere. Garden objects and constructions were reminders of other times and other places. Follies became popular (Kluckert 2000).

The layout of landscape style parks varied. The poetic movement preferred wild and romantic landscapes, while the influence of painters and paintings led to the picturesque style promoted by William Gilpin (1724-1804) (Batey 1996).

The designs of Lancelot 'Capability' Brown (1716-1783) included large undulating fields, spread-out tree clumps, a sober selection of planting, and an absence of decorative elements (Stroud 1975; Turner 1985; Kluckert 2000; Anonymous 2000). Brown's aim was to 'correct' nature in order to conform to an aesthetic ideal. His successor Humphry

Repton (1752-1818) designed more complex gardens containing flower beds, and also emphasised efficient access and circulation (Clifford 1962; Daniels 1999).

The following list shows some of the primary characteristics of the landscape style:
In terms of structure:
· continuity by means of sight lines and scenes; asymmetry; a sequence of settings; pause and focus;
· pictorial composition and a contrast between building and park

In terms of experience:
· vague boundaries; flowing space; picturesqueness; dynamic balance; continuity; successive experiences; intricate order

In terms of reference:
· harmony; delight in nature, both cultivated and uncultivated; drama; melancholy; pictures literature

In terms of design tools:
· clumps of trees, ha-ha's, bocages, rivers, waterfalls, brooks, rapids, streams, valleys, scenes, hills, slopes (Baljon 1992)

· Anonymous. 2001. Garden History. Journal of the Garden History Society, London, Theme Number 'Lancelot Brown' vol. 29 no. 1
· Baljon L. 1992. *Designing Parks*. Architectura & Natura Press, Amsterdam pp. 158-159
· Batey M. 1996. *Jane Austen and the English Landscape*. Barn Elms, London p. 68
· Clifford D. 1962. 'The great revolution of taste' pp. 123 ff. 'Humphry Repton' pp. 173-183 in: *A History of Garden Design*. Faber & Faber, London
· Crandell G. 1993. *Nature Pictorialized*. John Hopkins University Press, New York pp. 111 ff.
· Daniels S. 1999. 'Humphry Repton' & 'Landscapes of transition'. In: *Landscape Gardening and the Geography of Georgian England*. Yale University Press, New Haven
· Dixon Hunt J.; Willis P. 1975. *The Genius of the Place*. Paul Elek, London
· Hunt J.D. 2000. *Greater Perfections*. Thames & Hudson, London pp. 80 ff.
· Kluckert E. (ed). 2000. *Gardens of Europe*. Könemann, Köln pp. 370-377; 388-391
· Moore C.W. (et al). 1989. *The Poetics of Gardens*. MIT Press, Cambridge p. 46
· Saudan M.; Saudan-Skira S. 1987. 'Gardens to dazzle the eye'. In:

From Folly to Follies. Discovering the World of Gardens. Benedikt
Taschen Verlag, Köln pp. 63 ff.
- Stroud D. 1975. *Capability Brown.* Faber & Faber, London
- Turner R. 1985. *Capability Brown and the Eighteenth-century
English Landscape.* Weidenfeld and Nicholson, London

Some of the more conspicuous elements of a
romantic park were follies, ha-ha's and
hermitages. A 'folly' was originally a popular
name for a construction or building that
showed so many blunders that it had to be
razed (*Oxford English Dictionary*). The best
known follies are the silly and useless
structures that were built deliberately (and
became popular) in Romantic gardens and
parks, especially in 18th-century England and
Germany. In France they were called *fabriqués*
(*Oxford Companion*). They took the form of
Chinese bridges, Gothic sheds, pyramids,
mosques, Turkish baths, and primitive sheds,
all thrown together haphazardly, usually at
reduced scale, and often half finished. By
serving as a shepherd's village as well as a
second home, Queen Marie Antoinette's
Hameau in the park at Versailles was a folly
in a double sense.

A ruin such as an abbey, church, priory or
castle was also a popular type of folly. Not all
landowners were fortunate enough to have a
genuine, conveniently placed ruin, and had to
build their own. As well as being a feature of
visual interest in the view, this was also
intended to stimulate philosophical thoughts
on the frailty of man and the impermanence
of his creations (*Goulty*).

Through their references to other places
and other times, follies were supposed to
enrapture walkers. Memory, illusion and
nostalgia all played their role (Saudan 1997).
A walk through such a Romantic park was
like 'leafing through an encyclopaedia or
history book'. It was 'an endless catalogue of
surprise, pleasure and sheer delight' which
'sometimes [gave] way to more complex
mysteries, to higher demands'. There [was] a
strong connection with literary works
(Mosser 1991).

In contemporary architecture, follies are not
considered to be mere useless objects, even if
they are uninhabitable or unfit for a practical

use. They may serve as orientation points in a
complex space, or as exercise material for the
analysis of architectonic problems. Recent
examples are the follies in Parc de la Villette,
Paris, designed by Bernard Tschumi in his
winning entry for the international design
competition in 1982 (Baljon 1992).

A recent example of a 'serious folly' is found
in the imported remains of a Roman palace,
carefully reconstructed in the county of
Surrey England in the 1990, thereby re-
creating a building from 'a disorderly pile of
fragments' (Woodward 2002)

Ha-ha's are a boundary to a garden,
pleasure ground or park, which keep out farm
animals without interrupting the view from
within, and which are not seen until
approached closely. They consist of a ditch

A ha-ha at Wallington Estate, Northumberland, England.

185

Cross sections.

whose inner side is usually perpendicular and faced with stone, and whose outer side is sloping and turfed (*Goulty*).

This feature was developed in France and used at Versailles (*le saut de loup*, *la clairvoie*, or '*ah-ah*'), (*Oxford Companion*; Kluckert 2000) and first introduced into England by Charles Bridgeman (1690-1738) after William Kent (1685-1748) had discarded the notion that a garden was by definition an enclosed space. Kent 'broke with the idea of enclosure and saw the whole of Nature as a garden'. The motto was 'to leap the fence' (Rogers 2002; Thacker 1985). The result was 'the destruction of walls for boundaries, and the invention of *fosses* – an attempt then deemed so astonishing that the people called them Ha! Ha!'s to express their surprise at finding a sudden and unperceived check of their walk' (Turner 1985).

A hermitage is a solitary dwelling place for meditation in a garden; a feature of interest, often a folly. The hermitage was fashionable in several European countries during the 18th century (Woodward 2001). To amuse visitors, it was supposed to be used as the habitation of a hermit, but it often proved difficult to

A romantic park view in Wiersse Estate, Achterhoek, Gelderland, the Netherlands.

Park in Rotterdam designed by garden architect J.D. Zocher between 1852 and 1862.

find prospective hermits to occupy them; such people were obliged to let their hair and nails grow for a period of seven years, and were equipped with spectacles, a Bible and a sleeping mat (Clifford 1962). Some of the best known hermitages in England were at Stowe, Buckinghamshire, and Stourhead in Wiltshire (*Goulty*).

• Baljon 1992. *Designing Parks*. Architectura & Natura Press, Amsterdam pp.210, 211
• Clifford D. 1962. *A History of Garden Design*. Faber & Faber, London pp. 147-148
• Kluckert E.. 2000. *The Gardens of Europe*. Könemann, Köln p. 228
• Mosser. M. 1991. 'Paradox in the Garden: a brief Account of Fabriqués'. In: Mosser M.; Teyssot G.T. (ed). *The History of Garden Design*. Thames and Hudson, London pp. 263-280
• Rogers E.B. 2002.' Leaping the Fence'. In: *Landscape Design. A Cultural and Architectural History*. Abrams publishers, New York pp. 239 ff.
• Saudan M.; Saudan-Skira S. 1997. *From Folly to Follies*. Benedikt Taschen Verlag, Keulen
• Thacker C. 1985. 'Leaping the Fence'. In: *The History of Gardens*. Croom Helm, London p. 181
• Turner R. 1985. *Capability Brown and the Eighteenth-century English Landscape*. Weidenfeld & Nicholson, London p. 39
• Woodward C. 2001. 'Serious Follies'. In: *In Ruins*. Vintage, London pp. 136-159

Although the English landscape style was a source of inspiration for garden designers on the European continent, it was not copied directly. Would-be imitators in the Netherlands, for instance, faced a number of problems in their predominantly flat landscapes; extensive groundworks were needed to create the desired hummocks and slopes, the only uneven ground being found in dune areas and on the bulwarks around various cities that had been dismantled and converted to promenade parks (Cremers 1981).

Nonetheless, landscape-style gardens were laid out in the Netherlands from the last quarter of the eighteenth century, initially as part of the reconstruction of gardens of larger estates. The first example was the enlargement of the Classical layout the Beeckestein garden at Velzen, designed by J.G. Michael (1738-1800) (Oldenburger 1998). Two generations of prominent landscape architects, J.D. Zocher Sr (1763-1817) and J.D.

Zocher Jr (1791-1870), laid out many private gardens, and later created parks – including Amsterdam's Vondelpark – in a number of towns (Backer 1998). They were followed by L. Springer (1855-1940) (Moes 2002).

• Backer A. (ed). 1998. *De Natuur Bezworen* (i.e. *Nature conjured*). *Een inleiding in de geschiedenis van de Nederlandse tuin-en landschapsarchitectuur van de middeleeuwen tot het jaar 2005*. De Hef publishers, Rotterdam pp. 33 e.v.
• Cremers E. (et al). 1991. *Bolwerken als stadsparken* (i.e. *Bulwarks as urban parks*). *Nederlandse stadwandelingen in de 19de en 20ste eeuw*. Delft University Press.
• Moes W. 2002. *L.A. Springer Tuinarchitect Dendroloog*. Uitgeverij De Hef, Rotterdam
• Warnau H. 1990. 'Enkele aspecten van de romantiek in de tuinkunst. Ideeën in de achtergrond van de landschapsstijl' (i.e. *Some aspects of romanticism in garden design. Ideas on the background of the landscape style*). In: Groen Journal, Doetinchem no. 7 pp. 21 ff.
• Oldenburger C. 1998. *Gids voor de Nederlandse Tuin- en Landschapsarchitectuur Deel West*. De Hef, Rotterdam pp. 252-253

Landscape typology
see > type

Landscape values
see > value

187

Layer Overlay
see also > analysis, landscape, multiple use, palimpsest

'A sheet, quantity or thickness of material typically one of several covering a surface or body' (*Oxford English Dictionary*).

The natural stratification of a landscape is caused by geological forces which, over time, have added layers of rock, soil, and water bodies, on top of which natural vegetation and wildlife have developed and man's settlement patterns have been established. Put simply, a landscape may thus be described as constituting three layers: the physical, the biotic and the human. These can themselves be divided into a number of specific layers (McHarg 1969). The top, anthropogenic, layer can in turn be divided into older and younger settlement patterns. Still visible, often just below the surface of the land, are traces of the past, such as old land parcels, fossil roads, ruins and other relics. These are connected by memories, legends and stories.

Such traces can be recovered via field work, aerial photography and remote-sensing techniques (Deuel 1973), revealing the landscape's effective nature as a palimpsest – 'a parchment used again after earlier writing had been erased' (*Webster*). In many cases, the older writings on the parchment have not completely disappeared, but still remain visible through the new text. This is also what happens in landscapes where former

and new patterns are simultaneously visible (Corbez 1997). Of importance to historical research, this adds interest to the work of landscape planners (van der Valk 2000).

Urban centres can also be built up in a series of layers – underground as well as on the surface – that are made to form an interactive ensemble, thereby promoting multiple land-use. Early examples are the inner cities of Montreal in Canada and Philadelphia in the US (Bacon 1974).

A site design may be based on a projected basic geometric pattern or matrix, over which a new set of lines is projected, which at

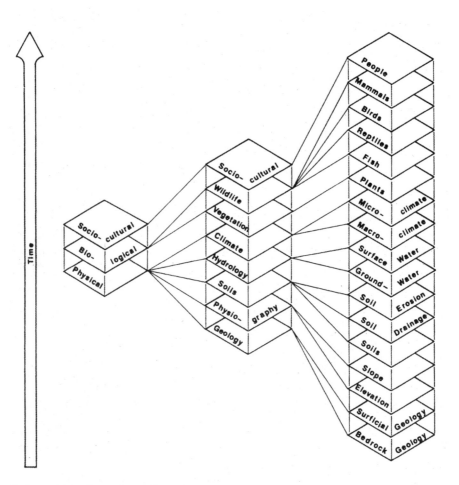

The 'layer cake' showing superimposed layers, from bedrock to settlement patterns.
Source: McHarg I. 1969: Design with Nature. The Natural History Press, New York

certain points form junctions with the bottom layer. The resulting graphic composition functions as an ordering framework for the design. This is called a deconstructivist approach to design. An internationally well-known example is the winning entry for the 1982 design competition for Parc de la Villette in Paris by Bernard Tshumi (Baljon 1992).

The term 'layer' can also be used in an abstract sense, such as that conveyed by the term 'layers of meaning'. It expresses the reaction of an observer, who in the course of time slowly discovers, unearths and attempts to understand the physical environment with its extremely complex set of relations (Thompson 1999).

Similarity between layers may become apparent when social networks are connected with geographic data – a 'world of layers' in which imagination, action and possession go hand in hand (Lengkeek 2002).

• Bacon E. 1974. 'Putting ideas to work – Philadelphia'. In: *Design of Cities*. Thames and Hudson, London pp. 264-304
• Baljon L. 1992. *Designing Parks*. Architectura & Natura, Amsterdam pp. 190; 206-212
• Corboz A. 1997. 'Het territorium als palimpsest'. In: de Jong E. (ed). *Tuinkunst 3*. Architectura & Natura, Amsterdam pp. 8-35
• Deuel L. 1973. *Flights into yesterday. The story of aerial photography*. Pelican Book, Harmondsworth, Middlesex
• Lengkeek J. 2002. *De wereld in lagen* (i.e. *The world in layers*). Inaugural address, Wageningen University.
• McHarg I. 1969. *Design with Nature*. Natural History Press. New York. pp. 103-115;
• Thompson I. 1999. *Ecology, Community and Delight. Sources of Values in Landscape Architecture*. Spon, London pp. 73-74

Foundations of excavated buildings in 's-Hertogenbosch, the Netherlands.
Photo: Frank Meijer

• van der Valk A. (et al). 2000. *Gespaard Landschap* (i.e. *Saved landscapes*). Amsterdamse Raad voor de Monumentenzorg.

Legibility

see also > landscape, language, layer, palimpsest, toponymy

To be legible means 'to be capable of being read' (*Webster*) and: 'clear enough to be read' (*Oxford Advanced*).

Applied to buildings, this means that observers can discern the parts, see how they join, and also understand the function of the whole. In a landscape, it means that people can identify and recognise the constituent parts, what goes on there, where 'places' are, and how the parts can be arranged in a coherent pattern (Grujard 1988; Lynch 1959; Spirn 1998).

Legibility is subject to the following conditions:
• Beholders should understand the 'vocabulary' and grammar of the landscape. In other words, they should be able to recognise not only the difference between field and meadow, houses and office buildings, but also between cover-sand ridges and river banks, moraine and marine sediments. They should be aware of its natural and cultural history. The greater their knowledge and the better their reading, the greater their enjoyment (Hunt 2000).
• Land-use types must be both visible and recognisable, and their relationship with terrain features must be evident. The function of a farm is read in the form of its barns and sheds, visible wheel ruts and compost heaps (Warnau 1993). 'Some landscapes are so full and rich with meaning that you can almost read them like a book, or leaf through them like a picturebook' (van Toorn 1998).

Expectations, insight, and the recognition of contrasts also helps one's reading of the landscape (Gandelsonas 1980). The same goes for stories that belong to a place or an area: one may speak of the 'narrative' aspects of a region. When an environment acquires a

189

place within the local culture and it becomes a 'place', it is connected with stories that show its value to the population. Thus, dikes are part of the stories about the dangers of flooding, and monuments tell stories about the past. Commercial tourism makes use of such stories – whether about Omaha Beach in Normandy, Hadrian's Wall in England, or the birthplace of famous people. 'We live within worlds of stories, and we use stories to shape those worlds. In history, fiction, lived experience, myth, anecdote, and stories all tell of origins, explaining causes, marking the boundaries of what is knowable, and exploring the territories beyond' (Potteiger 1998).

Many stories come to us through the names of fields, roads or towns. Toponymy explains the history of a place. Metaphors refer to places elsewhere. Names can also be rhetoric, such as those of boulevards and squares that refer to historic events or famous kings, generals, politicians and heroes. They tell us of happenings and people that were considered important enough to remember, though sometimes ideas and memories change, and names are replaced – for instance Mandela Boulevard replacing Stalin Allee (Hunt 2000).

A designer has many means at his disposal for telling stories. The park at Versailles is full of stories about King Louis XIV: '*Tout autant qu'un parc, Versailles est un livre. La bible par laquelle le roi-dieu, usant de tous les moyens possibles du récit (allégories, digressions, secrets, surprises...) et mêlant à la fête tous les personnages, divins, humains ou animaux, se raconte et s'engendre lui-même*' (Orsenna 2000).

• Gandelsonas M. 1980. 'On reading architecture'. In: Broadbent G. (et al). *Symbols and Architecture*. Wiley & Sons, New York pp. 243 ff.
• Grujard M. (et al). 1988. *Regarder et comprendre un paysage*. Jupilles Almann-Levy
• Hunt J.D. 2000. 'Word and image in the garden'. In: *Greater Perfections. The Practice of Garden Theory*. Thames & Hudson, London pp. 126 ff.
• Lynch K. 1959. *The Image of the City*. MIT Press pp. 2-3
• Orsenna E. 2000. *Portrait d'un homme heureux. André le Nôtre 1613-1700*. Fayard, Paris
• Potteiger M. ; Purinton J. 1998. *Landscape Narratives – Design Practices for Telling Stories*. John Wiley & Sons, New York

• Spirn A. 1998. *The Language of Landscape*. Yale University Press, New Haven pp. 15-18
• van Toorn W. 1998. *Leesbaar landschap* (i.e. *Legible landscape*). Querido publishers, Amsterdam
• Warnau H. 1993. 'Landschapsarchitectuur en de moderne stroming in de bouwkunde' (i.e. Landscape architecture and the modern movement in architecture). In: Smienk G. (ed). *Nederlandse landschapsarchitectuur. Tussen traditie en experiment*. Thoth publishers, Bussum p. 34

Light

see also > basin, colour, space

Light is a 'kind of natural radiation that makes things visible; source of light; also: understanding; enlightenment' (*Oxford English Dictionary*).

Light is connected with the origin of life. Every mythology and religion considers light as the beginning of reality. As during the Age of Enlightenment, it is a symbol of renewal. The truth is brought 'to light'.

Light makes objects, spaces and places visible, enabling designers to exploit its physical properties in manipulating the experience of space with contrasting light, shade and colours. Shadows are created in daylight under the canopy of trees, but also by objects and features of the natural terrain. They vary in brightness depending on the density of vegetation and the time of the day (Minnaert 1993; Lynch 1995). The manipulation of natural and artificial light, both within buildings and outdoors, is one of the main means for creating space, pattern and atmospheres (Anonymous 1997/1;

Light creates space, patterns and atmospheres. Sunlight between the planks in the wall of a barn in Twickel estate, Twenthe, the Netherlands.

Anonymous 1997/2).

As the sun moves through its daily arc, some places on a site may always remain in the shade, while other parts may be in the sun all day. Every planting plan is affected by the different light conditions that have to meet the requirements of different plants. In built-up areas, water and glossy facades mirror and reflect light, whereas trees provide shade and dappled light (Arnheim 1969; Amidon 2001).

Changes in lighting conditions indicate the course of time, per day and per season.

Atmospheric conditions determine the colour and brightness of light, as seen in the 'golden mists and tinted steam' in paintings by Turner (1775-1851) (Wilton 1979). While the moisture-laden atmosphere of England, for instance, creates an exaggerated aerial perspective that causes receding hills to fade in the distance, the clarity of the light in a dry desert climate makes distant mountains seem eerily sharp and close by (Moore 1989).

• Amidon J. 2001. 'Light, Colour, Texture'. In: *Radical Landscapes. Reinventing Outdoor Space*. Thames & Hudson, London pp. 10-37
• Anonymous. 1997/1. 'Light in Architecture' Theme Number

The reflection of light in water doubles the image of a building: the former World Trade Center, Manhattan, New York. Photographed in 1987.

191

Light reflecting from fountains makes open space between dense foliage visible from afar: Hyde Park, London.

Architectural Design Journal
- Anonymous. 1997/2. Topos European Landscape Magazine no. 20 Theme number 'Nightscape'. Callwey, München
- Arnheim R. 1969. 'Light creates space'. In: *Art and Visual Perception*. Faber Editions, London pp. 300-305
- Lynch D.K.; Livingston W. 1995. *Colour and Light in Nature*. Cambridge University, Press pp. 1-19
- Minnaert M. 1993. *Light and Colour in the Outdoors*. Springer, Verlag

- Moore C.W. (et al).1989. *The Poetics of Gardens*. MIT Press Cambridge pp.8-9
- Wilton A. 1979. 'Introduction'. In: Shanes E. *Turner's Picturesque Views in England and Wales*. Book Club Associates, London p. 5.

The effect of changing light on a landscape in the morning and at night: 1. effets de la lumière – le matin 2. Effets de la lumière – le soir.
Source: André E. 1879, l'Art des Jardins. Traité général de la composition des Parcs et Jardins. Masson, Paris p. 129

Mannerism

see also > eclecticism, illusion, Renaissance

'An often affected peculiarity of action, bearing, or treatment' (*Webster*).

'Style of 16th-century Italian art which challenged some of the classical rules of painting (e.g. by altering perspectives, showing people in distorted poses and using violently rich colours). It can be seen in the later works of Michelangelo. The term is also applied to architecture of the same period' (*Oxford English Dictionary*).

Art historians disagree on the nature of Mannerism. For some it is a form of degeneration, a fixed routine in which the great masters of the Renaissance are copied and imitated. Others see it as an attempt to improve the representation of natural form, and therefore find it worthy of praise, even if there are tendencies towards eclecticism (Janson 1966; Gombrich 1971).

Typical of Mannerism is the disintegration of the unified spatial composition that prevailed in Renaissance art. Scenes in paintings are decomposed, and secondary motives dominate while the central motive is devalued and suppressed (Hauser 1975).

A notable example of Mannerism in garden art is the Garden of Monsters at Villa Orsini in Bomarzo, Italy, dating from 1552. Illusionist techniques are used to deformed and exaggerated art objects. Monsters, dragons, giant fruit and other trivialities represent literary allusions. A lopsided building confuses the observer, just as some contemporary post-modern buildings do (Jellicoe 1975; Kluckert 2000).

Early Mannerism fell back on Renaissance ideals and its mathematical order, and was often based on individual preferences and local circumstances. In the Low Countries, the books of Vredeman de Vries (1526-1606) constituted an important catalogue of motives to choose from (Mehrtens 1991). During the 20th century, Mannerist tendencies could be identified in many fragmented Postmodern designs.

• Gombrich E.H. 1971 (second edition). 'Mannerism: the historiographic background'. In: *Norm and Form*. Phaidon, London pp. 99 ff.
• Hauser A . 1975. *Sociale geschiedenis van de kunst* (i.e. *The social history of art*). SUN reprint pp. 246-252
• anson H.W. 1966. 'Mannerism and other trends'. In: *History of Art*. Abrams, New York p. 374
• Jellicoe G. & S. 1975. *The Landscape of Man*. Thames and Hudson, London pp. 164-166
• Kluckert E. (red). 2000. *The Gardens of Europe*. Könemann, Köln pp. 84 ff.
• Mehrtens U.M. 1991. 'Johan Vredeman de Vries and the Hortus Formae'. In: Mosser M.; Teyssot G. *The History of Garden Design*. Thames and Hudson, London pp. 103-105

Enigmatic events, illusions and delusions are typical phenomena in the Garden of Monsters at Villa Orsini in Bomarzo Italy. This is Sacro Bosco, the lopsided house dating from 1552.

Source: Kluckert E. (ed). 2000. The Gardens of Europe. Könemann Köln p. 87

Map, Chart, Plan

see also > GIS, reduction

'A representation of the earth's surface or part of it; its physical and political features delineated on paper or other material, according to a definite scale or projection' (Goulty). 'Topography is the art or practice of detailing on maps or charts the natural and man-made features of a place or region, especially so as to show elevations. It is also the configuration of a surface, including its relief and the position of its natural and man-made features' (*Webster*).

The origins of cartography date back to the Greek philosopher Ptolemy in the second century B.C., whose work was rediscovered in 15th-century Italy. Ptolemy distinguished between two sub-disciplines in geography: topography, which concerned itself with the location of places; and chorography, which presented a graphic description or view of a landscape, and therefore belonged to the realm of art (Olwig 2002). The interchange between the two disciplines became apparent in the 17th century: like artists, cartographers used perspective images, and their maps resembled paintings (Alpers 1983; Cosgrove 1993).

Contemporary topographic maps register data that are needed for the typology and classification of landscapes, for the clarification of the origins of settlements, and for tracking down problems (Spirn 1998). The topography of a country contributes to

its identity. In the eyes of some patriots the identity of the Netherlands is manifest as 'a world of order and peace, sense and wisdom, where different forms fit into an overall mosaic' (Turin 1999).

The reading of landscapes may rely on direct observation as well as on the use of maps. 'Each map is a form of rhetoric. By emphasising certain aspects of reality as it was, or perhaps will be, and by representing these with the aid of certain selected symbols or colours, we evoke a response from the reader' (Ormeling 1997).

Maps never present an objective and overall image of a site or landscape, but are based on choices, and can even be misleading. There are various ways in which town plans can show the configuration of built-up areas: they may emphasise the dimensions of public outdoor space, or the distinction between public and private. They may pictorialise the relationship between volume and space, or between built-up areas and the surrounding landscape (Meyer 2002). The lines, planes, cross-hatchings or colours they

195

Painters used to draw maps: Architectura by Laurent de la Hye, 1630. Nijenhuis Museum, Heino, the Netherlands.

use must be translated to reality via legends.

Maps are made comparable by their simplicity, clarity and uniformity of basic units. Their icons tend to function only because of the existence of conventions about what they mean (Gombrich 1982).

The higher the scale of a map, the greater the reduction and abstraction of reality. Maps also represent a time-bound situation: they are quickly outdated and need periodic revision. These revisions provide the opportunity to study and compare successive stages of past development (Boudon 1991).

Standard maps versus special maps

Maps produced by surveyors for governments or other agencies have a standard legend, and aim to give an objective representation of the land surface measured

Leaping across the river Waal: graphic rhetoric of B&B landscape architects.

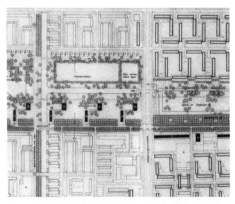

The sober design drawing of landscape architect W.C.J. Boer for Amstelpark in Buitenveldert, Amsterdam, 1957.

(Corner 1996). They are based on triangulation of the earth's surface, on aerial photographs, and, more recently, on remote sensing techniques. All these techniques have made it possible for man to create for himself an image of large parts of the world: 'the map offers a way of controlling both the contingencies of nature and the rivalries of human proprietors' (Cosgrove 1996).

However, the maps drawn by planners and designers to illustrate projected future situations are very different. Because individual designers use their own means of expression, standardisation is absent. Design drawings present a wide array of linguistic and graphic novelties – which hardly supports their main goal, which is to help transmit ideas and present conditions for developments; there is always the risk that the connection between an image and future reality will be lost (Hoogstad 1990).

'Mental maps' are based on individual and collective memories of existing local environments, and also of images of faraway places (Lynch 1960). Experiments in map-drawing from memory show just how differently distances, directions and dimensions are experienced and remembered. The influence of social differences and conflicts on the perception of accessibility and attainability may also be registered this way. Social and physical space are inextricably mixed (Gould 1974).

- Alpers S. 1983. *The Art of Describing. Dutch Art in the Seventeenth Century.* The University of Chicago Press
- Boudon F. 1991. 'Garden History and Cartography'. In: Mosser M.; Teyssot G. *History of Garden Design.* Thames & Hudson, London pp. 125-134
- Corner J. (ed). 1996. *Taking Measures across the American Landscape.* Yale University Press, New Haven
- Cosgrove D. 1996. 'The measures of America'. In: Corner J. *Taking Measures across the American Landscape.* Yale University Press, New Haven 3 ff.
- Cosgrove D. 1993. 'Venice and the mapping impulse'. In: *The Palladian Landscape.* Leicester University Press, pp.173-175
- Gombrich H. 1982. 'Mirror and map'. In: *The Image and the Eye.* Phaidon Press, London pp.172-189
- Gould P.; White R. 1974. *Mental Maps.* Pelican Book, Harmondsworth, Middlesex
- Hoogstad J. 1990. 'Architectural drawings'. In: *Space-time-motion.* SDU Uitgeverij, The Hague p. 68
- Lynch K. 1960. *The Image of the City.* MIT Press, Cambridge
- Meyer H. 2002. 'The composition of the town plan'. In:

Steenbergen C. (ed) *Architectural Design and Composition.* Thoth publishers, Bussum pp. 116-129
• Olwig 2002. *Landscape Nature and the Body Politic.* The University of Wisconsin Press. pp.32-40
• Ormeling F. 1997. 'De nieuwe kleuren van Nederland' (i.e. The new colours of the Netherlands). In: Stedebouw & Ruimtelijke Ordening, NIROV, The Hague no. 2 p.19
• Spirn A. 1998. 'The map is not the place; virtual landscapes'. In: *The Language of Landscape.* Yale University Press, New Haven pp. 204-205
• Turin M. 1999. 'Het vlakke land' (i.e. The flat land).In: *Album van de Nederlandse ruimte.* De Balie, Amsterdam pp.50-57

Margin

see > border

Mass Solid

see > volume

Matrix

see also > module, grid

'Something that gives form, foundation, or origin to something else enclosed in it' (*Webster*).

In a geometric layout of an outdoor space, the basic pattern of the plan is created by a matrix, often a regular or geometric grid connecting the dimensions of a house plan and the morphology of the surrounding landscape. Italian Renaissance gardens were often laid out on the basis of this principle (Steenbergen 1996). The matrix of the Dutch polder of Zuidelijk Flevoland penetrates the layout of the town of Almere-Buiten, linking its interior with the outlying districts.

A matrix may also serve as the geometric basis for a layout, but without forming a grid (Moholy-Nagy 1968). Matrices or grids in gardens may be visible as patterns formed by hedges and pavement, or in the regular spacing of trees. Their use dates back many centuries, and many applications have resulted in delightful solutions. However, when the continuity of the pattern demands a repetition of similar elements, problems can arise if varied orientations of slopes require different planting solutions (Treib 2002).

An entirely different concept is the matrix as a graphical 'arrangement of numbers, symbols etc in a rectangular grid' (*Oxford Advanced*), serving as 'an effective tool for identifying and communicating one-on-one relationships' (Motloch 2001). This has two or three coordinates along which all relevant factors dealt with in the design process are arranged in an orderly fashion by means of symbols, numbers or keywords, and can thereby be compared at a glance. Such an overview can also be used as a summary of the evaluation process. To check on the compatibility of various uses, for example, one can indicate a number of types of land-use on the two axes of a matrix, using a third axis to show the third dimension by presenting the environmental effects of types of land-use over time (McHarg 1963, Patri 1970).

• McHarg I.1963. *Design with Nature.* Natural History Press, New York p. 144
• Moholy-Nagy S. 1968. *Matrix of Man. An Illustrated History of Urban Environment.* Praeger, New York.

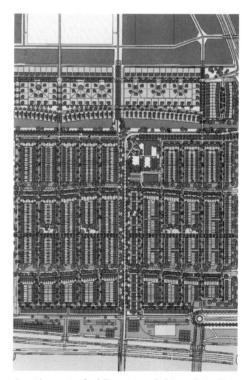

197

A matrix as a standard dimension underlying a design. Map of Almere-Buiten, the Netherlands.

• Motloch J.L. 2001. *Introduction to Landscape Design.* John Wiley, New York p. 290
• Patri T. (et al).1970. *Early Warning System. The Santa Cruz Mountains Regional Pilot Study.* University of California, Berkeley pp.163 -178
• Steenbergen C.; Reh W. 1996. *Architecture and Landscape.* Thoth, Bussum p. 45
• Treib M. 2002. 'The content of landscape form'. In: Landscape Journal, The University of Wiscosin Press, Urbana, Illinois no. 20:2-01

Maze

see > labyrinth

Meaning

see > sign

Metaphor

see also > analogy, association, landscape language, legibility, symbol, reference

'Use of a word or phrase to indicate something different from the literal meaning' (*Oxford English Dictionary*).

Metaphor is 'a figure of speech in which a name or descriptive term is transferred to some object both different from but analogous to that to which it is properly applicable' (Broadbent 1973). As in literature and the arts, metaphors in environmental design stimulate creative thinking by helping to form trains of thought that supplement or avoid logical reasoning. Two different objects or phenomena are connected through the

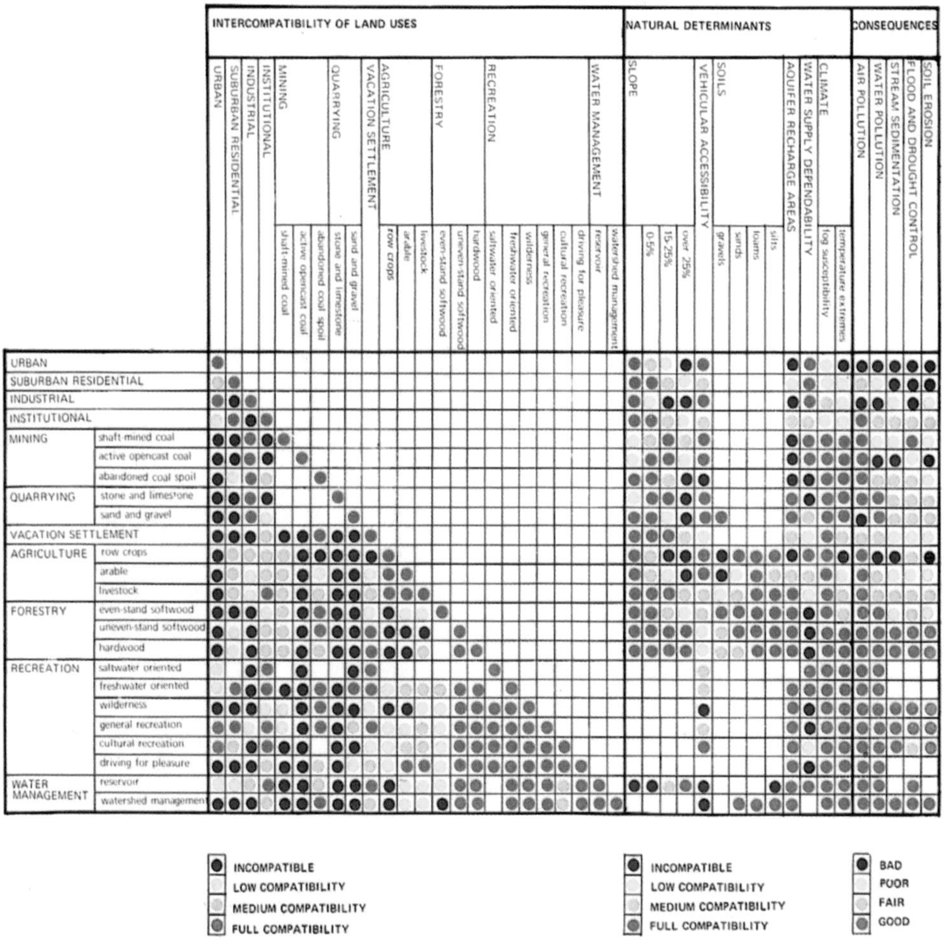

198

A matrix may present an overview of all the data supporting a design process.

Source: McHarg I. 1963. Design with Nature. Natural History Press New York

transformation of an image, which helps clarify a message, such as in 'a ship ploughs through the sea'.

Metaphors also help memorise events and things (Schacter 1996).

Writers and poets may be inspired to produce metaphors that capture the reality of an experience. Having observed the moon in daylight, Marcel Proust (1871-1922) wrote: 'Sometimes in the afternoon sky, a white moon would creep up like a little cloud, furtive, without display, suggesting an actress who does not have to 'come on' for a while, and so goes 'in front' in her ordinary clothes to watch the company for a moment, but keeps in the background, not wishing to attract attention to herself' (de Botton 1997).

Buildings and constructions may acquire a metaphoric charge when analogies with other objects are evident. Such analogies are not always unambiguous. The world-famous Sydney Opera House may represent a sailboat, a collection of shells, or even a group of copulating turtles (Jencks 1977).

Metaphors stimulate the experience of landscape and assist human orientation in space. People tend to project parts of the human body onto the visible environment: a river has a head and a mouth; a mountain

has a foot (Spirn 1998). To search for potentials of a site and to visualise design concepts, a designer may use various metaphors (Turner 1996). 'Leaping from metaphor to metaphor, attending to this aspect and then to that [...] the mind begins to understand the significance of decisions in all their important dimensions' (Lynch 1984).

Urban environments can be characterised by metaphors such as an arena (where people compete) or Babylon (where confusion and dissonance reign), a forum (where people meet and discuss), a jungle (a dangerous place) or a theatre (where people enact their roles) (Knox 2000). Well-known

Opera House, Sydney, Australia – metaphoric in more than one sense.

'Castle' houses in the Haverley quarter of 's-Hertogenbosch, the Netherlands, 1995. Architects: Soeters van Eldonk Ponec; landscape architects: Paul van Beek, H+N+S.

Photograph: Frank Meijer

metaphors in Dutch physical planning are 'Green Heart Metropolis' for the urban agglomeration in the western provinces, and 'Blue-Green String' for the sinuous marshy zones planned as part of 'New Nature' in the same area.

• de Botton A. 1997. *How Proust Can Change Your Life*. Vintage Books, New York p. 89
• Broadbent G.1973. *Design in Architecture. Architecture and the Human Sciences*. John Wiley & Sons, London p. 329
• Jencks C. 1977. *The Language of Post-modern Architecture*. Academy Editions, London pp. 40 ff.
• Knox P.; Pink S. 2000. *Urban Social Geography*. Prentice Hall, Englewood Cliffs (fourth edition) pp. 7-8
• Lynch K.; Hack G. 1984. *Site Planning* (third edition). MIT Press, Cambridge p. 128
• Spirn A. 1998. *The Language of Landscape*. Yale University Press, New Haven pp.19-20
• Schacter D.L. 1996. *Searching for Memory: the Brain, the Mind, and the Past*. Basic Books, London
• Turner T. 1996. 'Metaphorical Plans'. In: *City as Landscape. A Post-modern View of Design and Planning*. E&F Spon, London pp.79-90.

Metamorphosis

see also > dynamics, transformation

' A striking alteration in appearance, character, or circumstances' (*Webster*).

Urban and rural areas in Western Europe have undergone a metamorphosis many times in history. Dimensions, scale and layout have changed. Urbanisation and infrastructure have generated new urban landscapes, expressing a new economic reality. In rural areas, developments in agricultural production have led to changes in the layout of the land and the construction of new farm buildings.

Comparison of recent topographic maps with their older counterparts shows the extent of these changes (Baart 2000). In the past the metamorphosis of a landscape – which was usually gradual – resulted predominantly from decisions taken by many individuals working with limited central coordination. Nowadays, landscape change usually results from conscious intervention that is based on top-down planning and results in short-term changes. In this case the word 'transformation' is more applicable.

• Baart T. (et al). 2000. *Atlas of Change. Rearranging the Netherlands*. NAi publishers, Rotterdam

Mimesis

see also > abstract, landscape, representation

'Imitation, mimicry' (*Webster*). 'The imitation or representation of the real world in art and literature' (*Oxford English Dictionary*).

It is also called the 'eye-witness principle' or the (correct) imitation of nature (Gombrich 1982). Early art theory pronounced art to be the imitation of reality. However, by regarding paintings as a form of imitation that could be substituted by mirrors, Socrates (470-399 B.C) robbed art of its prestige. In his view, the cabinet maker was a higher level of artist than the painter, because he created form on the basis of an idea (Baumeister 1999).

In 17th-century painting, Realism and Naturalism not only aimed to create an exact reproduction of nature, they also attempted to re-present, to re-create an image held by the painter of reality. Mimesis is therefore more than mere copying. Contemporary abstract art has turned away from any likeness of reality; in contrast, magic realism evokes an atmosphere of doom, timelessness and decadence portrayed in realistic images (van der Blom 1997).

Throughout the history of garden design, the imitation of – and reference to – nature has been an essential pursuit, but literal reproduction has normally been avoided. Japanese garden art, for instance, is characterised by an enigmatic mixture of symbolic reference and direct, small-scale imitation (Kuck 1968).

• Baumeister T. 1999. *De filosofie en de kunsten* (i.e. *Philosophy and the arts*). *Van Plato tot Beuys*. Damon Best pp.21-23
• van der Blom A. 1997. *Nederlandse Schilderkunst. Tussen detail en grandeur* (i.e. *Dutch painting between detail and grandeur*). Atrium, Alphen aan de Rijn p. 229
• Gombrich E.H. 1982. *The Image and the Eye. Further Studies in the Psychology of Pictorial Representation*. Phaidon, Oxford pp. 252-254
• Kuck L. 1968 *The World of the Japanese Garden*. Walker Weatherhill, New York p. 226

The representation of a mountain, cascade and river in the garden of Daisen-in shrine in Kyoto, Japan.

Minimalism

see also > functionalism, modernism

A minimum is 'the least quantity or value possible or permissible'(*Webster*).

A minimalist design is characterised by the least possible complexity and reference. While, as a design style, it is related to the analytical approach taken in Modernism, it also has analogies with Classicism. Its forms are associated with purity, clarity, cleanliness, muted colours and an absence of clutter. References and symbolism are omitted, and natural materials moulded into geometric forms, thereby lending a space or object a sense of uniqueness. Directed inwards, it has sculptural elements of simple form, which usually bears little relation to their environment.

The roots of minimalism can also be found in oriental gardens with their limited range of plant materials (Bradley-Hall 1999). The style is now found in many Modernist designs, such as those by Dutch landscape architects Hans Warnau, (1922-1995) and Hein Otto (1916-1994) (Pohl 1983), and the American Peter Walker (Walker 1997; Weilacher 1996). Though these designers

attempt to 'tell a story with a minimum number of words', one might wonder whether this is not an ideal that leads to a denial of the roots of landscape architecture (Tischer 2000).

In Minimalist land art, the aim is to create three-dimensional objects that, when viewed

Makuhari Office Building, IBM, Tokyo, Japan. Landscape architect: Peter Walker.

Source: Walker. P. 1997. Minimalist Gardens. Spacemaker Press Washington DC

Railway-yard planting at Meerssen, the Netherlands. Landscape architect: Hein Otto, 1965.

from close quarters, 'disseminate an inimitable form of communication'. Form is reduced to perfection. Examples of work by contemporary artists include the spiral jetty of Robert Smithson in Utah, Michael Heizer's land art in the desert of Arizona and the garden sculptures of Henri Olivier (Weiss 1998).

- Bradley-Hall C. 1999. *The Minimalist Garden*. Mitchell Beazley, London
- Pohl N. 1983. 'The rediscovery of clarity in Dutch landscape architecture'. In Garten und Landschaft Journal no. 5 pp. 398-405; no. 6 pp. 482-488; no. 7 pp. 553-558, Callwey, München
- Tischer S. 2000. 'When minimalism leads astray'. In: Topos, European Landscape Magazine, Callwey, München no. 33 pp. 68-72
- Vroom M.J. (ed.) 1990. ' Slobbengors sportsfields in Papendrecht'. In: *Outdoor Space*. Thoth publishers, Bussum pp. 118-122
- Walker. P. 1997. *Minimalist Gardens*. Spacemaker Press pp.1-9; 17-23
- Weilacher U. 1996. 'Pop, Baroque and Minimalism'. In: *Between Landscape Architecture and Land Art*. Birkhäuser, Basel pp. 205 ff.
- Weiss A. 1998. *Unnatural Horizons*. Princeton University Press pp. 37-140

Model

see also > analogy, design instruments, simulation

A model is 'a representation of relevant characteristics of a certain reality, and a way to express properties of an existing object or system ' (Broadbent 1973). It is also 'a representation in three dimensions, usually on a smaller scale, of a building device, structure or tract of land to illustrate some proposal (Goulty).

Models have various uses in planning and design. In architectural design, a drawing and a scale model visualise reality through analogies in form between representation and reality.

Design models also help test theories. There are four types of model (Rowe 1991):
· A descriptive model explores the why and how of a design. It is what Steinitz calls a 'representational model' (Steinitz 1990).
· A predictive model attempts to find out about future developments that may occur

in the area under study.
· An exploratory model looks for connections between the present and the future which cannot be found by logical reasoning. Instead, trial and error, testing and checking are used to explore reality. The planner/designer 'jumps' to conclusions (Kleefmann 1984).
· A planning model simulates alternative development strategies, testing them by means of plans or designs (including predictive models). It is related to – and may rely on – a scenario. Such models are rarely conceived on their own: in most cases, several are set up simultaneously for comparison and evaluation. For practical reasons, they are limited in number to three or four.

Alternative planning models are based on carefully considered alternative solutions to a planning problem. These help operationalise choices – for instance a cheap one versus an expensive one, or one that is adapted to environmental conditions versus one that is purely functional and self-contained. Though such models may be compared, with the favoured one being recommended for implementation, they are mostly used to clarify the consequences of various choices.

In the Netherlands, radical choices are difficult to agree on, which is why the final choice is usually a compromise between various alternatives. In planning jargon this is called 'synthesis-modelling' (Vroom 1973). 'Everybody in Holland knows this game. Civil servants make extreme proposals and hastily withdraw them after everybody has reacted with indignation. In the next phase, new versions of the same thing come up that somehow meet the objections raised, together with a series of other alternatives. This is the basic model' (Pley 1999). This statement has plenty of illustrations, especially in the seemingly endless procedures involved in the planning of motorways and railways.

In landscape ecology, a model is a databank, a systematically ordered set of data that serves as a basis for predicting the effects of interventions in a landscape. There are

203

204

The five models in the 1971 Volthe de Lutte study:
1. Agriculture as the primary function. Conditions for agricultural production are optimised as far as circumstances permit. A certain amount of space is reserved for nature areas and outdoor recreation.
2. Nature conservation as the primary goal. Large areas are set aside for nature development.
3. Forestry as the primary function. Agricultural land is converted to woodland. The conservation of a few farming units helps to maintain some spatial diversity, and also supports nature conservation and outdoor recreation.
4. Outdoor recreation as the primary function. A number of bungalows and facilities for day-visitors are located in a scenic environment in which nature areas and woodlands are interspersed between farming units.
5. The synthesis model. In the Netherlands, making clear decisions is always difficult in the public domain, and there is always a search for compromise. In this case, a plan without much quality kept everybody happy.

Source: Bijkerk C. (et al). 1971. Landinrichting Volthe de Lutte. Verkenning – analyse – modellen. Studiegroep Volthe de Lutte. Landbouw Hogeschool Wageningen. pp. 76-90. 228

several types of model: expert systems, statistical models, simulation models and support systems for decision-making processes (Knaapen 1999).

• Broadbent G. 1973. *Design in Architecture*. John Wiley & Sons, New York pp. 79 e.v.
• Kleefmann 1984. *Planning als zoekinstrument* (i.e. *Planning as an exploratory instrument*). VUGA The Hague, pp. 106-109
• Knaapen J. 1999. 'Landschapsecologische modellen: instrumentarium' (i.e Landscape ecological models; the instruments). In: van Dorp D. (ed). *Landschapsecologie*. Boom, Meppel pp. 183 ff.
• Pley H. 1999. 'De ware kunst van het Nederlandisme' (i.e. The true art of Dutchness). In: *Tegen de Barbarij*. Prometheus, Amsterdam p.147
• Rowe P.G. 1991. *Design Thinking*. MIT Press, Cambridge pp. 163 ff.
• Steinitz C. 1990. 'A framework for theory applicable to the education of landscape architects (and other environmental professionals)'. In: Landscape Journal. The University of Wisconsin Press, Urbana, Illinois vol. 11 no. 1 pp. 136-143
• Vroom M.J. 1973. 'Volthe de Lutte: a systematic approach to land planning in scenic rural areas in the Netherlands'. In: Lovejoy D. (ed). *Land Use and Landscape Planning*. Leonard Hill Books, Aylesbury, Nottinghamshire

Modernism

see also > Functionalism, Minimalism, Postmodernism

'The theory and practices of modern art; an intentional break with the past and a search for new expression' (*Webster*). The concept of 'modern' ranges from 'contemporary' to 'new'. One modernises buildings, tools, and even society – and this helps improve things (Williams 1983).

Modernism represents a belief in the permanent progress of society in terms of knowledge and of social and moral values. It is the radicalised consciousness of modernity. It lives on in the realisation of a rupture with the past, with tradition and with close-knit communities. Reason is used to make the future a malleable one. 'Modernists [...] are at once at home in this world and at odds with it' (Berman 1992). In the cultural sphere, vertical differentiations may develop, such as between culture and daily life, between high and low culture, between scholarly and auratic art and popular pleasures, and between elite and mass forms of consumption (Urry 2002).

In architecture and painting, Modernism dates back to the 1920s, and the pioneering work of the Bauhaus in Germany and De Stijl in the Netherlands (Peter 1994). After the Second World War, the influence of Modernism on architecture and landscape architecture became dominant worldwide, emerging as a reaction to – and rebellion against – the dominance of academism and eclecticism in architecture, and Romanticism in landscape architecture. A search for 'authentic' form commenced (Colquhoun 1989).

Architect Le Corbusier (1887-1965) proposed to abolish the individuality of dwellings and, with the aid of new building techniques, to create a new form of housing, the so-called 'machines for living' (Le Corbusier 1959; Le Corbusier 1968). Earlier in the 20th century Mies van der Rohe (1886-1969) applied simple geometric form, fully exposed construction materials and large multifunctional spaces in his German pavilion for the World Exposition in Barcelona in 1929. Philip Johnson (1906-2003) applied the same principles in his own house in New Canaan, Connecticut during the 1950s (Luning Prak 1968). Walls no longer enclosed spaces, but were used as free-standing elements, dividing and articulating an open plan.

Modernism is also renowned for its design discipline, purity of lines, and clarity of form – all of which required a strong design talent.

After the Congrès Internationale d'Architecture Moderne (CIAM) Congress of 1926, the philosophy of urban design changed radically. A new model of urban development was launched that introduced a strict separation of functions, such as housing, traffic, industry and outdoor recreation. The interpenetration of urban areas and surrounding rural 'green' areas was also proposed. The concept of garden cities was expanded (Benevolo 1980).

The movement was strengthened not only by rational and stylistic considerations, but also by social ideals. Poor housing conditions and high mortality rates in industrial cities called for a different way of building – one with more light and air, and with better

Architect Philip Johnson's private house in New Canaan, Connecticut, USA. Built in the 1950s.

Mies van der Rohe's Barcelona Pavilion of 1929.
Photo: Harry Harsema

provisions for hygiene. Housing areas were thus laid out with multiple-storey apartment buildings set in public and 'communal' open space (Benevolo 1980). The closed housing block was replaced by open blocks, which from then on were designed as three-dimensional compositions (Galindo 2002).

As an integral part of the planning process, the British planner Sir Patrick Geddes (1854-1932) introduced the regional survey. The natural foundation of the landscape thereby became the basis for planning (Cook 1969; Geddes 1915). During the second half of the 20th century, planning teams were joined by the new disciplines of ecology and landscape ecology (McHarg 1998).

Modern landscape architecture was related to modern architecture and town planning. Historical styles were abandoned, the juxtaposition of the formal and the romantic layout discarded. New space concepts were developed, aiming for a 'fresh, original, contemporary approach to design problems'

(Walker 1994).

In Dutch landscape architecture, Modernism was also rooted in a social (and socialist) revival. Rather than laying out gardens for the affluent, the ideal became one of working on low-cost housing schemes in collaboration with urban designers. The founding of a professional organisation, the Dutch Association for Garden and Landscape Architecture in 1922, helped promote professional practice (Boer 1990)

In landscape design, typical elements of Romantic design – spectacular scenes, intricate settings, exuberant symbolism and the illusion of wide expanses – were all discarded. In contrast with the ideals of architects such as Le Corbusier, who wanted people to live in high-rise buildings in the midst of an undisturbed Arcadian scenery, the landscape architect emphasised simplicity, functionality and rectilinearity (Thompson 1999). Orientation in a well-structured space was considered important.

207

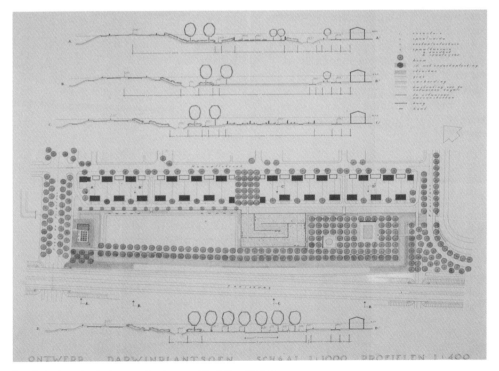

Darwinplantsoen Amsterdam, 1952. Landscape architect: Hans Warnau.

Meaning should not 'transcend the characteristics of place or context' (Treib 1993).

The designer of an outdoor space was concerned primarily with the composition of horizontal and vertical planes (Hauxner 2003). Symbolic content was deemed to be intrinsic to the forms of trees, plants, soils and building materials: 'plants speak for themselves'. References should be functional.

Whereas the monotony of its collective buildings caused modern architecture to lose its appeal, modern landscape architecture survived. This was due largely to the nature of its assignment and its material, but also to the fact that the discipline stuck to its own traditions.

The most important characteristics of the modern style in landscape architecture can be listed as follows (Baljon 1992):

In structural terms: Zoning by means of articulation and connection; disordered symmetry; a loose geometry; juxtaposition between building and surroundings.

In terms of spatial experience: Form connected with object; linkage of spaces; simultaneous experiences; a clear order.

In terms of reference: Pragmatism; efficiency; a lack of emotion; programmed facilities.

In terms of design tools: Avenues, loose groups of trees and shrubs, watercourses; play ponds, playing fields, sightlines, inclines, flower gardens; structures and constructions as ornaments.

• Baljon L. 1992. *Designing parks*. Architectura & Natura Press,. Amsterdam pp. 158-159
• Benevolo L. 1980. 'The modern city'. In: *The History of the City*. Scolar Press, London pp. 841-896
• Berman M. 1992. 'Why modernism still matters'. In: Lash S.; Friedman J. (ed). *Modernity & Identity*. Blackwell Publishers, Oxford pp. 33-57
• Boer W. 1990. 'Changing Ideals in Urban Landscape Architecture in the Netherlands'. In: Vroom M.J.; Meeus J.H.A. *Learning from Rotterdam*. Mansell/Nicholls, New York pp. 44-68
• Colquehoun A. 1989. *Modernity and the Classical Tradition*. MIT Press, Cambridge pp. 57-89
• Cook T.S. 1969. *City Planning Theory*. Philosophical Library, New York pp. 18-19
• Le Corbusier. 1959. *L'urbanisme des trois établissements humains*. Cahiers Forces Vives. Editions de Minuit, Paris
• Le Corbusier. 1968. *Towards a New Architecture*. Dover

publications, London
• Galindo J.; Sabaté J. 2002. 'The evolution of an open urban design method'. In: Steenbergen C. (et al) (ed). *Architectural Design and Composition*. Thoth publishers, Bussum pp. 146-155
• Geddes P. 1915. *Cities in Evolution*. Oxford University Press, New York (1940)
• Hauxner M. 2003. *Open to the Sky. The second phase of the modern breakthrough 1950-1970*. The Danish Architectural Press. Copenhagen
• Luning Prak N. 1968. *The language of architecture*. Mouton. Nijmegen pp. 162-169
• McHarg I., Steiner F.L. 1998. *To Heal the Earth. Selected Writings of Ian L.McHarg*. Island Press, Washington D.C. pp. 242-278
• Peter J. 1994. *The Oral History of Modern Architecture*. Abrams, New York
• Thompson I. 1999. 'The impact of Modernism on landscape architecture'. In: *Ecology, Community and Delight*. Spon, London pp. 96-100
• Treib M. 1993. 'Axioms for a modern landscape architecture'. In: Treib M. (ed). *Modern Landscape Architecture: A Critical Review*. MIT Press, Cambridge pp. 36-67
• Urry J. 2002. *The Tourist Gaze* (second edition). Sage Publications pp. 75-77
• Walker P.; Simo M. 1994. 'The Legacy of Landscape Architecture: Art or Social Service?'. In: *The search for Modernism in the American Landscape. Invisible Gardens*. The MIT Press, Cambridge pp. 2 ff.
• Williams R. 1983. 'Modern'. In: *Keywords. A Vocabulary of Culture and Society*. Fontana Books, London. pp. 208-209

Module

see also > matrix, grid

A standard or unit of measurement (*Webster*). [A course of study] composed of a number of several independent units from which students may select a certain number (*Oxford Advanced*).

A module may also be a standardised element or object that is produced separately and attached to others so as to form a building or a piece of furniture. The geometric scheme of the Renaissance garden at Villa Medici in Florence consists of a number of squares whose sizes are multiples of the squares inside the building. These are the modules for the layout (Steenbergen 1990). In this case module and matrix are synonymous.

The layout of monofunctional sites is often based on a repetition or addition of a specific module: in a cemetery, this module is the grave; in a car park, it is the car; in sports grounds the football field, tennis court, etc.

In many contemporary gardens, pavement

patterns are based on modules that help unify space. In Dutch city pavements, standard concrete tiles (30x30 cms) influence the scale of streetscape and even function as national emblems, albeit in a modest way. As they are laid in a sand bed and can quickly be lifted and replaced by hand, they are also very practical.

A modulor is the systematic division of the human form into golden section proportions, as devised by the architect Le Corbusier (Le Corbusier 1945). He assumed the height of a man to be 6 feet or 1.829 metres, a number he divided in accordance with the golden section so that the larger of the two parts is 1.130 metre, corresponding to the height of the navel. This distance can be divided to match other parts of the human frame. This series of proportions was the basis of many dimensions in Le Corbusier's building designs (Goulty).

• Le Corbusier. 1945. *Le Modulor : essai sur une mesure harmonique a l'échelle humanine applicable universellement a l'architecture et a la mecanique l'Architecture d'Aujour'hui.* Boulogne
• Steenbergen C. 1990. 'Villa Medici en de integrazione scenica'.

In: *De Stap over de Horizon.* PhD thesis, Delft Technical University pp. 29-41

Monument, Monumental

Something that serves as a memorial, especially a building, stone or statue erected in memory of a person or event. 2.) A natural feature or historic site set aside and maintained by the government as public property (*Webster*).

A historic estate is mostly an architectural monument, while older or abandoned factories may be listed as industrial monuments. Similarly, geomorphological features may be declared geological monuments, and abandoned agricultural land a nature monument.

All such objects have existed for a long time, and were taken for granted until, in the 20th century, society became conscious of their value and the authorities declared them to be monuments (van Voorden 2002). Listed monuments in the Netherlands are protected by law, and national budgets guarantee conservation and adequate maintenance.

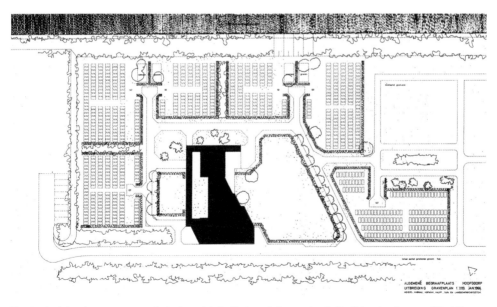

The standard size of a grave serves as the basic module for the layout of a cemetery in Hoofddorp. Landscape architect: Hans Warnau 1960.

Source: Vroom M.J. (ed). 1992. Outdoor Space. Thoth, Bussum

Monumental buildings are meant to impress. The Krupp
family's Villa Hügel at Baldeney, Germany.

210

In the Netherlands, monumentality is usually of modest
proportions. Front door of Casteelse Poort Museum,
Wageningen.

Memorials are a special type of monument,
designed and carefully located to
commemorate an important past event, and
thereby to preserve it in the collective
memory. They include war memorials and
objects commemorating special events
(Wasserman 2002).

Monumental buildings or outdoor spaces
are usually large and imposing dimensions
that simultaneously refer to the past.
However, some contemporary urban quarters
whose layout is monumental make no such
reference. For instance, they may consist of
large scale building blocks in a conspicuous
geometric form, such as the Antigone
quarter in Montpellier, France, designed by
the Spanish architect Ricardo Boffil (1939-
present)

Monumental historic gardens and parks are
laid out in straight lines and geometric
forms, effectively making grand gestures that
express wealth and power. The dimensions of
their spaces exceed those in the everyday
environment. Unity and stability in the
overall form allow for flexible detailing. Key
words are rigidity, clarity, transparency and
directedness.

• van Voorden F. 2002. 'Reconstruction of History; On the
  meaning of monuments'. In: Steenbergen C. (et al) (ed).
  Architectural Design and Composition. Thoth publishers,
  Bussum pp.130-145
• Wasserman J. 2002. 'Memory embedded'. In: Landscape
  Journal, The University of Wisconsin Press 21: 1-02

Mosaic
see also > pattern

As the borders of landscape units are often
vague, overlapping, or layered, landscape
patterns are not always clearly visible. In
many cases, landscapes can therefore better
be described in terms of networks and
mosaics. Meandering and branching systems
cut through and separate land surfaces, and
thereby form mosaics. These systems exist at
various levels of scale, from microscopic to
world-wide. They are created by the existence
of differences in physical conditions and also
the occurrence of energy currents. They are
heterogeneous in a spatial, structural and a

A mosaic of land patterns. North-eastern Canada from the air.

temporal sense (Bell 1999). In his book *Land Mosaics* ecologist Richard Forman describes the characteristic forms of borders between mosaics in nature (Forman 1995).

• Bell S. 1999. 'Mosaic landscapes'. In: *Landscape, Pattern Perception and Process*. Spon pp.30-34
• Forman R.T.T. 1995. *Land Mosaics*. Cambridge University Press. pp. 3-7

Motive
see > theme

Multiple use
see also > function, functionalism, layer, reconstruction

Multiple means 'containing, involving or consisting of more than one' (*Webster*).

One practical means of saving precious open space is by combining different types of land-use in one place or area. This can be achieved by alternative uses over time, or by permanently mixing a number of simultaneous uses. Such multiple use means

that, over time, the same piece of land is used more intensively – not the same thing as *intensive* use, which results from increasing density in the use of space.

Multiple use is thus a form of synergy, i.e. 'the interaction of two or more organisations, substances or other agents to produce a combined effect greater than the sum of their separate effects' (*Oxford English Dictionary*). It is a means to achieve higher environmental quality by providing added value vis-à-vis a 'normal' type of land use (Duineveld 2002).

In practical terms, multiple use may consist of re-allocating agricultural land in order to reserve space for natural process and outdoor recreation. In urban areas, parts of sports fields and cemeteries may be opened to the public as promenades. Car parks may be arranged in such a way that, after office hours, they are available for sports and play. An ancient example is found in the Ponte Vecchio in Forence: dating from 1345, this combines a river bridge with housing. So far, successful attempts to copy this principle have been rare (Janssen 2000).

Multiple land-use in a layered city: Tokyo.

Source: Blauwe Kamer. Magazine for Landscape and Urban Environment. Stichting Lijn in Landschap, Wageningen. August 2005 p. 28

An example from the Middle Ages: the Ponte Vecchio in Florence Italy with its houses and shops.

Multiple use can also be promoted by building in three dimensions. City centres in both North America and Western Europe have been constructed in layers, where not only traffic and parking facilities are placed underground, but also public squares (Bacon 1974).

- Bacon E. 1974. 'Putting ideas to work'. In: *Design of Cities*. Thames & Hudson, London pp. 264 ff.
- Duineveld M.; Lengkeek J. 2002. *Het beleefde land. Over beleving en meervoudig ruimtegebruik* (i.e. *The perceived land. On experience and multiple use*). Leerstoelgroep ruimtelijke analyse Wageningen University
- Jansen E.; Südmeier I. (ed). 2000. *Het gelaagde landschap. Meervoudig ruimtegebruik in perspectief* (i.e. *The layered landscape. Multiple use in perspective*). Uitgeverij Expertisenetwerk Meervoudig Ruimtegebruik, Utrecht

Mysticism

'The experience of mystical union or direct communion with ultimate reality. Vague guessing or speculation' (*Webster*).

The need for a mystique experience was felt strongly in the Romantic Age, whose gardens contained scenes that would evoke such feelings (Hunt 1975). Also dating from this period is the notion of 'intricacy' – that which is 'complex and enigmatic'.

In the rational world of the 20th century, the idea of mysticism became suspect and was therefore ignored. However, it never disappeared entirely: though Modernism abolished symbolism and ambiguity in theory, it never quite did so in practice. While the Dutch architectural movement De Stijl claimed to have generated a new and clear language, 'pointing the way towards an objective, general and serviceable language in plastic art' (Jaffé 1956), the writings of painter Mondrian (1872-1944) and architect van Doesburg (1883-1931) are particularly mystifying (Mondriaan 1956) (see *Constructivism*).

Mystical elements are evident in computer-generated designs by Postmodern architects such as Frank Gehry, visitors to such buildings often having to divine the what and why of their form.

- Hunt J.D. 1975. 'Joseph Addison'. In: *The Genius of the Place*. Paul

Unio Mystica by Johfra.
Source: Verkerke poster

213

Elek, London p. 138
- Jaffé H. 1956. *De Stijl 1917-1931 The Dutch contribution to modern art*. Meulenhoff publishers, Amsterdam p.8
- Mondriaan P. 1956. 'New art – new life'. In: Jaffé H.. 1956. *De Stijl 1917-1931 The Dutch contribution to modern art*. Meulenhoff Amsterdam pp. 211 ff.

Myth, Mythology

From the Greek *mythos*, i.e. a fable, story or tale; later given the meaning of 'what could not really exist or have happened' (Williams 1985).

There are two types of myth. The first is 'a usually legendary narrative that presents parts of the beliefs of a people, or explains a practice, belief or natural phenomenon'.

While myths are connected with religious images and rites, such as the Celtic ceremonies of the Druids, they are also expressed in landscape form and natural processes. Egyptian myths such as those of Isis and Osiris explain the fertility of river Nile. Greek myths and sagas that recounted the adventures of gods and heroes helped explain the relationships between the causes and effects of natural phenomena, which could not be clarified otherwise. Mountains and pyramids connected heaven and earth. 'Myth stood for history, a living collective reality, which could not be proved by rational means' (Weilacher 1996).

Although landscape was 'de-mythologised' at the beginning of the Enlightenment, Italian Renaissance gardens still contained many objects and elements of mythical origin, such as Bacchus and Hercules, and nymphs and dragons (Barker 1976; Jellicoe 1975; Schama 1995). The pastoral images in 18th-century English landscape gardens also contained mythical representations (Rowe 1991). The symbolic meaning of trees is known in all cultures and in the oldest myths; it was only during the 19th century that everything contrary to reality came to be called a myth.

214

The second type of myth is 'a false or unsupported belief' (*Webster*); a 'thing, person etc that is imaginary, fictitious or impossible: the myth of racial superiority, of a classless society of human perfectibility'(*Oxford English Dictionary*).

In Western cultures there is a powerful tendency to associate a country's image with the past, when – or so it is invariably pronounced – things were better than they are now. In the contemporary debate on environmental quality, one myth may in fact oppose another: that of technology as the solution to all problems versus the Arcadian myth of Gaia as Mother Earth (Pepper 1996).

• Barker M. (ed). 1976 *Pears Encyclopaedia of Myths and Legends*. Book Club Associates, London
• Jellicoe G. & S. 1975. *The Landscape of Man*. Thames and Hudson, London
• Pepper D. 1996. *Modern Environmentalism. An Introduction*. Routledge, London pp. 202-205
• Rowe G.P. 1991. 'Myths and Masks'. In: *Making a Middle Landscape*. MIT Press, Cambridge pp. 217 ff.
• Schama S. 1995. 'The Flow of Myth'. In: *Landscape and Memory*. Harper Collins, London pp.245 ff.
• Weilacher U. 1996. 'The power of myth'. In: *Between Landscape Architecture and Land Art*. Birkhäuser, Basel pp. 35-36
• Williams R. 1985. *Keywords. A Vocabulary of Culture and Society*. Fontana Paperbacks p. 210

Narrative

see > legibility

Nature

see also > aesthetics, ecology, ecocentrism, landscape, myth, Romantic, value, wilderness

'The phenomena of the physical world collectively, including plants, animals, the landscape and other features and products of the earth, as opposed to humans or human creations' (*Webster*).

The word nature comes from the Latin *natura*. In its earliest sense it was the essential character or quality of something; later, it became the constitution of the world (Williams 1986).

The history of the relationship between man and living nature is a complex one. During the Middle Ages, nature – the wilderness – was an indivisible whole, full of secrets and threats. It was both the object and the source of myths and sagas (Glacken 1967; Schouten 2005).

The Enlightenment brought a distinction between two natures: one that could be dispassionately dissected and 'measured' on the basis of scientific method, and another that was elevated and accessible. This marked a drastic change in man's attitudes (Lemaire 1970): from now on, nature was something he would both fear and love, while becoming ever more capable of manipulating it and subjecting it to his own purposes (Thomas 1983; Soper 1995). During the Romantic Age, 'elevated' nature was considered to be of great beauty, superior to human artefacts: it was in natural beauty that ethical and aesthetic values coincided, resulting in the sublime (Burke 1756).

While a culture constructs its own world by means of concepts, the concept of nature is also a social construct. In Western Europe, it has come to denote a type of place, whereas in other cultures it is – or was – rather a force, a primeval chaos (van Assche 2004). Nature as a place is experienced most of all when its counterpart is also present. The Dutch poet Gerrit Komrij puts it this way: 'No garden is possible without nature, and no nature without a garden'.

Since World War Two, attitudes have gradually changed, and man's primacy over nature has become a subject for debate (see *Ecocentrism*). Until the middle of the 20th century, the assumption that living nature could be neglected or even suppressed – 'derelict' or 'wild' land – was evident in many regional planning projects. In this period, many natural phenomena were lost – victims of ignorance and indifference. In the second half of the 20th century, attitudes began to change, with an increasing aversion to technology and urbanisation, and a growing preference for natural phenomena. This was the effect of 'a situation in which, in the eyes of many, culture – in the sense of cultivating nature – was accompanied by too many negative effects' (Lemaire 1970). Nature was re-discovered or even re-invented (Macnaughten 1998). Nowadays, while society holds various images of nature, there is a broad consensus on the need to protect, conserve or even to develop it.

Popular conceptions of nature may eventually produce a degraded definition whereby nature is 'everything that contains

Nature for the connoisseur: roadside vegetation in a Dutch nature area.

216

Nature to the Dutch urban dweller : a cow in a meadow standing near a ditch.

chlorophyll, is not made of brick and is free of motorised vehicles' (Ibelings 1999). A very different definition is the scientific one: 'all that orders and maintains itself, whether or not in connection with human activities, but never according to human objectives' (Schroevers 1980). Nature conservancy and management policies, however, are based on very human goals. In the Netherlands, for example, 'real' or 'authentic' nature no longer exists, except in the marine estuary along the Dutch coast, or in spontaneous vegetation along roadside verges and the edges of ditches.

If confusion is created by the contrasting definitions of nature, ecologists attempt to avoid it by introducing the need for bio-diversity. But in a densely populated country such as the Netherlands it is difficult to say how much bio-diversity is required – a dilemma that is apparent in the wide range of views on the 'why' and 'how' of nature conservation.

In gardens and parks, images of nature have been abundant throughout history, sometimes in the overall concept, and sometimes in special 'wilderness' features, such as the *boschi* of gardens of the Italian Renaissance (van der Ree 1992). Such images may variously serve as sources of inspiration, as examples, or as building material, but they are always altered, 'cultivated', symbolic, perfected. In different ways, such transformation has occurred throughout

217

New man-made nature at Blaauwe Kamer, river Rhine, the Netherlands.

successive periods in history (Jellicoe 1975).

Recent publications claim that the representation of nature in outdoor environments should be expanded to include the discoveries made in the natural sciences in the 20th and 21st centuries. As Jencks' demonstrates in Portrack, his garden in Scotland, colliding waves, atomic particles, fractals and DNA molecules can be represented in modelled groundform, and by sculptural elements and patterns (Jencks 2003).

• van Assche K. 2004. *Signs in time*. PhD thesis, Wageningen University pp. 98 ff.
• Burke E. 1756. *A philosophical Inquiry into the Origins of our Ideas of the Sublime and the Beautiful*. Oxford 1990
• Glacken C.J. 1967. *Traces on the Rhodian Shore. Nature and Culture in Western Thought from Ancient Times to the End of the Eighteenth Century*. University of California Press, Berkeley
• Ibelings H. 1999. 'Autolandschap'. In: Kolen (et al) (ed). *Landschap in meervoud*. (i.e. *plural landscapes*). Jan van Arkel, Utrecht pp. 49-56
• Jellicoe G. & S. 1975. *The Landscape of Man*. Thames and Hudson, London.
• Jencks C. 2003. *The Garden of Cosmic Speculation*. Francis, London
• Lemaire T. 1970. *Filosofie van het landschap* (i.e. *Landscape philosophy*). Ambo, Amsterdam p. 38
• Macnaughten P.; Urry J. 1998. 'Inventing Nature'. In: *Contested Natures*. Sage Publications pp. 32 ff.
• van de Ree P. (et al).1992. *Italian Villas and Gardens*. Thoth, Bussum p.124
• Schouten M.G.C. 2005. *Spiegel van de natuur* (i.e. *Mirroring nature*). KNNV publishers, Utrecht pp. 96 ff.
• Schroevers P.J. 1980. *Landschapstaal* (i.e. *The language of landscape*). Pudoc, Wageningen p. 94
• Soper K. 1995. *What is Nature?* Blackwell, Oxford pp. 42 ff.
• Thomas K. 1983. *Man and the Natural World*. Pantheon Books, New York.
• Williams R. 1986. *Keywords: A Vocabulary of Culture and Society*. Fontana Paperback, London

Nature conservation and development

see also > ecological design, ecological networks, nature

In the Netherlands, a 'feeling for nature' manifested itself during the second half of the 19th century (Biese 1905). A pioneering advocate of the protection of nature was the writer and poet Frederik van Eeden (1860-1932). Eventually, in 1901, this led to the establishment of the State Forest Service, which was charged with the acquisition and management of nature areas at a national level. A private initiative also led to the founding of the Society for the Conservation of Nature Monuments in 1905. Among the founders was the renowned educator and naturalist Jac. P. Thijsse (1865-1945). This Society successfully acquired and managed a variety of nature areas throughout the Netherlands (Anonymous 1956).

Several decades later, however, it is still being debated what should be protected, and how protected areas should be managed – a matter in which there are various ideals and visions. Five such visions have been formulated by the Dutch National Council for Environmental and Nature Research. These have resulted in the following policies (van Amstel 1988):

The classical vision

Under this vision, priority is given to protecting, managing and restoring – wherever necessary – natural and landscape values in designated areas whose rich natural diversity was largely the product of primitive farming techniques. Still isolated from their wider surroundings, these areas are now managed by controlling the natural succession of vegetation types, mainly through mowing and the removal of all unwanted growth. The objective is to maintain a maximum variety of species inside these areas. Management is in the hands of private nature conservancy organisations (sometimes government sponsored) or government departments.

The nature development vision

Under this vision, there are four objectives: to foster bio-diversity, to achieve both self-regulation and authenticity in natural process, and also to achieve completeness in ecological communities.

As minimal human influence is a prime condition for naturalness, this requires the setting aside of large areas of valuable (or potentially valuable) land, which can then be 'developed' for conservation purposes. Importantly, there should be both a strict separation between inside and outside, stimulation of a diversity of species, and a spontaneous introduction (and re-introduction) of new species. Active maintenance is avoided as much as possible. In principle, this results in a visually complex environment, beauty being the result of a natural order and not of human intervention.

Examples of this type are found in parts of the National Ecological Network.

The functional vision

This vision promotes harmony between nature conservancy goals and human exploitation, with functional management types helping to sustain valuable systems. The intention is to keep nature in balance with agriculture and other types of land-use, the underlying objective being to stimulate multi-functionality so as to achieve a landscape that is both varied and attractive. Management is in the hands of farmers, volunteers and other interested parties.

The eco-philosophical vision

This vision holds that the relationship between man and nature that was lost in recent times must be repaired through the introduction of an alternative lifestyle. This is organised in small-scale communities that live in harmony with nature; Mother Nature will care for everything.

The sustainable-technology vision

Here it is believed that, if further degradation of nature and the environment is to be stopped, society as a whole must change. Further increases in production and consumption must be discouraged. Better environmental conditions will be created partly through innovation, technological renewal and the development of sustainable sources of energy. Similarly, opportunities for nature conservation and development will be created by both the interweaving and separation of types of land-use.

Inherent to the eco-philosophical and sustainable-technology visions is the view that social change is necessary.

A dominant role in Dutch Government physical planning policy is played by the conservation of nature. This is evident not only in the official Nature Policy Plan, but also in the layout of those parts of the national ecological network in which 'new nature' is created through the large-scale reconstruction of rural areas, a policy contested by critical outsiders as well as insiders (Van der Windt 1998).

The continuing discussion on the subject – not to mention the opposing views on the course that should be taken in nature conservation – is underlain by the absence of an all-encompassing theoretical basis. As paradigms in biological and ecological theory changed frequently throughout the 20th century, there are now various schools of thought, each producing divergent answers to questions on the factors that underlie diversity in plants and animals, on the prime importance of such diversity, and of the influence of human action upon it. The scientific basis underlying Dutch nature management policy is therefore unclear (de Jong 2002).

- Van Amstel A.R. 1988. *Vijf visies op natuurbehoud en natuurontwikkeling* (i.e. *Five visions on Nature conservation and -development*). Publicatie RMNO no. 30 Raad voor Natuur en milieuonderzoek, Rijswijk pp. 16-25
- Anonymous. 1956. *Vijftig Jaar Natuurbescherming in Nederland* (i.e. *Fifty years of Nature Conservation in the Netherlands*). Vereniging tot Behoud van Natuurmonumenten, Amsterdam
- Biese A. 1905 (reprint undated). *The Development of the Feeling for Nature. In the Middle Ages and Modern Times.* Burt Franklin, New York pp. 1 ff
- De Jong M.D.Th.M. 2002. *Scheidslijnen in het denken over natuurbeheer in Nederland.* (i.e. *Dividing lines between ways of thinking on nature conservation*). Doctoral thesis, Delft University Press.
- Metz T. 1998. *Nieuwe Natuur. Reportages over een veranderend landschap* (i.e. *New nature. Reports on a changing landscape*). Ambo, Amsterdam pp 9-31.
- de Visser R. 1997. *Het Landschap van de landinrichting* (i.e. *The landscape of land consolidation*). Blauwdruk, Wageningen pp. 27-28
- van der Windt H.; Feddes F. 1998. 'Natuur, stad en land' (i.e. Nature, city and rural land). In: *Oorden van Onthouding. Nieuwe natuur in verstedelijkend Nederland.* NAi uitgevers, Rotterdam pp. 25-37

219

Network

see also > access, ecological network, nature conservation, node

'An interconnected or interrelated chain,

group or system' (*Webster*).

One of the most fundamental human interventions in landscapes involves staking out areas – creating the borders, edges, and limits that define or separate them – and laying out connecting lines such as waterways and cable or pipeline networks. Between them, boundary lines and connecting lines constitute networks.

Besides ecological networks, physical planners also distinguish urban, infrastructural and information networks (Anonymous 1999). One aspect of a 'network society' is the so-called 'network-city'. The simultaneous result of economic globalisation and of the technological revolution from which information technology emerged (Castells 1996), this is an agglomeration of urban centres and nodes that constitutes a housing and labour market with a variable supply of housing, employment and services. The emergence of urban networks is connected with a continuing increase in the scale of housing and industrial areas, accompanied by social detachment and rootlessness. Thanks to recent communication technology, economic and social activities are no longer tied to particular areas.

220

• Anonymous. 1999. *Ruimtelijke Verkenningen* (i.e. *Explorations in space*). Rijksplanologische Dienst, Ministerie VROM, The Hague pp. 127-133
• Castells M. 1996. *The Rise of the Network Society*. Blackwell Publishers, Oxford

Node

see also > infrastructure, network, place

'A point in a network or diagram at which lines or pathways intersect or branch' (*Oxford Advanced Dictionary*).

Nodes in urban networks were first defined by Kevin Lynch (1960) as points where lines of infrastructure converge and where activities concentrate. They include traffic interchanges and transfer points for people or goods, and vary in scale and complexity – from bus and railway stations, through railway marshalling yards to sea ports and international airports. As well being points of

interchange, they contribute to the image of cities in which they are located. Rather than being a traveller's final destination, most serve as places of transit.

Multimodal transport and the integration of transport systems at different levels of scale require the planning of a hierarchic pattern of nodes. Their layout is determined mainly by technical criteria. Their size often makes it difficult to fit them into their environment.

As at the railway station of Meerssen in the Dutch province of Limburg, minor nodes can be made visible by planting trees and hedgerows that help to accentuate lines and create spaces (Vroom 1992/1). Similarly, at the motorway interchange at Vianen, the alignment of surrounding land patterns is continued within the interior space – part of an attempt to make the node a visible part of its environment (Vroom 1992/2). And to create unity in a fragmented collection of verges, cars parks, other traffic areas, and areas for plane spotters, the planting plan at Amsterdam airport provided for the large-scale planting of a single tree species (see *Continuity*) (Harsema 2000).

• Harsema H. (ed). 2000 '400,000 birches in a field of clover'. In: *Landscape architecture and town planning in the Netherlands 97-99*. Thoth publishers, Bussum pp.156-159
• Lynch K. 1960. *The Image of the City*. MIT Press, Cambridge pp.72-78
• Vroom M.J. (ed). 1992/1. 'Garden of Meersen railway station'. In: *Outdoor Space*. Thoth publishers, Bussum pp. 114-117
• Vroom M.J. (ed). 1992/2. 'Planting plan for motorway interchange at Vianen'. In: *Outdoor Space*. Thoth publishers, Bussum pp. 190-193

Order

see also > composition, design, geometry, orientation, perception, system

'The arrangement or disposition of people or things in relation to each other according to a particular sequence, pattern or method. A state in which everything is in its correct or appropriate place' (*Oxford English Dictionary*).

According to Plato (428-348 BC), order was synonymous with 'cosmos', and was in opposition to 'chaos', which implies the absence of order. Plato stated that artefacts were constructed to bring the order and coherence of things to light, and that architecture was the ultimate way in which universal order could be reflected.

In natural environments: 'an (animal) organism to survive must be equipped to solve two basic problems. It must be able to answer the questions "what" and "where". In other words it must find out what the objects in its environment mean to it, whether any are to be classified as potential sources of nourishment or of danger, and in either case it must take the appropriate action of location, pursuit or flight. These actions pre-suppose what in higher animals and in man has come to be known as a "cognitive map", a system of coordinates on which meaningful objects can be plotted' (Gombrich 1979).

As part of the perception process in man, the search for order interacts with order in the environment. Man-made landscapes are all designed by the ordering hand of man, unlike nature, whose order is more complex and often difficult to see, and where irregularity seems to predominate. 'So deeply engrained is our tendency to regard order as the mark of an ordering mind that we instinctively react with wonder whenever we perceive regularity in the natural world' (Gombrich 1979). Order provides clarity: 'symmetry, rhythm and sequential dimensions enable us to reduce the enormous amount of visual information presented by an architectonic object to a comprehensible size and complexity' (Dijkstra 2001).

How much visual order is optimal? Too much leads to monotony, and thus boredom.

In the realm of physics, disorder or entropy is the counterpart of order: the universe tends to move from an ordered state to a disorderly one. In pictorial art, the ordering hand of the artist seems to be in a constant battle with natural forces (Arnheim 1971).

Order and coherence

In every spatial and social system there are fluctuating sub-systems. Even in an landscape that *appears* to be orderly, internal processes create change and disorder. Order and chaos coexist everywhere (Prigogine 1984).

Together with chaos theory and other new insights into the natural sciences, changing concepts of the nature of the universe have brought about changes in architectural form. Eventually, these may also affect the paradigms of landscape architects (Jencks 1995; Koh 2005), though, to date, the aim of

A carefully composed transition from regularity to randomness:' 'Gravel Stones' by Georg Nees.

Source: Gombrich E.H. 1979. The Sense of Order. Cornell University Press Ithaca, New York p. 94

landscape architects – classical and modern alike – has been to create coherence and to reduce complexity to points, lines and planes (Motloch 2001).

Coherence is 'the situation in which – or the degree to which – different things (objects or spaces) are connected, hang together' (*van Dale*). The existence of coherence or wholeness in outdoor space means that parts of the whole are visibly related. Coherence is expressed in terms of articulation, connection, rhythm and continuity. As Dutch architect-town planner Granpré Molière (1883-1972) once stated, 'Urban design means creating coherence: between town and country, and culture and nature. It is the connection between the individual and society [and] between the past and the present' (Bosma 1993).

The creation of order and harmony within a single spatial composition involves linking the elements of a plan, and forming a whole in which all the requirements and preconditions are united (Baljon 1992; Weiss 1998). Harmony means 'a correct adaptation of the parts in a whole as well as of that whole in the character and conditions of a site and its owner' (Repton 1806).

Several design tools can be used to create order: axiality, regularity, hierarchy, symmetry, correct proportions, and the use of a dominant theme or element (Beune 1990; Leupen 1997).

The ordering of objects in an environment can also tell a story, as Dutch author Maarten 't Hart observes in his novel *Droomkoningin*: 'In the distance I saw black vertical poles tied together with ropes onto which pieces of cork had been threaded. Upon coming closer I realised they were fishing nets. I looked from pole to pole, following the lines, each binding its own ripple of moonlight. Now it is all visible, I thought, that whole order of rope and wood and interleaved moonlight, to tell us what life is like. Look, there is a pattern, an orderly arrangement; it has something to say' (p.178).

By analysing natural patterns, a landscape planner may attempt to superimpose order onto the landscape, or to reinforce any order that already exists there (Sijmons 1998).

• Arnheim R. 1971. *Entropy and Art. An Essay on Disorder and Order.* University of California Press, Berkeley.
• Baljon L. 1992. *Designing Parks.* Architectura & Natura, Amsterdam pp. 119-121
• Beune F.; Thus T. 1990. 'Fragmentation of Urban Open Space'. In: Vroom M.J.; Meeus J.H.A.. *Learning from Rotterdam.* Mansell, London pp. 106-122.
• Bosma K. 1993. *Ruimte voor een nieuwe tijd.* NAi publishers, Rotterdam p. 201
• Dijkstra T. 2001. *Architectonische kwaliteit.* 010 publishers, Rotterdam
• Gombrich E.H. 1979. 'Order and purpose in nature'. In: *The Sense of Order.* Cornell University Press, New York pp.1-16
• Jencks C. 1995. *The Architecture of the Jumping Universe.* Academy Editions, London
• Koh J. 2004. *Ecological Reasoning and Architectural Imagination.* Inaugural address. Wageningen University

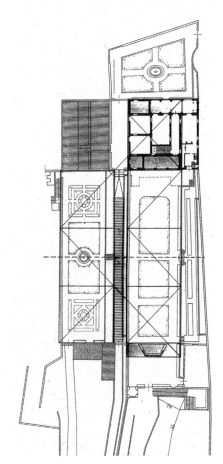

223

A geometric module serving as the basis for ordering the layout of Villa Medici in Fiesole Italy.

Source: Steenbergen C. 1990. *De stap over de horizon. Een ontleding van het formele ontwerp in de landschapsarchitectuur.* Dissertation Delft University of Technology

- Leupen B. (et al).1997. 'Order and composition'. In: *Design and Analysis*. Van Nostrand Reinhold, New York pp. 56-59
- Motloch J.L. 2001. 'Visual arts as ordering mechanism'. In: *Introduction to Landscape Design* (second edition). Wiley & Sons, New York pp. 134 ff.
- Prigogine I.; Stengers I. 1984. *Order out of Chaos*. Bantam Books, Toronto p. XV
- Repton H. 1806. *An enquiry into the changes of taste in landscape gardening to which are added some observations on theory and practice including a defence of the art*. J.Taylor, London (original edition)
- Sijmons D. (ed) 1998. *Landscape*. Architectura & Natura, Amsterdam
- Weiss A. 1998. 'Syncretism and style'. In: *Unnatural Horizons*. Princeton Architectural Press, New York pp. 9 ff.

between the two (Lynch 1971; Simonds 1997).

- Baljon L. 1992. *Designing Parks*. Architecture & Natura, Amsterdam p. 66
- Hidding M.C. 1997. *Planning voor stad en land* (i.e. *Planning for town and countryside*). Coutinho, Bussum pp. 39 ff.
- Kleefmann F. 1984. *Planning als zoekinstrument* (i.e. *Planning as a search tool*). VUGA, The Hague
- Lynch K. 1971. 'Organising Place and Action'. In: *Site Planning* (second edition). MIT Press, Cambridge pp. 25-44
- McHarg I. 1969. *Design with Nature*. Natural History Press, New York p. 144
- Simonds J.O. 1997. *Landscape Architecture. A Manual of Site Planning and Design. Third Edition*. McGraw-Hill, New York

Organisation

see also > access, design, determinism, function, matrix, order, structure

'The structure and arrangement of related and connected items (the spatial organisation of [...])' (*Oxford English Dictionary*).

Spatial organisation represents a complex totality of interrelated activities and uses, clustered into social, natural, technical and plastic and expressive entities. Such organisation can be defined as the so-called 'space-society system' (Kleefmann 1984; Hidding 1997). 'Organised space' is analogous to 'structured space', while 'ordered space' is normally a more static concept.

Rather than ordering space, landscape planning focuses primarily on guiding and organising processes, while in a site-planning process, activities are simultaneously organised and ordered, and types of land-use are distributed, combined and connected (Baljon 1992). The organisation of a layout begins with the brief in which types of land-use are described and quantified. The relationships between activities and terrain conditions are made visible in a matrix (McHarg 1969).

In principle, a plan can either be organised deterministically (where the 'what', 'how' and 'where' are determined by the site conditions) or functionally (where precedence is taken by the efficiency of activities or functional use). Most site-planning processes, however, seek a balance

Orientation *(in space and time)*

see also > composition, dynamic, perception, landmark, order, structure, vista

'The determination of the relative position of something or someone. In zoology: an animal's change of position in response to an external stimulus, especially with respect to compass direction' (*Oxford English Dictionary*).

All human beings want to know where they are – in space and time, in the fields of personal relationships and of nature, in the world of how things operate, and in the world of subtle intimations and emotions (Boulding 1969). 'Man's feeling about being properly oriented in space runs deep. Such knowledge is ultimately linked to survival and sanity. To be disoriented in space is to be psychotic' (Hall 1970).

To landscape architects, two types of spatial orientation are important.

The first is the observer's reaction to an environment: how he finds his bearings and orients himself. The second involves the position in space of an object (such as a building) – thus how it is oriented (to a street, a view, an open space).

With respect to the first type – the observer's reaction – an observer wants to know where he is, and how far he needs to go to his destination. Such spatial orientation requires a certain amount of order, including social order (see *Order*).

Various types of design tool, such as axis, sightlines and hierarchical path systems, help create the conditions for this. To the same end, the American architect Kevin Lynch introduced notions such as 'paths, nodes, edges, landmarks and districts', all elements in the environment that determine the image of a city and help analysing spatial conditions (Lynch 1960).

Similarly, orientation in time means not only that we know what to expect, but also that we remember what has happened before. Certainty and security in human existence are provided by an environment in which there is a visible relationship between the past, present and future. 'Change and recurrence are the sense of being alive – things gone by, death to come, and present awareness' (Lynch 1972). This explains the importance we attach to our heritage landscapes, which 'contain the debris and cradle the memory of innumerable past events' (Lowenthal 1985).

While most landscapes in the Netherlands contain visible traces from the past (see *Palimpsest*), 20th-century polders lack such a history, and thus represent a break with the past. Yet here, too, temporal and spatial orientation are possible. The layout of these polders, their overall scale, and the character of the buildings all point towards a unified concept, a central planning system – signs enough that these polders are part of a Dutch tradition (van der Wal 1997). Crops, roadside planting, paving materials, lamp-

posts, letterboxes and traffic signs are the same as in the rest of the country. The breach is not total after all.

With respect to the second type of spatial orientation, the orientation of a building means that it 'faces' a compass direction, a view, another building, a public square, or a landmark (Arnheim 1969; Lynch 1984). The front of a building, the most important side, is more usually oriented towards something than the rear is. A special historic example of a building that is oriented in four directions – 'enjoying beautiful views on every side' – is Palladio's Villa Rotunda in Vicenza, which dates from 1569 (Rogers 2001; Steenbergen 1996).

- Arnheim R. 1969. 'Form'. In: *Art and Visual Perception*. Faber Editions, London pp. 82 ff.
- Boulding K.E. 1969. *The Image*. Ann Arbor Paperbacks University of Michigan Press pp. 3-18
- Canter D. 1977. *The Psychology of Space*. The Architectural Press, London pp. 49-79.
- Gombrich E.H. 1979. *The Sense of Order*. Cornell University Press, Ithaca, New York pp. 1-3.
- Hall E.T. 1970. 'The anthropology of space: an organising model'. In: Proshanksy H.M. (et al). *Environmental Psychology. Man and his Physical Setting*. Holt Rinehart and Winston, New York p. 17
- Lowenthal D. 1985. *The Past is a Foreign Country*. Cambridge University Press
- Lynch K. 1960. *The Image of the City*. MIT Press Cambridge
- Lynch K. 1972. *What Time is this Place?* MIT Press Cambridge
- Lynch K.; Hack G. 1984. *Site Planning*. MIT Press Cambridge pp. 58-59; 153-192

225

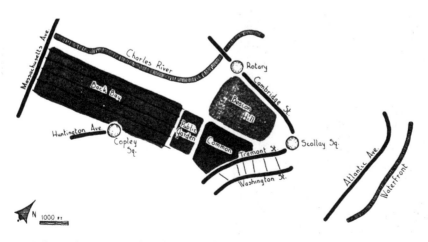

Orientation in the city of Boston, USA, as drawn by Kevin Lynch in 1960.
Source: Lynch K. 1960. The image of the city. MIT Press Cambridge p. 21

• Rogers E.B. 2001. *Landscape Design*. Abrams, New York p. 148
• Steenbergen C.; Reh W. 1996. *Architecture and Landscape*. Thoth Publising, Bussum p. 130
• van der Wal C. 1997. *In praise of common sense. Planning the ordinary. A physical planning history of the new towns in the IJsselmeerpolders*. 010 Publishers, Rotterdam

Ornament

see also > aesthetics, décor

'A thing used to or serving to adorn something but usually having no practical purpose [...]. Decoration added to embellish something, especially a building'. From Latin: *ornamentum* meaning equipment, ornament (*Oxford English Dictionary*).

In the view of Immanuel Kant (1724-1804), an ornament is 'what belongs to the representation of an object, not as an intrinsic part but as an external addition, adding to the pleasure of taste. It is ornamental because of its form, such as the frame of a picture or the cloth draped over a statue. When an ornament [...] is added merely in order to enhance the attractiveness of a painting, it is called a frill' (Kant 1790).

Before 1750, functional and ornamental aspects were interrelated. Because ornamentation was not regarded as an additional attribute, it was less superficial. During the 15th century, the word pulchritudo (literally 'beauty') was used by Leon Batista Alberti (1404-1472) to indicate a quality akin to 'clarity', which was dependent on the way an object 'fitted' (*Britannica*). Beauty and functionality were connected. 'The essence of the Italian Renaissance Garden is nature – selected, arranged and also fabricated into ornaments. Pergolas, trellis constructions, labyrinths, topiary, tree houses, mounts and grottoes all embellished gardens' (Lazarro 1990).

In French and Dutch 18th-century Classicist gardens, sculpture, sundials, grottoes, shell displays, *berceaux*, arcades and lattices were used both for ornamental purposes and as elements for structuring space (Kluckert 2000; Plumptree 1989). At that time, no distinction was made between the decorative (which also refers to other things) and the ornamental, i.e. pure adornment (Arnheim 1969; de Jong 1993).

20th-century Modernist Dutch landscape architects abhorred ornament and embellishment, preferring a minimalist design (Warnau 1993). In Post-modern design, ornament has made a comeback, not necessarily as an adornment, but also as a means for providing meaning and articulating space. 'It is designing as an elegant creation of a beauty which will order ephemeral phenomena – fitting out for a life in a Post-modern world' (Vuyk 1992).

Sundial at Huys ten Donck near Ridderkerk, the Netherlands.

• Arnheim R. 1969. 'Ornament'. In: Art and Visual Perception. Faber Editions, London pp. 134-140
• de Jong E. 1993. *Natuur en Kunst* (i.e. *Nature and art*). *Nederlandse tuin- en landschapsarchitectuur 1650-1740*. Thoth publishers, Bussum p.52
• Kant I. 1790. *Over Schoonheid* (i.e. *On beauty*). Boom, Meppel 1978. p. 64
• Kluckert E. 2000. *The Gardens of Europe*. Könemann, Köln
• Lazarro C. 1990. *The Italian Renaissance Garden*. Yale University Press, New Haven pp. 47-68; 131-160
• Plumptree G. 1989. *Garden Ornament. Five Hundred Years of History and Practice*. Thames and Hudson, London
• Vuyk K. 1992. *De esthetisering van het wereldbeeld* (i.e. *Creating an aesthetic world view*). Kok Agora, Kampen pp. 84

• Warnau H. 1993. 'Landschapsarchitectuur en de moderne stroming in de bouwkunde' (i.e. Landscape architecture and the modern movement in architecture). In: Smienk G. (ed). *Nederlandse Landschapsarchitectuur. Tussen traditie en experiment* .Thoth publishers, Bussum pp. 33 ff.

Oxymoron

see also > paradox, romantic

'A figure of speech in which apparently contradictory terms appear in conjunction'. From the Greek *oxumōron*, meaning: 'pointedly foolish' (*Oxford English Dictionary*). 'Faith unfaithful kept him falsely true' and 'dead alive' are both examples of oxymorons.

There is a clear relationship with the term 'folly' – also derived from 'foolish' – a folly often being a 'constructed ruin'.

Whether terms are contradictory also depends on definitions and interpretations. When 'true Nature' is defined as a phenomenon free of human intervention, the notion of 'nature management' is a contradictory one.

Recognising an oxymoron is not a matter of playing word games, but of seeing through ambiguities. An oxymoron may be used by an artist to expose one-sided opinions in a provoking albeit deceitful game. A well-known example is the Whitehead Institute Splice Garden in Cambridge, Mass., USA, a roof garden designed by landscape architect Martha Schwartz. This features plastic plant material laid out in two design styles: a French style, and a Zen style in which plants and stones are interchanged (Spirn 1998; Landecker 1997).

227

• Landecker H. (ed). 1997. *Martha Schwartz. Transfiguration of the Commonplace*. Spacemaker Press p.115
• Spirn A. 1998. *The Language of Landscape*. Yale University Press, New Haven pp. 230-231

Palimpsest

see > layer

Panorama

see also > space, vista

'A picture of a landscape or another scene, either arranged on the inside of a cylindrical surface round the spectator as a centre, or unrolled or unfolded and made to pass before him so as to show the various parts in succession. An unbroken view of the whole surrounding area. (*Oxford English Dictionary*).

The term is derived from the Greek *pan* ('all') and *hora* ('to see'). References to Panoramas date back at least as far as the time of Odysseus' travels (Crandell 1993/1). In Western Europe, the first description of a landscape panorama that was deliberately sought out is probably that of the Italian poet Petrarch (Francesco Petrarca; 1304-1374), who climbed Mont Ventoux in France in 1335, intending 'to see what so great an elevation had to offer' (Rogers 2001). Before that time, hostile environments represented danger and fear, effectively prohibiting repose and reflection there (Crandell 1993/2).

The first Italian Renaissance villas around Rome were situated in places that offered a panoramic view of the rural surroundings (Steenbergen 1996). Such a view from a high point extends to the horizon, but also encompasses lower areas nearby. There is a direct optical relationship between the elevation point of the observer, the vertical angle of view, and the degree to which objects are visible (Higuchi 1983).

The opening of the Eiffel tower in Paris in 1889 gave large numbers of people their first opportunity to view the landscape as a plane – a composition of lines, boundaries and nodes – rather than as a series of eye-level perspectives (Hughes 1980). Even now, the modern experience of the city is to see it as a tourist attraction, through coin-operated binoculars on top of a skyscraper. Here, the 'all-encompassing view becomes a first-rate aesthetic experience. In the panorama view, the observer takes delight in taking possession of the distance [...]. The panorama becomes the model for viewing towns, landscapes, history' (Boomkens 1998).

- Boomkens R. 1998. *Een drempelwereld* (i.e. *A threshold world*). NAi uitgevers, Rotterdam pp. 305 ff.
- Crandell G. 1993. *Nature Pictorialized*. Johns Hopkins University Press, New York pp. 37-40
- Crandell G. 1993/2. *Nature Pictorialized*. Johns Hopkins University Press, New York pp. 48, 73
- Higuchi T. 1983. 'Space-position relationships'. In: *The Visual and Spatial Structure of Landscapes*. MIT Press, Cambridge pp. 36 ff.
- Hughes R. 1980. *The Shock of the New*. BBC London
- Rogers E.B. 2001. 'Classicism reborn: landscape ideals of the Renaissance in Italy and France'. In: *Landscape Design, a Cultural and Architectural History*. Harry Abrams, New York p. 125
- Steenbergen C.M. 1996. 'Rome as a landscape theatre'. In: *Architecture and Landscape*. Thoth, Bussum pp. 85-91

229

Panorama of Rotterdam.

Photo: Hans Dijkstra. Source: www.blauwekamer.nl, panorama Jan Laan

Paradigm. Discourse

see also > theory, vision

'A world view underlying the theories and methodology of a particular scientific subject' (*Oxford English Dictionary*).

A paradigm can be viewed as a coherent set of assumptions about the reality around us, a *weltanschauung*, an implicit basic assumption. It represents 'the totality of the background information, the laws and theories which are taught to the aspiring scientist as if they were true, and which must be accepted by him if he in turn is to be accepted into the scientific community' (Pepper 1996).

In the natural sciences, paradigms are changeable over time (Kuhn 1970). A design theory is also based largely on a paradigm. Since the middle of the 20th century, new ideas based on systems theory, environmental consciousness and the ideal of sustainability have caused the paradigm in landscape architecture to shift. On the basis of these ideas, the way design problems are tackled has also changed (Ndubisi 1997; Rosenberg 1986).

Naturally, the paradigms of town planners have also changed, in the Netherlands as elsewhere. The traditional aim for unity, coherence and the enforcement of plans has been replaced by ideals and views on diversity, chaos and freedom to choose. The reductionist Cartesian approach to complex design assignments by dividing them into subordinate parts has been replaced by a more holistic approach (Motloch 1991). With the Post-modern application of ecological principles in the design of outdoor space, a new paradigm of 'holistic philosophy and evolutionary ethic' is coming into being (Koh 1982).

There is also a marked overlap between the definition of a 'paradigm' and the notion of 'discourse' as formulated by the French philosopher Michel Foucault (1926-1984). As, in Foucault's view, discourse makes part of reality accessible by constructing it, knowledge of reality is socially constructed – based in culture. 'Space, landscape and town are fields where many different discourses meet and are mingled' (Assche, 2004).

As Jacobs adds, 'an assumption underlying this characterisation of discourse is that meanings of parts of reality are not pre-given, but to a great extent socially constructed by different forms of communication. Communication is taken here in its broadest sense: it can be speech and written text in natural language, body-language and pictorial language. Behaviour can also be seen as a form of communication. The way a gardener maintains his garden, for example, is an expression of ideas about gardening and nature, an expression that can be interpreted by others, and hence a form of communication. By analysing different expressions of a group of people, the discourse of the group of people can be reconstructed, by formulating the underlying ideas that are inherent in the expressions' (Jacobs 2005).

• van Assche K. 2004. *Signs in time*. PhD thesis, Wageningen University p. 54
• Jacobs M. 2005. 'Daily natures in polyvocal societies: allotment-gardens in Rotterdam'. In: *The production of mindscapes*. PhD thesis, Wageningen University. In preparation
• Koh J. 1982. 'Ecological design: a post-modern design paradigm of holistic philosophy and evolutionary ethic'. In: Landscape Journal vol.1 no. 1, pp. 76-84.
• Kuhn T.S. 1970. *The Structure of Scientific Revolutions. Foundations of the Unity of Science*. The University of Chicago Press pp. 43 ff.
• Motloch. J. 1991. *Introduction to Landscape Design*. Van Nostrand Reinhold, London pp. 257-262
• Ndubisi F. 1997. 'Landscape ecological planning'. In: Thompson G; Steiner F. (ed.). *Ecological Design and Planning*. Wiley & Sons, New York p. 17
• Pepper D. 1996. *Modern Environmentalism. An Introduction*. Routledge, London pp. 260-264
• Rosenberg A.M. 1986. 'An emerging paradigm for landscape architecture'. In: Landscape Journal vol. 5 no. 2, ,The University of Wisconsin Press, Urbana, Illinois pp. 75-83

Paradox

see also > contrast, irony, oxymoron

'A phenomenon that exhibits some contradiction or conflict with preconceived notions of what is reasonable or possible. It is essentially absurd and false' (*Oxford English Dictionary*).

Life is full of paradoxical situations; human expressions and ways of reasoning contain improbabilities, vicious circles and infinite regression. The oldest known fully developed paradox is the statement by the Cretan Epimedes: 'all Cretans are liars'. Another well-known paradox is infinity as expressed in cartography: the more detailed the scale of a map, the longer the lines in a landscape, because when one draws at a scale of 1:1 and beyond, every curve must be drawn.

Our view of our environment is as full of apparent contradictions as the activities we undertake to change things. In our simultaneous exploitation and conservation of nature – or our attempts to do so – we display our desire to combine tradition and modernity, and to promote identity and diversity in the same place. Visitors to a Romantic park believe themselves to be in a natural setting, but are in a completely man-made environment. (Spirn 1998) Conversely, the spontaneous growth of very natural phenomena, such as weeds in a car park, is considered objectionable. In attempting to remove these weeds, municipal park departments have shifted from chemical

Getting your drinks from discarded bottles: Vondelpark, Amsterdam.

weed-killers to more 'environmentally friendly' means such as flame-throwers. These combinations of the natural and the artificial are paradoxical, as are the aggressive means applied and the language used.

So is the rubbish-bin in a park filled with discarded beer bottles and carrying the label 'minibar'.

Here, the paradox in form and meaning is intended to attract attention and stimulate reflection. A well-known example of a paradoxical statement in modern architecture is: 'less is more'.

• Spirn A. 1998. 'Cultivating Paradox'. In: *The Language of Landscape.* Yale University Press, New Haven p. 262-265

Paraphrase

see > reference

Park

see also > Functionalism, garden, landscape, Modernism, place, promenade, Romanticism, theme

'A large public garden in a town used for recreation. A large enclosed piece of ground, typically with woodland and pasture, attached to a country house. A large area of land kept in its natural state for public recreational use' (*Oxford English Dictionary*).

Parks and gardens have always been the result of a search for contact with nature, albeit of a cultivated and romanticised kind (Spirn 1984). Historically, the development of parks as an urban element has been a long and complicated process (Steenbergen 1993). Until the 18th century, Western European parks were privately owned and intended for the enjoyment of their proprietors. In Paris, the royal gardens of the Tuileries palace were opened to the public sometime during the 18th century. After that, public gardens began to flourish in many cities, and were included in master plans for urban development (Cleary 2002).

At the beginning of the 19th century, public parks emerged as pieces of ground laid out for public use in an urban setting (Chadwick

231

Complexity: Vondelpark Amsterdam, a park in the landscape style.

1966; Ponte 1990). Many of the urban parks that were laid out in cities in Europe and the USA still enjoy a world-wide reputation (Tate 2001). Vondelpark, the first urban park in Amsterdam, was laid out in 1877. Other Dutch city parks were also laid out as promenade parks, often on demolished ramparts or bulwarks, and furnished with decorative plant materials, curvilinear paths and ponds, all conforming to the principles of the landscape style.

Over the years, park layouts have reflected shifts in function, with the emphasis changing from public health in early parks to social reform in later years, followed yet later by active recreation. The present tendency is towards sustainable parks, in which human health goes hand in hand with ecological health, with stewardship being important for an art-nature continuum (Cranz 2004).

Parks are urban phenomena. While villages may have some greenery or woodland, parks belong to towns. The 20th century saw some particularly radical change in their design and use. The emphasis in German Volksparken was on sports and play, and large new parks such as Amsterdamse Bos

Monotony: Kanaleneiland, Utrecht in the 1970s; a Modernist park.

were laid out primarily as recreation areas (Andela 1981; Boer 1990; Polano 1991). During the 1960s, the need to cut maintenance budgets led to frugal planting plans that served solely to enclose and subdivide meadows, playgrounds and sports fields, and to screen cycle tracks and foot paths. The abundance of flowering trees shrubs and herbaceous plants so typical of the 19th century park was reduced to the occasional flower garden.

Currently, there are several trends in contemporary urban park design. In one of these, the layout of new parks is similar to that of urban squares, thereby creating open spaces that express urban culture; they are places to move through as well as to stay (Geuze 1993). Like the Post-modern Museum Park in Rotterdam, they are often full of symbolic elements (Wortmann 1993).

A different trend is to use ecological management principles to create representations of nature. Such ecological ideals are based on a concern for environmental processes that urban planners tend to have ignored in the past. Their use involves a new type of ecological aesthetic (Koh 1982; Hough 1995). Sometimes, however, these new ideals manifest themselves in particular forms of Mannerism. These ignore the fact that a park's success depends on people's search for meaningful experiences, which is based on a feeling of attachment to particular outdoor spaces. Such an experience can easily be hampered by any number of factors, including a decline in public safety, which might be countered by creating more interconnected multiple-use outdoor spaces (Jacobs 1965; Broadbent 1990).

Parks must be 'timely', because they spring from current concerns and address current use. At the same time they must be timeless (or untimely), because they are always designed for a future that cannot be known, and can only be predicted, if at all, by being predicated on our experience of the past (Hunt 2002).

The size, form and location of contemporary parks varies greatly. There are many types of outdoor space, at different scales and with various functions, such as green oases, buffer zones, and ecological networks (Huet 1993). Parks may consist of green inclusions within an agglomeration, encircle towns as green belts, or connect the inside and outside of a city (Tummers 1997). There are also the large territories with specific natural and/or cultural values that are managed and conserved under the status of national park (Anonymous 1997).

• Andela G. 1981. 'The Public Park in the Netherlands'. In: Journal of Garden History. An International Quarterly, Taylor & Francis, London vol. 1 no. 4, pp. 367-392
• Anonymous. 1997. 'Parks'. Topos European Landscape Magazine no. 19, Callwey, München
• Boer W.C.J. 1990. 'Changing ideals in urban landscape architecture in the Netherlands'. In: Vroom. M.J.; Meeus J.H.A. (ed). *Learning from Rotterdam*. Mansell/Nicholls publishing, New York pp. 44-86
• Broadbent G. 1990. 'Urban realities'. In: *Emerging Concepts of Urban Space Design*. Van Nostrand Reinhold, London pp. 138 ff.
• Chadwick G.F. 1966. *The Park and the Town*. The Architectural Press, London p. 19
• Cleary R. 2002. 'Public garden and City Planning'. In: Hunt J.D.; Conan M. (ed) *Tradition and Innovation in French Garden Art. Chapters of a New History*. The University of Pennsylvania Press, Philadelphia pp. 68-81
• Cranz G.; Boland M. 2004. 'Defining the sustainable park: a fifth model'. In: Landscape Journal. The University of Wisconsin Press, Madison, Wisconsin pp. 102-120
• Geuze A. 1993. 'Accelerating Darwin'. In: Smienk G. (ed). *Nederlandse Landschapsarchitectuur. Tussen traditie en experiment*. Thoth, Bussum pp.12-22
• Hough M. 1995. *Cities and Natural Process*. Routledge, London
• Huet B. 1993. 'A park est un parc ist ein Park'. In: Knuijt M. (et al) (ed). *Modern Park Design. Recent Trends*. Thoth publishers, Bussum pp. 28-32
• Hunt J. Dixon 2002. 'Reinventing the Parisian Park'. In: Hunt J.D.; Conan M. (ed). *Tradition and Innovation in French Garden Art. Chapters of a New History*. The University of Pennsylvania Press
• acobs J. 1965. 'The uses of neighbourhood parks'. In: *The Death and Life of Great American Cities*. Pelican Books, Harmondsworth, Middlesex
• Koh J. 1982. 'Ecological design: a post-modern design paradigm of holistic philosophy and evolutionary ethic'. In: Landscape Journal vol.1 no.1 pp.76-84
• Polano S. 1991. 'The Bospark, Amsterdam, and urban development in Holland'. In: Mosser M.; Teyssot G. *The History of Garden Design*. Thames & Hudson, London pp. 507-509
• Ponte A. 1990. 'Public Parks in Great Britain and the United States: from a Spirit of the Place to a Spirit of Civilization'. In: Mosser M.; Teyssot G. *The History of Garden Design*. Thames & Hudson, London p. 373-386
• Spirn A.W. 1984. 'The Search for Nature: Park, Suburb and Garden City'. In: *The Granite Garden*. Basic Books. pp. 29-37
• Steenbergen C. 1993. 'Teatro rustico. The formal strategy and

grammar of landscape architecture'. In: Knuyt M. (ed). *Modern Park Design*. Thoth publishers, Bussum
• Tate A. 2001. *Great City Parks*. Spon, London.
• Tummers L.J.M. ; Tummers-Zuurmond J.J. 1997. *Het Land in de Stad* (i.e. *The countryside in the city*). Thoth, Bussum pp. 145 ff.
• Wortmann A. 1993. 'The Museumpark, Rotterdam'. In: ARCHIS Journal, NAi, Rotterdam no. 1 pp. 28-39

Parterre

see also > pattern, theme

'A flower garden, particularly in the area adjoining the house, laid out in a regular ornamental manner' (Oxford Companion).

The *parterre de broderie* was introduced to Holland in the 17th century by Andre Mollet (de Jong 1993). It consisted of decorative patterns created by low box hedges set against a background of coloured soil, sometimes with bands of turf. *Parterres à l'anglaise* consisted of patterns cut out in lawns; these were easier to maintain.

• De Jong E. 1993. *Natuur en Kunst. Nederlandse tuin- en landschapsarchitectuur 1650-1740*. Thoth, Bussum

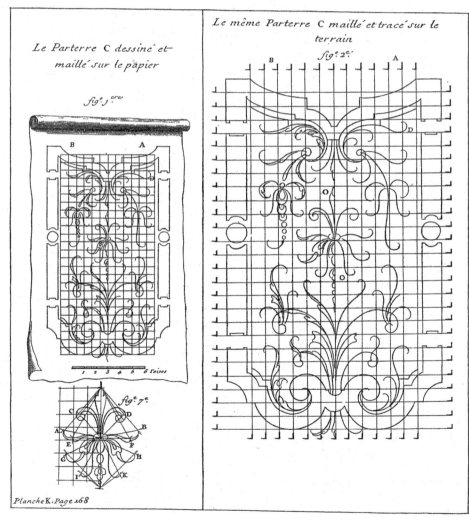

Parterre in plan as drawn in La theorie et Pratique du Jardinage by the illustrator Le Blond in 1709.

Source: Sørensen C.Th. 1959. Europas Havekunst. G.E.C. Gads Forlag, Copenhagen. pp.135 and 132

Pastiche

see also > authenticity, eclecticism, fashion, mannerism

'Artistic work consisting of elements from various sources' (*Oxford English Dictionary*).

A pastiche is generally considered to be a poor imitation of a work of art or antique, made in the style of some other artist. Examples of pastiche in garden design are found in designs by 16th-century Mannerists and 20th-century Postmodernists (Kluckert 2000). While they involve a nostalgic search for 'the perpetual present' – for images from elsewhere and from the past – they are also created without any knowledge of reality, and therefore view the past through 'our own pop images and stereotypes about the past which remain forever out of reach' (Urry 2002).

All this is related to an inability to invent new styles and words. Art becomes artifice, the endless recycling of past styles in fiction, film art and architecture. Old plots are 'plagiarised unashamedly, given an archaic feeling even when the setting may be a contemporary one' (Cooke 1990).

• Cooke P. 1990. *Back to the Future. Modernity, Postmodernity and Locality.* Unwin Hyman, London p. 110
• Kluckert E. 2000. *Gardens of Europe.* Könemann, Köln pp. 83 ff.
. Urry J. 2002. *The Tourist Gaze.* Sage Publications ,London p. 83

Pastoral

see also > arcadia, picturesque, poetic, Romanticism

'Used for or related to the keeping or grazing of sheep. Associated with country life, typically in a romanticised or idealised form'. A pastoral scene is an idyll in the sense of 'a poetical painting of the life of simple, unspoilt people, such as herdsmen and other country folk living close to nature'. Pastoralism is a typical trait of Romantic gardens and parks with their Arcadian images (*Oxford English Dictionary*).

The pastoral ideal was born in the 16th century, and is in essence more than a literary style. Its purpose was not merely to describe the life of a shepherd, with its simple and natural benefits, but also to imitate. The ideal

appealed to those seeking to escape reality, who ignored the hardships and dismal poverty of shepherds and farmers, believing instead that love achieved its natural fulfilment in a shepherd's world. In the description of a sunny dream world, shrouded in flute-play and bird's song in 'a landscape of crystal wells and shady groves' (Drabble 1979), there was also an erotic undertone. Originally the sensory delight of sun and summer, shadow and fresh water, flowers and birds prevailed. In later stages this was superseded by painting and a more conscious observation of nature (Huizinga 1919).

A well-known example from the 17th century is Queen Marie-Antoinette's *ferme ornée* at Versailles, with its rustic buildings

Painting of a forest scene by B.C. Koekoek, 1839.

Source: Loos W. (et al) (ed). Langs Velden en Wegen. De verbeelding van het landschap in de achttiende en negentiende eeuw. V+K Blaricum / Rijksmuseum, Amsterdam.p. 59

235

and flocks of sheep. A 19th-century example is Thoreau's Walden in New England, an idyllic place far from the urban scene. But even here the sounds of the city penetrated, giving rise to complex emotions described vividly in his famous book (Marx 1964; Thoreau 1854).

In the early 20th century, the primary pursuits of the emerging nature conservation movement in the Netherlands involved the restoration of pastoral landscapes (Keulartz 1995). At that time, 19th-century examples of a quiet countryside with its diversity of plants and wildlife were rapidly disappearing. As a countermeasure, selected areas were acquired so they could be farmed according to more traditional practices. Careful management made it possible to conserve marshland, together with its remaining pools and lakes, often surrounded by reed-land, osier-beds, grassland, and also heather lands with their sheep-pens. Such pastoral landscapes thereby became protected monuments.

• Drabble M. 1979. 'The Pastoral Vision'. In: *A Writer's Britain. Landscape in Literature.* Thames & Hudson, London pp. 47-104
• Huizinga J. 1919. *The Waning of the Middle Ages.* Wolters/Noordhof, Groningen
• Keulartz J. 1998. *The Struggle for Nature. A Critique of Radical Ecology.* Routledge, London
• Marx L. 1964. 'Sleepy Hollow'. In: *The Machine in the Garden.* Oxford University Press, New York pp. 3-33
• Thoreau H.D. 1854 (1973). 'Sounds'. In: *Selections from Walden.* Avenell Books, New York pp.73 ff.

Path

see > access

Patio, Court-yard

see also > garden

'An inner court open to the sky. Often a paved recreation area that adjoins a building' (*Webster*).

In Islamic architecture, the patio is included in the design of a building. It is usually square in plan, formal in layout, and in some cases is surrounded by an arcade. In desert climates, the inner court provides coolness, especially when it is equipped with a fountain, which stimulates air circulation (Schoenauer 1962; Rogers 2002).

During the early Middle Ages, the *hortus conclusus* was a refuge in the middle of a threatening wilderness; it combined a sense of safety with the enjoyment of fruit and of pleasure. As an open space in a dark woodland, it provided openness, a natural inner world, and a well-organised space (Aben 2002. Urban courts SOMETIMES adjoined royal palaces but might also be located between less prestigious housing blocks (Harsema 2002).

In contemporary densely built urban quarters, a patio garden provides a private and sheltered space (Alexander 1977; McHarg 1998).

• Aben R.; de Wit S. 2002. *The Enclosed Garden.* 010 publishers, Rotterdam EA 164
• Alexander C. (et al).1977. 'Courtyards which live'. In: *A Pattern Language.* Oxford University Press pp. 561 ff.
• Harsema H. (ed). 2002. 'Phoenix Garden Delft: Tranquil courtyard in a hectic city centre'. In: *Landscape architecture and town planning in the Netherlands. 99-01.* Thoth publishers, Bussum pp. 73-77
• McHarg I.; Steiner F.1998. 'The Court House Concept'. In: *To Heal the Earth. Selected Writings by Ian McHarg.* Island Press, Washington D.C. pp. 163 ff.
• Rogers E. 2001. 'Paradise on earth: the Islamic Garden'. In: *Landscape Design. A Cultural and Architectural History.* Harry Abrams publishers, New York
• Schoenauer N.; Seeman S. 1962. *The Court-Garden House* McGill University Press, Montreal

Safety and comfort in Begijnhof, Amsterdam.

Pattern

see also > composition, design, geometry, layer, map, mosaic, process, soil, theme

'A repeated decorative design. An arrangement or sequence regularly found in comparable objects or events' (*Oxford English Dictionary*). 'An arrangement of parts, elements or details that indicate a design, or somewhat orderly distribution in the landscape' (Goulty).

A pattern consists of a repetition of identical elements or motifs, such as those in a cloth or pavement. In French Classicist gardens, patterns were often used in a *parterre de broderie*, by which they were often characterised.

Geometric gardens, farmyards and gardens in the landscape style all have a characteristic pattern that helps identify them (Stauffacher 1988). The interconnected elements within such a pattern include arcades, paths, the façades of buildings, places for activities, steps and stairs on which people can sit around a central space. The internal connections and relationships within a pattern can be analysed and used to create a design programme. Pattern, structure and systems are therefore interwoven concepts.

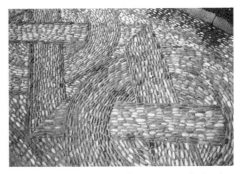

Decorative paving pattern at Villa Garzoni in Collodi, Italy.

Design patterns evolve during a design process and also appear as its final product. The layout of a site is fixed in a pattern drawn on paper. On a plan, such a pattern has a graphic composition that can be interpreted as a three-dimensional composition. The repetition of certain lines and planes in a composition may lead to the formation of a central motive or theme (Turner 1996/1).

In a more abstract sense, a pattern can be seen as a collection of objects and events that form a network 'Every place is given its character by certain patterns of events that keep happening there. These patterns of

237

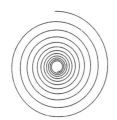

Patterns can be classified according to their geometric characteristics, such as bifurcations, meanders and explosions.

Source: Bell S. 1999. Landscape, Pattern, Perception and Process. Spon, London

events are always interlocked with certain geometric patterns in space' (Alexander 1977; Alexander 1979; Turner 1996/2).

A landscape pattern is represented on a map by the contours and borderlines of elements, areas and objects – all of them landscape components that are visible at eye level, or traceable by aerial survey or mapping techniques. Maps show lines, points, and planes by means of colours or hatchings. Landscape patterns tell tales. Some of them are geometric such as a spiral (like a snail shell), a form indicating growth. They can also be hierarchic: a branching river consists of a pattern indicating one-directional stream flow, and a meander shows how geophysical forces are at work (Stevens 1974; Bell 1999/1). Thematic maps show geomorphological, soil and vegetation patterns. Topographic maps also show settlement patterns (Bell 1999/2)

The analysis of a landscape pattern provides information on the composition of landscape elements at a given point in history. Comparison of older maps with more recent ones shows how and where changes in patterns have occurred over time (Baart 2000). As part of interdependent phenomena in natural and cultural processes, patterns evolve and change. While the changes that take place over time in geological and soil patterns may be hardly perceptible to the human eye, those in vegetation and land-use are evident within a human lifespan (Forman 1986).

• Alexander C. (et al). 1977. *A Pattern Language*. Oxford University Press, New York pp. IX-XVII
• Alexander C. 1979. *The Timeless Way of Building*. Oxford University Press, New York p. X
• Baart T. (et al). 2000. *Atlas of Change. Rearranging the Netherlands*. NAi publishers, Rotterdam
• Bell S. 1999/1. *Landscape, Pattern, Perception and Process*. Spon, London pp.11-29
• Bell S. 1999/2. 'Landform patterns'. In: *Landscape, Pattern, Perception and Process*. Spon London pp. 119 ff.
• Forman R.T.T.; Godron M. 1986. *Landscape Ecology*. John Wiley, New York
• Stauffacher Solomon B. 1988. *Green Architecture and the Agrarian Garden*. Rizzoli, New York pp. 12-17
• Stevens P. 1974. *Patterns in Nature*. Atlantic-Little, Brown Books, Boston
• Turner T. 1996. 'Structural friends of the pattern language'. In:

City as Landscape. Spon, London pp. 27 ff.
• Turner T. 1996. 'Patterns in use; footprints in the sand'. In: *City as Landscape*. Spon, London pp. 348 ff.

Perception

see also > aesthetics, character, dynamic, experience, image, perspective, phenomenology, sequence, value

'The ability to see, hear, or become aware of something through the senses. A way of regarding, understanding or interpreting something, a mental impression' (*Oxford English Dictionary*).

Human perception and the experience of spaces and objects involve the senses: hearing, feeling, smelling, seeing and balancing (Bell 1999). The most important of these for environmental designers is seeing – eyesight – which involves the optical mechanisms whereby the environment is perceived (Rock 1984; Prak 1979). The perception process can be divided into successive phases, such as the scanning of images by the eye, the reception and processing of stimuli, and the registration of all this in the memory (Gibson 1979; Porter 2002).

People are helped to recognise scenes by a wide range of memories – fear, delight, comfort, or other experiences (Schacter 1997). Remembering images from the past always involves a simplification of the real scene, part of the process whereby people form a mental map of their environment that will help them find their way during successive visits (Gould 1974). The creation of such maps is facilitated by the amount of order and structure present in the environment (Lynch 1960).

The processing of perceived stimuli includes the evaluation of the visible environment, whereby meanings are attached and actions prepared. The perception of objects in the environment – whatever their nature; anything from electrons to swans – is always based on a point of view, a theory, concept, or expectation, and possibly even a myth. These percepts scan the world like a searchlight, the direction of the beam of light determining

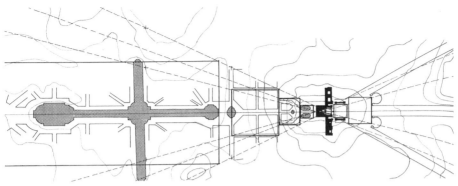

Plan of the park at Versailles, France. .

Source: Steenbergen C.; Reh W. 1996. Architecture and Landscape. Thoth Bussum.

Series of photos of the park at Versailles, showing changing perspective views.

The palace viewed from the main terrace.

Looking back from the bottom of the stairs.

View over the nearest fountain to the Grand Canal.

View back to the palace from a point beyond the fountain.

View of the palace from the lower terrace.

View of the Grand Canal over the second fountain.

what becomes visible and is recognised as a 'fact' (Koningsveld 1976). Such pre-conceived ideas, ideals, paradigms and theories thus mean that a person's perception of a particular scene may lead to different reactions over time (Meinig 1979).

This was also observed by Dutch author Nescio (1882-1961) when looking across the river to the town of Nijmegen: 'And from across the water the town rose up into the blue sky – the quay and the houses and more houses up the slope, protruding halfway or fully above one another [...] and somewhere a church, large, as a sign for God to recognise his town, with the two spired towers reaching up and up for more height. This is the way a poet reaches out from his poetic soul to a God who remains invisible in the blue sky. And yet the little poet had to laugh at the wonder in his eyes, because what he saw was nothing but a collection of hovels full of a puny life that was not even Dutch, but that of a small provincial small town' (Nescio 1933).

People want to explore a new environment and to claim space for themselves where will they feel comfortable, at home. A hostile environment is therefore remembered differently from a familiar and safe one. When children in a slum area of an American city were asked to draw a map of their daily

The tapis vert enclosed by boskets.

The tapis vert enclosed by boskets.

Transverse view through a bosket.

Fountains in front of the Grand Canal.

The Grand Canal.

View of the palace across the tapis vert.

environment from memory, they produced very different images, depending on their background and lifestyle (Gould 1974).

The visual perception of a particular environment may be static or dynamic. A geometric outdoor space may be designed primarily for viewing from a central point. Here the application of the rules of perspective is one of the chief means to induce a static experience of space (Higuchi 1983; Steenbergen 1996). The way the environment is perceived also depends on the use of instruments such as the camera obscura or the camera lucida with its prism: 'instruments do not merely follow theory but are capable of determining it' (Lee 2000).

Dynamic perception results from movement through space. In the great Park at Versailles, Paris, static and dynamic perception are both possible. From the main terrace behind the palace, the observer has a full view of the central axis all the way to its terminal point at the horizon. The descent down the stairways to the Grand Canal provides a view of lower terraces, side-rooms and cross-axis that were invisible from the top, and provides a succession of new experiences and views (see *Perspective*). Similarly, the sequence of images presented to the observer while strolling through the central part of a town may contribute to a delightful spatial experience (Cullen 1968). For all such reasons, designers of new infrastructure should always take account of travellers' dynamic perception of roadside elements (Appleyard 1964).

- Appleyard D. (et al).1964. *The View from the Road*. MIT Press, Cambridge
- Bell S. 1999. 'The perception of patterns'. In: *Landscape, Pattern, Perception and Process*. E & FN Spon, London pp. 39 ff.
- Cullen G. 1968. *The Concise Townscape*. The Architectural Press, London p. 17
- Gibson J.J. 1979. 'The theory of affordances'. In: *The Ecological Approach to Visual Perception*. Houghton Miffin Co, Boston pp. 127 ff.
- Gould P.; White R. 1974. *Mental Maps*. Pelican Books, Harmondsworth, Middlesex. pp. 30-37; 173-197
- Higuchi T. 1983. *The Visual and Spatial Structure of Landscapes*. MIT Press, Cambridge, Mass pp. 62 ff.
- Koningsveld H. 1976. *Het verschijnsel wetenschap* (i.e. *The phenomenon of science*). Boom, Meppel p. 101
- ee P.Y. 2000. 'The rational point of view: Eugène Viollet-le-Duc and the camera lucida'. In: Birksted J (ed.) *Landscapes of Memory and Experience*. Spon Press, London pp. 63-73
- Lynch K. 1960. *The Image of the City*. MIT Press, Cambridge
- Meinig D.W. 1979. The beholding eye. Ten versions of the same scene'. In: Meinig D.W. (ed). *The Interpretation of Ordinary Landscapes*. Oxford University Press, New York pp. 33-48
- Nescio. 1933 (1996). *Verzameld Werk* (i.e. *Collected Work*). Nijgh & van Ditmar, Amsterdam pp. 103-104
- Porter T. 2002. 'Taking the eye for a run; a sight for sore eyes'. In: Steenbergen C. (et al) (ed). *Architectural Design and Composition*. Thoth publishers, Bussum pp. 50-64
- Prak N.L. 1977. *The Visual Perception of the Built Environment*. Delft University Press
- Rock I. 1984. *Perception*. Freeman & Company, New York
- Schacter D.L. 1997. *Searching for Memory: The Brain, the Mind, and the Past*. Harper Collins, New York
- Steenbergen C.; Reh W. 1996. 'Viewpoint, perspective and horizon'. In: *Architecture and Landscape*. Thoth, Bussum pp. 42-45

Pergola, Trellis
see also > arcade

The meaning of the Italian word *pergola* is 'Any arbour, bower or close walk of boughs, mainly of vines'.

Pergola in the rose garden at Museum Boymans Rotterdam. 1959 Architects: van den Broek & Bakema.

Originally, a pergola consisted of a light timber construction of upright and cross-members that was strong enough to support only climbing plants. After the Italian Renaissance such structures became known throughout Western Europe. During the 17th century they were applied in garden design – by Le Nôtre and others – in combination with the *treillage*, an elaborately detailed vertical wall with gates and porticos. In the 19th century, the influence of architect Edwin Lutyens (1869-1944) ensured that they once again became an important element in garden architecture (Oxford Companion).

A pergola is very similar to a berceau, 'a tunnel-shaped trellis or a corridor made of pruned trees' (Backer 1998), the difference being that a pergola is usually constructed of wood or iron, while a berceau is formed entirely by living plants. In Classicist gardens, both were important components in the spatial composition. In contemporary gardens, pergola are still common, and are used not only to lend three-dimensionality to a path, but also to enclose or subdivide outdoor space (Alexander 1977).

• Alexander C. (et al). 1977. 'Trellised walk'. In: *A Pattern Language*. Oxford University Press pp. 809 ff.
• Backer M. (ed). 1998. *De Natuur bezworen*. De Hef Uitgevers, Rotterdam pp. 20, 101.

Perspective

see also > light, space, panorama

'The art of drawing solid objects on a two-dimensional surface so as to give the right impression of their height, width, depth, and position in relation to each other when viewed from a particular point'. Linear perspective is 'a type of perspective used by artists in which the relative size, shape and position of objects is determined by drawn or imagined lines converging at a point on the horizon'. An aerial perspective is that 'representing more distant objects as fainter and more blue' (*New Oxford Dictionary of English*).

'Perspective is based on the fact that light is normally propagated along straight lines and that we can therefore work out for any object in space what light rays from its surface will reach a given point' (Gombrich 1982).

In the 18th century Jean-Jacques Rousseau wrote: 'The delusion of perspective is needed to perceive space and to determine its subdivision. Without optical illusions, we would not be able to see distant objects; without a reduction in size and change in colour, we would not be able to gauge a distance, or rather, it would not exist for us. In

Linear perspective in ploughed land.

Perspective on the basis of diminishing sizes: sculpture at Herrenhausen park, Hannover, Germany.

the case of two trees of equal size, the one removed from us by a hundred feet seems as tall as the other at a distance of ten feet; we will situate them next to one another. If we perceived all dimensions of all objects as being of equal size, we would not see space, and everything would seem to be projected onto our retina' (Rousseau 1762/1980).

Applied for the first time in the early Italian Renaissance, perspective rules were often used in 17th-century Dutch paintings (Cosgrove 1993; Crandell 1993; Gombrich 1972). In architecture and garden design, the invention of perspective rules coincided with the birth of a new perception of space (Giedion 1967).

We perceive depth-in-space in various ways:
· in a stereoscopic view. The lens of the human eye projects two slightly different images onto the retina. These are processed inside the brain into a coherent three-dimensional image.
· in textural perspective. The apparent roughness in a rough extended surface (such as a cabbage field) decreases with distance. Nineteenth-century landscape architects exploited this phenomenon in park designs by putting large-leafed trees in the foreground and willowy trees in the background. The effect was that spaces looked larger than they actually were.
· in size perspective. Objects of the same size look smaller at a greater distance.
· in central perspective. Lines parallel to the view converge in depth, while lines crossing the view seem to be closer together. This effect can be exploited by making lines in the field converge, thereby creating the appearance of greater depth.
· in parallel perspective. Isometry or axonometry draws lines that remain parallel in the distance. There is no vanishing point and no horizon. A bird's-eye view shows the three dimensions of a building or a site at one glance. It shows space as if it were infinite (Montague 1998; Lockard 1974; Steenbergen 1996; Weiss 1998).
· in dynamic perspective. For motorists, objects near the roadside move out of view faster than objects at a distance.

The perception of depth in space depends largely on the quality and direction of light. As a result of the changing angle of sunlight during the day – and also during the seasons – the appearance of objects and spaces changes. Colour and brightness are also influenced by atmospheric conditions. In a dry desert climate, distances in the landscape look shorter than elsewhere (Moore 1989).

By providing deep shade, trees enhance the experience of space (Arnheim 1969; Amidon 2001). To enhance the perception of depth in their paintings, and also to create dramatic effect, Dutch landscape painters such as Rembrandt (1606-1669) used contrasting light and shade (*clair-obscur*).

Ever since their invention in the 15th century, the rules of perspective have been a favourite instrument for creating illusory spaces that fool the observer's eye and

243

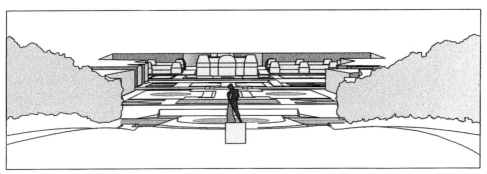

Central perspective at Vaux le Vicomte, Melun, France.

Source: Steenbergen C.; Reh W. 1996. Architecture and Landscape. The design experiment of the great European gardens and landscapes. Thoth, Bussum

control the experience of space (Steenbergen 1996). A classical example is Villa Barbaro in the Italian Veneto, which dates from 1565. Here, collaboration between architect Andrea Palladio (1508-1580) and painter Paolo Veronese (1528-1588) resulted in a connection between outdoor and indoor spaces, whereby 'entering a room means entering another time and another space. You are effectively removed from reality' (Andersson 2003).

Much later, the 17th-century parks at Versailles and Vaux-le-Vicomte used side screens, transverse axes, sight lines and changes in elevation to produce increasingly well-organised and complex compositions (Hamilton Hazlehurst 1980; Weiss 1998). One effective demonstration of this is an axonometric or isometric view which, at a single glance, shows the three dimensions of the park at Vaux (Steenbergen 1996).

Anamorphosis is a special example of perspective distortion. 'In the visual arts, [this is] an ingenious perspective technique used to give a distorted image of the subject represented in a picture when seen from the usual viewpoint, but so executed that if viewed from a particular angle, or reflected in a curved mirror, the distortion disappears and the image in the picture appears normal' (Britannica).

Combined with *trompe l'oeil*, anamorphosis has been used to create perspective effects in buildings (Dars 1979). Forms and patterns in

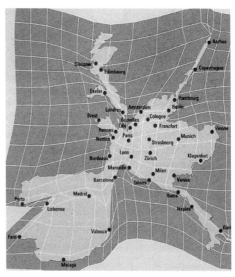

The effect of high-speed trains on travel times. Maps can also be drawn as anamorphoses.

Source: Ministerie VROM. 1999. Ruimtelijke Verkenning RPD. SDU, The Hague

floors or walls can be distorted to create surprising and misleading images that change according to the position of the observer.

Perspective views can also be manipulated in pavement patterns. Thus, the size of a terrace divided into a series of rectangles which enlarge with increasing distance from the observer looks smaller than it actually is (Steenbergen 1996).

Anamorphosis may also be used in national

The transformation of an image of St John at Patmos in an anamorphosis drawn on a wall. The figure stretches out towards the rear.

Source: Steenbergen C.M. 1990. De Stap over de Horizon. Dissertation, faculty of architecture, Delft University of Technology

or regional maps when measured distances are expressed in terms of the time needed to travel from A to B. Thus, compared to the standard map of western Europe, the map showing travelling distances between European cities by high-speed trains is distorted.

- Amidon J. 2001. 'Light, Colour, Texture'. In: *Radical Landscapes. Reinventing Outdoor Space*. Thames & Hudson, London pp. 10-37
- Andersson S.I. 2003. 'Gardens in Fantasy and Reality'. In: Kerkstra K. (ed). *The Landscape of Symbols*. Blauwdruk publishers, Wageningen pp. 41-62
- Arnheim R. 1969. 'Light creates space'. In: *Art and Visual Perception*. Faber Editions, London pp. 300-305
- Cosgrove D. 1993. 'Perspective'. In: *The Palladian Landscape*. Leicester University Press, Leicester pp. 199-200
- Crandell G. 1993. 'Centering the Spectator: the Renaissance'. In: *Nature Pictorialized*. Johns Hopkins University Press, New York pp. 59-72
- Dars C. 1979. *Images of deception*. Phaidon, London.
- Giedion S. 1967. 'The new space-conception: perspective'. In: *Space Time and Architecture*. Harvard University Press, Cambridge pp. 30-40
- Gombrich E.H. 1972. *The Story of Art*. Phaidon London pp. 171-172, 190-191.
- Gombrich E.H. 1982. 'Perspective: geometrical proof and psychological puzzle'. In: *The Image and the Eye*. Phaidon Press, London pp. 189-196
- Hamilton Hazlehurst F. 1980. *Gardens of Illusion*. Vanderbilt University Press, Nashville, Tennessee. pp. 17-45; 59-152
- Lockard W.K. 1974 (2001). *Design Drawing*. Pepper Publishing.
- Montague J. 1998. *Basic Perspective Drawing* (3rd edition). John Wiley & Sons, New York
- Moore C.W. (et al) 1989. *The Poetics of Gardens*. MIT Press Cambridge pp. 8-9
- Rousseau J.J. 1762. *Emile, of over de opvoeding*. Boom, Meppel

1980 pp. 136
- Steenbergen C.; Reh W. 1996. *Architecture and landscape*. Thoth, Bussum pp. 42-44, 149, 181
- Weiss A. 1998. 'Dematerialisation and iconoclasm'. In: *Unnatural Horizons. Paradox & Contradiction in Landscape Architecture*. Princeton Architectural Press, New York pp. .45 ff.

Phenomenology

see also > image, legibility, perception, values

'An approach that concentrates on the study of consciousness and the objects of direct experience' (*Oxford English Dictionary*).

Phenomenology might explain what, in its most common and fundamental sense, 'landscape' means to us: our belief that through our sight, hearing and movements – in short, our presence – a world arises before us. There is an inseparable connection between subject and object. With every thread of our existence, we are connected with the world around us (Lemaire 1999). In this way, phenomenology is diametrically opposed to the Descartian separation of subject and object which, for instance, underlies landscape evaluation techniques that attribute objects with properties such as goodness and beauty.

245

- Lemaire T. 1999. 'Een wijsgerige wandeling door het landschap' (i.e. A philosopher's walk in the countryside. In: Kolen J.; Lemaire T. *Landschap in meervoud*. Jan van Arkel, Utrecht

The difference between a design by Capability Brown and a picturesque design for the same site, according to Richard Payne Knight.

Source: Sørensen C.Th. 1959. Europas Havekunst. G.E.C. Gads Forlag, Copenhage

Picturesque

see also > Arcadian, composition, pastoral, poetic, Romanticism

'Resembling a picture: suggesting a painted scene' (*Webster*).

As early as the 15th century, a picturesque landscape or a picturesque scene was defined as a view of a man-made landscape or a garden that looked similar to painting (Andersson 2002).

Dutch landscape painters and the French painters Nicolas Poussin (1594-1665) and Claude Lorrain (1600-1682) all had a strong influence on the English clergyman-painter William Gilpin (1724-1804), whose sketchbooks contained images of scenery from all over England and, in combination with his written observations, made the landscapes of Britain at the time known to a larger public (Batey 1996; Rogers 2001). In these drawings and his paintings, rural scenes were filtered in order to look safe and pleasant: any unpleasantness – such as manure heaps, horseflies or aggressive bulls – were absent. Though such omissions often require quite an effort on the part of the artist (Turner 1985), a benign gloss was superimposed on reality (Hunt 1992).

The compositional rules for the picturesque landscape style as applied in the design of estate grounds were derived from painting, with a foreground, a middle-ground and a background, the whole scene being framed in side screens (Stauffacher 1988). The picturesque image of reality on canvas was later inverted by Uvedale Price (1747-1829), who claimed that landscapes and parks should be laid out according to picturesque ideas (Price 1810). In England the 'Picturesque Style' partly preceded and partly overlapped 19th-century Romanticism (Reh 1995).

During the second part of the 18th century, the picturesque style spread throughout Europe, known variously as *jardin anglais*, *ferme ornée*, *Englischer Garten* and *giardino inglese*, and with many transitions between a picturesque layout and a geometric one (Hunt 2002).

In 20th-century landscape planning, the picturesque ideal was at odds with the Functionalist approach of landscape architects that was then dominant, which opposed official planning policies that called for the planting of tree-belts or hedges as a means of screening unsightly elements in rural areas. In the Functionalist view, such measures worked against their ideal of a landscape that was legible and clearly structured.

- Andersson S.I. 2003. 'Gardens in fantasy and reality – learning from Villa Barbaro'. In: Kerkstra K. (ed) *The landscape of symbols*. Blauwdruk publishers, Wageningen
- Batey M. 1996. 'Enamoured of Gilpin on the Picturesque'. In: *Jane Austen and the English Landscape*. Barn Elms, London
- Hunt D.J. 1992. *Gardens and the Picturesque. Studies in the History of Landscape Architecture*. MIT Press, Cambridge
- Hunt J.D. 2002. *The Picturesque Garden in Europe*. Thames & Hudson, London
- Price U. 1810 (reprint 1971). *Essays on the Picturesque. On the Use of Studying Pictures for the Purpose of Improving Real Landscape*. Maerman, London
- Reh W. 1995. *Arcadie en metropolis*. Ph.D thesis Technical University Delft pp. 41 ff.
- Rogers E.B. 2001. *Landscape Design. A Cultural and Architectural History*. Abrams, New York pp 252 ff.
- Stauffacher Solomon B. 1988. *Green Architecture and the Agrarian Garden*. Rizolli, New York pp. 14-15; 31-40; 74-86
- Turner R. 1985. *Capability Brown*. Weidenfeld & Nicholson, London pp. 33 ff.

Place

see also > adaptation, context, garden, identity, layer, park, pattern, square, system

'Particular area or position in space occupied by somebody or something. City, town or village. Building or area of land used for a particular purpose. A natural or suitable position for something. Rank, position or role in society' (*Oxford English Dictionary*).

'To be at all – to exist in any way – is to be somewhere, and to be somewhere is to be in some kind of place' (Casey 1997). An environment in which a number of phenomena are assembled can be called a place. Individual, visible and tangible phenomena such as trees and houses are rarely self-contained; in various ways, they are connected or related. Some of these phenomena may include or contain others. A forest contains trees and also constitutes an environment for trees. A town is a collection of buildings with movements and activities in between. Activities and events 'take place', which means that every happening occurs in some locality.

Places of natural origin ('natural places') are determined by topography, water, vegetation. In a country such as the Netherlands, only semi-natural places exist. These occur at different scales, from landscape type to landscape element.

Places of a cultural origin ('man-made places'), also called *genius loci*, exist where the configuration of human settlement has adapted to the natural environment and where its architecture determines the type of space (Hunt 1975; Norberg-Schulz 1980). People live there, feel at home and sustain social and emotional ties.

'The place is always limited; it has been created by man and set up for his special purpose' (Norberg-Schulz 1971).

However, a 'limited' place can also be quite large, such as the urbanised zone of the Randstad region in the Netherlands. This metropolitan area can be seen as a *lieu de mémoire*, embodying 'the visual evidence of how mass culture has brought the historical delta landscape to life' (Taverne 1994).

A place may be found in a small corner: Genoa, Italy.

A private space can be created anywhere. At the edge of a lake at Slijk Ewijk, the Netherlands.

We recognise a place in its combination of characteristics and meanings (Canter 1977; Motloch 2001). The most meaningful places are those in which culture merges with nature.

These places have a strong social or emotional density; as they are saturated with history, they contain a certain amount of non-transparency. They constitute the real *genius loci*, defined by Alexander Pope (1688-1744) as 'The presiding deity or spirit; the tutelary god or attendant spirit of a place. Every place is unique by its physical composition and the way in which it is experienced; and it should be the objective of every perceptive and sensitive observer to be aware of the special character of a place; and every landscape designer to enhance and not to destroy that unique quality.'

The title 'place-maker' conferred upon the 18th-century English landscape architect Lancelot 'Capability' Brown (1716-1783) may therefore be seen as a most flattering statement (Batey 1996).

A place is rarely an indivisible whole. Instead, it normally consists of a series of places between which people move along paths. While desert nomads keep moving from one place to another over long, predetermined routes, the inhabitants of a unified place called 'home' move their positions during the day between smaller places such as the living room, the kitchen, the desk and the bedroom. All such places are centres in an organised world 'connected by an intricate path, pauses in movement, markers in routine and circular time' (Tuan 1977). 'In a life-span, a man now – as in the past – can establish profound routes only in a small corner of the world' (Tuan 1974). There is a complex relationship between time and space, in which movement, change, memory and rootedness all play a role. Space, time, path and place therefore belong to the core concepts of landscape architecture.

Places also have a social dimension. Events 'take place'. Relations between people in society are such that each person knows 'his place' in the local order – a 'standing' related to factors such as material wealth, social prestige, character and blood relations, and

A meaningless place with a farm cart used as a planter.

A cultural place: a settlement related to its environment. Strmica, Slovenia.

legible in external attributes such as clothing and behaviour, and in the location and character of dwellings (Casey 1997; van der Woud 1998).

The counterpart of a place is the 'non-place' or '*non-lieu*', a location perceived only through the eyes of a passer-by, for which people feel no particular attachment. Non-places are anonymous and exchangeable. They vary between monotonous suburban districts (Rowe 1991), local bank counters and supermarkets, railway stations and petrol stations, the 'catering places'. They are without a history and are completely transparent (Augé 2000).

The increase in the number of non-places in our mobile society may be seen as a threat to the real places, but, to some, these derided landscapes have a specific quality. Painter Edward Hopper (1882-1967) found poetry in them, his paintings suggesting a consistent interest in different kinds of travelling place (de Botton 2003). There is also the possibility that a non-place may eventually develop into a real one. Where people meet, where farewell and welcoming occur simultaneously, as at airports and railway stations, there is generally an atmosphere of emotional involvement (Hajer 2000).

Pseudo-places are different. Unlike 'real' travellers who undertake a journey to unknown and unfamiliar places that require interpretation and much effort to explore, tourists depart for remote places that have been selected from the package deal of travel agencies. These have been inspected in travel brochures and are visited as part of guided tours. Recognition is pre-programmed and immediate (Fussell 1980).

Finally there is the 'vacant' or 'dishonest' place – an outdoor space laid out with the intention of creating certain atmospheres and moods that bear no relation to the environment of the place, or may even be in conflict with it. One example is the 'silent bird-sanctuary' adjoining a motorway near Rotterdam: laid out around a lake created as the by-product of sand-extraction activities, it is equipped with bird-watching facilities that allow the visitor to observe waterfowl in the middle of the noise and stench of heavy

250

traffic (ten Hooven 1999).

- Augé M. 2000. *Non-places. Introduction to an Anthropology of Supermodernity.* Verso, London
- Batey M. 1996. 'A mere nothing before Repton'. In: *Jane Austen and the English landscape.* Barn Elms, London pp. 80.
- de Botton A. 2003. 'On travelling places'. In: *The Art of Travel.* Penguin Books, London pp. 31-62
- Canter D. 1977. *The Psychology of Place.* The Architectural Press, London pp. 6-12
- Casey E.S. 1997. *The Fate of Place. A Philosophical History.* University of California Press, Berkeley p. ix p. 313
- Fussell P. 1980. 'Tourism and anti-tourism'. In: *Abroad.* Oxford University Press.
- Hajer M.; Reijndorp A. 2000. *In search of a new public domain. Analysis and strategy.* NAi publishers, Rotterdam pp. 44 ff.
- ten Hooven M. 1999. 'De stilte wordt eenzaam in het landschap' (i.e. Silence becomes loneliness in the landscape). In: Kolen J.; Lemaire T. *Landschap in meervoud.* Jan van Arkel, Utrecht pp. 31-33
- Hunt J.D.; Willis P. 1975. *The Genius of the Place.* Paul Elek, London
- Motloch J. 2001. 'Sense of Place'. In: *Introduction to Landscape Design.* Van Nostrand Reinhold, London pp. 193 ff.
- Norberg-Schulz C. 1971. *Existence, Space and Architecture.* Studio Vista, London p. 19
- Norberg-Schulz C. 1980. *Genius Loci.* Academy Editions, London. pp. 6-76
- Rowe P.G. 1991. 'Placelessness or Place?'. In: *Making a Middle Landscape.* MIT Press, Cambridge pp. 56 ff.
- Taverne E. 1994. 'The Randstad. Horizons of a diffuse city'. In: ARCHIS. Journal for architecture, urbanism and visual arts, NAi, Rotterdam pp. 26-51
- Tuan Yi-Fu. 1974. Topophilia. *A Study of Environmental Perception, Attitudes and Values.* Prentice-Hall Inc. Englewood Cliffs, New Jersey p. 100
- Tuan Yi-Fu. 1977. 'Time and place'. In: *Space and Place. The Perspective of Experience.* Edward Arnold publishers, London pp. 179 ff.
- van der Woud A. 1998. *Het Lege Land* (i.e. *The empty land*). Contact, Amsterdam pp. 322-323

Poetic

see also > aesthetic, Arcadia, landscape style, pastoral, picturesque, Romanticism

'Writing in language chosen and arranged to create a particular emotional response through meaning, sound and rhythm. A quality that stirs the imagination. A quality of ease and grace' (*Webster*).

Poetry – in Greek, *poisis* – literally means 'to make, to create', especially a poem. Whereas musicians may produce concepts such as harmony and rhythm, and the landscape painter compositions of landscape images, the wording of emotions is the domain of the poet (Drabble 1979). Poetry has always had a strong influence on garden art; a garden, like a piece of music, is a poetic composition (Moore 1989; Hunt 2000). Alexander Pope (1688-1744) was a poet as well as a gardener.

A poetic perception of landscape is closely connected with Romanticism. During the Romantic Age, melancholy, sentiment, fear, tragedy, heroism and sublime experiences were often intermixed such that they could hardly be distinguished from one another. They were epitomised in landscapes with solitude and places of horror, dark pinewoods, grottoes, ruins and 'wuthering heights' (Batey 1996).

An 18th-century painter was 'a poet in colours, effects, lines and shapes, and in his vision nature should not be viewed as through a mirror, but portrayed subjectively through the individual poetic understanding of the artist' (de Leeuw 1997).

Poetic expression is visible in the 'genius of the place'. A new aesthetics of contemporary landscape architecture should be based on a connection between feeling, functionality and meaning (Spirn 1988). An example of such a connection may be found in the poetic garden 'Little Sparta' near Edinburgh, Scotland, laid out and owned by the artist Ian Hamilton Finlay (Weilacher 1996).

* Batey M. 1996. 'The Gothic imagination'. In: *Jane Austen and the English Landscape*. Barn Elms, London pp. 40 ff.
* Drabble M. 1979. *A Writer's Britain. Landscape in Literature*. Thames and Hudson, London
* Hunt J.D. 2000. 'Gardens in Word and Image'. In: *Greater Perfections. The Practice of Garden Theory*. Thames & Hudson, London pp. 143-179.
* de Leeuw R. 1997. 'De verbeelding van het landschap in de achttiende en negentiende eeuw' (i.e. The pictorialisation of landscapes in the 18th and 19th century). In: Loos W. (et al). (ed). *Langs Velden en Wegen*. V+K Publishing, Blaricum pp. 20-21
* Moore C.W. (et al). 1989. *The Poetics of Gardens*. MIT Press, Cambridge, Preface and pp. 13 ff.
* Spirn A.W. 1988 'The poetics of City and Nature: towards a new aesthetic for urban design. In: Landscape Journal, The University of Wisconsin Press, Urbana, Illinois pp.108-126
* Weilacher U. 1996. 'Poetry in Nature Unredeemed'. In: *Between Landscape Architecture and Land Art*. Birkhäuser, Basel

Polarity

see also > border

Polar means 'diametrically opposite' (*Webster*).

In most landscapes, polar opposites exist in terms of form, location, meaning or substance. Examples include land/water, urban/rural, culture/nature, high/low, front/back. These extremes often contrast sharply in a particular spot or along a borderline or edge – when, for example, the surf breaks on a rocky coast. Polar opposites

251

The front and rear facades of 19th-century dwellings in Wageningen, the Netherlands.

may also be connected via a gradual transition zone or by such transitory elements as the succession of elements on a beach – from surf to sand bank, to groyne, to dune base and slope, and finally to the top of a dune.

In some Dutch polders there are polar opposites between front and rear – in the built-up ribbon developments along the main road on one side, and the rear limits of land parcels on the other side. The built-up front part is characterised by complexity and intensive small-scale land-use. The rear part of the land is accessible via narrow roads

Dunes and surf connected by dam and stairway. The extremes are dry and wet, high and low. The Westerscheldt near Zoutelande, the Netherlands.

that give access to open pastureland offering distant views. This is the more natural part, reserved for cattle and other animals. It has a simple layout, an extensive use, and a quiet atmosphere (Coeterier 2000). These extremes are at some distance from each other, and are connected by a sequence of land parcels of gradually increasing size. The recognition of this polarity is an important condition for successful landscape planning.

In buildings, polar opposites are found in the contrast between front and back. As fronts are often part of street facades, they are the most representative and the best-maintained parts. A prominent front door and a decorated facade contribute to a display of affluence, and may often refer to history. The backs of buildings often look less well kept (Bloomer 1977).

Front gardens are often laid out in a 'representative' way. Part of the face of a dwelling, they contribute to the expression of affluence and well-adapted citizenship. While the front is formal and socially oriented, the back yard is the place for informal family activities (Jackson 1995];Yi-Fu-Tuan 2002).

- Bloomer K.C.; Moore C. 1977. *Body, Memory and Architecture*. Yale University Press, New Haven pp. 1 ff.
- Coeterier F. 2000. *Hoe beleven wij onze omgeving* (i.e. *How we experience our environment*). Published by the author, Wageningen ISBN 90-9014237-1 p.109
- Jackson J.B. 1995. 'Ghosts at the door'. In: *Landscape in Sight. Looking at America*. Yale University Press, New Haven pp. 107-109
- Yi-Fu Tuan. 2002. 'Landscape at a microscale: home and garden'. In: Olwig. K.R. *Landscape Nature and the Body Politic*. The University of Wisconsin Press pp. xii-xiii

Polder

see also > dam, dike, geometry, heritage, island

'A tract of low land reclaimed from a body of water, (as the sea) [Dutch]' (*Websters*). This definition is amplified in the Dutch dictionary: 'a piece of land or an area enclosed by channels within which the water level is artificially controlled by means such as windmills or pumps. Polders can be divided into marine polders or reclaimed

land, river polders and peatland. Polders are usually managed collectively by regional water boards' (*van Dale*).

While the wide expanses of a Dutch polder landscape may be a unique sight, and thus be one of the country's national emblems, the water-management system which maintains their function is also specifically Dutch (van de Ven 1993).

Although parts of the Netherlands' medieval polder landscape are still intact, much of it has been transformed by urbanisation and land-reconsolidation plans. All of it, however, owes its existence to the 16th-century technology that first made it

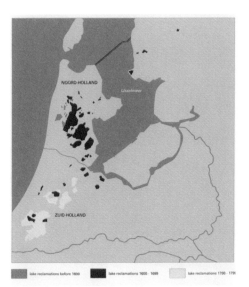

253

Map of the Netherlands showing areas of reclaimed land.

Source: van de Ven G.P. (ed) 1993. Man-made Lowlands. History of Water Management and Land Reclamation in the Netherlands. Matrijs publishing, Utrecht. p. 132

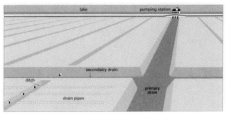

Schematic representation of the water-management system in a polder.

Source: van de Ven G.P. (ed) 1993. Man-made Lowlands. History of Water Management and Land Reclamation in the Netherlands. Matrijs publishing Utrecht p. 248

possible to create new land by draining lakes – an advance which was extended in the 17th century by the invention of the windmill. The new land was laid out in geometric patterns (Lambert 1971).

In the 20th-century polders, many polders were reclaimed when the Zuiderzee was closed in order to create the freshwater IJsselmeer. These polders are characterised by multiple land-use and extensive urbanisation (van der Wal 1997).

• Lambert A.M. 1971. 'The Golden Age'. In: *The Making of the Dutch Landscape*. Seminar Press, London pp. 179-228
• van de Ven G.P. (ed). 1993. *Man-made Lowlands. History of Water Management and Land Reclamation in the Netherlands*. Matrijs publishing, Utrecht pp. 131-136; 185-204; 237-286
• van der Wal C. 1997. *In Praise of Common Sense. Planning the ordinary. A physical planning history of the new towns in the IJsselmeerpolder*. 010 publishers, Rotterdam

Postmodernism

see also > eclecticism, map, modernism, symbol

'Modern architecture died in St Louis Missouri at 3.32 p.m. (or thereabouts) on July 15, 1972, when the infamous Pritt-Igoe scheme, or rather several of its slab blocks, was given the final coup de grâce by dynamite. Previously it had been vandalised, mutilated and defaced by its black inhabitants' (Jencks 1977).

Apparently, the ideals of Modernism in architecture had failed, to be replaced by a

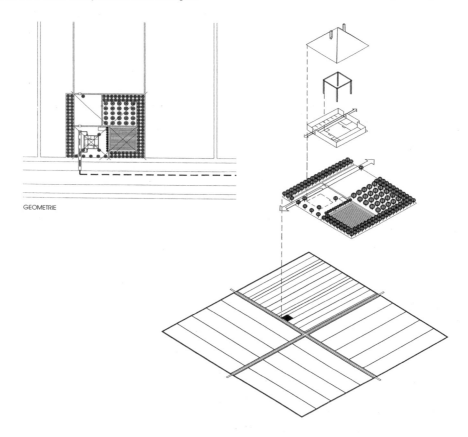

GEOMETRIE

A square farmhouse fitting into the geometric pattern of a reclaimed polder in the province of Noord-Holland, the Netherlands.

Source: Reh W.; Steenbergen C. (ed). 1999. Zee van Land. De droogmakerij als architectonisch experiment. Faculty of Architecture at Delft University of Technology p. 43

new movement.

Postmodernism is a movement 'critical of the general, centralised, purposive and distanced characteristics of modern thought' (Cooke 1990). It involves the denial of certainties that are the basis for total planning, such as the creation of wholes, hierarchic procedures and hierarchic patterns, all dependent on the existence of a central authority. It means that the vertical differentiation of the Modernist cultural sphere is discarded. Art forms are no longer characterised by uniqueness, originality and singularity, but are mechanically and electronically reproduced (Urry 2002).

In architectural theory, Postmodernism means a rejection of the Functionalist and purist ideals associated with modern architecture, and with the principles and ideals of movements such as De Stijl in Holland, the Bauhaus in Germany, and the concepts of architects such as Le Corbusier (1887-1965) and Mies van der Rohe (1886-1969). Underlying the rise of Postmodernism is the degeneration of these Modernist ideals into a monotonous and sterile architecture, which made a countermovement inevitable:

'It was time to redefine the modern canon, and to open the floodgates to all the drama, rhetoric playfulness, irony, weirdness, inconsistency, multivalence and extravagance, that their votaries of 'the Style' had worked so hard to keep out' (Berman 1988).

Among the influential publications that voiced discontent and introduced the movement were those of Jane Jacobs (Jacobs 1961) and Robert Venturi (Venturi 1966). Post-modern design is based on the view that the world is not an orderly and well-organised whole, but disintegrating, fragmented, full of contrasts and with a surprising individual expression. From then on – or at least until the next countermovement – the emphasis would be on a multitude of symbols, metaphors and references (Harvey 1990).

Architect Robert Venturi puts it this way: 'Signs and symbols prevail over spatial composition, the ephemeral, the fleeting [...]. Alienated objects which emanate a feeling of estrangement heighten the awareness of the observer [...] but for whom and for how long? Meaning can be enhanced by breaking the order; the exception points to the rule [...]

255

Exuberant presentation of the design of Schouwburgplein, Rotterdam. 1988. West 8 landscape architects.

contrast supports meaning [...] an artful discord gives vitality to architecture' (Venturi 1977). In landscape architecture, obscure and mysterious references are reintroduced, legible to insiders only.

Post-modern space is an autonomous phenomenon and can be created on the basis of purely aesthetic motives without any relation to social objectives. Although the random borrowing of forms and symbols from the past leads to a suspicion of unrestrained eclecticism, such criticism is ignored by the Post-modern designer.

Some observers point to other negative features: 'a Post-modern landscape will be silent and contain dark corners; it is transparent and without any history, an almost ultimate product of a technocratic society' (Lemaire 1999).

In 21st-century Dutch landscape architecture, the difference between 'Modern' and 'Post-modern' or 'Neo-modern' is a relative one. Movements in architecture are never homogeneous anyway, but they share the urge to control form and space, to lay down precisely, to detail carefully. 'Postmodernism is not anti-modern or reactionary', says Charles Jencks (1987). The aesthetic rules are similar, but there is more flair and self-confidence. Dogmas on social equality and the primacy of nature are viewed with some scepticism. The rendering and presentation of design proposals also change. Precise ink drawings are replaced by exuberant three-dimensional representations.

• Berman M. 1988. 'The experience of modernity'. In: Thackara J. *Design after Modernism*. Thames and Hudson, London p. 45
• Cooke P. 1990. *Back to the Future*. Unwin Hyman, London p.94
• Harvey D. 1990. *The Condition of Post-Modernity*, Blackwell, Oxford pp. 43, 66
• Jacobs J. 1961. *The Death and Life of Great American Cities*. Pelican Book, Harmondsworth, Middlesex
• Jencks Ch. 1977. *The Language of Post-modern Architecture*. Academy Editions, London
• Jencks C. 1987. *Post modernism. The New Classicism in Art and Architecture*. Academy Editions, London
• Lemaire T. 1999. 'Een wijsgerige wandeling door het landschap' (i.e. A philosophical walk through the landscape). In: Kolen J.; Lemaire T. (ed). *Landschap in meervoud*. Jan van Arkel, Utrecht
• Urry J. 2002. *The Tourist Gaze* (second edition). Sage Publications, London pp. 75-77

• Venturi R. 1966 (second edition 1977). *Complexity and Contradiction in Architecture*. Museum of Modern Art, New York pp. 16 ff.
• Venturi R.; Scott Brown D.; Izenour S. 1972 (revised edition 1977). *Learning from Las Vegas: the Forgotten Symbolism of Architectural form*. The MIT Press, Cambridge pp. 7 et seq.

Process

see also > dynamic, framework, layer, design method

'Something going on. A natural phenomenon marked by gradual changes that lead to a particular result. A series of actions, operations or changes leading to an end' (*Webster*).

A design process involves a succession of steps: from inventory and the formulation of objectives – based on a concept – all the way to the final product (Motloch 2001; Rutledge 1971).

Our landscapes are constantly subjected to short and long-term processes such as day and night, the monthly progress in seasonal time, the annual cycle of seasons connected with growth, propagation and death of organisms. There are also climate changes over centuries and geologic processes over millennia (Motloch 2001).

In contrast to these natural cycles, human action results in linear processes. Population growth and technological development result in irreversible changes in the landscape. Constant change is also brought by urbanisation, accessibility, the adaptation of agricultural production, and developments in land-use.

The character of landscapes is therefore dynamic, which means that any attempt to conserve or freeze an existing situation will require quite an effort, and usually be unsuccessful. All one can do is attempt to guide development through management policies and planning instruments, for example by creating structural frameworks within which a continuous process can be guided and controlled (den Ruijter 1999).

There is a marked difference between the design of a building, which results in the construction of an object that is more or less fixed, and that of an outdoor space such as a garden or a park, which merely marks the beginning of a long-term process of growth and change (Leatherbarrow 2004).

• Leatherbarrow D. 2004. *Topographical Stories. Studies in Landscape and Architecture.* The University of Pennsylvania Press, Philadelphia pp.131-133
• Motloch J.L. 2001. *Introduction to Landscape Design.* Van Nostrand Reinhold, London pp. 49-56; 286-301
• den Ruijter M. 1999. 'The Netherlands: processes versus static states'. In: Topos. European Landscape Magazine, Callwey, Munich no. 27 pp. 2-40
• Rutledge A.J. 1971. 'Site Design Process'. In: *Anatomy of a Park.* McGraw Hill Company, New York pp. 91-105

Promenade

see also > access, boulevard, flâneur

'A leisurely walk or ride, especially in a public space for pleasure or display. A place for strolling' (*Webster*).

Promenades as places to saunter or stroll became popular in 17th-century France. The activity of promenading was defined as 'to move around on foot while conversing in an agreeable way' (Rabreau 1990). 'Promenading has less to do with seeing the countryside, or

with recreation, edification or communing with nature than with communication, amusement, conversation and entertainment' (Schröder 2002). It was also considered to contribute to citizens' health (Cleary 2002).

While a promenade or esplanade normally consists of a tree-lined avenue, it may also be a walkway with attractive views and points of repose along a river, through a park, or – as at Promenade des Anglais in Nice – along the seafront (Rabreau 1990). Over the centuries, promenades in Paris have evolved from green

Promenade along Lac de Bourget, Aix-les-Bains, France.

257

Bulwark and promenade in Hulst, Zeeland, the Netherlands.
Photo: Frank de Josselin de Jong

walks along the city's edge to built-up streets in its interior: boulevards (Cleary 2002).

The concept of promenade was introduced to many towns in the Netherlands during the 19th century when derelict bulwarks and fortifications were razed. To create a pleasant urban environment for wealthy citizens in Rotterdam, broad promenades were laid out along the edge of the central urban district. As well as ponds, there were tree-lined lawns between 50 and 100 metres in width, all flanked by imposing mansions. The work was combined with the construction of a new system of canals that would improve the city's water management system (Hooimeijer 2001).

Cities today have promenades in various forms and at all scales (Schäfer 2002).

• Cleary R. 2002. 'Public Gardens and City Planning'. In: Hunt J.D.; Conan M. (ed) *Tradition and Innovation in French Garden Art*. The University of Pennsylvania Press, Philadelphia pp. 68-81
• Hooimeyer F.; Kamphuis M. 2001. *The Water Project. A nineteenth-century walk through Rotterdam*. 010 publishers, Rotterdam
• Rabreau D. 1991. 'Urban Walks in France in the Seventeenth and Eighteenth Centuries'. In : Mosser E.; Teyssot G.T. *The History of Garden Design*. Thames & Hudson, London pp. 305-316
• Schäfer R. (ed.) 2002. 'Promenades'. Special Issue. Topos

European Landscape Magazine no. 41, Callwey, München
• Schröder C.F. 2002. 'For the pleasure of the people'. In: Topos European Landscape Magazine no. 41, Callwey, München pp. 63-64

Proportion

see also > aesthetics, geometry, measure, module, scale

'The relation of one part to another or to the whole with respect to magnitude, quantity or degree' (*Webster*).

Proportions are based on measurements that are expressed in numbers. A harmonious composition requires correct proportions. The term 'harmony' stems from musicology and stands for 'pleasant to hear', but is also connected with combinations of pitch and frequency that can be laid down in numbers (Hindley 1976). 'For buildings with a tight and regular physical order it is natural for the designer to seek a matching order of divisions and relationships for the eye; and one way to do this is through a visual proportional system' (Licklider 1965).

The theory of proportions has been an object of interest for architects ever since

The inner-city promenade laid out as part of a dignified housing area. Westersingel, Rotterdam in 2003.

antiquity. Vitruvius drew the proportions of the human body, which he then transposed to spatial dimensions. As Leonardo da Vinci (1452-1519) wrote: 'Vitruvius, the architect, has it in his work on architecture that the measurements of man are arranged by nature in the following manner: four fingers make one palm and four palms make one foot; six palms make a cubit; four cubits

make a man, and four cubits make one pace and twenty-four palms make a man; and these measurements are those of his building' (March 1998). In turn, Alberti (1404-1472) applied his 'Canons of Proportion', which was based on musical systems and partly on geometric form.

In the plastic arts, garden art and architecture, an important tool for creating harmonic composition was the Golden Section, which was deemed to be 'perfect' because it could be reproduced infinitely (Eco 2005). During the Italian Renaissance, a rational system of dimensions and proportions – with a preference for the square – was the basis for the layout of villas and gardens (Steenbergen 1990). During the 20th century, architect Le Corbusier (1887-1965) reverted to this system in his publication *Le Modulor* (Corbusier 1945).

In an undulating terrain, the layout of a park cannot be based on the rules of the Golden Section. Instead, other rules of thumb are applied. For example, in order to create an agreeable composition in rolling terrain, dense woodland should relate to open space in a proportion of one to three (Bell 1993).

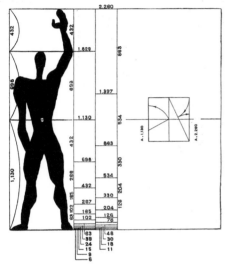

Le Corbusier's Modulor.

Source: Blake P. 1960. Le Corbusier. Aula, Utrecht

Soit un rectangle de largeur *l* et de longueur *L*.

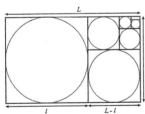

Si ce rectangle répond à la propriété suivante :

$$\frac{L}{l} = \frac{l}{L-l}$$

cette proportion se retrouve dans le rectangle obtenu en déduisant un carré du rectangle initial.

The Golden Section.

Source: Orsenna E. 2000. Portrait d'un homme heureux. André le Nôtre 1613–1700. Fayard, Paris

• Bell S. 1993. *Elements of Visual Design in the Landscape.* Spon London pp. 145-150
• Le Corbusier. 1945. *Le Modulor : essai sur une mesure harmonique a l'échelle humaine applicable universellement a l'architecture et a la mécanique. l'Architecture d'Aujour'hui,* Boulogne
• Eco U. (ed). 2004. *History of Beauty.* Rizolla, New York. Chapter III
• Hindley G. (ed). *The Larousse Encyclopedia of Music.* Hamlyn, London
• Licklider H. 1965. 'Proportional systems'. In: *Architectural Scale.* The Architectural Press, London
• March L. 1998. *Architectonics of Humanism. Essays on Number in Architecture.* Academy Editions, London pp. 107, 272 ff.
• Steenbergen C. 1990. *De Stap over de horizon* (i.e. *The step over the horizon*). PhD thesis, Delft University pp. 22 ff.

Public Space, Public domain

see also > behaviour, environmental determinism, place, space

'Public space is the stage upon which the drama of communal life unfolds' (Carr 1992).

Public space can be described from various points of view. The first is administrative and legal: by whom is it managed, for whom, and with which consequences? While, in principle, public spaces are accessible to everyone, this accessibility is subject to a gradual transition: from the public streets, squares and parks managed by public authorities, through places such as railway stations and town halls, which have regular periods of closure; to shopping malls, exhibitions and theme gardens and other spaces which are exploited on a permanent basis (Hajer 2000).

The design of an outdoor space is strongly influenced by ownership and management. Semi-public spaces requiring entrance fees can be laid out in a more refined and vulnerable manner than the freely accessible spaces where wear and tear – not to mention vandalism – call for robust equipment. One negative development is the increasing commercialisation of such spaces, where the paying user is welcome but many public activities are barred or suppressed (Zukin 1997).

A second view of public space is the historical and social one. Public outdoor spaces have always been connected with urban life (Jacobs 1961). In ancient Athens,

people could experience the complexity of urban life in the Agora, where cultural, religious, commercial, social and leisure activities were mixed. Public space was also the public domain – much appreciated, much visited, and full of activities, memories and meanings, even if it was not open to the public at all times or on all occasions (Hajer 2001). Because no social group can survive without opportunities for lasting informal contacts, contemporary outdoor public space should offer similar opportunities (Alexander 1977; Gehl 1996).

French urban squares dating from the time of Napoleon III and his prefect Georges Haussmann (1809-1891) were designed for the *grande parade* and the display of central authority. The scenes and atmospheres created here did not belong to the commonplace world of citizens. These places belonged to what Jackson (1984) calls 'the political landscape' – the complex array of a large-scale urban environment with its infrastructure and other central public facilities, all laid out and controlled by central authority.

In the Netherlands, public spaces are primarily utilitarian in character, and have

Public square in Venice Italy, seen from above.
Photo: Frank Meijer

not been designed to impress. They form the 'urban theatre' (Reijndorp 1996). But there – and in much of Europe – the public domain now seems less and less open to the general public, as it is being appropriated by business interests or marginal activities (Fliert 2000). Drastic changes have followed functional separation and increases in scale; the concept of urban open space has been expanded and now covers whole urban regions with expanding facilities for outdoor recreation and consumption (Hemel 1999).

The increasing damage caused by abuse and vandalism means that some public parks and squares have recently been reconstructed in a spectacular way, out of a belief that a multilateral and lively atmosphere will attract more visitors. Two Dutch examples are Museumplein in Amsterdam, designed by Sven Ingvar Andersson (Harsema 2000) and Schouwburgplein in Rotterdam, designed by West 8 landscape architects. Apparently the idea still holds that the right sort of planning and design of outdoor space will be beneficial in terms of improved behaviour of users. Sometimes these aims are achieved, either temporarily or in the long term.

- Alexander C. (et al). 1977. 'Common areas at the heart'. In: A Pattern Language. Oxford University Press p. 618
- Carr S. (et al).1992. *Public Space*. Cambridge University Press p. 3
- Fliert B. 2000. 'Public space: goods for sale'. In: Topos European Landscape Magazine, Callwey, München no. 33 pp. 6-17
- Gehl J.; Gemzøe L. 1996. *Public Spaces – Public Life*. Danish Architectural Association, Copenhagen
- Hajer M.; Reijndorp A. 2001. *In search of a public domain. Analysis and strategy*. NAi publishers, Rotterdam
- Harsema H. (ed.) 2000. 'Abstract buildings in a green city square'. In: *Landscape architecture and town planning in the Netherlands 97-99*. Thoth, Bussum pp. 194-197
- Hemel Z.; van Uum E. 1999. 'Open ruimte wordt openbare ruimte' (i.e. Open space becomes public space). In: Van der Wouden R. (ed). *De Stad op Straat*. Sociaal en Cultureel Planbureau, The Hague p. 90
- Jackson J.B. 1984. *Discovering the Vernacular Landscape*. Yale University Press, New Haven pp. 34-38
- Jacobs J. 1961. 'The uses of neighborhood parks'. In: *Life and Death of Great American Cities*. Penguin, Harmondsworth pp. 99 ff.
- Reijndorp A.; Nio I. 1996. *Het stedelijk theater. Ruimtelijk beleid en openbare ruimte* (i.e. *The urban theatre. Planning policy and public space*). Thoth, Bussum
- Zukin S. 1997. 'Landscapes of economic value'. In: Benedikt M. Center 10: Architecture and Design in America. The University of Texas Press, Austin pp.135 ff.

261

Museumplein Amsterdam. 1995. Landscape architect: Sven Ingvar Andersson.
Photo: Frank Meijer

Quality

see also > aesthetics, diversity, experience, flexibility, function, identity, image, orientation, sustainable, value

'Peculiar and essential character: nature. An inherent feature: property. Degree of excellence: grade. Synonyms are property, attribute' (Webster).

The quality of an object is normally determined by its appropriateness for a certain purpose. In order to establish this appropriateness, we need criteria, their nature depending on the objectives or type of use being pursued. Thus, for a tool, one might think in terms not only of its purchase and maintenance costs, but also of its long-term durability, its dependability, and the ease with which it can be handled. As the amount of time and money invested in an object can be counted, these criteria are quantifiable.

We may also attempt to determine quality on the basis of such non-utilitarian considerations as beauty, amenity, composition or significance. How such quality can be determined is a matter of values and debate; in this domain, quantitative criteria do not exist.

Though quality may be difficult to define, it is usually easy to recognise. Robert Pirsig (1977) relates the story of a teacher who asks his students to tell him what quality is. They do not know. He then invites them to inspect and rate, in terms of poor to excellent, examples of their fellow students' project-work. When a large majority of them come to the same conclusion, it is clear that they do apparently know what quality is after all...

One way of examining quality in environmental design is by examining the different approaches taken to it by those concerned with architecture, landscape and the environment.

Architectural quality

According to architects, quality depends on five factors:
· the connection between form and function
· the relationship between a building, its site, and the surroundings of both
· the clarity of the concept

· the way in which associative meanings are dealt with
· the way in which measurements and proportions are applied (Dijkstra 2001)

Landscape quality

According to the Dutch Ministry of Agriculture, landscape quality can be established on the basis both of intersubjective assessments and objective, quantifiable criteria. The Ministry's 1991 Landscape Policy Document (Anon 1991), specifies landscape quality not only as being valuable from an aesthetic point of view and as well-functioning in an ecological sense, but also as having a sound economic and functional basis. However, while the document states that landscape quality is the product of the ways in which these three conditions are met and of how they relate, it does not indicate the content and meaning of the notion of 'valuable', nor by whom this is determined...

As aesthetic quality is dependent on human perception, which is determined by so many different factors, it is therefore difficult to fathom. One such factor is the degree to which something is perceived as 'belonging'. Another is the cultural background of the observer.

Observing the panorama of a typical English landscape around Salisbury, Mr Stevens in Kazuo Ishiguro's *Remains of the Day* reflects: 'I distinctly felt that rare, yet unmistakable feeling – the feeling that one is in the presence of greatness [...]. And yet, what precisely is this greatness? [...] I would say that it is the very lack of obvious drama or spectacle that sets the beauty of our land apart. What is pertinent is the calmness of that beauty, its sense of restraint'.

Landscape quality as perceived here is connected with English history and culture, reflecting the behavioural code and view of reality of a typical Englishman – which differ markedly from the concerns that are sometimes seen as characterising other nationalities: e.g. the spectacular for an American, grandeur for a Frenchman or the common or prosaic for a Dutchman. These landscape qualities are not therefore an intrinsic trait of landscapes, but exist only because people attribute meanings, and because meanings depend on the image we

263

have of the world around us.

There is therefore no such thing as an objectively determined all-round landscape quality. The purpose and usefulness of landscape quality assessments for planning purposes may thus be debatable.

Environmental quality

This quality includes both the natural environment and the environment in which people live.

While it is assessed from various points of view that do not recognise the predominance of a single all-encompassing quality, distinctions can be made between quality that is 'true', 'just' and 'truthful'.

· True (or verifiable) quality is assessed on the basis of objective analysis of physical reality and a search for measurable causes and effects. One example of it is found in soil maps, from which suitability maps can be derived for various uses within planning.
· 'just' (or correct) quality is assessed on the basis of existing criteria or generally accepted standards. Environmental Impact Statements are based largely on these criteria.
· Truthful (or 'honest') quality depends on emotions, intentions, desires – in a word, feeling. Thus, for example, the sea should be pure and clean, and – as we saw in 1995 in the case of the Brent Spar oil-drilling platform – the Shell oil company should not dump abandoned equipment in the deep sea, even if no measurable harm is done by it. One of the best-known champions of this concept of quality is Greenpeace.

True quality and honest quality often conflict, especially when people prefer to rely on their own 'gut feeling', for example when they mistrust scientific findings that claim a certain process will not have negative effects (Jacobs 2002, 2004).

Another way to look at quality is by distinguishing between the 'dynamic' and the 'static'.

Each has a positive side and a negative side. Dynamic quality is attributed to objects and places which people value highly at a certain moment. It is associated with the new, the exciting, surprising, futuristic .The marketplace brings a constant supply of new products – the latest tunes, the newest forms, the ultimate designs. However, after the initial excitement has died away, these objects and phenomena become boring, and they are discarded, abandoned. In which context Post-modern architecture is a very dynamic phenomenon...

Static quality is attributed to objects and an environment that have been present for a long time; these things are familiar, durable – and sometimes their presence and value are not noticed until they have disappeared. Classical architecture and music have a stable and durable quality. Great monuments are always there to be visited and admired, but not all static environments are exciting – they can also inspire boredom. Due to the lack of a market place, cities in countries ruled by a dictatorship are lacking in dynamic quality, are therefore static and boring (Pirsig 1991). In general, environmental quality will thus depend on the balance between static and dynamic quality.

As landscape architecture has to deal with both aspects, landscape master plans lay out durable structures in the form of frameworks surrounding areas in which dynamic change occurs (Sijmonds 1990). However, not only do urban environments suffer considerable wear and tear, our requirements of them evolve over time. Declining levels of quality usually therefore mean that complete neighbourhoods must be reconstructed within the time-span of one generation (Harsema 2000).

· Anonymous. 1991. Visie Landschap (i.e. Landscape Policy Document). Ministerie LNV, The Hague pp. 16-19
· Dijkstra Tj. 2001. Architectonische kwaliteit (i.e. Architectonic quality). Uitgeverij 010, Rotterdam pp. 22, 23
· Harsema H. (ed). 2000. 'Reconstruction of urban areas' in: Landscape architecture and town planning in the Netherlands 97-99. Thoth, Bussum pp. 45-53
· Ishiguro K. 1989. *The Remains of the Day*. Faber & Faber, London
· Jacobs M. 2002. Landschap 3. Alterra, Wageningen University and Research Centre
· Jacobs M. 2004. 'Metropolitan matterscape, powerscape and mindscape' in: Tress G&B. (et al) (ed). Planning Metropolitan Landscapes: Concepts, Demands, Approaches. DELTA series 4, Wageningen University and Research Centre.
· Pirsig R.M. 1974. Zen and the Art of Motor Cycle Maintenance. An Inquiry into Values. Harper Collins, New York/London
· Pirsig R.M. 1991. Lila. An Inquiry into Morals. Bantam Books, New York
· Sijmons D. 1990. Regional planning as a strategy. In Landscape and Urban Planning, Elsevier, Amsterdam no. 18 pp. 265-273

Recognition

see also > identity, image, structure

To recognise means 'to be able to identify somebody or something that one has seen or heard before; to know somebody or something again' (*Oxford Advanced*)

To know something 'again' refers to a memory of phenomena one has seen earlier. Although this memory is helpful in imagining or conceiving something (Schacter 1996), there are limits to the amount of visual impressions the human memory can store. This is because only the dominant elements are retained.

Orientation within urban space is underlain by a shared, communal image of cities; this consists of a collage of images determined by a number of characteristic and dominant elements (Lynch 1959). While recognition may be facilitated by repeated exposure to the same environment, an environment will also need a certain amount of internal coherence or structure.

Recognition is also connected with the identity of the objects or spaces perceived, in which a role is played by projections and visual anticipation. The recognition of familiar images may provide a feeling of certainty – which may either be pleasurable or boring (Gombrich 1954). On the other hand, a completely new sensation caused by an unanticipated event may cause a shock effect that is very stimulating and creates new interest. History shows that new developments in technology and the arts provided exciting news. These included inventions such as the steam turbine in 1884 and the electromotor and pneumatic tyre in 1888, but also paintings by Picasso (1881-1973) and the utopian architecture of Le Corbusier (1887-1965) (Hughes 1980).

- Gombrich E. 1954. *Art and Illusion*. Phaidon Press, London
- Hughes R. 1980 *The shock of the New*. BBC publications ,London
- Lynch K. 1959. *The Image of the City*. MIT Press, Cambridge pp. 46 ff.
- Schacter D. 1996. *Searching for Memory: the Brain, the Mind, and the Past*. Harper Collins, London

Reconstruction

see > restoration

Reduction, Reductionism

see also > *analysis, image, perception, recognition, system*

'Change something to a more general or basic form' (*Oxford Advanced*).

In perceiving the environment, the human eye and brain are confronted with an overload of stimuli that cannot be processed simultaneously. To help the observer to recognise and remember, a complex image is therefore reduced to its main outlines.

This need for simplicity is exploited by artists and designers who also reduce their images and forms to the main outlines, thereby allowing the viewer to complete the picture. Prominent examples in the Netherlands are the *Miffy* children's books by

'Portrait of Hansje' by Bart van der Leck.

Simplified plan of the Paris Metro.

Dick Bruna, and some of the paintings by Bart van der Leck (1876-1958), a member of De Stijl, the Dutch New Plastic Art Movement established in 1917 (Jaffé 1956). In the plastic arts, reduction as a form of visual coding is a well-known phenomenon (Gombrich 1982).

In maps and plans of landscapes and towns, the real situation on the earth's surface is presented in reduced form. In regional planning, such a reduction of reality is inescapable, as a planner or designer will draw some of the main outlines on the topographical maps that are needed for a design proposal. Attempts to make use of all available data would lead nowhere: in order to develop new concepts, information must be reduced and side-issues ignored (de Jong 1992).

Reductionism is 'the tendency to analyse, or principle of analysing, complex things into simple constituents' (*The Concise Oxford Dictionary*).

Modernist environmental design is associated with a reductionist view which holds that the social and physical environment is reducible to a combination of so-called 'basic elements' that can be subjected to objective observation and scientific diagnosis. On the basis of such research, the environment can thus be comprehended and subjected to control.

Landscape or site analysis, as one of the constituent parts of a design process, is a reductionistic activity. Before attempting any design activity that will change the function and composition of a landscape or site, a landscape architect needs to understand the 'how' and 'why' of the existing functions. But because the human mind cannot possibly understand the full complexity of all the social and environmental processes in a landscape, this landscape is dissected – or reduced – to its constituent parts. These are separately studied and evaluated, with the aim of combining them anew at a later stage of the design process (Steiner 2000).

Problems arise when the relationships between the dissected parts are unknown or ignored, and when the analysis fails to include personal, social and cultural factors. Without an additional creative input by designers, neither does an emphasis on logic and deduction lead to design solutions. For all such reasons, the Modernist approach to design and planning became suspect – explaining why Postmodernist design advocates holism as a new and better approach: 'the reductionist view of the environment and its exclusive and elitist view of environmentalist design' must be replaced by an holistic, 'all-inclusive' approach (Koh 2004, 2005).

Values, meanings and artistic imagination must be included in the design process. Even if it is not yet clear how designers can learn to understand the processes and relationships in complex environments, and then apply their knowledge in a new design methodology, this new approach may be a marked improvement.

• Gombrich E. 1982. 'Image and code'. In: *The Image and the Eye.* Phaidon, London pp. 278-197
• Jaffè H.C.L. *de Stijl 1917-1931. The Dutch contribution to modern art.* Meulenhoff, Amsterdam pp. 45-49
• de Jong T. 1992. *Kleine methodologie voor ontwerpend onderzoek* (i.e. *A methodology for design research*). Boom, Meppel p. 59
• Koh J. 2004. *Ecological Reasoning and Architectural Imagination.* Inaugural Address, Wageningen University
• Koh J. 2005. 'Ecological Design. A New Post-Modern Design Paradigm: One of Holistic Philosophy and Evolutionary Ethic'. In: Topos: Periodiek van het Laboratorium voor de Ruimtelijke Planvorming Jaargang 15 no. 2 Wageningen University
• Steiner F. 2000. *The Living Landscape.* McGraw Hill, New York pp. 13-17

267

Reference, Referential images

see also > design tools, image, symbol

To refer is 'to place in a certain class so far as cause, relationship, or source is concerned. To have a relation or a connection' (*Webster*).

Whether old or new, most parks and gardens refer to other worlds, both in their layout and by means of the objects and ornaments displayed in them. These other worlds may be rural, 'natural', exotic or faraway. A sequence of spaces in a park is laid out in such a way that optical illusions 'create zones of virtual realities to be surfed or promenaded at will by the visitor' (Hunt 2002).

Inversely, the outside world may be

The seaport paraphrased: Schouwburgplein, Rotterdam, with gantries, funnels and ship's decks. West 8 landscape architects, 1988.

Reproducing an imagined past. Poster produced by the World Wildlife Fund in 1987, showing an ideal natural landscape to be created in the flood plain of the river Rhine.

paraphrased in a designed outdoor space – the definition of 'paraphrase' being 'to express the meaning of (a word, phrase, passage, or work) in other words, usually with the object of fuller and clearer expositions' (*Oxford English Dictionary*). However, in Las Vegas, Nevada, some buildings refer almost all too directly to their

Las Vegas, the gambling city.

The Dutch polder landscape paraphrased: Garden at the IGA International Horticultural Exhibition 1964 in Hamburg. Landscape architect: M.J. Vroom.

function of gambling hall.

In Rotterdam's Schouwburgplein, cranes and ventilation shafts paraphrase the seaport with its derricks and ships decks. The Dutch garden at the 1964 IGA Horticultural Exposition in Hamburg paraphrased the Dutch landscape with its quays and long, straight polder ditches (Hauxner 2003).

To illustrate design proposals, pictures of environments that exist elsewhere can be used as referential images. Sketches, photographs and collages of photographs of outdoor spaces or landscapes can all help graphically and illustratively to show the intentions of the design.

More abstract historical or geographical references may serve as reminders of past situations or developments. However, as such references are sometimes used as examples to be imitated, they risk being interpreted as objectives for contemporary developments (Sijmons 1998). Some nature managers in the Netherlands obtain their references and dreams from imagined landscapes in Roman times, attempting to re-create the situation when humans were a rare species in the lowlands.

269

• Hauxner M. 2003. *Open to the Sky.* Danish Architectural Press, Copenhagen pp. 183-184
• Hunt J.D. 2002. 'Reinventing the Parisian Park'. In: Dixon J.D.; Conan M. (ed). *Tradition and Innovation in French Garden Art. Chapters of a New History.* The University of Pennsylvania Press p. 204
• Sijmons D. 1998. 'Referentiebeelden: misbruik wordt gestraft' (i.e. The abuse of references will be punished). In: = *Landschap.* Architecture & Natura, Amsterdam pp. 94-96

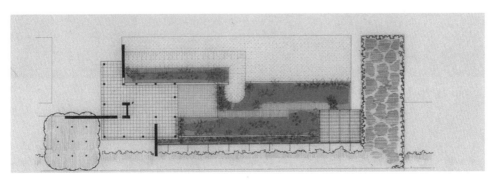

Renaissance

see also > Arcadia, Classicism, geometry, hill,
Mannerism, perspective, proportion

'The movement or period in Europe
between the 14th and 17th centuries marked
by a revival of interest in classical arts and
literature and by the beginnings of modern
science. Also: the neoclassic style of
architecture prevailing during the
Renaissance' (*Webster*).

In 15th-century Italy, landscape-as-space
was 'rediscovered' as an object of
architectonic manipulation. The building of
villas outside such cities as Florence, Rome
and Venice was prompted by a search for the
Arcadian life among wealthy citizens, who
sought sensory delight in representations of
a lost but perfect world. The thoughts and
ideals expressed in early Renaissance
gardens are manifest in the work of the
artistic all-rounder Leon Battista Alberti
(1404-1472).

Gardens were laid out on terraced slopes,
and enclosed spaces were opened up to
distant views (Lazarro 1990; Thacker 1985).
Architect Andrea Palladio (1508-1580)
designed *belvederi* – villas with excellent
views – for landowners in Veneto,
emphasising 'a choice of a healthy location
with clean air and clean water in a beneficial
nature' (Cosgrove 1993; Leupen 1997; Rogers
2001).

The basis for the theory of proportions lay
in the mathematical dissection of space as
related to the dimensions of the human
body. Geometric schemes underlay the layout
of outdoor spaces, which were related to the
distant horizon through the rules of
perspective (Shepherd 1953; Steenbergen
1996; Kluckert 2000). The prime objectives
were the creation of unity and coherence.

'Renaissance art does not allow the viewer
[...] to stop to inspect details or to detach a
single element from the overall composition.
[Instead] he is forced to absorb all parts in
one single observation' (Hauser 1975).

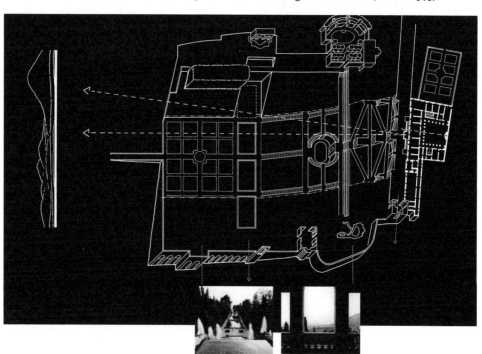

A geometric diagram underlies the plan, simultaneously creating optical space that guides the spectator's view to the horizon.
Plan of Villa d'Este, Tivoli, Italy.

Source: Steenbergen C.; Reh W. 1996. Architecture and Landscape. The design experiment of the great European gardens and landscapes.
Thoth, Bussum

- Cosgrove D. 1993. 'The villa in Palladio's Four Books'. In: *The Palladian Landscape*. Leicester University Press pp 98 ff.
- Hauser A. 1975. *Sociale geschiedenis van de kunst* (i.e. *A social history of art*). SUN, Nijmegen p. 191
- Kluckert R. 2000. 'The Italian Renaissance garden'. In: *The Gardens of Europe*. Könemann, Köln pp. 50 ff.
- Lazarro C. 1990. *The Italian Renaissance Garden*. Yale University Press, New Haven pp. 100-108
- Leupen B. (et al). 1997. 'Representation and utility'. In: *Design and analysis*. 010 publishers, Rotterdam pp. 73-76
- Rogers E.B. 2001. *Landscape Design*. Harry Abrams, New York pp. 147-148
- Shepherd J.C.; Jellicoe G.A. 1953. *Italian Gardens of the Renaissance*. Alec Tiranti, London
- Steenbergen C.; Reh W. 1996. *Architecture and landscape*. Thoth, Bussum
- Thacker Chr. 1985. 'The Renaissance Garden in Italy'. In: *The History of Gardens*. Croom Helm, London pp. 95 ff.

Renovation, Revitalisation

see > restoration

Representation

see also > design instruments, drawing, image, imagination, mimesis, reference

'An artistic likeness or image. A sign or symbol of something.' (*Webster*) Individual objects or whole landscapes may be represented in paintings, drawings or photographs. Representation differs from imitation because in every image a part of reality is left out (*Britannica*).

Seventeenth-century Dutch landscape painters strove to represent reality as exactly as possible. 'They perceived their role as capturing or receiving what is seen, and representing it just as the eye does' (Crandell 1993). A designer is able to exercise control because he has mastered the art and craft of producing representations through drawings, sketches, diagrams, and thereby may influence (or manipulate) others (Franck 1994).

There is a distinction between the representation of images and the 're-presentation' of meanings, ideas and ideals in the design of outdoor spaces (Hunt 2000). Cascades in Renaissance gardens re-present rivers; rocky mountains are re-presented in rock gardens. Some of the fountains designed by landscape architect Lawrence

Halprin show a backdrop of stone re-presenting a mountain wall.

Re-presentations also relate to the way we perceive the world around us and to the stories we connect with them. The folders of tourist organisations show tourist-oriented representations of scenic areas; tourists also see representations of landscapes through the windscreens of their cars or the windows of touring coaches. They can also stay home

271

Rocky mountains may be re-presented in rock gardens and fountains. Hell's Gate in Kenya, and fountain designed by Lawrence Halprin in San Francisco.

and 'take possession of the world' through their TV screens (Urry 2002).

• Crandell G. 1993. *Nature Pictorialized*. Johns Hopkins University Press, New York. pp 101-102
• Franck K.A.; Schneekloth L.H. 1994. 'Representing'. In: *Ordering Space. Types in Architecture and Design*. Van Nostrand Reinhold, London p. 29
• Hunt J.D. 2000. 'Representations'. In: *Greater Perfections. The Practice of Garden Theory.* Thames & Hudson, London pp.76-115
• Urry J. 2002. 'Globalising the Gaze'. In: *The Tourist Gaze*. Sage Publications, London pp.141-161

Research

see also > analysis, behaviour, design, landscape planning, quality, value

'Investigation or experimentation aimed at the discovery and interpretation of facts; revision of accepted theories or laws in the light of new facts, or practical application of such new or revised theories or laws' (*Webster*).

Various disciplines, each with its own vantage point, conduct academic research on the aspects of landscapes that can be objectively registered, 'measured' and described. Such aspects include the genesis of landscapes, and the natural and antropogenic patterns and processes within them.

The results of this type of research in landscape design and planning have various practical applications, such as written reports, Geographic Information Systems data-banks, and suitability maps based on the analysis of soil conditions (McHarg 1969). If an area survey or analysis is intended to serve as the basis for a design or planning project, it contains the collection of relevant data, analysed in relation to the objectives stated and means available.

Over the last fifty years, analytical techniques that support the design and planning process have developed enormously. For example, the social sciences have researched the relationship between the landscape and man's perceptions, behaviour, attachments, and value systems. But while the results have created greater insight into the relationship between man and his environment, they do not provide

criteria for landscape quality or design quality (see *Value*, *Quality*).

Throughout Western history, the relationship between science and art in architecture has been the subject of debate, with reason and geometry opposing sensibility and emotion. In the 20th century, reasoning seemed to have won: the mythical, metaphorical depth of the natural and cultural worlds seemed to have been neutralised, and to have been subjected to instrumentation and control (Corner 1990). But while contemporary landscape architects may be tempted to rely on scientific theory and technique, it is an impossible proposition, as no usable science of design has ever been developed (Schon 1985).

In an attempt to define the roles of the arts and sciences in research, Appleton (1986) describes three examples of 'areas of investigation' in which art of scientific method are applied:

1.) areas that rely principally on 'scientific' evidence, such as those which explain the distribution of natural vegetation through the study of environmental conditions.

2.) areas that draw on 'mixed' evidence from the arts and the sciences, such as those involved in the reconstruction of past landscapes.

3.) areas where evidence from the arts predominates, such as research on the human experience of landscape through the analysis of paintings and literary sources.

<<WITREGEL>>

Landscape architecture research in the strictest sense of the word involves exploring possible future developments or situations with the aid of scenarios, models and simulations (Steenbergen 2002). Situations and conditions that are not yet recognisable are presented in such a way that their usefulness can be tested in relation to stated objectives (Kleefmann 1984). A repetitive process that goes through a series of rounds of deliberation and consultation, it provides a planning process with precision and accuracy, making it possible to articulate, simulate and define vague political intentions, which can thus be converted into actions.

272

By analysing the design process – the logic of the successive steps taken as well as that of the architectonic composition – design research explores the way designs have been composed. The combination of design research with research in the natural and social sciences results in a transition from 'survey before planning' to 'survey while planning' (Sijmons 2002).

• Appleton J. 1986. 'The role of the arts in landscape research'. In: Penning-Rowsell E.; Lowenthal D. (ed). *Landscape Meanings and Values*. Allen and Unwin, London pp. 26-38
• Corner J. 1990. 'A discourse on theory I: Sounding the Depths – Origins, Theory and Representation'. In: Landscape Journal. The University of Wisconsin Press Madison, Wisconsin pp. 61- 78
• Kleefmann F. 1984. *Planning als zoekinstrument*. Uitgeverij Vuga, The Hague
• McHarg I. 1969. *Design with Nature*. Natural History Press, New York.
• Schon D. 1985. *The Design Studio. An Exploration of its Traditions and Potentials*. RIBA Publishing Ltd, London p. 31
• Sijmons D. 2002 'Voldongen fictie. De potenties van het regionaal ontwerp'. (i.e Accomplished fiction. The potentials of regional design). In: *Landkaartmos en andere beschouwingen over landschap*. Uitgeverij 010, Rotterdam pp. 242-252
• Steenbergen C. (et al). 2002. *Architectural Design and Composition*. Thoth publishers, Bussum pp. 22-25

Restoration, Reconstruction, Renovation

see also > heritage, monument

How can objects from the past be conserved or preserved? Unless constant care is given, everything old will decay and perish. Even in the recent past, such care hardly existed. 'In many places the most horrible and disturbing things have happened. What remains on the spot is no more than the wind-blown listlessness of land reallocated by developers and nature managers, without any historic anchors' (Pley 1999).

Even if we do care, the effects of our efforts may not be what we expect: 'however faithfully we preserve, however authentically we restore, however deeply we immerse ourselves in bygone times, life then was based on ways of being and believing incommensurable with our time' (Lowenthal 1985).

The terms restoration, renovation and reconstruction have different but somewhat overlapping meanings, and are often confused in daily use. Each is examined in turn below.

Restoration

The term restoration refers to 'work of restoring a ruined building, work of art, etc. to its original condition' (*Oxford English Dictionary*). The restoration of ancient buildings that have undergone repeated alterations and additions over the centuries is a hazardous assignment, because the question 'why' always needs to be raised: 'It would be worthwhile to judge the restoration of old buildings as a lack of faith in contemporary design, and as a sign of the degeneration of the art of building as a means of a builder's self-expression,' says Dutch architect Habraken (1961).

Another question concerns the choice of the former state to which one wishes to restore a building. Choices are made and old forms 'made up' (Ex 1996). The authenticity of the restored object is questionable, partly because, more often than not, the materials used differ from the originals (Jackson 1980; van Voorden 2002; van der Woud 1996).

The conservation and 'sprucing up' of isolated relics in a changed environment also brings a rupture with the past and a loss of continuity over time (Lynch 1972). If notice boards offering historic information are added for the illumination of tourists, any sense of alienation will be reinforced (Urry 1990). 'My prime objection against the current practice of restoring and preserving monuments and historic buildings is that history is invented', says Dutch historian van der Woud (van der Woud 2002). The prime consideration seems not to be what a monument looked like in the past but how it *ought* to have looked.

During the restoration of older gardens and parks whose main outline is still intact the (supposed) intentions of the original designer are carefully copied. Later changes are removed, sometimes with questionable results. An important principle for park restoration should therefore be to intervene as little as possible.

Two fine Dutch examples of restored parks

273

are the park in the Groeneveld estate in Baarn (Vroom 1990) and the garden at Neercanne castle in Limburg (De Jong 1996; Harsema 2000).

- Ex N.; Lengkeek J. 1996. 'Op zoek naar het echte' (i.e. In search of the real). In: Vrijetijdsstudies jrg. 14 no. 1 pp. 24 ff.
- Habraken N.J. 1961. *De dragers en de mensen. Het einde van de massawoningbouw* (i.e. *The bearers and the people. The end of mass-produced housing schemes*). Scheltema & Holkema, Amsterdam pp. 23-24
- Harsema H. (ed). 2000. 'Historic gardens with a contemporary play on lines'. In: *Landscape architecture and town planning in the Netherlands 97-99*. Thoth, Bussum pp. 220-223
- Jackson J.B. 1980. *The Necessity for Ruins, and Other Topics*. University of Massachusetts Press, Amherst pp. 89-102.
- de Jong E. 1996. 'Restoration of Baroque Gardens. The Unesco Conference on Neercanne'. In: *Tuinkunst 2*. Architectura & Natura, Amsterdam
- Lowenthal D. 1985. *The Past is a Foreign Country*. Cambridge University Press p. xvi
- Lynch K. 1972. *What Time is this Place?* MIT Press, Cambridge, Mass pp. 29-37
- Pley H. 1999. 'De ware kunst van het Nederlandisme' (i.e. The true art of Dutchism). In: *Tegen de Barbarij*. Prometheus ,Amsterdam pp. 144
- Urry J. 1990. 'Gazing on History'. In: *The Tourist Gaze*. Sage Publications pp. 104 ff.
- van Voorden F. 2002. 'Reconstruction of history; on the meaning of monuments'. In: Steenbergen C. (et al) (ed). *Architectural Design and Composition*. Thoth publishers .Bussum pp. 146-155
- Vroom M.J. (ed). 1990. 'Groeneveld castle park in Baarn'. In: *Outdoor Space*. Thoth. Bussum pp. 88-91
- van der Woud A. 1996. 'De ethiek van onthouding. De beoefening van het niets-doen bij restauraties' (i.e. The ethics of abstention. The practice of doing nothing while restoring). In: ARCHIS Journal no. 6 pp.32-36.
- van der Woud A. 2002. 'Ik word bang voor die collectieve liefde voor alles wat er is, en die geringe belangstelling voor wat er komen moet' (i.e. This new love for the present and the lack of interest in what should come, scares me). In: Neuvel K. *De uniformering voorbij*. Meinema. Zoetermeer pp. 72-73

Renovation

Renovation is 'the repair, renew and adaptation of buildings, gardens and parks to changed requirements' (*van Dale*).

It involves a process of repair and replacement whereby parts of a dilapidated building are kept intact, and thus usable. An urban park on the decline, and even unfit for use due to the lack of adequate maintenance, is thereby brought to life again. Renovation or revitalisation thus involves changes in the original plan, resulting – for some parts – in a new layout. Old trees are replaced and pavements and ponds subjected to major repair (van der Ham 1998).

The renovation of public parks often meets with resistance and protest on the part of the local population, which views these measures as destructive (Rooijen 1984).

Parts of urban districts are also subject to renovation. Since the 1980s, residential renovation – also called reconstruction – has been carried out in a number of cities in the Netherlands where older neighbourhoods have become very run down, sometimes to the point of complete degradation. Projects vary in nature, from the renovation of building facades, to demolition and reconstruction.

In the vast majority of cases, these operations are limited to individual building complexes. But in the western districts of Amsterdam dating from the 1950s, the plans are much larger in scale. Over the period from 2002 to 2015, a number of apartment buildings are being – or will be – razed and replaced by different type of housing. Others are extensively renovated. The layout of the main infrastructure will be adapted to new needs and new underground piping and cabling networks installed, all to help create a renewed physical environment (Harsema 2002).

Reconstruction

The reconstruction of parks and gardens is an extreme form of restoration or renovation. To re-construct means 'to construct again, to rebuild, to remodel' (*Webster*).

When almost nothing of an original building or site remains, reconstruction is unavoidable (Jacques 1997). In the case of a historic park or garden, a completely new layout must be developed on the basis of extensive and reliable documentation. The original situation is re-created using materials and construction methods similar to those used when the original layout was constructed. This can only be done through the collaborative effort of a team of specialists.

The results of one such process can be seen

Renovation of a park, resulting in a different layout. Masterplan of Zuiderpark in Rotterdam, 2001.

Palace gardens, Het Loo near Apeldoorn: a 17th-century Classicist park reconstructed from scratch during the 1980s.

Photo: Harry Harsema

in the palace gardens of the palace of Het Loo near the Dutch town of Apeldoorn, which were rebuilt from scratch. In this case, it was chosen to re-create the gardens as they had been laid out at the time of King William III (1650-1702). This decision led to the destruction of the existing, fully developed 19th-century landscape style park (Asbeck 2000). 'Choices must be made and priorities set, all guided by an understanding of the spirit of the place, the original conception, and the elements that contributed to its artistic quality' (Spirn 1994). A special problem encountered during a reconstruction plan is created by the fact that part of the original plant collection is no longer available (Hernández-Bermejo 1991).

• van Asbeck J. 2000. 'The formal garden at Het Loo'. In: Mosser M.;Teyssot G. (ed). *The History of Garden Design. The Western Tradition from the Renaissance to the Present Day*. Thames & Hudson. London pp.178-180
• van der Ham R.; Pars H. 1998. *Het Grote Park. Geschiedenis van het Zuiderpark 1908-1998* (i.e. *The large park. History of Zuiderpark 1908-1998*). 'De Nieuwe Haagse' publishers, The Hague pp.249 ff.
• Harsema H. (ed). 2002. 'Western garden suburbs – Amsterdam: Old districts in a new world'. In: *Landscape architecture and town planning in the Netherlands 99-01*. Thoth publishing. Bussum pp. 48-55
• Hernández-Bermejo E. 1991. 'Botanical Foundations for the restoration of Spanish-Arabic Gardens'. In: Tjon Sie Fat L.; de Jong E. (ed). *The Authentic Garden*. Clusius Foundation p.158
• Jacques D. (ed). 1997. 'The techniques and uses of garden archaeology'. In: Journal of Garden History, Taylor & Francis, London vol. 17 no. 1 (special issue)
• van Rooijen M. 1984. *De Groene Stad. Een historische studie over de groenvoorziening in de Nederlandse Stad* (i.e. *The green city. An historic survey of green spaces in Dutch cities*). Cultuurfonds van de Bank voor Nederlandse Gemeenten pp.147-148.
• Spirn A. 1994. 'Texts, Landscapes and Life'. In: *Tilegnet Sven Ingvar Andersson*. Arkitektensforlag, Copenhagen p.110.

Rhythm

see > dynamic

Romanticism

see also > landscape style, pastoral, picturesque, poetic, utopia, wilderness

'A literary, artistic and philosophical movement marked by emphasis on the imagination and emotions and especially by an exaltation of primitive and the common people, appreciation of nature, and interest in the remote or melancholy' (*Webster*).

'Romanticising' still means 'to believe that things are better and more beautiful than they are in reality'. In 17th-century English the word 'romantick' meant 'as in romances', i.e. 'untrue, unlikely, exaggerated, fantastic' (*Britannica*).

Romanticism, nature and landscape

During the 18th century, a division became manifest between different concepts of nature. During the Age of Enlightenment, physical nature was seen as matter that could be objectively dissected and analysed. The world had thereby become demystified and prosaic. As a reaction, a longing arose for a new mythology that would support the belief that 'Nature is the spirit of what is good, beautiful and true in the world' (Thacker 1985). Jean-Jacques Rousseau (1712-1778) stressed the importance of reverie and the power of the imagination, and believed in the innate goodness of 'natural man' (Rogers 2001).

The Romantic Movement was also clearly a reaction against the changes in society that had accompanied the emergence and expansion of industrial capitalism in the 18th century. As some saw it, factories and mass production 'degraded and despoiled' the environment (Pepper 1996). The analogy with the situation in the 20th century is striking.

Under the Romantics, nature became exalted, sublime: the object of artistic exploration. Jean-Jacques Rousseau and Johan Wolfgang Goethe (1749-1832) were both ardent lovers of nature. Soon after 1700, landscapes perceived as 'irregular, strange, and fantastic; primitive, untamed, and wild; varied, changing, and contrasting' were labelled as Romantic. A search began for the wilderness, the untouched virgin landscape – for 'delectable horror' as a sublime experience (Schama 1995). As Henry David Thoreau wrote: 'We can never have enough of nature. We must be refreshed by the sight of inexhaustible vigour, vast and titanic features, the sea-coast with its wrecks, the wilderness with its living and its decaying trees, the thunder cloud, and the rain which lasts three weeks and produces freshets. We need to witness our own limits transgressed, and some life pasturing freely where we never wander' (Porter 1962).

The antagonism between a dispassionate, scientific view of nature and the more emotional attitude that originated in the Romantic Age has persisted until today. The Romantic critique of urbanisation, industrialisation and of civilisation in general, has been repeated endlessly in the 20th and 21st century, when every expansion of industrial sites, each new technical innovation was initially being refused as "unnatural". This embracing of nature and aversion to culture may be regarded as a phenomenon whose cause lies in an ever-increasing "cultivation". It is the consequence of a situation in which many people view culture – the cultivation of nature – as getting out of control (Lemaire 1970).

The Romantic Movement had a strong influence on garden design and laid the groundwork for various subsidiary varieties of the landscape style (Rogers 2001).

• Lemaire T. 1970. *Filosofie van het Landschap* (i.e. *Philosophy of landscape*). Ambo, Amsterdam p. 47
• Pepper D. 1996. *Modern Environmentalism. An introduction.* Routledge, London p. 189
• Porter E. 1962. '*In Wildness Is the Preservation of the World'.* Quotations from Henry David Thoreau's writings with photographs by Eliot Porter. Sierra Club & Ballantine Books, New York p. 58
• Rogers E.B. 2001. 'Sense and sensibility'. In: *Landscape Design. A Cultural and Architectural History.* Harry Abrams, New York pp. 232- 280
• Schama S. 1995. 'Vertical Empires, Cerebral Chasms'. In: *Landscape and Memory.* Harper Collins, London pp. 447-478.
• Thacker Chr. 1985. 'Leaping the Fence'. In: *The History of Gardens.* Croom Helm, London p. 181

Rural Countryside

see also > landscape, Romanticism, suburbia, urbanisation

'Of or relating to the country, country people or life, or agriculture' (*Webster*).

The term 'rural' is normally seen as the

277

'Landschap met waaiende bomen', van Gerard van Nijmegen (1804).

Uit: Loos W. (et al) (red). Langs Velden en Wegen. V+K, Blaricum / Rijksmuseum Amsterdam. Blz. 96

opposite of urban – a contrast that dates back several centuries and is based on the existence of rival powers that espoused different values. 'To the one side were the absolutist, purist and universalist aspirations of court and monarch, to the other side the customs and traditions, the rights and obligations of the people; to the one side, high art and artifice, to the other side, closeness to earth and organic wholesomeness' (Yi-Fu Tuan 2002). The royal courts as the centre of the political system of a country determined the layout and organisation of the rural land (Olwig 2002).

The contemporary definition of rurality differs from one European country to another. In some countries it is related to population density, with varying standards in terms of the number of people per square kilometre (Hoggart 1995). In Dutch physical planning policy, rurality is not considered a question of population density but of 'atmosphere'. In 2001, rural areas accounted for about 75% of the country's landmass. It is the opposite of the urban – and official policy aims at keeping it that way. Agriculture, protected nature areas and outdoor recreation belong there.

However, the last fifty years have brought drastic change to rural areas (Baart 2000; Bethe 1997) – the result of the large-scale transformation accompanying the arrival of new 'economic carriers' such as industrialisation, urbanisation, land consolidation and road construction projects. It also followed the increasing migration of urbanites to the countryside, when people seeking a rural idyll started occupying farmhouses and cottages, or built new villas there. The conversion of many farms into second homes caused a considerable loss of authenticity in rural architecture, an effect that was exacerbated by the arrival of many holiday camps and bungalow parks (Metz 2002). As a result of these developments, the rural Netherlands is – despite official planning policy – increasingly becoming a 'rurban field' in which the distinction between town and country is slowly evaporating.

In several Western European countries, the image of rurality is associated with 'the countryside', representing 'a bucolic vision of an ordered, comforting, peaceful, and, above all, deferential past'. This image is however 'fundamentally a constructed one, comprised of elements that never existed together historically' (Urry 2002).

While repose, beauty and nature in rural areas are seen as qualities deserving protection in the Netherlands, the rural in France is perceived as land to be ordered, where natural resources must be 'tamed' and exploited (Bunce 1994). In landscape design, this principle is manifest in the urge to *'géométriser l'espace'*. It is an expression of what French landscape architects see as the cultivation of the natural landscape, the clearing of forests, the establishments of paths through hill country, the marking out of plots of land, routes and lines. It is a way of 'taking possession of the terrain, and an expression of how mankind conquers nature' (Almekinders 1994). These differences in attitudes also affect national policies. In France, for instance, physical planning is much more centrally organised than elsewhere in Europe (Davies 1989).

• Almekinders B.; Knuyt M. 1994. 'Park design as theatre'. In: Archis Journal. Architecture, Urbanism, Visual Arts. No. 5. NAi, Rotterdam pp. 46-55
• Baart T. (et al). 2000. *Atlas of Change. Rearranging the Netherlands*. NAi publishers, Rotterdam
• Bethe F.H. (ed). *Rural Areas and Europe. Processes in Rural Land Use and the Effects on Nature and Landscape*. Ministry of Housing, Planning and the Environment. National Spatial Planning Agency, The Hague
• Bunce M.F. 1994. *The Countryside Ideal: Anglo-American Images of Landscape*. Routledge, London
• Davies H.W.E. (et al). 1989. Planning Control in Western Europe. Department of the Environment, Her Majesty's Stationery Office. London pp. 409-442
• Hoggart K. (et al). 1995. *Rural Europe. Identity and Change*. Arnold, London
• Metz T. 2002. *Fun! Leisure and landscape*. NAi publishers, Rotterdam pp.191-194
• Olwig K.R. 2002. *Landscape Nature and the Body Politic. From Britain's Renaissance to America's New World*. The University of Wisconsin Press Madison, Wisconsin
• Urry J. 2002. *The Tourist Gaze*. Sage Publications, London p.87
• Yi-Fu Tuan. 2002. 'Court versus Country'. In: Olwig K.R. *Landscape Nature and the Body Politic*. The University of Wisconsin Press, Urbana, Illinois pp. xvi-xii

Scale

see also > dimension, proportion, reduction

Scale is 'the relation between the actual size of something and the map, diagram etc. which represents it' (*Oxford Advanced*). It is also 'the proportion between a distance on a map and the corresponding distance on the ground. It may be expressed in words as a divided line or as a representative fraction. A rough distinction is often made between small-scale maps in which a large area is represented and large scale maps or plans' (*Goulty*).

The amount of detailing in a design is related to the scale of the map used. At the higher level of scale, lines and planes can be reproduced on maps in a simplified way, and are indicated fairly roughly. Further detailing of maps requires more precision. In mapping coastlines and watersheds at a more precise scale, the cartographer encounters more and more curves, points and indentations – a phenomenon related to the existence of 'fractals', i.e. mathematical figures that can be endlessly repeated when they are enlarged. In mathematics fractals are 'any of a class of complex geometric shapes that commonly exhibit the property of self-similarity' and 'a self-similar object is one whose component parts resemble the whole' (*Britannica*).

In nature, some fractals are seemingly infinite in their repetitive form, while others – such as trees, rivers systems or blood vessels that branch out into smaller patterns – are finite structures (Hovelijn 2001). These examples indicate the need to adapt the scale of inventory maps to the scale of the proposed design. Designing simultaneously at different levels of scale therefore requires special skills.

While a landscape plan may be drawn at a scale of 10,000, the layout of a square with its paving and lighting details requires designs to a scale of 1:2 – in other words, accurate to the last centimetre. Special skills are required to span these extremes of scale. Landscape architects claim it as their exclusive domain.

Scale is also 'a standard by which something can be measured or judged' (*Webster*).

Differences between the proportions of spaces and objects allow us to estimate their size, especially when fixed within certain proportions, or related to a certain standard, such as the human body. Doors and windows in the façade of a building allow us to grasp the size of the whole. Over-sized doors such those as found in churches and palaces are intended to make us feel humble. A garden terrace looks smaller when paved with large tiles (Motloch 2001).

However, the existence of such a thing as a 'human scale', meaning that some scales are more 'human' than others, may be denied. Sizes as the spectator experiences them are 'illusory': there is no simple correspondence between the spectator's impression of size, and dimension – size – as it can be measured on a building. The apparent size of a division, shape or space is affected by the other size-relationships that serve as cues in the same view. A lack of cues makes the recognition of

Contrasting scales of gate and door in Piazza del Popolo, Rome.

Photo: Frank Meijer

Design details: pavement, Schouwburgplein Rotterdam. West 8 landscape architects.

Landscape patterns around Zieuwent-Harreveld, province of Gelderland, the Netherlands. The situation in 1880 compared to that in 1970. The intermediate scale has disappeared.

Source: Landscape and Urban Planning Journal. Elsevier, Amsterdam, no. 18 1990

sizes of spaces difficult, making these spaces appear to be 'scale-less' (Licklider 1965).

Scale has an impact on our sense of well-being. In reference to the Renaissance garden, Shepherd and Jellicoe (Shepherd 1953) wrote: 'In practice, sympathy to surroundings, the most important asset to the peace of any garden, was obtained in many ways. The most natural bond was scale.'

The scale of landscapes

The experience of scale in a landscape depends on the degree of enclosure determined by land form, planting or buildings (Bell 1993). 'When people normally speak of landscape scale, they are referring to its bigness, its enormity relative to themselves. The limitless immensity of the landscape is felt to be spacious, sweeping, vast, enveloping and engaging of the subject' (Corner 2002).

In rural areas in the Netherlands it is sometimes possible to perceive hierarchy on three interrelated scale levels. The local level is represented by buildings and farmyards whose dimensions are usually related to the size of the human body. At the intermediate level, clusters of buildings enclose larger spaces. At the regional level, vistas or panoramic views to the horizon provide connections with the outside world. When these three levels of scale are no longer visible at a single glance, the landscape is no longer called 'open' (Vroom 1986).

In modern agricultural landscapes, the loss of the intermediate scale level creates an increasing sense of uniformity, a loss of diversity that is also apparent in the ecological sense (Kerkstra 1990).

• Bell S. 1993. *Elements of Visual Design in the Landscape.* Spon, London pp.150-156
• Corner J. 2002. 'Representation and landscape'. In: Swaffield S. *Landscape Theory. A Reader.* The University of Pennsylvania Press, Philadelphia

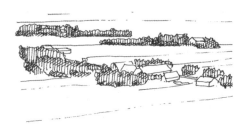

Levels of scale in Midden-Delfland, province of Zuid Holland, the Netherlands. 1. Local level 2. Intermediate level 3. Regional level.
Source: Landscape and Urban Planning Journal. Elsevier, Amsterdam, no. 12 January 1986

Manipulated scale: miniature shed makes the surrounding park look larger. Huys ten Donck near Ridderkerk, the Netherlands

• Hovelijn I.; Schultmeyer J. 2001. *Fractals*. Epsilon publishers, Utrecht
• Kerkstra K.; Vrijlandt P. 1990. Landscape planning for Industrial Agriculture: a proposed Framework for Rural Areas'. In: Landscape and Urban Planning Journal, no. 18, Elsevier, Amsterdam 1990 pp. 275-287
• Licklider H. 1965. *Architectural Scale*. The Architectural Press, London
• Motloch J.L. 2001. 'Scale'. In: *Introduction to Landscape Design*. John Wiley & Sons, New York pp. 115 ff.
• Shepherd J.C.; Jellicoe G.A. 1953. *Italian Gardens of the Renaissance*. Tiranti, London p.12
• Vroom M.J. 1986. 'The perception of dimensions of space and levels of infrastructure and its application in landscape planning'. In: Landscape and Urban Planning Journal no. 12, Elsevier, Amsterdam pp. 337-352

Scenario

see also > model

'Imagined sequence of future events' (*Oxford Advanced*). Also 'a prediction based on a set of assumptions and applied to make comparisons with other scenarios on the basis of a different set of assumptions. The comparisons are often made between the best and worst cases' (*Goulty*).

In physical planning, a scenario is an illustrated forecast of long-term developments within a region or in a whole country, combined with an analysis of the conditions supporting economic, demographic or technological trends. Expected changes in attitudes, standards and values in society may also be considered. All these assumptions make scenarios uncertain and vulnerable; one might call them 'experiments in thoughts about the future' (Schoute 1995; van der Cammen 1986).

283

A scenario is normally one of a series of alternative forecasts intended to provide an insight into opportunities and to clarify consequences, and thereby to provide a basis for a well-considered choice. Although contributions to transparent decision-making will be made if a scenario is underlain by clearly defined starting points, it is impractical if the alternative options are too extreme. In practice, planning is normally a matter of compromise: the need for solutions that satisfy the greatest possible number of parties excludes extreme differences between scenarios.

Some scenarios for developments in the province of Noord-Brabant, the Netherlands, until 2050: 'Historic town' by Rob Krier and Jos Cuypers; 'Systematic ordering' by H+N+S landscape architects, and 'New identities' by MDRDV architects.

Source: Blauwe Kamer Magazine. Stichting Lijn in Landschap, Wageningen, no. 1 1999, pp. 20 ff

In landscape planning, many scenarios have a three-dimensional aspect, and when referring to landscape development at a regional level they may resemble spatial models (Bhalotra 1994). The maps which are produced by Dutch planning departments to show scenarios at a national level, however, are normally suggestive rather than illustrative. To explain intentions without being too explicit (as this might otherwise lead to land speculation and unwanted debate), they are drawn schematically, using abstract conventions such as arrows, circles and cross-hatching.

At a regional level, more clarification of intended development is unavoidable. In 1988, for example, the authorities in the Dutch province of Noord-Brabant wished to explore 'probable, possible and desirable' developments in various parts of the province. To formulate objectives and make choices, they invited a number of planners and designers to draw up a range of scenarios. These were illustrated by recognisable settlement patterns with elements such as housing blocks, belts of woodland and other objects, that facilitated

discussion of their contents (Guinée 1999).

- Bhalotra A. 1994. 'From scenario to plan'. In: Schoute J. (et al) (ed). *Scenario studies for the rural environment.* Kluwer Academic Publishers, Dordrecht pp. 91-97
- van der Cammen H. 1987. *Nieuw Nederland. Onderwerp van Ontwerp.* (i.e. *The new Netherlands. Object of design*) Stichting Nederland Nu als Ontwerp Staatsuitgeverij (i.e. Foundation Netherlands Now as a Design Assignment. Government Publishing Office), The Hague
- Guinée A. 1999. 'De Ruimtelijke Toekomst van Noord Brabant. Ontwerpers schetsen scenario's voor 2050' (i.e. The future of Noord Brabant. Designers sketch scenarios for 2050) in: Blauwe Kamer Journal, Wageningen, no. 1 1999 pp. 20-27.
- Schoute J.F.T. (et al) (ed). 1995. *Scenario Studies for the Rural Environment.* Kluwer Academic Publishers, Dordrecht

Scene, Stage, Staging

see also > association, coherence, composition, legibility, reference, space

'A stage setting. A view or site having pictorial quality. The place of an occurrence or action' (Webster)

A garden or a park as a scene is a three-dimensional composition of settings, tableaux and views with references, symbols and stories. It is the landscape as a theatre, a stage (Spirn 1994). The staging – or *mise-en-*

A scene as an architectural composition, portrayed by Vredeman de Vries in his Scenographia of 1560
Source: Mosser M.; Teyssop G. The History of Garden Design. Thames & Hudson, London p. 103

scene – of a site may be designed in one of three contexts: rational, expressive or pictorial. Rational staging means expanding the geometric scheme of a building or a site into the environment, the surrounding landscape. Examples are found in those Italians villas in which, due to the superimposition of a matrix on the landscape, congruence has been created between the dimensions and scales of indoor and outdoor elements.

Expressive staging involves a reference to nature or to other times and places. Various tools can be used, such as ponds and cascades, sculptures and boskets (Steenbergen 1990).

Pictorial staging is used in the English landscape style garden, where built forms are adapted to the natural morphology of the landscape (Reh 1996). The notion of scenography was introduced by Vredeman de Vries (1526-1606). In his book *Scenographia, sive perspectivae* of 1560 he showed scenes with décor-like architectural settings, using the rules of perspective to fit objects logically into the surrounding space (Mehrtens 1990).

- Mehrtens M. 1990. Johan Vredeman de Vries and the Hortum Formae. In: Mosser M.; Teyssop G. *The History of Garden Design.* Thames & Hudson, London pp. 103-105
- Reh W. 1996. *Arcadie en metropolis* (i.e. *Arcadia and metropolis*). PhD, Delft Technical University p. 197
- Spirn A. 1994. 'Texts, landscapes and life'. In: *Sven Ingvar Andersson Festskrift.* Arkitektensforlag, Copenhagen p. 111
- Steenbergen C.M. 1990. *De stap over de horizon* (i.e. *The step across the horizon*). PhD thesis, Delft Technical University. p. 36

Scheme, Plan, Diagram, Outline, Schedule

see also > concept, construct, drawing, matrix

'A graphic sketch or outline. A concise statement or table. A plan or programme of action. A systematic or organised design' (*Webster*). A graphic sketch or preliminary outline is a drawing showing a simplified or generalised image of the construction, composition or function of some object (*van Dale*). By indicating the main outline or contours of elements and objects, schematic drawings for the design of outdoor spaces

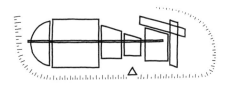

Schematic drawing of the site plan of the Ahold headquarters in Zaandam. Design by Lodwijk Baljon 1988.
Source: Vroom M.J. 1992. Buitenruimten/Outdoor Space. THOTH, Amsterdam

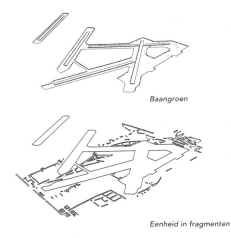

Baangroen

Eenheid in fragmenten

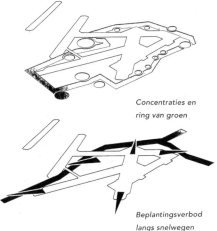

Concentraties en ring van groen

Beplantingsverbod langs snelwegen

A number of schematic drawings explain the main motifs and themes in the planting design for Schiphol airport. From top to bottom: vegetation along runways, unity in fragments, concentrated and circumferential planting, and a planting ban along motorways.
West 8 landscape architects.
Source: Blauwe Kamer Magazine. Stichting Lijn in Landschap, Wageningen, no. 2 1996

help explain the overall composition.

A table or diagram shows the main points of the logic underlying a final plan. It is a concise statement that orders facts, events, conclusions or actions. It may serve as a guideline for action by providing a brief survey of all factors concerned. A matrix can also serve as a diagram (McHarg 1969; Motloch 2001). It helps show the successive steps in the implementation of a design, as well as the time schedule to be followed.

- McHarg I. 1969. *Design with Nature*. Natural History Press, New York p. 144
- Motloch J.L. 2001. *Introduction to Landscape Design*. John Wiley & Sons, New York pp. 290-291

Semiotics
see > sign

Sentiment, Sentimentalism
see also > image, Romanticism

'An attitude, thought or judgement prompted by feeling. Refined feeling, delicate sensibility. Emotional idealism. A romantic or nostalgic feeling' (*Webster*).

Sentiments are connected with the enjoyment of art, nature, and life, for which they are also a condition. While they are often associated with the emotionally turbulent Romantic Age, they are equally important in the 21st century, especially when assessing environmental quality and our feeling of connectedness with the place we live in. 'The term topophilia couples sentiment with place' (Yi-Fu Tuan 1974). Human life without sentiment is unthinkable.

Sentimentalism is an exaggerated

A well-protected grave.
Photo Frank Meijer

286

Appealing honey-sweet images.
Source: Bijhouwer: Waarnemen en ontwerpen, 1954, p. 8

expression of feeling, representing false sentiment intended, consciously or unconsciously, to mislead. It indicates superficial involvement and insincere emotions. Advertisements for new cars, for example, are often located in a virginal landscape, thereby glorifying precisely the values that are directly threatened by the object being advertised.

Sentimentalism is closely connected with the notion of kitsch, 'cheap and showy vulgarity or pretentiousness in art, design etc' (*Oxford English Dictionary*), such as garden gnomes in the shape of Donald Duck, Mickey Mouse or a well-known politician. Kitsch is associated with sugary images and thus with bad taste. 'Whenever an artistic expression or object becomes a commonplace object and part of our daily routine to such a degree that everyone agrees on its achievement in terms of beauty or representation, it easily becomes kitsch' (Lengkeek 1994).

Kitsch, however, can also be consciously employed to promote renewal and change in value-judgements, even if its effect are only temporary. Examples include the quasi-military uniforms and stately cars used by The Beatles pop group in the 1960s, which were intended as a provocative parody. Advertising generally makes shrewd use of directly appealing images that use kitschy effect to catch the eye (Dorfles 1968). Some theme parks with historicising scenes use figures in traditional clothing that move around and behave in ways evocative of former times. Here, information, nostalgia and kitsch are inextricably mixed (Metz 2002).

• Dorfles G. 1968. *Kitsch. An Anthology of Bad Taste*. Studio Vista, London.
• Lengkeek J. 1994. *Een meervoudige werkelijkheid* (i.e. *A multiple reality*). PhD thesis, Wageningen University p. 48
• Metz T. 2002. *Fun! Leisure and landscape*. NAI publishers Rotterdam pp. 108-120
• Yi-Fu Tuan. 1974. 'Topophilia and Environment'. In: *Topophilia*. Prentice Hall, Englewood Cliffs, N.J. pp. 92-112

Shape

see > form

Sightline, Vista

see also > axis, composition, orientation, perspective

A sightline is 'the direct line of vision between the eye of an observer and the object seen. The central line of sight is the line of vision that bisects the view' (*Goulty*).

A sightline thus connects a point of view with the horizon or any point in between. In contrast with an axis or a vista, it needs no guiding framework; what happens between the point of observation and any point on the horizon is of no significance. Instead, the visibility of a distant point or landmark is essential.

As they help an observer to determine his position in space, sightlines are instruments that help control space. Within enclosed spaces, they are used to determine a layout (Vroom 1992); outside, sightlines or regulating lines that connect main features or other conspicuous points are used to situate buildings. Such a set of regulating lines creates coherence within a site (Broadbent 1990; Harsema 2000).

Axis and vistas are framed sightlines. They offer 'a distant view through or along an avenue or opening' (*Webster*). The frames may consist of pillars or columnar trees such as the cypresses in the gardens of the Italian Renaissance. They may also consist of an opening in a hedge or a wall, a foreground aperture through which the observer looks to the horizon (Shepherd 1953; Simonds 1977).

287

Vista through concrete wall of a bunker on the beach of Calais, France.

Photo: Frank Meijer

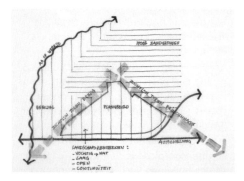

The location and size of the opening are important: 'the more open it is, the more obvious; the more it shouts, the sooner it will fade' (Alexander 1977). Landscape paintings and photographs always show a framed view in which a tableau is selected (Crandell 1993).

A vista may also be created by the view down an avenue, or, as in a 17th-century French parks, down an axis flanked by woodland or buildings to a distant view of a prominent object on the horizon. In landscape-style parks designed by Lancelot 'Capability' Brown (1716-1783), the main view from the house was framed by an asymmetric vale (Turner 1985).

• Alexander C. (et al). 1977. 'Zen view'. In: *A Pattern Language*. Oxford University Press pp. 641 ff.
• Broadbent G. 1990. *Emerging Concepts in Urban Space Design*. Van Nostrand, New York p. 301
• Crandell G. 1993. *Nature Pictorialized. 'The View' in Landscape History*. Johns Hopkins University Press, New York
• Harsema H. (ed). 2000. 'Breda town centre expands onto former barracks site'. In: *Landscape architecture and town*

Site of Esso headquarters in Breda, with sightlines to landmarks on the horizon. Design by landscape architect Yvonne Horsten, 1985.

Source: Vroom M.J. (ed). 1992. Outdoor Space. Thoth, Bussum p. 97

planning in the Netherlands 97-99. Thoth, Bussum pp. 54-57
- Shepherd J.C.; Jellicoe G.A. 1953. *Italian Gardens of the Renaissance.* Tiranti, London. p. 23
- Simonds J.O. 1997. *Landscape Architecture* (third edition). McGraw-Hill, New York pp. 221-223
- Turner R. 1985. *Capability Brown.* Weidenfeld & Nicholson, London p. 81
- Vroom M.J. (ed). 1992. 'Site of the Esso-Benelux headquarters near Breda'. In: *Outdoor Space.* Thoth, Bussum pp. 96-99

Sign, Meaning, Significance

see also > association, emblem, experience, metaphor, perception, reference, symbol, icon

A sign is 'a mark having a conventional meaning and used in place of words or to represent a complex notion'. Meaning is the general term used of anything requiring or allowing interpretation. Significance applies specifically to 'something that is conveyed as a meaning often obscurely or directly' (*Webster*).

A sign makes a fact or a message available for sensory perception. It may have a permanent connection with what is being signified (such as 'where there's smoke there's fire'), or it may be based on agreements within a certain social group or culture, as with traffic signs (Coates 1988). A sign may be a symbol (see *Symbol*).

The world is full of meaning for everybody and the attachment of meaning to objects or events is an inherent part of the perception process. 'Man is an animal suspended in webs of significance he himself has spun' (Geertz 1973). The meaning of objects depends on the place they occupy within a larger context. In perceiving the environment, people always look for an answer to questions such as 'What is that?' or 'What does it mean to me?' Signs, whether or not consciously affixed, help answering these questions. In complex situations such as road junctions and airport buildings, they may even dominate over space and form, all while providing orientation to travellers (Broadbent 1990).

They may be clearly recognisable, like those along the highway strip in the USA that have been so eloquently described by Venturi and others: 'The sign for the hotel Monticello, a silhouette of an enormous Chippendale highboy, is visible on the highway before the hotel itself. This architecture of styles and signs is antispatial; it is an architecture of communication over space; communication dominates space as an element in the architecture and in the landscape' (Venturi 1977; Yi-Fu Tuan 1993; Zube 1970).

In other cases they must be 'discovered' by careful observation, by association. Some

289

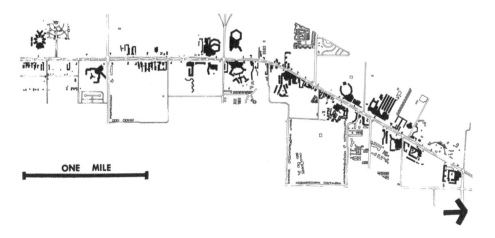

ONE MILE

Signs dominate space. Highway strip in Las Vegas.

Source: Venturi R. (et al). 1977. *Learning from Las Vegas: The Forgotten Symbolism of Architectural Form.* MIT Press, Cambridge

signposts along motorways may carry an ambiguous message, like those advertising McDonald's restaurants, which indicate not only efficient service and a certain type of inexpensive menu, but the 'McDonaldisation' of society: fast-food joints for hurried travellers and the disappearance of alternative cultures of dining in a mobile Post-modern society.

Tourists are always looking for signs that refer to pre-supposed environments, such as the 'typical' English garden, the 'real' French chateau, or the 'German' beer-garden (Urry 1990). How we perceive a landscape or the world around us depends on the way we relate to it (Craik 1986). This understanding has changed over the centuries, which is why the architecture of older towns and buildings do not carry the same meanings for us as those that were originally intended (Norberg-Schulz 1983; Jencks 1980).

The primary functions of a building may get lost, or be replaced; secondary functions with different meanings may take over. The Parthenon in Athens is no longer understood as the place of worship for which it was built, but as the fundamental exemplar of Greek architecture. Antique lamps outside suburban homes have preserved their primary function – to illuminate – but they have been taken out of their original context and now signify a Romantic past (Eco 1980). While gardens may be seen as a miniaturised cosmos, as an imagined ideal world, they are made up of very ordinary materials (Riley 1988).

In 20th-century Modernist parks and gardens, signs were banned. Recently, they have come back into vogue as a means of marking spaces and referring to special events (Høyer 1993).

In information theory, signs are defined as messages. When a person perceives a sign, his interpretation depends on his own disposition and the context in which the sign is seen. In the perception process, the order is as follows: transmitter - sign - content - receiver - interpreter - disposition - context - effect.

The general theory on the communication

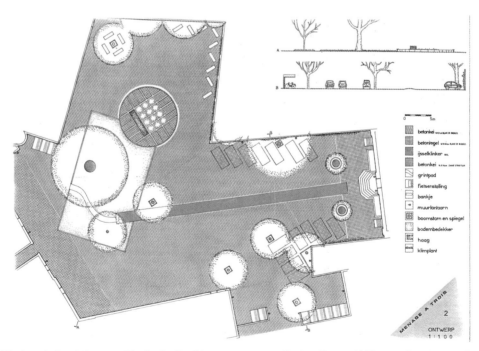

Winning entry in a design competition for the site of the government tax collection office at Middelburg, with a coin inserted into the pavement. Design by M.A.M. Kuipers and M.A. Looye, 1987.

of signs and messages is called semiotics, also defined as 'the science occupying itself with the value of a sign, with sign structures and with the relation between a sign and the object signified' (*van Dale*). In the design world, signs are used in graphic representations. Icons used to be religious images, but nowadays are specially designed symbols on maps, or the ideograms used in airport and railway-station signage to direct travellers to platforms, waiting rooms and other facilities.

Signs function at three levels of abstraction:
· The level of signs and their combination: syntax. This is the formal study of signs, the inventory, the rules of combinations such as in grammar. Graphic presentations made by landscape architects belong to this level.
· The level of reference to the real world: semantics. This is the content of signs as well as the context or the circumstances in which they are transmitted. In architecture, semantics involves a reference to the functi-on of something, to the status of a homeowner, or to another world (Spirn 1998).
· The level of the use and the effect of signs: pragmatics. This is the response, the behavi-our of people in response to the signs they receive. The design of an outdoor space is meant to influence the behaviour of people, by facilitating, conditioning or determining it (see *Behaviour*).

· Broadbent G. 1990. *Emerging Concepts in Urban Space Design*. Van Nostrand Reinhold, New York pp.248-252
· Coates N. 1988. 'Street signs'. In: Thackara J. (ed.) *Design after Modernism*. Thames and Hudson, London pp.107 ff.
· Craik K.1986. 'Psychological Reflections on Landscape'. In: Penning-Rowsell E.C.; Lowenthal D. (ed.) *Landscape Meanings and Values*. Allen and Unwin, London pp. 48-62
· Eco U. 1980. 'Function and Sign: the Semiotics of Architecture'. In: Broadbent G. (et al) (ed.) *Signs, Symbols and Architecture*. Wiley & Sons, New York pp. 28-29
· Geertz C. 1973. *The Interpretation of Cultures*. Basic Books, New York p. 5
· Høyer S. 1993. 'Paradise does not care about religion'. In: *Modern park design. Recent trends*. Thoth, Bussum pp. 103-114
· Jencks C. 1980. 'The architectural sign'. In: Broadbent G. *Emerging Concepts in Urban Space Design*. Van Nostrand Reinhold, New York
· Norberg-Schulz C. 1983. *Meaning in Western Architecture*. Rizolli, New York
· Riley R. 1988. 'From Sacred Grove to Disney World'. In: Landscape Journal, The University of Wisconsin Press, Urbana, Illinois vol. 7 no. 2 pp.136-147
· Spirn A.W. 1998. 'Rules of Context: Landscape Grammar'. In: *The Language of Landscape*. Chapter 6. Yale University Press, New Haven pp.168-190
· Urry J. 1990. *The Tourist Gaze. Leisure and Travel in Contemporary Societies*. Sage Publications, London p.12
· Venturi R. (et al). 1977. *Learning from Las Vegas: The Forgotten Symbolism of Architectural Form*. MIT Press, Cambridge pp. 3-19
· Yi-Fu-Tuan. 1993. 'The Strip'. In: *Passing Strange and Wonderful*. Island Press, Washington D.C. pp. 158-160
· Zube E. (ed.) 1970. *Landscapes. The Writings of J.B. Jackson*. The University of Massachusetts Press pp.55-73

Simplicity

see also > complexity, Modernism, Postmodernism

Simplicity was one of the main hallmarks of Modernism, and its pursuit was related to the world-view that prevailed at the time it emerged. In 1954, S. Giedion wrote: 'Both artistic expression and scientific research have now come to employ methods that completely dematerialise the object they are investigating. Both seek to study primary elements: science concentrates upon particles so infinitely small that they can only be apprehended intellectually, art upon the very simplest formal shapes. Both are creating a new image of the world' (Giedion 1954).

Some forty years later, Charles Jencks wrote: 'one index of the most valuable art is its invitation to the imagination,' adding 'evolution proceeds from the simple to the complex'. In Postmodernist architecture, complexity has become highly valued because 'both passion and reasoning are simultaneously combined and tuned up' (Jencks 1995).

· Giedion S. 1954. *Walter Gropius. Work and Teamwork*. Reinhold Publishing Company, New York p. 39
· Jencks C. 1995. *The Architecture of the Jumping Universe*. Academy Editions, London

Site analysis

see > analysis

Site

see also > analysis, design, design method, place

A site is 'the actual or planned location (as of a building or town). The place or scene of something' (*Webster*). Site planning 'involves plans for specific developments in which precise arrangement of buildings, roadways, utilities, landscape elements, topography, water features, and vegetation are shown' (*Britannica*). In other words it is the art of arranging an external physical environment in complete detail.

In his standard work *Site Planning*, Kevin Lynch (1962) states: 'The site is a crucial aspect of the environment. It has an impact that is biological, social and psychological. It sets limits to the things that people can do, and makes possible their doing what they otherwise could not.'

The notion of 'site' is related to that of 'place'. 'A forest site is not simply the place where the forest stands; in its full connotation, the name is a qualitative expression of place in terms of forest growth [...]. In this sense the physical area is the sum of all natural resources that man has at his disposal in the area. It is beyond his power to add to them; he may 'develop' them, ignore them in part, or subtract from them by exploitation' (Sauer 1963).

• Lynch K. 1962. *Site Planning*. MIT Press Cambridge, Mass
• Sauer C.O. 1963. 'The morphology of landscape'. In: *Land and Life*. University of California Press, Berkeley p. 325

Sketch

see > drawing

Soil, Earth, Ground, Bottom

see also > geomorphology, hill, map, layer, mosaic, pattern

The soil is 'the upper layer of the earth in which plants grow.' It is also 'the territory of a particular nation' (*Oxford English Dictionary*). Ground is 'the bottom of a body of water; sediment at the bottom of a liquid; material that serves as a base (foundation); the area around and belonging to a building'

(*Webster*).

In planning policy and environmental design various functions and meanings are attached to soil and ground, especially as a foundation and as a creator of space.

Soil a foundation

The bearing capacity of soils is related to its compressibility (i.e. to its soil mechanics); knowledge of this capacity helps find the best place to build (Lynch 1984). In the western Netherlands, for example, past urbanisation took place mainly where soil stability would allow it. Farming was limited to those places were soils were cultivable and livestock would not get bogged down. The

Slopes along a valley of Alnwick Castle Park, Northumberland, England. Designed by Lancelot 'Capability' Brown.

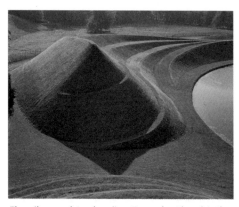

The soil as a sculptural medium. Terraced earthwork in the 'Garden of Cosmic Speculation', designed by Charles Jencks in 1990.

Source: Richardson T. (ed). 2000. The Garden Book. Phaidon, London

distribution of settlements was therefore related to soil differentiation, which in turn lent places their identity (Lambert 1971; McHarg 1969).

Modern engineering techniques make it possible to drain and stabilise soils, and thus to adapt them for the construction of roads and buildings. One result of this is increasing uniformity in settlement patterns.

As part of the upper layer of the earth's crust, the soil is a product of erosion and sedimentation, whereby oxidation, decomposition, precipitation and evaporation lead to the weathering of minerals and the formation of humus. Variations in topographic conditions have created various soil types, each carrying a variety of plant communities and land-use types. This diversity in soil formation is one of the key determinants of biodiversity. As soil formation and landscape formation are synonymous, knowledge of these soil types helps explain the genesis of landscapes (de Bakker 1979; Edelman 1950).

Soil as a creator of space

According to their genesis, ground form and changes in level have their own order. In the Netherlands, marine and fluvial erosion and sedimentation prevail. There are thus parallel ridges formed by previous riverbeds, parallel and horseshoe-shaped wind-deposits such as cover-sand ridges, and the escarpments along river channels formed by lateral moraine ridges.

Similarly, a hierarchy of scale and elevation has been created by branching streams; space has been formed by hills and valleys, plains, dikes and mounds (see *Geomorphology*); and land has been enclosed and defined by earth banks – often with hedgerows, which usually characterise older landscapes (see *Hedge*).

Landscape architects use earth volumes for sculptural effects; in 18th-century landscape-style parks there are some striking examples. 'The ground [...] is cast into an infinite number of elegant shapes, in every gradation from the most gentle slope to a very precipitate fall' (Turner 1985).

- de Bakker H. 1979. *Major soils and soils regions in the Netherlands*. Pudoc Centre for Agricultiral Publishing and Documentation, Wageningen.
- Edelman C.H. 1950. *Soils of the Netherlands*. North Holland Publishing Co., Amsterdam (with provisional soil map)
- Lambert A. 1971. 'Rural settlement'. In: *The Making of the Dutch Landscape*. Seminar Press, London pp. 49 ff.
- Lynch K.; Hack G. 1984. *Site Planning* (third edition). MIT Press Cambridge, Mass, Appendix A: 'Soils' pp. 379 -384
- McHarg I. 1969. *Design with Nature*. Natural History Press, New York pp.140-143
- Turner R. 1985. *Capability Brown and the Eighteenth-Century English Landscape*. Weidenfeld & Nicholson, London p.79

Sound/noise

see also > orientation, wall

Sound is 'the sensation experienced through the sense of hearing. A particular auditory impression'. Noise is 'loud, confused or senseless shouting or outcry. A sound that lacks agreeable musical quality or is noticeably unpleasant' (*Webster*).

To humans and animals alike, sounds are helpful for orientation in space and time. In many cities, church bells, traffic noise and ships' sirens are all part of a permanent background rumble. Soundmarks inform the traveller as much as landmarks: not only do loud signals warn of danger, there are pleasant sounds (birdsong and breaking waves, which act as reminders of nature) as well as unpleasant ones (barking dogs, lawn mowers and traffic noises, which belong to the bustle of daily life) (Dawson 1988).

In gardens, subtle sounds are produced by the movement of pedestrians on gravel, by falling water, and by acoustic reflections between walls. Because some plants are attractive to birds, which bring their own sounds, a garden designer may create the conditions for them (Dee 2001; Moore 1989). In Classicist gardens such as the Tivoli gardens near Rome, fountains, cascades and water organs are major sources of agreeable sound. Within an enclosed court, the silence can be blissful, and since the 1950s it has been precisely the exclusion of urban noises that has made the court house concept popular in many European countries (McHarg 1998).

In many rural areas, the sounds of wind,

rain, animals and some agricultural activities still prevail, but traffic noise is now heard over increasing distances.

As the sounds produced in the daily environment change over time, many of them now belong to history. The rasp of scythes, the jingling of milk cans, the rattle of iron hoops on cobbles, and the sounds of the steam locomotive are almost entirely lost.

Because contemporary sounds often turn into noise, designers have to pay more attention to the prevention of excessive noise than to sound as a source of sensory delight. Conventionally measured in terms of decibels, noise levels can sometime be harmful to the ear (Lynch 1984). In most cases, however, noise is more likely to be no more than a mere nuisance – the result of the wrong sound in the wrong place, sounds often being associated with places and environments (social and otherwise) from which people wish to dissociate themselves.

The drowning of natural sounds by industrial noise in rural areas began in the nineteenth century with the arrival of industrialisation and the construction of railways. The Americans Thoreau and Hawthorne were among the first to complain publicly about the noise they heard from passing trains, which disturbed the illusions they may have held about life in a natural or pastoral environment (Thoreau 1854; Marx 1964).

Many a contemporary holidaymaker seeks peace and quiet in rural surroundings, especially when the area visited is labelled as a 'sanctuary'. A Dutch study showed that sounds of mechanical origin are acceptable in rural places only when they seem to 'belong' and are part of the local background rumble, such as those produced by river barges or farm tractors (Coeterier 2001). Only for specific social groups of certain age categories do extremely noisy events such as car races, air shows or discos apparently form an attraction.

Environmental legislation provides rules and regulations that set noise thresholds and specify the equipment for reducing its

Sound barriers along a Dutch motorway.
Photo: Frank Meijer

impact. Industrial and traffic noise can be reduced by planting woodland and sinking roads below ground level, or through measures to reduce noise production at source. However, more and more motorways and railways are now hidden behind highly visible sound barriers, which, even if they are made of transparent material, have an enormous impact on travellers' perception of landscapes (Harsema 2000). As a result, infrastructure is becoming an increasingly alien element in the landscape.

- Coeterier J.F.; de Boer T.A. 2001. *Ruimte, Rust en Stilte. Beleving door burgers en indicaties voor beheer en beleid* (i.e. *Space, relaxation and silence. The perception of citizens, with indications for managers and politicians*). Alterra-rapport no. 423, Wageningen
- Dawson K.J. 1988. 'Flight, Fancy and the Garden's Song'. In: Landscape Journal no. 7, The University of Wisconsin Press, Urbana, Illinois pp.170-175
- Dee C. 2001. 'Detail'. In: *Form and Fabric in Landscape Architecture*. Spon Press, London pp.188-210
- Harsema H. (ed). 2000. 'Kleinpolderplein: Rotterdam seen through glass and acrylic'. In: *Landscape architecture and town planning in the Netherlands 97-99*. Thoth publishers, Bussum pp.152-155
- Lynch K.; Hack G. 1984. 'Noise'. In: *Site Planning (third edition)*. MIT Press, Cambridge pp. 412-419
- Marx L. 1964. 'Sleepy Hollow 1844'. In: *The Machine in the Garden. Technology and the Pastoral Ideal in America*. Oxford University Press, New York pp.1-33
- McHarg I. 1998. 'The court house concept'. In: *To Heal the Earth*. Island Press, Washington DC pp. 163-174
- Moore C.W. (et al).1989. *The Poetics of Gardens*. MIT Press, Cambridge p. 40
- Thoreau H.D. 1854 'Sounds'. In: *Walden or Life in the Woods*. Crown Publishers, New York 1973 pp. 73-92

Source, Fountain

see also > basin, grotto, stream, water

A source is 'the point of origin of a stream of water. Fountainhead'. A fountain is 'a spring of water issuing from the earth (or) an artificially produced jet of water' (*Webster*). In Mediterranean countries, the village fountain fed by artesian sources was once the prime supplier of water, its basin constituting the centre of household activities and daily social events. The scenes in Marcel Pagnol's *Manon des Sources* (1953) centre around the village fountain.

Throughout the history of garden design,

the source or fountain has symbolised the origin of running water – the source of life – and often refers to the birth of Venus. 'Sources of water – springs, wells, mountain peaks that precipitate the rain – have gathered about them an air of power and mystery [...]. They have always seemed an appropriate symbolic beginnings for gardens' (Moore 1989).

The creators of 15th-century Italian villa gardens with their grottoes, fountains, sculptures and cascades assumed that visitors would be familiar with the legends of Ovid en Virgil (70-19 B.C.) and with the heathen myths known at the time, represented by titans, gods, nymphs and heroes (Lazarro 1990; Schama 1995).

At that time, the construction of fountains was dependent on technical innovations that allowed for the piping of water and the use of aqueducts. The complex systems at Villa d'Este in Tivoli and also at Villa Lante at Bagnia and Caprarola are high points in fountain design (Kluckert 2000). Fountains were the principal elements in these gardens, often in combination with cascades; they were also the central point of the iconographic programme (Oxford Companion; Shepherd 1953). In terms of dimensions, these cascades were modest compared to later examples such as the giant cascades at Wilhemshöhe in Kassel (Dittscheid 1991).

A special element in French Classicist gardens was the nymphaeum: 'a monumental fountain or a building where water was piped into basins' (Hamilton Hazlehurst 1980; Orsenna 2000).

Famous 20th-century fountains include those designed by landscape architect Lawrence Halprin in Portland, Oregon, with their references to the region's rivers, cascades and wild mountain torrents (Halprin 1969; Spirn 1988). These fountains combine metaphorical allusions with sensory impressions such as coolness, freshness, rustle and murmur, and also reflected light. Consciously designed to produce these effects, they are also based on the latest technological developments (Minnaert 1993).

Contemporary functional cascades in the

295

Netherlands include the fish ladders in rivers and streams that have undergone architectonic treatment (Harsema 1996).

• Dittscheid H.C. 1991. 'The Park of Wilhelmshöhe'. In: Mosser M.; Teyssot G. 1991. *The History of Garden Design*. Thames and Hudson pp. 359 ff.
• Halprin L. 1969. *The RSVP Cycles. Creative Processes in the Human Environment*. Braziller, New York pp. 57 ff.
• Hamilton Hazelhurst F. 1980. *Gardens of Illusion. The Genius of André le Nostre*. Vanderbilt University Press pp. 84 ff.

• Harsema H. (ed). 1996. 'Fish-ladders in the Meuse'. In: *Landscape architecture and town planning in the Netherlands 93-95*. Thoth publishers, Bussum pp.186-189
• Kluckert E. 2000. *The Gardens of Europe*. Könemann, Köln pp. 77 ff.
• Lazarro C. 1990. *The Italian Renaissance Garden*. Yale University Press, New Haven pp. 87-100, 131-160
• Minnaert M.G.J. 1993. *Light and Color in the Outdoors*. Translated by L. Seymoor. Springer Verlag, New York
• Moore C.W. (et al). 1989. 'Creating climates'. In: *The Poetics of Gardens*. MIT Press, Cambridge

In Mediterranean countries, the local fountain with its washing basin played an important role in village life. La Fontaine publique, pen drawing and watercolour by Hubert Robert, 1770.

Source: Huisman P. L'aquarelle française au XVIIIe siècle. Bibliothèque des Arts, Paris

• Orsenna E. 2000. 'Le contentement des fontaines'. In: Portrait d'un homme heureux. André le Nôtre 1613-1700. Fayard, Paris pp.79 ff.
• Schama S. 1995. 'The flow of myth'. In: *Landscape and Memory*. Harper Collins, London pp.245 ff.
• Shepherd J.C.; Jellicoe G.A. 1953. *Italian Gardens of the Renaissance*. Tiranti, London p. 22
• Spirn A. 1988. 'The poetics of City and Nature: Towards a New Aesthetic for Urban Design'. In: Landscape Journal, The University of Wisconsin Press, Urbana, Illinois pp. 120-121

Space

see also > dimension, Modernism, panorama, perspective, place, scale, vista

'A limited extent in one, two or three dimensions. An extent set apart or available (parking space). A boundless three-dimensional extent in which objects and events occur and have relative position and direction' (*Webster*).

In our daily life, space has a positive meaning: we want space to live, to feel free, to grow, to see distant objects, to be able to choose. We profit from the existence of urban open space in terms of social, health, environmental and economic benefits (Woolley 2003). World-wide, there is a demand for more space for all sorts of activities (Anonymous 2001).

Space can be experienced as being 'full'. 'Fullness [...] can be a relative thing, until it becomes absolute, when pigs begin to bite off each others tails,' states Dutch journalist Montag in the *NRC Handelsblad* newspaper of 12 December 2003. Space is also connected with 'place' – i.e. a space with a special meaning – especially when people occupy and appropriate it, and adapt it for their uses (Yi-Fu Tuan 1977).

The experience of landscape is determined largely by the degree of enclosure (Bell 1993). This may be man-made, or the result of natural processes. 'The perception of space, our position in space and the way we frame a view are critical conditions of design' (Lavoie 2005).

Larger spaces are associated with openness, which is defined as 'free or far from boundaries or restrictions; permitting passage or access; having openings or spaces. Not enclosed or covered' (*Webster*).

Openness is an important asset: a place in which one can look away from one's own viewpoint, and experience space and distance. 'Designing public open space is an important branch of site planning'.

However, as John Irving (1985) states in *The Cider House Rules*, people want variation between enclosure and openness, 'Living on land where you can occasionally see a long way provides the soul with a perspective of beneficially expansive nature'. Openness in built-up areas can be suggested by creating views and vistas. But it is also associated with accessibility, with spaces being open to the public or closed, where private and public space is separated and some spaces are only open at certain times, like public buildings and some parks (Lynch 1984).

Openness may also be expressed in the form of buildings, parks or other spaces. They may be inviting or forbidding, superimposed or grown, free versus conditioned. There is a connection between the degree of openness and the narrative quality of an environment, its legibility (Potteiger 1998).

'Architecture is the meticulous creation of space' (van de Ven 1980; Motloch 2001) and landscape architecture is the art of creating outdoor space. Space should be used economically; it should be conserved and fostered. A poorly designed and poorly managed urban environment contains a great deal of 'lost space' that has been reduced to 'voids'. Such wasteful surroundings provide a negative experience (Trancik 1986).

297

• Anonymous. 2001. *Vijfde Nota Ruimtelijke Ordening (Fifth Report on Spatial Planning)* Ministerie VROM, The Hague pp.117 ff.
• Bell S. 1993. *Elements of Visual Design in the Landscape*. Spon, London pp. 150-156
• Irving J. 1985. *The Cider House Rules*. Jonathan Cape, London p. 26
• Lavoie C. 2005. 'Sketching the landscape: exploring a sense of place'. In: Landscape Journal 24:1-05, University of Wisconsin Press pp. 13-31
• Lynch K.; Hack G. 1984. *Site Planning* (third edition). MIT Press Cambridge pp.325-328
• Motloch J. 2001. 'Spatial development'. In: *Introduction to Landscape Design*. Van Nostrand Reinhold, London pp. 184 ff.
• Potteiger M.; Purinton J. 1998. 'Opening'. In: *Landscape Narratives. Design Practices for Telling Stories*. John Wiley, New

York pp.75 ff.

- Trancik R. 1986. *Finding Lost Space. Theories of Urban Design.* Van Nostrand Reinhold, London pp.1-20
- Yi-Fu Tuan 1977. *Space and Place. The Perspective of Experience.* Arnold, London
- Van de Ven C. 1980. *Space in Architecture.* van Gorcum, Assen p. XI
- Woolley H. 2003. *Urban Open Spaces.* Spon, London

Space, form and dimension

There are various concepts of space: of social space, physical space (the continuum to which the laws of physics apply), architectonic space, abstract space, and absolute space (homogeneous, infinite, or relative, the latter defined in terms of measures and coordinates). We have an impression of absolute space when at sea: 'freedom, awe and the attraction of a distant horizon are the attributes of oceanic space awareness: universal, timeless and footloose' (Lefebvre 1992; Aben 2002).

On land, the space we need for our various activities is located in all manner of areas, and has to be surveyed, determined, enclosed, and subdivided. Two questions consistently arise: how much land is available for a particular use, and how can the activities in question optimally be fitted into it? The answer to these questions lies in the ordering of land-use – not only in the functional sense – but also in a visibly unified composition, with a particular form and carefully studied dimensions (Braham 1985; Ekkers 1990).

Spatial forms can be categorised in terms of curvilinear, angular, irregular, axial, radial concentric, organic etcetera (Trancik 1986; Krier 1988). Each of these forms is associated with a particular expression that combine geometric and social rules (formal, static, informal, dynamic, etc) (Broadbent 1990).

Differently sized spaces affect our spatial perception. When large and small spaces adjoin, some sort of interaction is suggested. 'When large spaces are experienced as being added to smaller, this has an expanding effect; when small spaces are experienced as being added to larger, this has a confining effect' (Hoogstad 1990).

Until the 14th century, people lived in limited, enclosed spaces (Aben 2002). A jump to an expanded view of the horizon was made by Petrarch, the Italian poet Francesco Petrarca (1304-1374), who climbed Mont Ventoux in France in 1336 to observe the panoramic view from the top. His only motive was 'to see what so great an elevation had to offer'. We have here 'a new and much bolder human perspective of the terrestrial landscape than that of the medieval individual, who, with gaze turned inward, contemplated only the visionary landscape of paradise' (Rogers 2001). [**delete Lemaire]

In parts of the Netherlands, widespread urbanisation has created an apparent lack of space; the public sees the country as overcrowded. However, statistics show that only 11% of the total surface of the country has been built upon (Anonymous 1999). The perception of crowdedness may be caused less by the extent of urban expansion than by the way built-up areas and infrastructural works are distributed over the landscape.

The objective of national planning policy is to conserve 'open space', not by conserving visually open space as such, but by preventing the expansion of built-up areas

The enclosed space at Catharijne Convent, Utrecht, the Netherlands.

and infrastructure, and by protecting nature areas, woodland and outdoor recreation facilities (Anonymous 1988). The concept of open space has thus shifted from the Euclidian meaning in terms of geometric properties and of dimensions to the types of use and the value attached to them (Albers 1997). While the space-consuming growth of infrastructure is much deplored, there is little awareness of the fact that infrastructure is indispensable for the access to – and the enjoyment of – open space.

Spaces within built-up areas are enclosed by various means such as roofs, vertical walls and columns (Ching 1979). The sense of enclosure is currently being reduced by the increasing use of transparent and light-reflecting building materials. When continuous spaces are formed between the mirroring walls of glass-covered high-rise buildings – as in many downtown areas in major cities around the world – a loss of orientation points will follow. A city thus risks becoming 'a hall of mirrors in which passers-by are dizzied into oblivion' (Gregory 1994).

This may be the hallmark of Post-modern 'heterotopia': the multifaceted space, 'with a multitude of localities containing things so different that it is impossible to find a common logic for them, a space in which everything is somehow out of place' (Gregory 1994).

- Aben R.; de Wit S. 2002. *The enclosed garden*. 010 publishers, Rotterdam pp. 14; 27 ff.
- Albers G. (et al). 1997. *Open Space in Urban Areas*. ARL, Hannover.
- Anonymous. 1988. *Vierde Nota over de Ruimtelijke Ordening* (i.e. *Fourth Report on Spatial Planning*) Ministerie VROM, The Hague p.113
- Anonymous. 1999. *Statistisch Jaarboek* (i.e. *Annual Statistical Report*). Centraal Bureau voor de Statistiek, Voorburg p.26
- Braham M. 1985. 'Principles of design. Part 3: Spatial design; organisation of space'. In: Landscape Design. London no. 6/85 pp. 11-15
- Broadbent G. 1990. 'The logic of informal space'. In: *Emerging Concepts in Urban Space Design*. Van Nostrand Reinhold, London pp. 21-23
- Ching F.D.K. 1979. *Architecture: Form, Space & Order*. Van Nostrand Reinhold, London pp. 110-152
- Gregory D. 1994. 'Strange lessons in deep space'. In: *Geographical Imaginations*. Blackwell, Oxford pp. 150-154
- Hoogstad J.1990. *Space-time-motion*. SDU, The Hague p. 21
- Krier R. 1988. 'On architectonic form'. In: *Architectural*

Composition. Academy Editions, London pp. 41-68
- Lefebvre H. 1992. *The Production of Space*. Blackwell, Oxford
- Rogers E.B. 2001. *Landscape Design. A Cultural and Architectural History*. Abrams, New York p. 125
- Trancik R. 1986. *Finding Lost Space*. Van Nostrand Reinhold, London pp.101

Space, scale and hierarchy

Space is connected with scale; there is a recognisable hierarchical relationship between the dimensions of a space (or a building) and those of a standard unit such as the human body. A distinction can be made between 'personal space', with distances of 30-100 centimetres; 'social space', from one to four metres; and 'public distance', from four metres to the horizon (Motloch 2001).

The perception of space in landscape at 'public distance' is governed by a number of critical distances, the so-called thresholds. One such threshold is the stereo threshold, i.e. the distance at which the relative position of the object to its surroundings can still be perceived. Another is the movement threshold: the distance within which a moving observer only just perceives an object as moving in relation to its background. This threshold is estimated at 1,400 metres. A third threshold is the visibility threshold, which depends on luminance of the sky, the contrast between an object and the sky, the degree of 'meteorological visibility', the dip of the horizon, and the size of the object. This can be calculated in each individual case (Nicolai 1971).

A conscious search for hierarchical space in landscape was manifest in the plans for the first of the new polders in the former Zuiderzee in the early decades of the 20th century. A sequence of spaces was designed, ranging from the paced-out farmyard, through the land parcel, to open fields and the horizon. The visibility of a hierarchic sequence of spaces is an important criterion for determining the distinction between an 'open' and an 'enclosed' landscape (Vroom 1986).

- Motloch J.L. 2001. *Introduction to Landscape Design* (second edition). Wiley & Sons, New York pp.112-121

In 1336, Petrarch was the first human being to climb Mont Ventoux in France solely in order to enjoy the view.

'A hall of mirrors in which passers-by are dizzied into oblivion': Manhattan N.Y.

• Nicolai J. 1971. *De visuele invloed van woonplaatsen op het open landschap* (i.e. *The visual impact of settlements on open landscapes*). PhD thesis, Delft Technical University pp. 155 ff.
• Vroom M.J. 1986. 'The perception of dimensions of space and levels of infrastructure and its application in landscape planning'. In: Landscape Planning Journal, Elsevier, Amsterdam pp. 337-352

Space and time

Cubism was the movement in painting that recognised the impossibility of perceiving spaces from a stationary point of view. The true nature of space could only be experienced by a moving observer: 'Space = Time x Movement' (Hoogstad 1990).

In modern architecture this principle led to the removal of enclosing walls and the introduction of continuous space within buildings, also called 'cubic space' (Giedion 1948). In town planning, the free-standing high-rise apartment buildings standing on pylons – introduced by architect Le Corbusier (1887-1965) – looked as if they barely touched the ground (Broadbent 1990).

In Post-modern architecture, a different space-time concept has emerged. This is called 'volumetric space', which is predicated

An urban square as part of an important pedestrian route from the central railway station to city hall. Spuiplein, The Hague, the Netherlands. Designed by Joan Busquets in 1995.
Source: Landscape Architecture and Town Planning in the Netherlands 95-97, Thoth, Bussum p. 139

on the idea that reality cannot be understood through a reductivist objectivity, but only through a holistic acceptance of phenomena as they appear. ´Sense of place is impossible in space without here-there, me-you, us-them, inside-outside definition. The conceptual categories of inside and outside connote the existence of enclosing space separation and are thus volumetric' (Condon 1988).

• Broadbent G. 1990. *Emerging Concepts in Urban Space design*. Van Nostrand, Reinhold London p. 264
• Condon P.M. 1988. 'Cubist Space, Volumetric Space and Landscape Architecture'. In: Landscape Journal, The University of Wisconsin Press, Urbana, Illinois vol. 7 no. 1 pp. 1-14
• Giedion S. 1948. *Space Time and Architecture. The Growth of a Tradition*. Harvard University Press, Cambridge pp. 430-450
• Hoogstad J. 1990. *Space-time-motion. Prolegomena to architecture*. SDU, The Hague pp. 22; 42

Square, Plaza
see also > place, space

'An open place or area formed at the meeting of two or more streets' (*Webster*).

Squares are part the architecture of cities; some of them are famous works of art in their own right. 'St Peter's Square in Rome, St Mark's in Venice, and Place Vendôme in Paris are as generally known and admired as Leonardo da Vinci's Mona Lisa, Michelangelo's Moses, and Rembrandt's Night Watch. These squares are undoubtedly as much 'art' as any painting, sculpture or individual work of architecture [...]. It is only of secondary importance to this effect whether and to what extent in each instance specific functional demands are fulfilled' (Zucker 1959).

Many squares are 'representative' places; they express an idea, or lend identity in a spectacular way, such as the Post-modern Piazza d'Italia in New Orleans (Moore 1980). They may be designed to impress with their monumental buildings, or serve as parade grounds, like the Baroque squares in many European cities (Broadbent 1990). During the twentieth century, most city squares were taken over by motorised traffic. In the last thirty years, enormous efforts have been devoted to winning them back for pedestrian

301

use, a process that has led to the layout of many carefully designed open spaces (Gehl 2001).

In Dutch cities, most squares are traditionally utilitarian in character, having served as market places with names such as Veemarkt, Vismarkt and Kalvermarkt (i.e. cattle market, fish market and calf market). This does not prevent some of them from being extremely beautiful. Some squares fronting town halls are more representative, such as Dam square in Amsterdam and Grote Markt in Groningen. Due to the scarcity of land and the high density of buildings in towns, they are of modest dimensions (van der Woud 1998).

Squares provide a special sense of freedom for pedestrians and cyclists, who are able to roam about freely and are not restricted in their movements as they are by the pavements and cycle lanes elsewhere in the city. Squares are therefore important public places (Gehl 1996).

The design of new urban squares is mostly undertaken as part of the layout of whole new urban districts or neighbourhoods, such as the new expansions after the Second World War. They also may be the result of a reconstruction plan for a city centre or an urban renewal project, such as Schouwburgplein in Rotterdam (Harsema 2000/1) and Heuvel in Tilburg (Harsema 1998). In some cases, the reconstruction of a square is limited to a revision of its pavement pattern and furniture, as in the centre of Zutphen (Harsema 2000/2). A precise detailing is characteristic of these designs.

• Broadbent 1990. *Emerging Concepts in Urban Space design.* Van Nostrand Reinhold, London pp. 49 ff.
• Gehl J.; Gemzøe L. 1996. *Public spaces – public life.* Danish Architectural Association, Copenhagen
• Gehl J.; Gemzøe L. 2001. *New City Spaces.* The Danish Architectural Press, Copenhagen
• Harsema H. (ed). 1998. 'The squares in central Tilburg'. In: *Landscape architecture and town planning in the Netherlands 95-97.* Thoth, Bussum
• Harsema H. (ed). 2000/1. 'Squares with a history within sight of the port of Rotterdam'. In: *Landscape architecture and town planning in the Netherlands 97-99.* Thoth publishing, Bussum pp. 176179
• Harsema H. (ed). 2000/2. 'Facelift revives worn-out town centre'. In: *Landscape architecture and town planning in the Netherlands 97-99.* Thoth publishing, Bussum pp. 180-183
• Moore C. 1980. 'Piazza d'Italia'. In: Architectural Design Journal. Papadakis, London no. 5/6. pp. 20 et seq.
• Rasmussen S.E. 1951 *Towns and Buildings.* MIT Press, Cambridge, Mass
• van der Woud A. 1998. *Het lege land* (i.e. *The empty land*). Contact, Amsterdam pp. 307 ff.
• Zucker P. 1959. *Town and Square. From the Agora to the Village Green.* MIT Press Cambridge, Mass

The urban square as a parade ground: Ottawa, Canada, 1976

Stream

see also > barrage, basin, dike, source, grotto.

'A body of running water flowing on the earth, a steady succession, a constantly renewed supply' (*Webster*). Current or direction of something flowing or moving' (*Oxford English Dictionary*).

Since ancient times, rivers have been connected with myths and sagas; they represent the primordial symbols of life and death. The natural cycle of source, fall, stream, mouth and basin represent phases of human life. 'To see a river was to be swept up in a great current of myths and memories that was strong enough to carry us back to the first watery element in our existence in the womb. And along that stream were borne some of the most intense of our social and animal passions: the mysterious transmutations of blood and water, the vitality and mortality of heroes, empires, nations and gods' (Schama 1995).

The archetype consists of the four rivers that emanate in the Garden of Eden and run in four directions (Prest 1981). The orthogonal pattern of this archetype formed the basic model for many later gardens (Moore 1989). Rivers such as the Nile and Rhine are connected with myths and sagas such as those of Osiris and the Lorelei. They represent a rich cultural heritage: 'their shores are besprinkled with venerated ruins or the palaces of princes' (Schama 1995). They represent connecting lines and barriers (the Rhine to the Roman legions, for example).

As long as rivers are not harnessed in dikes, weirs and groynes, streams form landscapes, because erosion and sedimentation create a constantly changing topography (van de Ven 1993).

In symbolic form, the world-wide water-cycle has been represented in the layout of gardens for many centuries. 'Waters seem to

303

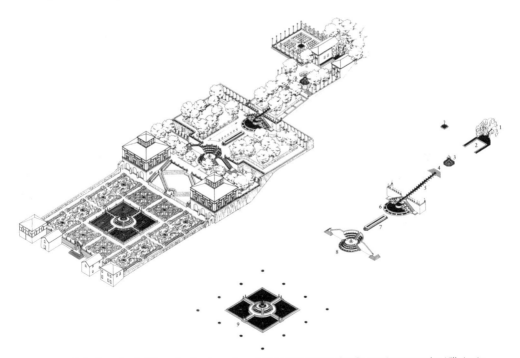

'Pilgrimage with the flow of water'. The natural water cycle symbolised and abstracted in the Renaissance garden. Villa Lante, Bagnaia, Italy: 1. the source: a fountain falling out of the wild forest; 2. pool flanked by pavilions; 3. fountain with masks, vases and dolphins; 4. cascade; 5. stepped ramp; 6. fountain with cascades and river gods; 7. stone dining table; 8. fountain of Little Lamps; 9. fountain with Cardinal Montalto's arms.

Source: Moore C.W. (et al). 1989. The Poetics of Gardens, MIT Press, Cambridge pp. 145 146

provide some of the more exciting and inventive movements of garden representation' (Hunt 2000). 'The shapes formed not only in natural movement but also those of captivity have inspired man to fashion water as a work of art' (Jellicoe 1966). In Renaissance gardens, the natural cycle is represented by the combination of source, fountain, fall, cascade and mirroring pond.

Cascades, a series of small stepped waterfalls, may range in scale from the small and elaborately sculpted channel in the garden of Villa Lante (Moore 1989) to the grandiose works at Wilhelmshöhe in Kassel, Germany (Kluckert 2000), where the difference in height between the head of the cascade and its termination is more than two hundred metres, over a distance of more than a thousand metres (Oxford Companion). This ensemble usually forms the 'water axis' of the layout (Halprin 1972; Schama 1995). Villa Lante in Bagnaia

demonstrates the story of the river as a 'pilgrimage with the flow of water' (Moore 1989).

In French formal gardens, water is presented 'in a sequence that depicts an ever-diminishing rush of movement, ending as a reflecting pool on the horizon. Nature is represented in the garden as a scientific classification system' (Steenbergen 1996).

During the 20th century, the abuse of rivers

The floodplain of the river Rhine as it looked in January 1995.

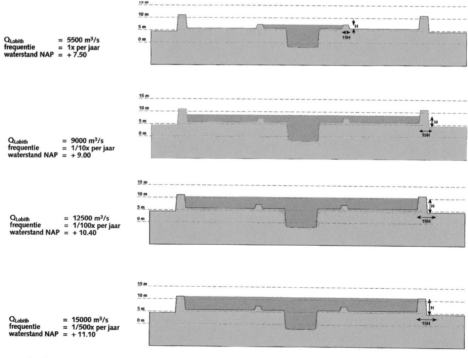

Q_{Lobith} = 5500 m³/s
frequentie = 1x per jaar
waterstand NAP = +7.50

Q_{Lobith} = 9000 m³/s
frequentie = 1/10x per jaar
waterstand NAP = +9.00

Q_{Lobith} = 12500 m³/s
frequentie = 1/100x per jaar
waterstand NAP = +10.40

Q_{Lobith} = 15000 m³/s
frequentie = 1/500x per jaar
waterstand NAP = +11.10

Water levels in the main Dutch rivers are becoming increasingly difficult to control. Four levels connected with different rates of runoff are presented here in cross-section.

Source: Ministry of Transport and Water Control, The Hague

as sewage disposal channels became an environmental hazard. Successful measures to stop this meant that contemporary river landscapes in some countries are now beginning to represent the ideal of new ecological zones – the 'blue lines' within the greenways that connect and form nationwide ecosystems (Fabos 1995).

A contemporary example of a park layout as a metaphor for 'stream' is the Guadelupe River Park in San Jose, California, where a strip of land parallel to the river is laid out for use as a city park that will survive floods. The form of the park expresses a series of currents and interruptions that show an analogy with a river bed. Ecological process and form, natural forces and cultural expression have thus been made to go hand in hand (Treib 2002) – and also a promising alternative to parts of the Dutch Ecological Network, whose gaps tend to make it resemble a misshapen Gruyère cheese.

• Fabos J.G. (ed). 1995. Greenways. Special Issue Landscape and Urban Planning, Elsevier, Amsterdam vol. 33 nos. 1-3
• Halprin L. 1972. 'Running water'. In: Cities. MIT Press, Cambridge pp. 339 ff.
• Hunt J.D. 2000. Greater Perfections. The Practice of Garden Theory. Thames & Hudson, London pp. 85-89
• Jellicoe G. 1966. 'Water'. In: Studies in Landscape Design. Volume II. Oxford University Press, London pp. 17-25
• Kluckert E. 2000. Gardens of Europe. Könemann Köln p. 309
• Moore C.W. (et al). 1989. The Poetics of Gardens. MIT Press, Cambridge pp. 144 -147
• Prest J. 1981. The Garden of Eden. Yale University Press, New Haven pp. 11 ff.
• Schama S. 1995. 'Streams of consciousness'. In: Landscape and Memory. Harper Collins pp. 245 ff.; pp. 349; 365.
• Steenbergen C.; Reh W. 1996. Architecture and landscape. Thoth publishers, Bussum p. 15
• Treib M. 2002. 'The Content of Landscape Form (The Limits of Formalism)'. In: Landscape Journal The University of Wisconsin Press, Urbana, Illinois. 20:2-01 pp. 119-140
• van de Ven G.P. (ed). 1993. Man-made Lowlands. History of water management and land reclamation in the Netherlands. Matrijs, Utrecht

Structure
see also> coherence, order, pattern, system
'Something made up of interdependent parts in a definite pattern of organisation. The arrangement or relationship of elements (as particles, parts or organs) in a substance, body or system' (Webster).

In the building industry, structure is related to the construction of edifices such as buildings or bridges. A more general definition is 'the mutual relation between parts or elements within a whole determining its nature' (Williams 1985). There are many applications of the term, such as those in language, technology, biology, geology, or organisations. In a number of cases the definition overlaps with that of 'system' and 'pattern'.

A structure differs from a system in that the first is a permanent framework, whereas a system can be open or closed. And while a pattern is just an orderly group of elements, 'a structure has three distinguishing features: it forms a whole, it consists of transformations, and is self-organising' (de Jong 1987).

Outdoor space can be structured by a framework of interconnected lines, walls or volumes that combine to form a unit. 'The function of structure is to give something to hold on to for human perception – to bring order into the information presented to us in such a way that we can form an image to be stored in our memory' (Dijkstra 2001).

A structure is perceived by everybody in the same way, forming hierarchical connections with main and sub-structures. Structures can be finite, complete, or infinite and expandable. They can also be 'strong' or 'weak'. If a strong structure is only partly finished or visible, it can be completed in only one particular way, while a weak structure is

305

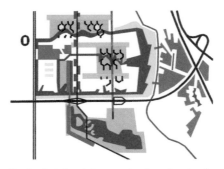

Structural relations between water channels and park systems in the south-eastern district of Amsterdam. Design proposal by Harm Veenenbos, 1988.

somewhat unpredictable (Hiele 1981).

Urban green structure

This the interconnected totality of parks, greenways, public gardens, promenades and paths within a town. In older towns these structures have grown piecemeal over time, while in newly constructed urban areas they have been conceived and laid out as part of the total town structure (van der Wal 1997).

A Dutch municipal 'green structure plan' is a long-term policy plan for the layout and management of the public green area. Within it, strong points and weaknesses are registered. Design proposals focus on making lasting improvements to the quality and coherence of the whole.

There are several criteria for the structural quality of urban outdoor space:
· utility: the space should be suitable for different activities.
· sphere and identity: planting should be adapted to the ecological conditions.
· coherence and orientation: there should be a visible connection between vegetation, buildings and infrastructure; routing should be logical, providing orientation in space.
· representation: plants and details should be carefully maintained, and exotic plants identified.
· ecological sustainability: comparable ecosystems should be interconnected, both within the town and in the urban fringe.
· public safety: traffic systems should be separated, and there should be lighting at night (Meeus 1992).

Landscape structure

Landscape structure is the physical, permanent, visible structure, the supporting main frame without which landscape could not function. This natural structure, also called 'deep structure', is the result of geological and climate factors (Spirn 1998). In landscape ecology, the terms patch, corridor and matrix are parts of landscape structure (Forman 1986).

Man-made structure is visible in the arrangement of horizontal networks, such as roads, canals, railroads and land lots. Structures that create enclosure consist of

walls, fences, dikes, plantations and buildings (*Britannica*). They form patterns and compositions which can be registered on maps, including mental maps. They contribute to an aesthetic experience (Gould 1974; Higuchi 1983).

Planning procedures may also be 'structured'. A structured planning process is founded on fixed rules and procedures. These rules are derived from the physical conditions, the brief and the technical and financial and political opportunities, procedures and constraints.

A landscape structure plan is a master plan for designated rural areas. It brings coherence and connectedness in a continually changing environment. Rather than laying down the creation of conditions for change in a definite plan, it creates certain emphases.

· Dijkstra T. 2001. *Architectonische kwaliteit* (i.e. *Architectonic quality*). 010 publishers, Rotterdam
· Forman R.T.T.; Godron M. 1986. *Landscape Ecology*. John Wiley, New York
· Gould P.; White R. 1974. *Mental Maps*. Penguin Books, Harmondsworth, Middlesex
· van Hiele P.M. 1981. *Struktuur* (i.e. *Structure*). Muusses, Purmerend
· Higuchi T. 1983. *The Visual and Spatial Structure of Landscapes*. MIT Press, Cambridge pp. 6-24
· de Jong T. 1987. *De structurele samenhang van architectuur begrippen* (i.e. *The structural coherence of architectural terminology*). Delft University Press pp. 75-76
· Meeus J.H.A. (et al). 1992. *Groenstructuurplan Tilburg*. Dienst Publieke Werken, Tilburg pp. 5-14
· Spirn A. 1998. *The Language of Landscape*. Yale University Press, New Haven pp. 104-106; 155-159
· van der Wal C. 1997. *In praise of common sense. Planning the ordinary. A physical planning history of the new towns in the Ijsselmeerpolders*. 010 publishers, Rotterdam
· Williams R. 1985. *Keywords. A Vocabulary of Culture and Society*. Fontana Paperback, London

Style

see also > landscape style, Modernism, Renaissance

'Manner that is typical of a particular writer, artist, etc, or of a particular literary, artistic etc period' (*Oxford Advanced*)

Historical design styles in architecture and garden design are rooted in the culture of a time in the past, such as Classicism, which reverted to examples from ancient times; and landscape style in the Romantic Age. Style periods succeed one another and react to each other. 'Every style period develops new concepts that refer to earlier times or other places, or what may be expected in the future' (Dijkstra 2001).

Style is an essential part of an environmental design. A purely functional design is by definition lacking in style.' Style is a way of thinking which contradicts the belief that pre-ordained functions can give the necessary directions to facts and that the problem consists merely of giving form to certain functions' (Broadbent 1990). While ecological design, with its emphasis on the maintenance and guidance of natural process and its extremely varied appearance may be 'a typical manner of doing', it can hardly be seen as having an artistic character. From the point of view of formal aesthetics it is therefore more a design method than a design style.

In the field of architecture, Frank Lloyd Wright (1867-1959) demonstrated an individual and consistent manner of designing. This was recognisable in much of his work, to the extent that he created an individual design style. His pupils applied the same formal language as their master did, thereby creating a design school.

Whenever a group of prominent designers adopt a common way of expressing themselves on the basis of a well-considered philosophy, ideal, or appealing utopian view, a design style may well spread over large parts of the world. Names such as Mies van der Rohe (1886-1969), Walter Gropius (1883-1969) and other architects are thus connected with the International Style of the Modernist period. In contexts such as this, style is 'the architectonic expression of the spirit of the time of a people and its culture, as well as climate and geography' (van der Woud 1997).

While the overall manner of expression may be consistent, there are always undercurrents within a design style – individual ideals that lead to a personal interpretation and different elaboration of design assignments. Within the English landscape style, for instance, there was a marked difference between the work of Lancelot 'Capability' Brown (1716-1783) and that of Humphry Repton (1752-1818) (Hunt 1992; Kluckert 2000).

The term 'fashion' indicates changing

307

A fashionable design in which standard street details have been omitted in favour of loose arrangements and extreme informality. Bloemenbuurt, Leiden, the Netherlands.

preferences which, unlike style, are not based on an ideal or a paradigm. It is 'a popular style at a given time or place' (*Oxford Advanced*).

In landscape architecture, the relationship between fashion and style is complicated, as it may be fashionable to design a park in a certain style. Two examples of fashionable trends in Modernist architecture were Brutalism and Neo-realism.

The cosy-looking informal layout of Dutch neighbourhoods in the 1970s – such as Almere-Haven, which in plan looks like a collection of cauliflowers – was a highly fashionable phenomenon that was quickly superseded (van der Wal 1997). In garden design, the use of conspicuous new plant varieties or of newly developed construction materials – open concrete blocks, wooden railway sleepers (i.e. railroad ties) – may briefly cause a stir before they become 'outdated'.

· Broadbent G. 1990. *Emerging Concepts in Urban Space Design.* Van Nostrand Reinhold, London p. 169
· Dijkstra T. 2001. *Architectonische kwaliteit.* Uitgeverij 010, Rotterdam
· Hunt J.D. 1992. *Gardens and the Picturesque.* MIT Press, Cambridge pp. 3-16
· Kluckert E. 2000. *Gardens of Europe.* Könemann, Köln pp. 370-390
· van der Wal C. 1997. 'Almere-Haven'. In: *In praise of common sense. Planning the ordinary. A physical planning history of the new Towns in the IJsselmeerpolders.* 010 Publishers, Rotterdam pp. 213 ff.
· van der Woud A. 1997. *Waarheid en karakter* (i.e. *Truth and character*). *Het debat over de bouwkunst 1840-1900.* NAi publishers, Rotterdam pp. 97

Styling (to compose, to formalise)

see also > concept, construct, style

'To cause to conform to a certain style. To design and make in accord with the current fashion' (*Webster*).

In landscape architecture, the activity of styling is not a matter of choosing a style. It is something that develops during the design process, something that crystallises under the influence of the brief. It involves a search – with the aid of analogies – for familiar situations, for exemplary plans and historic styles. It is the collection and selection of

prototypes, followed by their transformation. It has a close bearing with the character, content and technical aspects of the assignment. It is based on the ideas of the designer about the way he thinks a design should be elaborated (Baljon 1992).

The styling of objects such as cars and vacuum cleaners is an entirely different activity; this means creating an attractive and fashionable outward form for a product, but without changing the essential parts – the 'mass-produced image of individuality at the factory' (Jencks 1972).

· Baljon L. 1992. *Designing Parks.* Architectura et Natura, Amsterdam pp. 135-138
· Jencks C.; Silver N. 1972. 'Standardized consumption'. In: *Adhocism. The Case for Improvisation.* Secker & Warburg, London pp. 58-63

Suburbia

see also > arcadia, urbanisation

A suburb is 'the residential area adjacent to a city or large town' (*Webster*).

The origins of the suburban villa-landscape lie in Rome, two thousand years ago. For affluent citizens, rural life at that time was not a flight from an urban existence but a complementary existence (Rogers 2001).

In the Netherlands, suburbanisation originated at the end of the 19th century – just before the construction of railways – when developers bought up building sites in towns such as Bussum and Hilversum near Amsterdam. Affluent citizens of Amsterdam built new villas with spacious gardens, effectively creating contemporary extensive residential neighbourhoods (de Jong 1999) that transformed the landscape into picturesque parks with winding roads and changing scenery with fanciful gardens and irregular ponds.

During the 20th century, the movement of people from the urban centres to rural settings became a more widespread phenomenon. Thanks precisely to their ability to meet the demands of modern life, expanding cities lost much of their attractiveness, causing a growing stream of citizens to move to places where the enervating bustle of city life had not yet penetrated (Ibelings 1999).

In the United States, the exodus of the population from inner cities was of a different order. A massive movement to the suburbs, in which lower income-groups also participated, was stimulated by developers who filled vast low-cost housing schemes with customised catalogue-built bungalows. In the eyes of European town planners, the monotony of these suburbs with their lack of

public outdoor space and other facilities made them places of horror. They stand for 'urban sprawl' (Mumford 1963).

In reality, the social cohesion in these neighbourhoods was much stronger than a superficial inspection might suggest (Jackson 1970; Gans 1972). As in the USA, the Netherlands' network society increasingly demonstrates 'community without propinquity' (Webber 1969).

From an international point of view, 'suburbia' represents a life-style, a ideal housing situation in which the vicinity of an urban centre, the presence of greenery, and traces of rural life all make important contributions to a sense of well-being (Silverstone 1997; Rowe 1991).

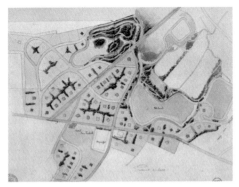

Suburban development Oud Bussum, designed by landscape architect Leonard Springer in the 1920s.

Source: Ibelings H. 1999. Nederlandse Stedenbouw in de 20ste eeuw. (Dutch town planning in the 20th century). NAI publishers Rotterdam

• Gans H.J. 1972. *Planning and Social Life: Friendship and Neighbour Relations in Suburban Communities.* Pelican Books, Harmondsworth, Middlesex pp. 123 ff.
• Ibelings H. 1999. *Nederlandse Stedenbouw in de 20ste eeuw* (i.e. *Dutch town planning in the 20th century*). NAi publishers, Rotterdam p. 6
• Jackson J.B. 1970. 'The many guises of suburbia'. In: Zube E. (ed). *Landscapes. The Selected Writings of J.B. Jackson.* The University of Massachusetts Press, Amherst pp. 113-115
• de Jong E. 1999. 'Living in a green setting. The history of an ideal'. In: ARCHIS Journal 1999/10, NAi, Rotterdam pp. 26-34
• Mumford L. 1963. 'Suburbia and beyond'. In: *The City in History.*

The spectre of urban sprawl in the USA as illustrated by Ian McHarg.

Source: McHarg I. 1963. Design with Nature, The Natural History Press, New York

Secker and Warburg, London pp. 482-513
• Rogers E.B. 2001. *Landscape Design. A Cultural and Architectural History.* Abrams, New York pp. 86-96
• Rowe P.G. 1991. *Making a Middle Landscape.* MIT press, Cambridge, Mass
• Silverstone R. 1997. *Visions of Suburbia.* Routledge, London.
• Webber M. 1969. 'Order in Diversity: Community without Propinquity'. In: Proshansky H. (et al) (ed). *Environmental Psychology. Man and his Physical Setting.* Holt Rinehart and Winston pp. 533-548

Survey

see > analysis

Sustainable, Durable

see also > quality, restoration

To sustain is 'to keep up: prolong; to bear up under: endure'. Durable means 'able to last a long time' (*Webster*). Sustainable development of the environment means to ensure that it meets the requirements of present generations without endangering the opportunities for coming generations to do the same (Anonymous 1989).

Sustainability can be promoted in a number of ways:

· In the interests of ecological sustainability, various instruments (such as the establishment of ecological networks) can be used to promote biodiversity and the long-term sustenance of lifecycles (de Bruin 1987).

· to promote the economical use of resources such as minerals and fossil energy, houses can be insulated and the use of wind and water energy be increased.

· to further technical and economic sustainability, pollution, acidification and over-manuring as they affect soils, water and the atmosphere can all be reduced, and the use of strong, dependable and durable materials be encouraged (Countryside Commission 1997)

· environmental quality in rural and urban areas can be maintained (see *Quality*) (Meeus 1990).

· to safeguard water quality and the water supply, measures can be taken against flooding and to promote water retention. These may involve water purification and the con-

Ecological engeneering as a contribution to the ecological network; Stram at Lievelde, Achterhoek.
Photo: Peter van Bolhuis, Pandion

scientious management of ground water (Vroom 1994).

Sustainable town planning has the objective of creating living areas that provide residents with long-term satisfaction and a sense of well-being. Such policies therefore promote:
· the use of building and construction materials whose production, application and maintenance do not have negative environmental effects
· high-density building
· much reduced use of private cars
· the recycling of water, the separation per neighbourhood of purified water and run-off, and the purification of water using natural processes such as helophytes (Tjallingi 1996).

· Anonymous. 1989. *Nationaal Milieubeleidsplan (National Environmental Policy Plan)*. Ministerie VROM, The Hague pp. 7-11
· de Bruin D. (et al). 1987. *Ooievaar. De toekomst van het Rivierengebied* (i.e. *Stork: the future of the river landscape*). Gelderse Milieufederatie, Arnhem pp. 99-110
· Countryside Commission 1997. *Agricultural Landscapes: a Third Look*. Technical Report, Walgrave, Northampton
· Meeus J. (et al). 1990 'Agricultural Landscapes in Europe and their Transformation'. In: Vroom M.J. (ed). Changing Agricultural Landscapes of Europe. Special Issue Landscape and Urban Planning, Elsevier, Amsterdam Vol 19 nos. 3-4 pp. 289-352
· Vroom M.J. (et al). 1994. 'Landscape planning and water management in the Netherlands'. In: Ekisitcs: the problems and science of human settlements. Volume 61 number 364-365 pp. 10-21
· Tjallingi S. 1996. 'Designing a water system'. In: *Ecological Conditions. Strategies and Structures*. Environmental Planning. IBN Scientific Contributions 2. IBN- DLO, Wageningen pp. 242-268

In garden design, durability means securing form and space for long-term use, making certain that the designer's intended layout stays in place. Without proper management, gardens and parks rapidly deteriorate; when maintenance is done without any understanding of the designer's intentions, they quickly change beyond recognition. Some landscape architects therefore make sure their contract includes their supervision for a period of some years after the design has been implemented (Ruys 1981).

Italian Renaissance gardens have stayed intact for centuries, partly because of careful maintenance and restoration, but also because of the use of durable materials –

311

As durable elements in Renaissance gardens, walls, steps and balustrades have survived centuries of wear and tear. Villa Vicobello, Siena.

Drawing by Lodewijk Wiegersma

stone – in terraces, landings, steps, walls and fountains. In these gardens, plants and plant beds are contained within a durable framework (van der Ree 1992; Steenbergen 1996).

Gardens and parks designed in a free or Romantic style are the least durable: they depend on the effort and expertise of managers to keep their characteristic layout and appearance. Without adequate maintenance these parks inevitably lose their original quality (Vroom 1992). Most of the gardens designed by 'Capability' Brown (1716-1783) are now in a decrepit state (Turner 1985).

• van der Ree P. 1992. *Italian Villas and Gardens*. Thoth Bussum pp. 47-131
• Ruys M.; Zandvoort R. 1981. *Van Vensterbank tot Landschap* (i.e. *From windowsill to landscape*). Moussault, Bussum pp. 85-93.
• Steenbergen C.M.; Reh W. 1996. *Architecture and Landscape*. Thoth, Bussum
• Turner R. 1985. *Capability Brown and the Eighteenth-century English Landscape*. Weidenfeld & Nicholson, London pp. 118 - 129
• Vroom M.J. (ed). 1992. *Outdoor Space*. Thoth, Bussum pp. 88-90

'Save water, shower with a friend.' Poster of Philadelphia Water Co, USA.

Symbol

see also > metaphor, sign, reference

'Something that stands for something else. Esp. something concrete that represents or suggests another thing that cannot in itself be represented or visualised.' 'A letter character, or sign used to represent a quantity, position, relationship, direction or something to be done. Instead of a word or a group of words' (*Webster*).

'Because there are innumerable things beyond the range of human understanding, we constantly use symbolic terms to represent concepts that we cannot define or fully comprehend' (Jung 1964).

Symbols are intimately linked with our spiritual, inner world and with religion. They can assume any imaginable form, including pictures, metaphors, sounds, gestures, colours, myths and personifications (Geertz 1973). The primordial symbols of religion and myth have a long history – also in features of the landscape, such as holy mountains, dolmens and megaliths (Ogrin 2003).

Even if we are not conscious of it, symbolism is present in all the phenomena around us. All designed landscapes and sites are full of references to far-off places and bygone events. The world of man is not only a world of things, it is a world of symbols in which the difference between reality and imitation is unreal in itself (Gombrich 1964). 'Symbolism is perhaps the single most important link between students of landscape in the arts and the sciences' (Appleton 1986).

There is a difference between a symbolic landscape and what we call a 'landscape of symbols'. 'The symbolic landscape is concerned with a single idea only, the great historic example being the Persian garden which brought heaven to earth. The landscape of symbols, on the other hand is one that has within it a symbol (or symbols) of sufficient intensity to endow it with a special significance' (Jellicoe 1970). Among the oldest symbols are the collections of monoliths at Avebury, Carnac and Stonehenge, and also the megalithic burial places in the Netherlands.

Symbolism as a movement in the 19th-century plastic arts preceded Art Nouveau (Gerhardus 1978). In architecture, the symbolism of a building or construction is that part of its outward appearance which indicates or refers to a different reality or another object. The Eiffel Tower and the Tower of London are urban symbols. A modern office block is the symbol of progress and dynamism, but also of globalisation and capital flows, thereby representing the image of the city (Yi-Fu Tuan 1974).

To many people, the cooling towers of nuclear plants emitting clouds of steam over rural areas symbolise radiation and danger – and therefore look threatening.

One counterpart is the wind-turbines, which symbolise environmentally benign ways of generating electricity.

Throughout the history of landscape architecture, the use of symbols has changed. In the Romantic age, buildings, ruins, and sculptures referred to ancient times, to elsewhere. The Modernist movement abhorred symbols because form was supposed to follow function – and plants 'spoke for themselves', making additional references superfluous. And yet all designed form, each line a designer draws on paper expresses something. A straight line is 'positive, powerful', a winding line 'indirect, plodding', an arrow 'formal, dogmatic' (Simonds 1997). In Post-modern design, symbols are once again used exuberantly, often 'citing' earlier style periods

Symbols of dynamic progress, of globalisation and capital flow: bank building in Rotterdam.

- Appleton J. 1986. 'The role of the arts in landscape research'. In: Penning-Rowsell E.; Lowenthal D. *Landscape Meanings and Values*. Allen and Unwin, London. pp. 39-40
- Geertz C. 1973. *The Interpretation of Cultures*. Basic Books, New York pp. 87-124
- Gerhardus M.; Gerhardus D. 1978. *Symbolism and Art Nouveau*. Phaidon, London pp. 5-14
- Gombrich E.H. 1964. *Art and Illusion*. Phaidon, London
- Jellicoe G.A. 1970. "The landscape of symbols'. In: *Studies in Landscape Design. Volume III*, Oxford University Press pp. 1 -16
- Jung K. 1964. *Man and His Symbols*. Aldus Books Doubleday, New York p. 21
- Ogrin D. 2003. 'Symbolism in landscape artefacts'. In: Kerkstra K. (ed). *The landscape of symbols*. Blauwdruk, Wageningen
- Simonds O. 1997. *Landscape Architecture*. McGraw Hill, New York. p. 193
- Yi-Fu Tuan. 1974. *Topophilia. A study of Environmental Perception, Attitudes, and Values*. Prentice Hall, Englewood Cliffs, N.J. pp. 192-201

313

Symbols of radiation and danger: cooling towers of nuclear plant in France.

Symmetry
see also > Classicism, geometry

'Balanced proportions, also beauty of form arising from balanced proportions. Correspondence in size, shape, and relative position of parts on opposite sides of a dividing line or median plane or about a centre of axis' (*Webster*).

Bilateral symmetry occurs when the opposite sides mirror; radial symmetry means that objects are arranged around a central point. Vertical symmetry occurs when images are reflected in still waters (Wöbse

2002). In natural environments, symmetry is only visible at the micro scale, such as in snow flakes, some fruit and plant leaves.

'Being precise and disciplined in plan, symmetry requires precision in detail. Bold in concept, it demands bold forms. The symmetrical plan becomes a structural framework, compartmentalising site features and functions' (Simonds 1997).

Symmetry symbolises stateliness and importance, and therefore has a social function, without which it would be merely a boring phenomenon (Ching 1979). 'Wherever symmetry is useful to the soul, and may assist her functions, it is agreeable to her, but wherever it is useless, it becomes distasteful, because it takes away variety; therefore things that we see in succession ought to have variety, for our soul has no difficulty in seeing them. Those on the contrary that we see in one glance, ought to have symmetry' (Repton 1806), citing Montesquieu (1689-1755).

Examples of symmetrical axes in squares and parks include paths and avenues, ponds and canals. They may be part of a geometrical composition, foreshortened in perspective view, such as in the Classicist parks in France. A composition that looks symmetrical at first sight acquires added interest if it is being slightly off-balance. A 'deranged' symmetry such as shown in the Chateau at Chambord is of higher complexity: the longer one looks the more there is to discover.

Asymmetry is not only a visual phenomenon, it is also connected with phenomena that are unbalanced in form or

Total symmetry in Champ-de-Mars, Paris.

314

Disordered symmetry at Chateau Chambord on the Loire, France.

in meaning. Examples include Modernist neighbourhoods, their well-ordered housing terraces with backyards laid out in a kitsch fashion that refers to a pastoral landscape (Rowe 1991).

• Ching F.D.K. 1979. *Architecture: Form, Space & Order.* Van Nostrand Reinhold, London pp. 342-349
• Repton H. 1806. *An enquiry into the changes of taste in landscape gardening, to which are added some observations on theory and practice including a defence on the art.* J. Taylor, London
• Rowe P. 1991. 'Modern pastoralism'. In: *Making a Middle Landscape.* MIT Press Cambridge pp. 232-234
• Simonds O. 1997. *Landscape Architecture.* McGraw Hill, New York pp. 249-253
• Wöbse H.H. 2002. 'Symmetrie'. In: *Landschaftsästhetik.* Eugen Ulmer Verlag pp. 38-39

Synthesis

see also > coherence, landscape analysis, montage, reduction

'The composition or combination of parts or elements so as to form a whole' (*Webster*).

Landscape analysis techniques developed in the USA (McHarg 1969; Steiner 2000) and also applied in the Netherlands are used to systematically dissect the landscape into its component parts, so as to gain a better insight into the functioning of these parts.

The problem for the landscape analyst is how to assemble the dissected parts into a new synthesised whole – a new situation imagined by the planner or designer – in which each component finds a place. To find a synthesis, the logical process of analysis has to be combined with a search, vision or idea; a creative jump.

Such a process is not without methodological pitfalls. The dissected elements must be reassembled in a new context. Functional requirements must be met, meanings have to be attached, and rational and sensory components must be combined into a new whole. There is no standard recipe to be followed; every assignment is a new adventure. In this process, knowledge and feeling, detachment and involvement converge. It is the culminating phase of a design (Baljon 1992).

In regional planning, where rational and

functional considerations are more dominant, a synthesis phase can best be described as an exploratory activity in which one may choose between 'projection' – extrapolation from existing tendencies – or a search for an entirely new solution by means of creative jump (Kleefmann 1984).

• Baljon L. 1992. *Designing Parks.* Architectura & Natura, Amsterdam
• Kleefmann F. 1984. *Planning als zoekinstrument* (i.e. *Planning as a search instrument*). VUGA Uitgeverij, The Hague pp. 106-108
• McHarg I. 1969. *Design with Nature.* The Natural History Press, New York
• Steiner F. 2000. *The Living Landscape.* McGraw Hill, New York

System

see also > fit, hierarchy, structure

'A set of connected things or parts forming a complex whole, in particular: a set of things working together as parts of a mechanism or interconnected network' (a railway system, a heating system, a park system) (New Oxford Dictionary of English).

'In the world around us objects exist that are interrelated in such a way that together they form an independent whole. This is what one calls a system' (Hanken 1973).

Systems exist at all levels of scale, the largest known being the solar system. A system may be composed of sub-systems that have a specific task or function, such as the heating system in a building. In order to understand complex systems, we create simplified models such as topographical maps, or mathematical models in which the structure of the original is made explicit. There are descriptive systems and also normative systems that have a purpose, one example being the organisation and tools needed for baking bread.

These systems may change or evolve, when a production process or a product is improved and adapted to new needs, such in the manufacture of automobiles or bicycles (Jencks 1972). The application of systems analysis has had enormous effects on industrial production, especially for military applications (West Churchman 1968).

Relations within a system can be

315

The evolution of the bicycle. The interrelation between sub-systems such as wheels, saddle, handlebars, frame and pedals slowly stabilises over time, eventually creating the most functional tool.

Source: Jencks C.; Silver N. 1972. Adhocism. The case for improvisation. Secker & Warburg, London p. 42

uncomplicated. For example, the efficiency with which household tools are produced and used can easily be analysed, as can the durability of these tools.

More complex environments are more difficult to dissect in their components and relations, and an analysis of such systems is feasible only with the aid of a computer (Alexander 1964). In such cases, reduction and simplification are needed. Environmental systems – 'collections of items believed to belong together' – are parts of wholes which are in turn parts of larger whole, from locality to universe. The larger, these wholes the more difficult they are to understand. During the 1960s, the conviction arose in the design professions that all relations in space would prove to be hierarchical, like the branches of a tree. This turned out not to be the case, as 'a city is not a tree'; separate elements need not be part of a larger one, but can also exist side by side, forming networks.

This is illustrated in the following example: (Alexander 1988). 'In Berkeley, at the corner of Hearst and Euclid street there is a drugstore, and outside the drugstore a traffic light. In the entrance to the drugstore there is a newsstand where the day's papers are displayed. When the light is red, people who are waiting to cross the street stand idly by the light; and since they have nothing to do, they look at the papers displayed on the newsstand which they can see from where they stand. Some of them just read the headlines, others actually buy a paper while they wait.'

According to Alexander this is a system,

A bicycle designed by Leonardo da Vinci around 1500.

because 'this effect makes the newsrack and the traffic light interdependent; the newsrack, the papers on it, the money going from people's pocket to the dime slot, the people who stop at the lights and read the papers, the traffic light, the electric impulses which make the lights change, and the sidewalk which the people stand on form a system – they all work together'.

The newsrack, the traffic lights and the sidewalk are the permanent, stable parts of the system: design products. The rest of the story, however, escapes the controlling hand of the designer, because people react differently to what they see, depending on the circumstances. The result is an open system, self-organising, creative and constantly evolving over time.

Soon after the publication of these views, attempts were made to design a neighbourhood that was based on a systematic analysis of all the imaginable relations within such a unit. However, it proved to be impossible to pin down all these interactions, even with the use of the largest computer then available (Hanson 1969). Intuitive steps and design experience were needed after all.

'Often, when a competent practitioner [...] constructs a basis for coherent design in a building site [...] he does something for which he cannot give a complete or even a reasonably accurate description. Practitioners make judgements of quality for which they cannot state adequate criteria; display skills for which they cannot describe procedures or rules' (Schon 1985).

Urban environments and whole landscapes may be viewed as systems. This helps in understanding many causes and effects, but a full grasp of all the relations that are involved remains unattainable. There are simply too many sub-systems to consider with too complex a set of relations. We may succeed in analysing and only partly understanding some sub-systems – water management systems or traffic systems, perhaps – while the complexity of eco-systems still keeps eluding us. Neither will we ever be able to fully understand, control or predict capricious weather systems that

depend so much on accident, coincidence and other unpredictable occurrences. 'Biological and social systems are open, which means that the attempt to understand them in mechanistic terms is doomed to failure' (Toffler 1984).

In view of our inability to understand all landscape process, it is advisable that we exercise modesty and pragmatism in the application of systems theory in landscape planning. The best we can do is to try and deal with landscape change on the basis of trial and error. The conclusion of all this is that 'the idea of a fully controlled planning practice which avoids unpleasant surprise is based on erroneous thought, even at the level of nature conservation' (Koningsveld 1988).

In its extreme consequence, such a systems approach, when applied in urban and rural planning, may lead to a conflict with the basic values of a free and democratic society, as it harbours the ideology of a government-controlled environment and society.

'We know the world as an organism, not a machine. We also know that a genuinely created world must be independent of its creator; a planned world (a world that fully reveals its planning) is a dead world' (Fowles 1965).

- Alexander C. 1964. *Notes on the Synthesis of Form*. Harvard University Press, Cambridge pp. 60 ff
- Alexander C. 1988. 'A city is not tree'. In: Thackara J. *Design after Modernism*. Thames and Hudson, London pp. 67-84
- Fowles J. 1965. *The French Lieutenant's Woman*. Signet Book, New York p. 81
- Hanken A.F.G.; Reuver H.A. 1973 *Inleiding tot de Systeemleer* (i.e. *Introduction to systems theory*). Stenfert Kroese, Leiden p.10
- Hanson K. 1969. 'Design from linked requirements in a housing problem'. In: Broadbent G.; Ward H. *Design Methods in Architecture*. Lund Humphries, London
- Jencks C.; Silver N. 1972. *Adhocism. The Case for Improvisation*. Secker & Warburg, London p.42
- Schon D. 1985. *The Design Studio. An Exploration of its Traditions and Potentials*. RIBA Publications Ltd, London p. 16
- Toffler A. 1984. 'Science and change'. In: Prigogine I.; Stengers I. *Order out of Chaos*. Bantam Books, New York
- West Churchman C. 1968. *The Systems Approach*. Delta Book, New York pp. 3-48
- Koningsveld H. 1988. Planning en (on)zekerheid. De samenleving als experiment of als technocratie (i.e. Planning and uncertainty. Society as an experiment or as a technocracy). In: PLAN. Maandblad voor ontwerp en vormgeving, Stichting Plan, Stam tijdschriften, The Hague 1-2 pp. 32-33

Taste

see also > aesthetics, style, sentiment

'Critical judgement, discernment, or appreciation' (*Webster*)

'The word taste [refers to] that quick discerning faculty or power of the mind by which we accurately distinguish the good, the bad or the indifferent' (Williams 1985). It involves the ability to judge the beauty of an object or a space without relying on fixed rules. Only people with 'correct' judgement have taste. 'I mean by the word Taste no more than that faculty or those faculties of the mind, which are affected with, or which form a judgement of, the works of imagination and the elegant arts' (Burke 1990).

While taste is something personal, it can also be based on collective judgements; it depends on imagination and leads to immediate and prompt reactions. It also has a social function: people may be classified according to whether or not they have good taste – by the ownership of 'a tasteless interior', for example (Baumeister 1999). Paradoxically enough, the display of refined bad taste may lead to attractive kitsch (Donà 1988).

One can distinguish between popular taste, bourgeois taste and a 'higher, intellectual level' of taste. The avant-gardist reacts to all 'simpler' types of taste by adhering to the taste of the intellectual (Bourdieu 1979).

One possible hallmark of good taste is simplicity of form, a strong need for ornamentation being considered dangerous, as it blinds the eye, dulls the mind and makes the mind lazy. 'The attractions of richness and splendour are for the childish; a grown-up person should resist these blandishments and opt for the sober and the rational' (Gombrich 1979). In music as well as in the arts and architecture, simplicity, severity and restraint are connected with Classicism and the classic. These are also one of the principles on which modern architecture is founded.

In politics and the social realm, according to Dutch philosopher Kees Vuyk, taste has now become associated with personalities and their styles of behaviour. In religion, taste means enjoying certain atmospheres – listening to blissful words and beautiful music, experiencing silence, and being immersed in decorative rituals: mystique (Vuyk 1992).

Taste changes over time. In 19th-century England, an emotional debate about

319

— L'arc de triomphe du mauvais goût. — D'après J.-C. Loudon.

Bad taste is a timeless phenomenon.

Source: André E. 1879. L'Art des Jardins. Traité Général de la Composition des Parcs et Jardins. Masson, Paris

'Changes in Taste' in landscape gardening was conducted between contemporaries such as Uvedale Price (1747-1829) and Humphry Repton (1752-1818), who drew comparisons with former times (Daniels 1999; Repton 1806). However, taste is timeless – especially bad taste (André 1979).

- André E. 1879. *L'Art des Jardins. Traité Général de la Composition des Parcs et Jardins.* Masson, Paris pp. 91-104
- Baumeister T. 1999. *De filosofie en de kunsten* (i.e. *Philosophy and the arts*). Damon, Best pp. 216 ff.
- Bourdieu P. 1979. *La Distinction. Critique sociale du jugement.* Les Editions de Minuit, Paris
- Burke E. 1990. (reprint). *Essays on the Sublime and the Beautiful.* Cassell, London
- Daniels S. 1999. 'Changes of Taste'. In: *Humphry Repton.* Yale University Press, New Haven pp.139 ff.; 112-114; 126
- Donà C. 1988. 'Invisible design'. In: Thackara J (ed). *Design after Modernism.* Thames & Hudson, London p. 153
- Gombrich E.H. 1979. 'Issues of Taste'. In: *The Sense of Order.* Cornell University Press Ithaca, New York. pp. 17 ff.
- Repton H. 1806. *An enquiry into the changes of taste in landscape gardening, to which are added some observations on theory and practice including a defence of the art.* J.Taylor, London
- Vuyk K. 1992. *De esthetisering van het wereldbeeld* (i.e. The aestheticising of a world view). Kok Agora, Kampen pp. 55 ff.
- Williams R. 1985. *Keywords. A Vocabulary of Culture and Society.* Fontana Paperback, London

Terraces in the garden of Dartington Hall, Devon, England. Designed by C. Percy.

Source: Richardson T. (ed) 2000.The Garden Book. Phaidon London p. 89

Terrace

see also > access, margin

'A flat roof or open platform. A relatively level paved or planted area adjoining a building. A raised embankment with the top levelled. A row of houses on a raised ground or a sloping site – also one of a series of banks or ridges formed in a slope to conserve moisture and soil for agriculture' (*Webster*).

In most parts of the world, a home can be built only after the land has been levelled. This is arguably the first and most fundamental act of construction in relation to the topography of the landscape: 'every terrain that has been transformed into a terrace serves as the physical and conceptual foundation for the accommodation and enactment of a broad range of topographical purposes, from the most mundane to the

Terraces fronting Chateau Neercanne, province of Limburg, the Netherlands.

Source: Landscape Architecture and Town Planning in the Netherlands 97-99. Thoth, Bussum, p. 221

Terraced landscape: rice fields in Bali, Indonesia.

The raised terrace as a central element in a symmetrical composition: Holkham Hall Norfolk, England. Designed in 1734 by William Kent.

Source: Steenbergen C.; Reh W. 1996. Architecture and Landscape. The design experiment of the great European gardens and landscapes. Thoth, Bussum. p. 224

most elevated' (Leatherbarrow 2004).

The terraces constructed outside 16th-century Italian villas were intended as extensions to the building that would provide a panoramic view over the landscape; at the same time they symbolised power and human dominance over nature. In many Classicist villas, the terrace or landing – enclosed by a balustrade – was reached via imposing symmetrical stairways that led up to the main entrance to the house via a portico, 'a roofed space, [...] often with detached or attached columns and a pediment' (*Penguin*). Connecting the inside and the outside, it formed a central point in the Classicist-symmetrical composition.

One of the first large terrace gardens to be constructed was at Villa Medici in Fiesole, its shape making the villa stand out as an independent architectonic type. Among the most famous terraces of the 16th century were probably those of Villa d'Este at Tivoli, which dated from 1550 (Lazarro 1990). The terraces of 17th-century French gardens laid out by André le Nôtre are not only much larger, but their position in relation to the rolling landscape is also quite different, connections with the surroundings via avenues and water bodies making them part of a coherent composition (Steenbergen 1996).

In the Netherlands, terraced gardens are fairly rare, due mainly to the flatness of the terrain. Some examples dating from the 17th century are found on sloping sites at Neercanne near Maastricht (Harsema 2000) and on the Warnsborn estate in the Achterhoek region.

In 18th century, England Lancelot 'Capability' Brown (1716-1783) banned terraces from his gardens, instead siting his villas in open meadows without any margin. Terraces were reintroduced by Humphry Repton (1752-1818), who used them as a transitional zone between house and garden (*Oxford Companion*).

In small contemporary urban gardens, a terrace is often a dominant element whose paving pattern is carefully adapted to the size and scale of the whole.

In high-density housing areas, a small roof-terrace is one of the few places where potted plants can be grown outdoors. Such terraces were introduced on a more imposing scale by the architect Le Corbusier (1887-1965), for instance in the Unité d' Habitation at Marseille (Le Corbusier 1933).

Terraced landscapes are found in mountainous regions in parts of Europe and elsewhere, and are among the most prominent examples of landscapes modelled by man. They have been constructed in places where stones are plentiful and the slopes otherwise too steep for tilling (Ambroise 1988; Alexander 1977). In tropical rice-paddy – or *sawah* – landscapes, terraces are retained by earth walls (Moore 1989).

Like that of hedgerow landscapes, the sustainment of terraced landscapes is based in a primitive economy with low labour costs. Many contemporary terraces are therefore falling into disrepair, with a resulting loss of historical, ecological and cultural values.

- Alexander C. (et al). 1977. 'Terraced slopes'. In: *A Pattern Language*. Oxford University Press pp. 791 ff.
- Ambroise R. (et al). 1988 *Paysages de terrasses*. Edisud Aix en Provence
- Le Corbusier. 1933. *La ville radieuse: éléments d'une doctrine d'urbanisme pour l'equipement de la civilisation machiniste*. Editions de l' Architecture d'Aujourd'hui, Boulogne
- Harsema H. (ed). 2000 'Historic gardens with a contemporary play on lines'. In: *Landscape architecture and town planning in the Netherlands 97-99*. Thoth publishers, Bussum pp. 220-223
- Lazarro C. 1990. *The Italian Renaissance Garden*. Yale University Press, New Haven pp. 100-108
- Leatherbarrow D. 2004. 'Levelling the land'. In: *Topographical Stories. Studies in Landscape and Architecture*. The University of Pennsylvania Press, Philadelphia pp. 114 ff.
- Moore C.W. (et al). 1989. *The Poetics of Gardens*. MIT Press Cambridge pp. 27-28
- Steenbergen C.; Reh W. 1996. *Architecture and Landscape*. Thoth Bussum p. 163

Texture

see also > perspective

'Something formed by or as if by weaving; the structure, feel and appearance of a textile that result from the kind and arrangement of its threads; similar qualities dependent on the nature and arrangement of the constituent particles (e.g. a gritty or a fine texture)' (*Webster*). 'The way a surface, substance or fabric feels to the touch, i.e. its thickness, firmness, roughness, etc' (*Oxford English Dictionary*).

Although the notions of texture and structure are closely linked in these definitions, the idea of a surface roughness, and of visibility and tactility (including that in outdoor space) seems to be dominant in daily use. These effects are produced by the varying distances between particles that are part of a pattern on an object's surface. As formed by vegetation, crops or ploughed furrows, landscape textures may appear to be rough or smooth, coarse or fine (Motloch 2001). With increasing distance between an observer and an object or a horizontal plane, the perceived size of particles is smaller. This produces a perspective effect.

In outdoor space, the sizes of leaves of individual trees and shrubs can create a texture that greatly influences the perception of size and scale. By putting coarse-leaved plants or trees in the background of a scene and fine-leaved plants in the foreground, a designer can make a space look smaller; by reversing these positions, it can be made to look larger (Bell 1993). Different textures can therefore be used to manipulate the scale and character of outdoor spaces.

· Bell. S. 1993. *Elements of Visual Design in the Landscape*. Spon, London pp. 61-67
· Motloch J. 2001. 'Texture'. In: *Introduction to Landscape Design*. Van Nostrand Reinhold, London pp. 199 ff.

Theme, Motif

see also > garden, pattern

' A subject of discourse, artistic representation, or musical composition' (*Webster*).

One of the meanings of the word 'theme' as it applies to the design of outdoor space is the standard form that is repeated and manipulated in a composition in order to give shape to the spatial structure and to influence spatial experience and reference. Themes are the abstract components of a style, the instrument between intention and material (Baljon 1992).

'In many works of art there is a dominant theme, or motif, which stands out and upon which the other portions are centred. This theme is then varied in different ways in other portions of the work. This is a special case of unity-in-variety: if every line in a work

323

The varying texture of crops helps the perception of depth in space. Gerendal, Limburg, the Netherlands.

of music or literature were entirely novel and different from the other ones, there would be enormous diversity but no unifying connecting links; whereas if there were simply a repetition of the initial theme or of entire sections of the work [...] there would be unity but no variety. Both unity and variety are preserved by having central themes, with other material that is related to them (unity) but not identical with them (variety)' (*Britannica*).

One example of a theme in a Classicist garden design is the termination of a parterre in an arched-shaped hedge or fence, which was sometimes used in Renaissance gardens and in 17th-century French gardens. The arch was supposed to provide an aristocratic effect expressing status and dignity (de Jong 1993).

A theme in the sense of 'a subject of talk, a piece of writing, a topic' (*Oxford English Dictionary*) is expressed in a thematic garden characterised by certain plants or a certain type of use, or in a theme-park where a

certain topic is dealt with (Kuitert 1988; Pohl 1995). Landscapes can also be dissected into their component parts, as represented in thematic maps showing one aspect of reality, such as a soil map, a water map, a road map.

A Dutch example of a theme-park is the *heempark*, a public garden or park that contains only indigenous plants; these have been usually collected in different parts of the country and planted on specially prepared soils in a free, Romantic composition. The Dutch archetype is Thijsse's Hof in Bloemendaal, which was designed in 1925 by park architect Leonard Springer (1855-1940) (Moes 2002). It was followed by Thijssepark in Amstelveen, which was laid out after 1940. Both were named after Jac P. Thijsse, the father of the nature movement in the Netherlands (1865-1945) (Woudstra 1997)

Some other theme parks in the Netherlands have cultural aims, such as Archeon in Alphen-aan-den Rijn, where archaic dwellings and tools are exhibited; or a commercial objective, such as Efteling

Heempark: the theme here is a collection of native species of herbaceous plants. Thijssepark, Amstelveen, the Netherlands, 1940-1972. Landscape architect: C.P.Broerse.

pleasure park near Kaatsheuvel. Whatever their aim, most charge an admission fee (Pohl 1995). Certain developments – such as porno shops, street festivals, outdoor music festivals, Gay Pride parades, and other events that subject some older inner-cities to the tourist gaze – sometimes create an atmosphere similar to that of a theme park (Metz 2002).

* Baljon L. 1992. *Designing Parks*. Architectura & Natura, Amsterdam p.135
* de Jong E. 1993. *Natuur en Kunst* (i.e. *Nature and art*). Thoth, Bussum p.153
* Kuitert W. 1988. *Themes, Scenes and Taste in Japanese Garden Art*. Gieben Publishers, Amsterdam pp. 3-63
* Metz T. 2002. *Fun! Leisure and landscape*. NAi publishers, Rotterdam pp. 90 ff.
* Moes C. 2002. *L.A. Springer. Tuinarchitect Dendroloog*. De Hef, Rotterdam pp. 82-85
* Pohl N. 1995. 'Der Themapark'. In: *Der kommende Stadtpark*. PhD thesis Technical University Delft pp. 84-87
* Vroom M.J. (ed.) 1992. *Outdoor Space*. Thoth, Bussum pp. 110-113
* Woudstra J. 1997. 'Jacobus P. Thijsse's Influence on Dutch Landscape Architecture'. In: Wolschke-Bulmah. (ed.) *Nature and Ideology*. Dumbarton Oaks, Washington pp. 155-185

Threshold

see also > margin

Thresholds are relatively limited spaces located either between larger spaces or at the entrance of buildings. Like margins or edges, they connect space, but are concentrated in one location. They are found in transitional spaces, entrances, interspaces, gates and frames, steps and balconies. Some are indicated by subtle changes in pavement,

A subtle threshold between a side street and a main road in Newcastle-upon-Tyne, UK.

where one pauses or takes a step (Dee 2001).

In an abstract sense, thresholds are moments of decision in a design process when minimum requirements from a brief must be specified: 'so much of this or that' (Lynch 1984).

* Dee C. 2001. 'Thresholds'. In: *Form and Fabric in Landscape Architecture*. Spon Press, London pp. 169-187
* Lynch K.; Hack G. 1984. *Site Planning* (third edition). The MIT Press Cambridge p. 114

Time

see > dynamics, process

Topography

see > analysis

Topology

see > analysis

Topos

see > place

325

Toponymy

see also > landscape language, legibility, place

'Taxonomic study of place-names, based on etymological, historical and geographical information. A place-name is a word or words used to indicate, denote or identify a geographical locality such as a town, river or mountain. Toponymy divides place-names into two broad categories: habitation names and feature names. A habitation name denotes a locality that is inhabited, such as a homestead, village or town, and usually dates from the locality's inception. Feature names refer to natural or physical features of the landscape and are subdivided into hydronyms (water features), oronyms (relief features) and places of natural vegetation growth (e.g. meadows, glades and groves)' (*Britannica*).

Vernacular field names are important sources of information and should therefore be part of every landscape analysis; they tell a story about the natural genesis and the history of settlement patterns. The study of these names provides insight into the 'genius of the place' (Braham 1985).

In more recent times, however, many field, place or street names have been ordained by authorities, who have preferred to use them to commemorate historical or contemporary events, such as wars, or persons of national or international importance, such as politicians or generals (Potteiger 1998). Such names are thus connected with the history of a nation rather than of a region or a place – though a disoriented traveller may sometimes be able to deduce the identity of a place from a fairly new street name: for instance, the name 'Avenida Touroperador Neckermann' will suggest he is in a major tourist resort in Spain.

Gardens, or different sections with a garden, may also bear names referring to their character or to other places. Sometimes, these also help visitors to find their way around or to put them in a certain mood. One example is the Elysian Garden at Stowe,

in Buckinghamshire, England. Other names (such as 'rose garden' or 'herb garden') refer to the dominant vegetation type, or denote the design style. In oriental gardens, names are also used to evoke certain moods (Hunt 2000).

• Braham M. 1985. Principles of design. Part 2. Spatial design: space and landscape. In: *Landscape Design*. Landscape Design Trust Reigate, Surrey, no. 2 pp. 95
• Hunt J.D. 2000. 'Word and Image in the Garden'. In: *Greater Perfections. The Practice of Garden Theory.* Thames & Hudson, London pp.16 ff.
• Potteiger M.; Purinton J. 1998. 'Naming'. In: *Landscape Narratives. Design Practices for Telling Stories.* John Wiley, New York pp. 75 ff.

Transformation, Transfiguration
see also > adaptation, metamorphosis, sign

To transform means 'to change in composition, structure or character' (*Webster*).

'Architects do not invent anything, they transform reality' (Frampton 1998).

Thanks to the transformation of a site that results when a design is implemented,

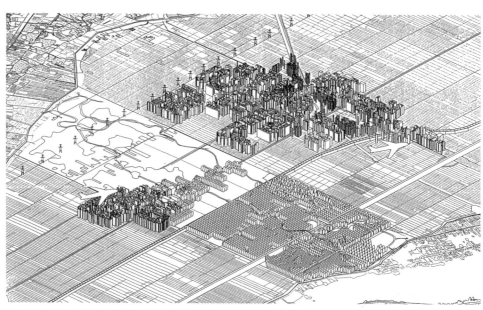

The transformation from rural to urban in the Haarlemmermeer polder near Amsterdam requires the careful harmonisation of dimensions and scale.

Source: Reh W.; Steenbergen C. (ed). 1999. Zee van Land. De droogmakerij als architectonisch experiment. Faculty of Architecture at Delft University of Technology

entirely new types of use are integrated within, or superimposed upon, the existing topography. Unlike metamorphosis, when change is the result of spontaneous endogenous processes, it is the result of conscious intervention.

A Classical example of a radical transformation is the 17th-century French garden at Vaux-le-Vicomte, designed by André le Nôtre: 'All vestiges of earlier buildings were erased, and the countryside was subjected to the most rigorous discipline, in the process of which hills were moved and levelled, valleys filled or made, and streams detoured and channelled into new waterways' (Hamilton Hazelhurst 1980).

A 19th-century example is the network of boulevards constructed by the Paris City Prefect Baron Haussmann, which broke through the medieval pattern of central Paris (Tietz 1998).

In the Netherlands, various 20th-century land-reconsolidation schemes brought about transformations in rural areas. Urbanisation as a 'transformation of a landscape to a subsequent stage of development' may be a lofty ideal, but if it is to be achieved in an harmonious way the planner needs to carefully adjust dimensions and scales (Steenbergen 2002).

Transfiguration is 'a change of form and appearance, especially a glorifying or an exalting change' (Webster). An ancient biblical example is the resurrection of Christ in a divine form as painted by Raphael around 1520. Such a mutation does not necessarily involve any change in form by the person or object perceived; instead, it results from a shift in perception, to which a changed meaning is attached (Meyer 1998). Mount Fuji in Japan is not solely a natural phenomenon: the many drawings and paintings that have been made of it over centuries and, connecting it with religious themes, have effectively transfigured into an icon (Weiss 1998).

• Frampton K. 1998. 'Place-form and Cultural Identity'. In: Thackara J (ed). *Design after Modernism*. Thames and Hudson, London p. 59
• Hamilton Hazelhurst F. 1980. *Gardens of Illusion. The Genius of*
André le Nostre. Vanderbilt University Press, Nashville, Tennessee. p 17
• Meyer E. 1998. *Martha Schwartz. Transfiguration of the Commonplace*. Spacemaker Press, Washington D.C.
• Steenbergen C.; Reh W. 2002. 'Critical transformation of the villa landscape'. In: Steenbergen C. (et al). (ed). *Architectural Design and Composition*. Thoth publishing, Bussum pp. 202-207
• Tietz J. 1998. *Geschiedenis van de architectuur in de 20ste eeuw* (i.e. *20th-century architecture*). Könemann, Köln p. 41
• Weiss A. 1998. *Unnatural Horizons*. Princeton Architectural Press New York p.140

Tree

'A woody perennial plant having a single usually tall main stem with few or no branches on its lower part' (*Webster*).

Trees have always been used to provide shade, to screen, and to form space (Halprin 1972; Anonymous 1996). They have played an important role in the history of human civilisation, not only by providing fuel and construction material, but also for their religious and symbolic value ('the tree of knowledge', 'the tree of forbidden fruit') and also in myths and sagas. Their original mythical function may have been that of the centre of the earth – a living axis standing on top of a mountain, reaching into heaven (Yggdrasil, the tree of life) (Eliot 1977). In the Middle Ages, the presence of trees on a site often signified a holy place (Schama 1995).

The artist-parson William Gilpin (1724-1804) named the possible results of combining trees in park design – clumps and interspersed lawns, belts, copses, open groves, and forests (Meyer 1992).

Over the centuries, the treatment of trees has varied considerably in Western Europe, the stress lying sometimes on their practical uses, and sometimes on their expression of symbolic values. When feudal systems predominated, trees were regularly trimmed in order to supply farmers with wood; eventually, this created gnarled, untidy trunks. In the great Classical gardens, trees were trimmed into geometric shapes, signifying man's dominance over nature. Meanwhile, kings ordered their foresters to grow straight slim trees that would provide timber for shipbuilding.

327

A break with the social practices that had been common during feudal times came with Romanticism, which held up the ideal of a beautiful and healthy society living amidst a beautiful and healthy nature. This brought a radical change in agricultural techniques that was accompanied by an abhorrence of the practice of tree trimming. In the Romantic Age, a tree was free to spread its branches, with no obstruction to disturb its growth (Luginbühl 2002).

The 20th century stressed the need for uniformity in the size and form of trees, especially when they were used for roadside planting. Extensive use was made of clones of poplars, elms and ashes that could guarantee the identical forms and heights needed to avoid distracting travellers. But during the 20th century, trees in urban areas also became the symbol of sustainable nature. Emotional public resistance against the thinning and felling of old tree stands in public parks suggests that trees had regained something of their previous sacredness.

In some cases, ancient trees may be legally protected as monuments (Hermand 1994). The Dutch Forest Act actually forbids trees to be cut down without specific permission, and every felled tree must be replaced by a successor in the vicinity.

A solitary tree sometimes features prominently in a field, or next to a farm building: 'In undifferentiated open landscapes, the single tree focuses an awful and undifferentiated plane on a centre. It makes a here and a there out of a nowhere' (Franck 1994).

· Anonymous. 1996. 'Trees'. Topos European Landscape Magazine no. 16, Callwey, München
· Eliot A. 1976. *Myths* . McGraw-Hill Book Co Maidenhead, England
· Franck K.A.; Schneekloth L.H. 1994. *Ordering Space. Types in Architecture and Design.* Van Nostrand Reinhold, London pp.

'The difference between here and there [...]'.
Photo: Frank Meijer

Dominant tree in botanical garden in Barcelona. Garden designed by Carlos Ferrater, Bet Figueras and José Luis Canosa. Laid out in 1999.

88-89
- Halprin L. 1972. 'Trees for all Seasons'. In: *Cities*. MIT Press, Cambridge pp. 163 ff.
- Hermand J. 1994. 'The death of the trees will be the end of us all'. In: Journal of Garden History Taylor & Francis, London vol. 14 no. 3 pp. 147-157
- Luginbühl Y. 2002. 'The Tree. Rural Tradition and Landscape Innovation'. In: Hunt J.D.; Conan M. (ed). *Tradition and Innovation in French Garden Art. Chapters of a New History*. The University of Pennsylvania Press, Philadelphia. pp. 82-92
- Meyer E. 1992. 'Situating Modern Landscape Architecture'. In: Swaffield S. 2002. *Landscape Theory. A Reader*. The University of Pennsylvania Press, Philadelphia pp. 167-172
- Schama S. 1995. 'The Verdant Cross'. In: *Landscape and Memory*. Harper Collins, London pp. 214 ff.

Type, Typology

'A specimen or series of specimens on which a taxonomic species or subspecies is actually based. A general form or character common to a number of individuals that distinguishes them as an identifiable class. A particular kind, class, or group (*Webster*).

'Type' is derived from the Greek *typos*: 'impression'. Once used to refer to a character in the sense of a typographic letter, it now denotes the essential character of a whole group of objects or persons (de Jong 1983). The typing of objects, places, landscapes – and also people: 'unwanted types' – involves the identification of common traits that allow us to order, arrange and classify – something we need to do when we become acquainted with the world around us, and when we give it names. 'A type can be an ideal or an original archetype, or a sample or history of representative cases, or a set of delimitating rules and regulations' (Krieger 2000).

In spatial planning there are three main types, the first being place types, which describe concrete inhabitable places, such as farms and houses, on the basis of their characteristics. The second are imaginary types, which are abstract and conceptual, consisting of words and ideas. The third are conceptual types, which are classification systems used to describe, explain and prescribe.

A typology erases the individual characteristics of objects, leaving only general traits. Like the taxonomy of Linnaeus, it thereby lays the basis for a classification system (Franck 1994).

In architectural theory, a type is a basic form that is repeated in different designs. Typologies are systematic descriptions of characteristics that help us understand the logic of existing spatial patterns (de Jong 1983) that will develop over time according to the conditions around them. Analysis of parts of Venice thus showed that types of dwellings develop their specific features only within the built fabric, while the urban fabric develops its specific features only within the urban structure. The whole of the urban organism can therefore be understood only in its historical perspective (Leupen 1997).

While the typology of urban public squares may thus be based on geometric characteristics, cross-sections and the nature of enclosing walls (Broadbent 1990), a landscape typology will describe territorial units that are internally consistent; such units were formed in history and can be clearly defined. Meanwhile, a typology of land patterns in the Netherlands will show differences between parallel and concentric patterns in sandy landscapes and geometric patterns in polder landscapes.

In flat landscapes, a landscape typology based on a purely spatial configuration creates the following subdivision:
- totally enclosed spaces, such as those inside woodlands
- spaces bordered on two sides, such as those in a landscape with hedgerows
- a divided space with a screen between two open spaces
- a continuous open space in which objects are spread out (Wassink 1999).

A thematic typology describes landscapes from a particular point of view, such as geology, land-use or management. In the Netherlands, basic distinctions fall into two basic sub-types, one consisting of geomorphological landscapes, soil types and geo-botanical landscapes, the other of water-management districts, such as valleys and polders (van de Ven 1993). Merging these sub-types into an overall typology is a

329

somewhat arbitrary undertaking that provides no insight into the ecological function of the landscape.

In the Netherlands there are also polythematic classifications, which are based on a combination of natural factors, spatial characteristics and historical developments, and which enables landscapes of dunes, artificial mounds, rivers and reclaimed polders to be distinguished (Bijhouwer 1977). Classification at a European scale reveals open marine landscapes, open and enclosed Mediterranean landscapes, bocage and semi-bocage landscapes, and also mountain and delta landscapes (Meeus 1990).

This sort of typology represents a 'vague', indefinite order containing ample transition zones and overlapping areas. As all these subdivisions are based on historical developments, it is also dated. Recent periods have seen the emergence of new distinctions, such as those between historical and newly developed nature areas.

Because contemporary planning and design

Bocage

Semi bocage

330

Montados

Kampen

Montagnes

Highlands

A typology of European landscapes.

Source: Meeus J. (et al) 1990 'Agricultural Landscapes in Europe and their Transformation'. In: Vroom M.J. (ed). Changing Agricultural Landscapes of Europe. Special Issue Landscape and Urban Planning. Elsevier. Amsterdam. Vol 19 nos. 3-4 fig. 10-22

assignments cannot be based on a typology rooted in historical developments, a new approach is needed. New tools may provide the answers, such as digital information systems in which all sorts of basic information of soils, land-use, movements and processes are collected and processed in direct relation to the planning objectives of large-scale projects.

• Bijhouwer J.T.P. 1977. *Het Nederlandse Landschap* (i.e. *The Dutch Landscape*). Kosmos, Amsterdam.
• Broadbent G. 1990. *Emerging Concepts of Urban Space Design.* Van Nostrand Reinhold, London p. 190
• Franck K.A.; Schneekloth L.H. 1994. 'Type: prison or promise?'. In: *Ordering Space. Types in Architecture and Design.* Van Nostrand Reinhold, London pp. 15 ff.
• de Jong T. 1983. *Inleiding tot de architectuurtypologie.* Delft University Press
• Krieger M. 2000. 'Types'. In: *What's Wrong with Plastic Trees?* Praeger, New York pp. 56-57
• Leupen B. (et al). 1997. *Design and Analysis.* Van Nostrand Reinhold, New York pp. 131 ff.
• Meeus. J.H.A. (et al). 1990. 'Agricultural Landscapes in Europe and their Transformation'. In: Landscape and Urban Planning no. 18, Elsevier, Amsterdam pp. 289-352
• van de Ven G.P. (ed) 1993. *Man-made lowlands.* Matrijs, Utrecht

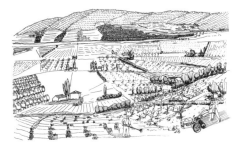

Coltura

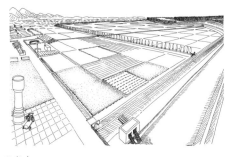

Delta's

331

Huertas

Open fields

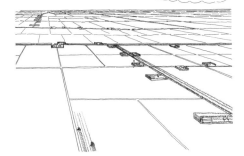

Polders

Open land mediterrana

Urban, urbanisation

see also > inversion, rural, suburbia

Urban means 'relating to or characteristic of the city'. 'Urbane' denotes the social aspects of city life in the sense of 'smoothly courteous or polite' (*Webster*).

Urbanity represents all those moral and aesthetic values that were lacking in pre-modern agrarian society, such as openness, mobility, diversity, collectiveness and unpredictability (Boomkens 1999).

The urbanisation of land is both a morphological phenomenon (i.e. in which a concentration of buildings appears) and a social one (i.e. when the experiences and behaviour of people on this land change). In its morphological sense, the process of urbanisation involves not only the expansion of urban concentrations, but also of the spread of individual constructions. Power-lines and other infrastructure appear in the countryside where, due to the fact that they signify urbanity, and thus represent aliening and highly visible intrusions, they do not 'belong'.

The Dutch Central Bureau of Statistics distinguishes five classes of urbanity, which, according to population density, range from 'highly urbanised' to 'barely urbanised'. A sixth class is 'non-urban'. In 2000, 'non-urban' accounted for less than twenty percent of the total population; together with the 'barely urbanised' category, it accounted for 40%.

In the meantime, the expansion of greenhouses and modern, mechanised farming means that modern agriculture is also 'urbanising'. In the Netherlands, as in many other countries, the urbanisation of rural areas is viewed as an environmental problem, as it brings noise, pollution and stress, all of which conflict with the Arcadian ideals of peace and quiet, nature, and pastoral life (Bunce 1994; Ibelings 1999).

Although Dutch planning policy aims to separate the urban and the rural, this has not been very successful (Anonymous 2001). Attempts by the Ministry of Agriculture to blend the two harmoniously have achieved results that are patchy at best (Anonymous 1995).

The ethics and sentiments of the majority urban population are beginning to invade traditional rural life. They are expressed mainly in the form of legal and financial instruments that restrict farming practices and hunting, and which lead to the conversion of agricultural land into 'new nature'.

- Anonymous. 1995. *Balans Visie Stadslandschappen* (i.e. *Vision on urban landscapes*). Ministerie van Landbouw, Natuurbeheer en Visserij, The Hague
- Anonymous. 2001. *Vijfde Nota Ruimtelijke Ordening* (i.e. *Fifth Report on National Planning*). Ministerie van Volkshuisvesting Ruimtelijke Ordening en Milieu, The Hague p. 100
- Boomkens R. 1999. 'Van de grote stad ging een onbestemde dreiging uit'. in: Van der Wouden R. (ed). *De stad op straat*. Sociaal en Cultureel Planbureau, The Hague
- Bunce M.F. 1994 The Countryside Ideal: Anglo-American Images of Landscapes. Routledge, London
- Ibelings H. 1999. *Nederlandse Stedenbouw in de 20ste eeuw* (i.e. *Dutch city planning in the 20th century*).NAi uitgevers, Rotterdam

333

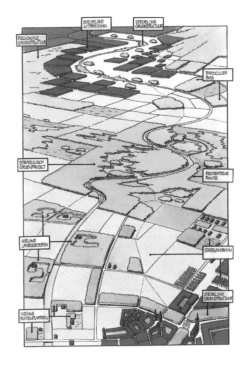

Selective urbanisation of the Dutch landscape as proposed by the Ministry of Agriculture and Nature Conservation in its policy document 'Nota Stadslandschappen' of 1995.

Utopia

see also > behaviour, design concept, modern

'A place of ideal perfection, especially in laws, government and social conditions. An impractical scheme for social improvement' (*Webster*). The notion is based on the book *Utopia* by Thomas Moore (1478-1535), which was published in 1516 and describes a society that was ideal but unfeasible. A utopia is by definition an impractical scheme.

There have been various literary descriptions of utopian landscapes, in which people live in perfect harmony with nature. They outline a variety of scenes, including exotic paradises, Eldorados, idyllic jungles or wildernesses and cultivated gardens.

'Utopias are perfect environments of the future – imagined places with perfection defined variously in economic, physical, political, and social terms. Their rationale is double-coded: they function both as a critique of existing society and a vision of a possible future. They inevitably tend towards caricature – the gross simplification of social reality' (Freestone 2000).

The many types of utopia are based in myth. All contain a high degree of moralism, intending to implement far-reaching changes in society, by force if necessary. They envisage a maximum of harmony and collective happiness, which they expect to obtain by means of an efficient social restructuring (Eaton 2001; Harvey 2000). Past examples have ranged from Communism to Fascism, and have often have degenerated into oppression and terror. No utopia is very far removed from its opposite extreme, dystopia: a 'future state of deplorable nature' (*van Dale*). 'The over-confidence leading to attempts to bring heaven on earth makes us convert the good earth into hell' (Popper 1967/1974).

Examples of utopian town planning can be found in the housing units or estates designed or inspired by architect Le Corbusier (1887-1965). One such project is the Bijlmermeer neighbourhood in the south-eastern sector of Amsterdam. This was built in a period when living and housing were regulated by bureaucratic, top-down, means

The utopias created by Modernists often proved to be impractical: the south-eastern district of Amsterdam, as it was conceived during the 1950s.

– when, in essence, residents were expected to behave in accordance with the ideals of the planners. It consisted of high-rise apartment buildings in a neighbourhood where functions were strictly separated, and people had to rely totally on communal facilities, including outdoor green space. Due largely to poor safety, the area was soon plagued by anti-social and criminal behaviour. In recent years, most apartments have been razed, and the neighbourhood is now being transformed according to more traditional models.

However, any architecture without ideologies or a utopian vision is also far from ideal, as it tends to lead to rigidity and cultural impoverishment. How such ideologies should be put into practical solutions is a matter of continuous debate (Broadbent 1990; Tafuri 1978).

- Broadbent G. 1990. 'Neo-rationalists'. In: *Emerging Concepts in Urban Space Design*. Van Nostrand Reinhold pp. 157 ff.
- Eaton R. 2001. *De ideale stad* (i.e. *The ideal city*). Mercator, Antwerp p. 16
- Freestone R. 2000. 'Utopias'. In: Knox P.; Ozolins P. *Design Professionals and the Built Environment*. John Wiley & Sons, New York Chapter 18.
- Harvey D. 2000. 'The spaces of utopia'. In: *Spaces of Hope*. Edinburgh University Press pp. 133-196
- Popper K. 1967 (reprint 1974). *De armoede van het historicisme* (i.e. *The poverty of historicism*). Aula 523 Het Spectrum, Utrecht p. 8
- Tafuri M. 1978. *Ontwerp en Utopie* (i.e. *Design and Utopia*). Sunschrift 117. SUN, Nijmegen

The traffic system.

Amsterdam: high-rise apartment buildings with public grounds.

335

Value

see also > aesthetics, authentic, experience, heritage, language, legibility, quality, sentiment, vision

'The regard that something is held to deserve. The importance or preciousness of something. The material or monetary worth of something. The usefulness of something considered in respect to a particular purpose'. Also 'a person's principles or standards of behaviour. One's judgement of what is important in life' (*Britannica*).

Human values exist in many forms, and may be practical, moral, aesthetic, economical, religious, ecological or otherwise. They are related to human experience, self-expression, mastery, contribution and excellence (Kane 1997). 'Every aspect of human experience is pervaded with value. This makes the concept of value itself one of the most complex and difficult notions' (Johnson 1999).

Values can be divided into two main categories: the objective and normative. Objective values are related to material worth and practical use. They can be measured or expressed in quantities such as numbers of square metres or sums of money. Property that is 'of value' is worth a lot of money (Rowe 1991).

Normative values are expressed in terms of quality, amenity, excellence or beauty, and are much more difficult to establish. They are based on shared opinions within a certain culture, both of an elite and of ordinary citizens who may think primarily in terms of propriety – in other words, of being correct in terms of their social or moral behaviour.

In *Bodily Harm*, Margaret Atwood (1988) describes such propriety as follows: 'The objects in the house [...] clocks, vases, end-tables, cabinets, figurines, cruet sets, cranberry glasses, china plates [...] were considered important because they had belonged to someone else. It was understood that you could never sell these objects or give them away. [...] They weren't beautiful, most of them. They weren't supposed to be. They were only supposed to be of the right kind: the standard aimed at was not beauty but decency.' Here, ethical and moral values

dominate and the solicitude for objects and for other people and their happiness is important (Kane 1999).

Values are not therefore properties of objects or spaces, but are attributed by man. 'Good is a property not of objects, but of concepts,' states psychologist Abraham Maslow (1908-1970) (Hartman 1959). This means, for instance, that every attempt to establish landscape values on the basis of empirical landscape analysis techniques is doomed to fail. 'Patterns of culture do not operate in accordance with the laws of physics' (Pirsig 1991). Differences in cultures, over time and between places, result in different value systems.

Landscape architects deal with three main aspects of value: historical values, natural value, and landscape value. Each is outlined briefly below.

Historical values

see also > heritage, culture

The narrative value of a landscape or a place is connected with the existence of a background story, of historical events. There may be examples from recent history, such as battlefields or wartime bunkers. At a local scale there are also places in the everyday environment that contain the memories of its inhabitants (Potteiger 1998).

However, history goes back further than living memory. 'What are the valued attributes, what are the aspects of bygone times that enable us to confirm and enhance identity, to acquire and sustain roots, to enrich life and environment, to validate or to escape from an otherwise overbearing present?' asks historian David Lowenthal. He describes four traits that seem to him especially valuable to distinguish the past from the present.

The first of these is antiquity. The very fact that things or objects are old makes them valuable: they may represent our heritage, our roots – an unspoilt past.

The second trait is continuity: the sense of enduring succession that is often manifest in places or areas where, in a distant past, human settlement left its marks on the landscape. Continuity expresses the conjunction of the whole, or parts of the past.

The third trait is termination: the past is appreciated because it is over; what happened in it has ended. Termination gives a sense of completion, of stability, of a permanence that is lacking in the present.

The fourth trait is sequence: time is linear and directional, the past covers a length of time that can be ordered, segmented and explained. To recognise that certain things happened before others enables us to shape memory, secure identity and generate tradition (Lowenthal 1985).

Natural values
see also > nature

These are natural processes that are important for our well-being, and sometimes even for our survival. They can be analysed and dissected. When such values are objective, they can be assessed by criteria such as rarity, diversity or biodiversity. When they are ethical or aesthetic, however, a lack of objective standards makes them much harder to pin down. Often, to underline their significance, they are thus labelled 'intrinsic' – and thereby become sacrosanct.

Though the rating of natural values has usually served to support protective measures, recently they have also been used to support active measures in the sense of 'made' or 'constructed' nature, for instance in the form of laid-out ecological networks (Anonymous 1998).

Landscape values
see also > landscape

In policy-documents issued by the Dutch government, landscape values are defined either in a very broad sense that includes natural and historical values, or otherwise as purely aesthetic values. The criteria for evaluating the latter have been derived from those applied to natural values (such as diversity, variety and rarity), thereby creating a risk that empirical methods will be used in a misleading way.

A world-wide survey of farm landscapes conducted in 2004 expressed the values and benefits of these landscapes in terms that varied according to location, climate zone and geological factors, all combined with land-use. Its criteria included scenery, biodiversity, cultural heritage, wildlife habitat, flood mitigation, water quality, water supply, recreation benefit, plant diversity, bird species, open space and habitat etc (Terwan 2004).

There is a marked emphasis in the criteria applied here on the degree of 'naturalness'. While some of these may be useful in the conservation of certain sites, they do not support planning and design in new living environments, where other criteria of beauty apply. Dutch journalist S. Montag touched on this subject in an article in the *NRC Handelsblad* newspaper of 21 May 1994: 'Seen from the air or from the ground, most of the Netherlands is beautiful. It does not possess the beauty of the untouched. It is beautiful in places because of its cool balance, the calculated layout of town and countryside that allows nature some space without giving it free rein.'

Over the last thirty years, landscape evaluation techniques have expanded enormously. Such an evaluation may address the rating of actual economic values (i.e. price) or potential values (suitability maps). It is directly applicable in the design process (McHarg 1969; Steiner 1999).

Due to the uncertainties involved in the calculation of many variables, the use of empirical methods in landscape evaluation often leads researchers to dubious results. Questions sometimes arise about the statistics used: for example, how many species of plants and animals have really disappeared in recent history, how exactly does the exploitation of underground gas and oil reserves affect the situation on the surface?

There is also the fact that scientists have their own views on reality. In the field of environmental quality, dispassionate views are extremely rare. 'I see facts as an almost infinite landscape of details and distant views, which we can see only partially through a distorted window called science. The objects in the landscape are there, but

338

the man-made window determines what we see' (Plasterk 2000).

• Anonymous. 1998. *Natuurbeleidsplan* (i.e. *Nature policy plan*). Ministerie LNV, The Hague
• Atwood M. 1988. *Bodily Harm*. Seal Books McLelland-Bantam Inc. Toronto p. 54
• Hartman R. 1959. 'The Science of Value'. In: Maslow A.H (ed). *New Knowledge in Human Values*. Harper & Row New York p. 19
• Johnson M.L. 1999. 'Metaphors of value'. In: Benedikt M (ed). *Center 11. Architecture and Design in America. Value 2* The University of Texas Press Austin p. 5
• Kane R. 1997. 'Four Dimensions of Value: from Experience to Worth'. In: Benedikt M (ed). *Center 10. Architecture and Design in America. Value*. The University of Texas Press. Austin pp. 9-15
• Kane R. 1999. 'Values and Metaphors'. In: Benedikt M (ed). *Center 11. Architecture and Design in America. Value 2*. The University of Texas Press Austin pp. 33-39
• Lowenthal D. 1985. *The Past is a Foreign Country*. Cambridge University Press. pp 52-63
• McHarg I. 1969. *Design with Nature*. Natural History Press New York. pp. 103-115; 127-152.
• Pirsig R. 1991. *Lila. An Inquiry into Morals*. Bantam Books p. 60
• Plasterk R. 2000. 'Bach en het buideldier'. In: *Leven uit het Lab*. Prometheus Amsterdam pp. 54
• Potteiger M., Purington J. 1998 *Landscape Narratives*. John Wiley & Sons New York
• Rowe P.G. 1991. *Design Thinking*. MIT Press Cambridge
• Steiner F. 1999. 'Suitability Analysis'. In: *The Living Landscape*. McGraw Hill New York pp.187-226
• Terwan P (et al). 2004. *Values of Agrarian Landscapes across Europe and North America*. Reed Business Information Doetinchem, the Netherlands

Vision, Outlook

see also > concept, design style, nature conservation, paradigm, utopia

'Ability to view a subject, problem etc. imaginatively; foresight and wisdom in planning' (*Oxford Advanced*).

In spatial planning and design, a vision will often project a future state of affairs. It may also describe the long-term outcome desired for developments currently being planned. The purpose of an official 'Vision Document' is to enable a planner – or even a whole community – to determine what such a development should become, and to start considering the best ways to bring this about.

For individual designers, a vision contains ideals and notions about the environment they wish to create. Although it may be based on aesthetic ideals, these are rarely independent of other considerations (Pohl 1992), and concern matters such as the way society functions (or should function) and the relationship between man and nature (Keulartz 1998). Such visions may be utopian in nature.

Both Modernism and Postmodernism have an optimistic outlook on the future, as well as a belief in the effectiveness of creativity and technology in solving social and environmental problems in an era of dynamic development (Harvey 1989). A more pessimistic outlook on the future is underlain by the ideals of the Romantic Age, in which technology was rejected on the grounds of being 'unnatural' (Huizinga 1945). Nowadays, endless planning procedures are just one result of the fundamental conflict between urgently needed renewal and the desire to protect and conserve (Provoost 1995).

Examples of Dutch policy documents that contain visions of a desired state of affairs are the Landscape Policy Document (Ministry of Agriculture) which summarises both the preconditions for landscape quality and the measures needed to develop or conserve a 'good' landscape over the next thirty years.

A planning document with an international scope is the 'Spatial Vision for North West Europe', whose aim is to establish a broader scale of analysis that will enable countries to consider their position in relation to transnational trends in spatial development (Anonymous 2001).

• Anonymous. 2001. *A Spatial Vision for North West Europe*. Ministry of Housing, Spatial Planning and the Environment. National Spatial Planning Agency, The Hague
• Harvey D. 1989. *The Condition of Postmodernity*. Basil Blackwell Oxford pp.10-38
• Huizinga J. 1945. *Geschonden wereld*. Tjeenk Willink Haarlem p.188
• Keulartz J. 1998. *The Struggle for Nature. A Critique of Radical Ecology*. Routledge London
• Pohl N. 1992. 'Horizontal articulation in landscape'. In: Topos no. 1 September 1992 pp. 42-47
• Provoost M. 1995. 'A "grand projet" for the Netherlands. The love-hate relationship between railway, road, landscape and city'. In: Archis Journal NAI publishers Rotterdam 3 pp. 68-80.

Vista

see > sight line

Volume, Mass

see also > form, openness, space.

A volume is a 'space occupied. Measure of a bounded space especially in cubic units. A usually shapeless body or mass'. A mass is 'a quantity of matter or the form of matter that holds or clings together in one body. Greatness of size' (*Webster*).

Landscape volumes and masses such as rock formations, hills, buildings and woodlands protrude visibly above ground level. Of these, only buildings and woodlands are malleable, which explains why designers use their volumes to create and model outdoor spaces. Mass is the counterpart of space, involving density in contrast to openness.

Large volumes such as those of forests carry meanings: while they are associated with protection or cover, they also may be viewed as threatening. Dense woodlands used to be places where wild animals, thieves and

highwaymen would hide, and where most people hardly dared to go (Schama 1995). Even today, footpaths in dense forests must be marked carefully in order to guide and reassure visitors who are afraid of losing their way. Most contemporary park visitors prefer the edges of woodland to the interior (Appleton 1975).

In the flat Dutch open polderland, volumes are isolated elements such as farmyards, villages or mounds that are spread out in space. They constitute landmarks and symbolise security in an open land that is exposed to the sun, wind and water (Bijhouwer 1977).

• Appleton J. 1975. 'Prospect and refuge theory'. In: *The Experience of Landscape*. Wiley & Sons New York pp. 70-74.
• Bijhouwer J.T.P. 1977. 'Het terpenlandschap'. In: *Het Nederlandse Landschap*. Kosmos Amsterdam pp. 21 ff.
• Schama S. 1995. 'Living in the woods: laws and outlaws'. In: Landscape & Memory. Harper Collins London pp. 142-143

In an open landscape the volume of an isolated farm with its shelterbelt stands out in space.
Photo: Veenenbos en Bosch landscape architects

Wall

see also > hedge, edge, space, volume.

A wall is 'a structure, as of brick or stone, raised to some height and meant to enclose or shut off a space. A material layer enclosing space' (*Webster*).

Indoors or out, walls enclose, bound, define, delimit or confine space. They have always been associated with the notion of the enclosed garden, the Hortus Conclusus. During the Middle Ages, gardens enclosed by a protective wall created relatively safe enclaves in the hostile and unsafe wilderness. The interior space was set apart, well-organised and clearly defined. Those who lived there planted trees, flowers and vegetables (Aben 1998).

In a similar way, contemporary enclosed gardens delimit private and protected space in a crowded and noisy urban environment. Around the world, gardens are contained, enclosed and subdivided by walls of many forms and materials. Whether solid, transparent, straight or curvilinear, these walls determine the character of outdoor spaces (Hauxner 2003).

A masonry wall built of local pebbles betrays the proximity of river deposits. Limousin, France.

A wall of local material: bamboo fence in Kyoto, Japan.

Old walls may bear traces of a long history: Plaça del Rei, Barcelona.

The choice of construction material is often determined per locality or region. Natural or vernacular materials contribute to the *couleur locale*, often in a literal sense. A Dutch brick wall with its standard-format bricks is as typical of the local scene as stone walls are in mountainous areas. Plastered walls in conspicuous colours are found in Mediterranean areas and in Britain (Lancaster 1986), while pebble-in-mortar walls are typical of river landscapes. Similarly, bamboo fence are the emblem of the Japanese garden (Carver 1955).

At a regional scale, larger outdoor spaces are partitioned off by roadside trees, hedgerows, earth banks and woodland fringes. These edges may form characteristic images (Lynch 1960; Moore 1989).

• Aben R.; de Wit S. 1998. *The Enclosed Garden. History and development of the Hortus Conclusus and its reintroduction into the present-day Urban Landscape.* 010 publishers, Rotterdam pp.10 .
• Carver N.F. 1955. *Form and Space of Japanese Architecture.* Shokokusha Tokyo
• Hauxner M. 2003. 'Walls and water surfaces'. In: *Open to the Sky.* Danish Architectural Press pp.168 ff.
• Lancaster M. 1986. *Britain in View. Colour in the Landscape.* Quiller, London
• Lynch K. 1960. The Image of the City. MIT Press pp. 62 ff.
• Moore C.W. (et al).1989. *The Poetics of Gardens.* MIT Press, Cambridge pp. 31-33

Water
see > barrage, basin, dike, source, stream

Wilderness
see also > nature, Romanticism

A wilderness can be 'a wild or uncultivated and uninhabited region or tract of land' or 'a piece of ground in a large garden or park, planted with trees, and laid out in an ornamental or fantastic style, often in the form of a maze or labyrinth' (*Goulty*).

Throughout the history of Western civilisation, the relationship between man and wilderness has been complex. 'Since the beginning of man's existence on earth, the wilderness has engendered two sorts of reaction: hostility and fear on one hand, and

A living wall: hedge in Vaux le Vicomte, Melun, France.
Photo Bleeker & Nauta

Wi

a sense of protection on the other' (Jackson 1994). For many centuries, the urge to control wilderness and exploit its resources resulted in the clearing of forests, the reclamation and cultivation of land, and thus a drastic reduction in the area of 'wild land'. At times, however, mystical sentiments would express themselves in a need to conserve or create wild places (Thomas 1983). In many parks and gardens, such places would also serve as a place to hide from the daily and all too artificial environment (Thoreau 1854/1973; Marx 1964; Rowe 1991).

In 15th-century Italian Renaissance gardens, special places were set aside – or created –

In Classicist park designs, the wilderness served as the counterpart to the geometric layout. *Royal Gardens of La Granja, San Idelfonso, Segovia, Spain.*

Source: Mosser 1990: The History of Garden Design, Thames & Hudson, London p.171

with an irregular layout and dense vegetation. These places formed the so-called *barchi*, which were used as hunting grounds, or the *boschi*, in which curvilinear paths in irregular copses represented a true wilderness (Lazzaro 1990; Mosser 1990; Hunt 2000). In the 19th century, the publication of Charles Darwin's *The Origin of Species* contributed to a change in values based on the insight that nature is not something to fight and dominate, but underlies human existence (Oelschlaeger 1991).

In some European countries where management problems are presented by the abandonment of agricultural land, it has to be decided whether or not cultivation should be discontinued and trees should be planted, or whether a new wilderness should be allowed to develop. After such abandonment, the cultural landscape will slowly be transformed by natural dynamics, but will continue to show the impacts of former cultivation (Küster 2004).

The true nature of the primeval wilderness is still a matter of debate between naturalists and historians. The idea that a dense and closed primeval forest covered much of western Europe for much of history is nowadays being superseded by images of a relatively open park landscape, where open meadows were maintained by the grazing of animals (Vera 1997).

In 18th-century England the notion of wilderness ranged from that of a sublime, desolate and savage landscape ('to weep on the rocks of roaring winds') to the type of domesticated natural-looking labyrinth described by Jane Austen (1775-1817), containing footpaths aligned by trees and coniferous hedges. These hedgerows provided 'ample space to narrow grounds with deception innocent' (Batey 1996).

During the 20th century, the moors in parts of England were viewed as sublime examples of wilderness, and large areas were therefore designated as protected landscapes. The experience of wilderness on these moors is determined by characteristics such as 'wildness', openness, asymmetry and homogeneity, where traces of human intervention are absent and walkers are free to roam the high grounds, (Shoard 1982). However, in Europe and North America, the basic premise that real wilderness and signs of human presence do not go together makes it very difficult to preserve or create wild areas:

'I placed a jar in Tennessee
And round it was, upon a hill
It made the slovenly wilderness
Surround that hill.
The wilderness rose up to it,
And sprawled around, no longer wild'
Wallace Stevenson (Weiss 1998)

The contemporary longing for wilderness has influenced the layout of gardens and parks as much as it did in the past, though it remains to be seen whether the creation of wilderness in a park is possible. As Dutch landscape architect Mien Ruys (Ruys 1981) states, 'A wild garden is in itself an irreconcilable contrast. A garden is by definition an enclosed, fenced-in space; and the notion of 'wildness' implies the unbounded, unrestricted.' This is confirmed by Birksted: 'A garden running wild undermines the concept of garden' (Birksted 2000).

To a large extent, an ecological garden is based on a different concept than a Dutch *heempark* (see *Garden*). Heemparks avoid complete wildness, but provide a suggestive appearance through the management and control of indigenous plants collected elsewhere (Ruff 1979; Hough 1995).

An abandoned garden reverts to wilderness.

345

Makeblijde garden at Houten, Utrecht, the Netherlands. Designed by Bakker & Bleeker landscape architects.
Photo: Harry Harsema

META J. VROOM

- Batey M. 1996. 'The Gothic imagination' and 'The familiar rural scene'. In: *Jane Austen and the English Landscape*. Barn Elms, London pp. 40 ff.; p.25
- Birksted J. 2000. 'Cézanne's property'. In: *Landscapes of Memory and Experience*. Spon Press, London pp. 77-86
- Hough M. 1995. *Cities and Natural Process*. Routledge New York
- Hunt J.D. 2000. 'The idea of a garden and three natures'. In: *Greater Perfections. The Practice of Garden Theory*. Thames & Hudson London pp. 32-75
- Jackson J.B. 1994. 'Beyond wilderness'. In: *A Sense of Place, a Sense of Time*. Yale University Press, New Haven pp. 73-91
- Küster H. 2004. 'Cultural landscapes'. In: Dieterich M.; van der Straaten J. 2004. *Cultural Landscapes and Land Use. The Nature Conservation-Society Interface*. Kluwer Academic publishers, Dordrecht pp. 1-11
- Lazzaro C. 1990. 'Nature without geometry'. In: *The Italian Renaissance Garden*. Yale University Press, New Haven pp. 109 - 130.
- Marx L. 1964. 'Sleepy Hollow'. In: *The Machine in the Garden*. Oxford University Press. pp. 3-33
- Mosser M.; Teyssot G. (ed.) 1990. *The History of Garden Design*. Thames and Hudson, New York pp. 91 ff.
- Oelschlaeger M. 1991. *The Idea of Wilderness. From Prehistory to the Age of Ecology*. Yale University Press, New Haven pp. 1-30
- Rowe P.G. 1991. 'Myths and Masks'. In: *Making a Middle Landscape*. MIT Press, Cambridge pp. 217 ff.
- Ruff A.R. 1979. *Holland and the Ecological Landscapes*. Deanwater Press Stockport, Cheshire
- Ruys M.; Zandvoort R. 1981. 'De wilde tuin'. In: *Van Vensterbank tot Landschap*. Moussault, Bussum pp. 87 ff.
- Shoard M. 1982. 'The lore of the moors and primary conditions for wilderness'. In: Gold J.R.; Burgess J. *Valued Environments*. Allen & Unwin, London pp. 55 ff.
- Thomas K. 1983. 'Cultivation or wilderness?'. In: *Man and the Natural World*. Pantheon Books, New York pp. 254 ff.
- Thoreau D. 1854 (reprint 1973). 'The Ponds'. In: *Selections from Walden*. Avenell Books pp.120-136
- Vera F. 1997. *Metaforen voor de wildernis: eik, hazelaar, rund en paard*. Ph.D thesis, Wageningen University
- Weiss A.S. 1998. *Unnatural Horizons. Paradox & Contradiction in Landscape Architecture*. Princeton Architectural Press, New York pp. 140-141

Wind

see also > experience, dam, dike, dynamic

The prevailing westerly winds have a striking effect on the landscapes of the Low Countries. The direct physical effect of wind erosion and sedimentation is visible in the dune coast, inland sand ridges and loess deposits which between them form the Aeolic landscapes (Anonymous 1965).

The indirect effect of strong winds on landscape form is caused by wave action along the sea coast and inland lakes. To protect the low-lying land, defensive measures such as dikes, barriers, levees and quays are required – highly visible in such terrain. (van de Ven 1993)

An even stronger effect is had by the protective planting screens planted out around cropland, farms, housing and recreation areas all over the country. As well as providing shelter for man, plants, animals and buildings, these screens, hedgerows, shelterbelts and scattered woodland lots add to the scale, diversity and character of the landscape.

As a source of energy, wind propels sailing boats and turns windmills and wind turbines. Highly valued representatives of Dutch national heritage, historic windmills have become a national emblem. For centuries, they supplied the energy needed to drain the land and to grind the grain. Their individual characteristics were usually the product of local or regional circumstances, and thus contributed to the diversity and identity of the various landscape types.

Modern wind turbines are more contested, and not only because of their appearance. While they are labelled as an 'environmentally friendly' source of electricity, they are hooked up to the national power networks, and thus have no local ties; they are anonymous. Problems are also caused by their noise and by birds that fly into their rotors. In short, as representatives of modern technology, they are not always welcome in rural settings (Hekkema 1996; Herngreen 2002).

To answer such problems, landscape planners prefer to concentrate them in large numbers in a limited numbers of selected areas, both inland and offshore. The arrangement of the turbines is strictly regimented, whether in grids, linear patterns or otherwise (Bosch 1994; Harsema 1998; van Dooren 2003).

Wind also bears an association with newness, progress, modern life and dynamic movement. Since the 1930s, aerodynamic form has been used in the design of all sorts of objects, not only those requiring low wind-resistance such as speeding cars, trains and aeroplanes. Static objects such as refrigerators, washing machines and irons were also streamlined (Giedion 1969).

In the 21st century, Computer Aided Design allows architects to use construction techniques that support streamlined forms in the design of new buildings (Anonymous 1998).

• Anonymous. 1965. *De Bodem van Nederland. Toelichting bij de Bodemkaart van Nederland Schaal 1:200.000* (i.e. *Soils of the Netherlands. Explanation of the soil map of the Netherlands*) Stichting voor Bodemkartering, Wageningen pp. 189-197; 249-257
• Anonymous. 1998. *Kas Oosterhuis, architect.* Uitgeverij 010, Rotterdam
• Bosch J. 1994. 'Molens hebben de wind tegen'. (i.e. *Wind turbines with the wind right in their teeth*). In: Blauwe Kamer, Wageningen no. 6 pp. 39-39
• van Dooren N.; van Leeuwen R. (ed.) 2003. 'Windturbines, IJsselmeergebied'. In: *Alle Hosper Landschapsarchitect 1943-1997.* Uitgeverij 010, Rotterdam pp. 142-145
• Giedion S. 1969. *Mechanization Takes Command.* Norton & Company, New York pp. 603-611
• Harsema H. 1998. 'Windturbines in the landscape'. In: *Landscape architecture and town planning in the Netherlands 95-97.* Thoth, Bussum pp. 74-77
• Hekkema H. 1996. 'Windmolenparken overschrijden de grenzen'. (i.e. *Windturbine parks are crossing borderlines*). In: Blauwe Kamer, Wageningen no. 3 pp. 6-7
• Herngreen R. 2002. 'Landschappen van wind. Nut, noodzaak en esthetiek van windturbines in het Nederlandse landschap'. (i.e. *Wind Landscapes. The use, necessity and aesthetics of wind turbines in the Dutch landscape*). In: Blauwe Kamer, Wageningen no. 1 pp. 23-27
• van de Ven G.P. (ed.) 1993. *Man-made Lowlands. History of water management and land reclamation in the Netherlands.* Matrijs, Utrecht

Using brushwood to slow wind erosion on the Dutch coast.

Detail of a windblown dune.

347

Protective planting around a farmyard.

Wind turbines near Enkhuizen, the Netherlands.

Alphabetical list of key words

349

About the author

Meto Vroom (1929) was Professor of Landscape Architecture at the Department of Spatial Planning at the Agricultural University in Wageningen, the Netherlands, from 1966 to 1995.

He obtained a Master's degree in Landscape Architecture at the University of Pennsylvania, Philadelphia, USA in 1957, and a Master of Science in Agriculture at the Agricultural University in Wageningen in 1959. During the 1960s he worked at the Floriade horticultural exhibition in Rotterdam, the Department of Parks in Amsterdam and, from 1963, as a landscape consultant with the State Forest Service.

From 1974 to 1977 he served as Chairman of the Research Committee of the International Federation of Landscape Architects (IFLA). Between 1988 and 1996 he was a member of the Education Committee of the European Foundation for Landscape Architecture (EFLA), and Chairman of its Advisory Panel, which dealt with the recognition of professional schools. His other appointments included membership on the editorial committee of Elsevier's *Landscape and Urban Planning Journal*, and on the National Advisory Council of the Dutch Ministry of Transport and Water Control.

In 1993 he became a member of the Scientific Advisory Board for the Le-Nôtre Project of the European Council of Landscape Architecture Schools, and also Chairman of the Landscape Architecture Europe Foundation.

His teaching experience has included visiting professorships and guest-lectures in various countries; his publications have included a number of articles in international journals. He was the editor of the book *'Outdoor Space': Environments* designed by Dutch landscape architects in the period since 1945.

351

Edited by
Uitgeverij Blauwdruk, Schip van Blaauw,
Generaal Foulkesweg 72
6703 BW Wageningen, The Netherlands

Text
Meto J. Vroom

Unless attributed otherwise, all photos by
Meto J. Vroom

Text editing
David Alexander in collaboration with
Maarten Ettema and Anne Marie Roetgerink

Design
Michel Backus en Harry Harsema,
Grafisch Atelier Wageningen

Printing
Ludwig Auwer, Donauwörth, Germany
Printed on acid-free paper produced from
chlorine-free pulp. TCF ∞

This book is also available in a Dutch
language edition published by Uitgeverij
Blauwdruk (ISBN 90-75271-15-8)

© 2006 Birkhäuser – Publishers for
Architecture, P.O. Box 133, CH-4010 Basel,
Switzerland
Part of Springer Science + Business Media

ISBN-10: 3-7643-7525-6
ISBN-13: 978-3-7643-7525-6

9 8 7 6 5 4 3 2 1
www.birkhauser.ch

A CIP catalogue record for this book is available from the Library
of Congress, Washington D.C., USA

Bibliographic information published by Die Deutsche Bibliothek.
Die Deutsche Bibliothek lists this publication in the Deutsche
Nationalbibliografie; detailed bibliographic data is available in
the Internet at: http://dnb.ddb.de.